Journalism Ethics

Practical and Professional Ethics series

Published in conjunction with the Association for Practical
and Professional Ethics

General Editors
Robert Audi, University of Notre Dame
Patrick E. Murphy, University of Notre Dame

Published in the Series

Practical Ethics
Henry Sidgwick
With an Introduction by Sissela Bok

Thinking Like an Engineer
Michael Davis

Deliberative Politics
Edited by Michael Macedo

From Social Justice to Criminal Justice
Edited by William C. Heffernan and John Kleinig

Conflict of Interest in the Professions
Edited by Michael Davis and Andrew Stark

Meaningful Work
Mike W. Martin

From Morality to Mental Health
Mike W. Martin

The Price of Truth
David B. Resnik

Playing Politics with Science
David B. Resnik

Journalism Ethics
Edited by Christopher Meyers

Journalism Ethics

A Philosophical Approach

EDITED BY CHRISTOPHER MEYERS

OXFORD
UNIVERSITY PRESS

2010

OXFORD
UNIVERSITY PRESS

Oxford University Press, Inc., publishes works that further
Oxford University's objective of excellence
in research, scholarship, and education.

Oxford   New York
Auckland   Cape Town   Dar es Salaam   Hong Kong   Karachi
Kuala Lumpur   Madrid   Melbourne   Mexico City   Nairobi
New Delhi   Shanghai   Taipei   Toronto

With offices in
Argentina   Austria   Brazil   Chile   Czech Republic   France   Greece
Guatemala   Hungary   Italy   Japan   Poland   Portugal   Singapore
South Korea   Switzerland   Thailand   Turkey   Ukraine   Vietnam

Copyright © 2010 by Oxford University Press, Inc.

Published by Oxford University Press, Inc.
198 Madison Avenue, New York, New York 10016

www.oup.com

Oxford is a registered trademark of Oxford University Press

Library of Congress Cataloging-in-Publication Data
Journalism ethics : a philosophical approach / edited by Christopher Meyers.
     p. cm. — (Practical and professional ethics series)
Includes bibliographical references and index.
ISBN 978-0-19-537080-5; 978-0-19-537079-9 (pbk.)
1. Journalistic ethics. I. Meyers, Christopher, 1957–
PN4756.J665 2010

174'.907—dc22   2009012873

9 8 7 6 5 4 3 2 1

Printed in the United States of America
on acid-free paper

This book, like all else in my life, is dedicated to Donna

Preface

"Journalism ethics? Har, har, har! It's a comedy book, huh?" Words to that effect were the almost universal reaction when I told folks I was working on this project. Comments about oxymorons were often quick to follow, along with multiple complaints about the speaker's hometown paper or TV news. In short, and surely not a surprise to anyone reading this, the general public's reaction to journalism and journalism ethics is intensely negative.

The only other common response came almost exclusively from working or former reporters: "Why bother? Traditional news, or at least traditional newspapers, are dead in the water."

Both reactions are, I think, mistaken. Yes, the ethics of journalism has no shortage of issues and horror stories; its practitioners undoubtedly could do a far better job of reporting ethically. These same judgments, though, apply just as well to the ethics of business, medicine, law, and, for that matter, the academy. If anything, reporters are more self-reflective and self-critical, as individuals and as a profession, than are all other groups with which I've worked.[1]

Further, despite dire warnings, I'm reasonably optimistic about newspapers' viability. Their death knell has been rung many times before, particularly at the advent of the television age, and yet they consistently revamp and prevail. The current challenges are undeniably acute: competition from online media, deep distrust of mainstream media's credibility and trustworthiness, a generally non-reading public, and an under-thirty population who say they get their news, if at all, from sources other than mainstream media; these factors all incline toward a pessimistic outlook. But as the chapters in this book attest in both direct and implied ways, we would all be far worse off without newspapers. Despite their many problems—ethical, political, economic—they remain vital to democratic societies and to individual communities.

Or at least the historical purposes and activities of newspapers, of traditional journalism, are vital. And despite the grand potential of online reporting, the work to date strongly suggests it won't be a viable replacement, not in its current forms, at any rate. Both mainstream media and new media will undoubtedly change—sometimes in ways that enhance the ethical values discussed below, sometimes (often) not.

Those among you who are currently news professionals, are in training, or teach, will decide which of those "sometimes" prevail. The array of forces currently changing journalism is complex and powerful, but it is not determinative. How journalism is practiced—via whatever medium—will be up to its practitioners; the public will always need information: to vote, to avoid scoundrels, to evade danger, to have one's beliefs challenged, or just to suggest where to eat and which movies to watch.

Journalism has ably, if not always perfectly, filled that role. This book is thus mostly about mainstream media, or at least about the traditional model of journalism, especially as it has been present in newspapers. While that model has been responsible for a slew of ethical debacles (think Jayson Blair, Janet Cooke, Jack Kelley, *Dateline NBC*[2]), it has also produced some of the most important stories in history, including Watergate and the Pentagon Papers. That model is also the driving force behind the heroic efforts of the *Times-Picayune*'s finding a way to scrape together a paper amid the devastation and flooding of Hurricane Katrina, and of *60 Minutes II* and Seymour Hersh's bravely breaking the Abu Ghraib scandal.[3] It is also reflected in the day-to-day willingness to take on controversial but vital causes, stories that won't go down in history but make all the difference in people's lives.[4]

Maybe I'm just desperately holding on to old ways, fingernails dragging as I'm pulled into a new journalistic model. To my mind, though, today's pressing question is not so much whether needed information is printed on a page, broadcast, or delivered digitally, but whether it is *believable*. Is its author committed to accuracy over ideology? Has it been properly researched and sourced? Has it been influenced by material gain, personal reward, or corporate profit? In short, can its recipients *trust it*?

The answer, of course, is that information is trustworthy if its sources are, and while the last forty years have seen a serious decline, mainstream media has historically held that status because it has insisted on methods and processes that merited it. Economic factors and a slippery slope of compromises have made it harder for mainstream media to sustain the most ethically important of those methods, while new media have not yet sufficiently established alternative standards; that is, they've not yet discovered how to gain trust in a nonhierarchical, largely editor-free world. Hence the need for books like this one, intended to remind reporters—current and in training—of the real reason for journalism and the most ethical methods for practicing it.

Whereas trustworthiness is earned through a number of means—for example, competency, communication skills, one's history, and one's associates—being ethical is clearly indispensable. It is almost never the case that one is seen as both unethical and worthy of trust.

What, then, does it mean to be ethical? The foundations are rooted in character, in the basic rules and attitudes one learns at mama's or papa's knee. But character is not fixed; one chooses—every day and throughout life—the kind of person one will be. Further, character simply provides motivation—to want to do the right thing, to seek out the right information, to analyze appropriately, and to act accordingly. Figuring out what to do with a complex problem requires one to determine what is at stake (i.e., what facts *and* values), who will be affected and in what ways, what options exist and what their likely consequences are, whether the problem is endemic to the practice, whether judged solutions will prevail or be used merely as window dressing, whether acting upon one's conclusions presents too great a personal risk, and whether the choice is consistent with how one wishes to define oneself. In other words, as I will repeatedly stress throughout the book, *ethics is hard work.*

This conclusion, admittedly, reflects my disciplinary bias. While an interest in practical ethics often begins with dramatic cases or problems, without the right foundation, answers will be unreliable and, often, superficial. To move beyond such superficialities, one must develop an informed and sophisticated theoretical and conceptual foundation. I have taught ethics—theoretical and applied, academic and in-setting—long enough to appreciate the power of gut moral reactions[5] and the associated belief that extensive ethical analysis is unnecessary to making good choices. But such gut reactions are merely the beginning of what must be a careful reasoned analysis.

I readily grant that philosophers are prone to take tough problems and make them far harder, sometimes unnecessarily so. Further, as I argue at length elsewhere,[6] there is nothing much worse than being asked to provide an ethics consultation in a professional setting, only to devote one's efforts to showing everyone how the case is much more complex than they originally thought, and then walking away without giving a clear recommendation. This, the once-standard philosophical approach to practical ethics, does a disservice both to the setting's professionals and, I think, to philosophy.

Practical ethics problems generally *are* complicated, demanding of careful reasoned scrutiny, rooted in sound conceptual and theoretical analysis. But they also have answers, or at least they have better and worse ones. Discerning the difference requires, as noted, a clear understanding of what's at stake, which in turn requires a clear understanding of the concepts and values. One cannot, for example, criticize a reporter for not being objective unless one knows just what that concept *means*.[7] Ditto for "privacy," "conflict of interest," "professional," and so on.

Hence this book's structure: Section One provides those theoretical and conceptual foundations, set within an informed journalistic backdrop, while Section Two is more practice oriented. The book was conceived as a text for journalism ethics or philosophy of journalism courses at the grad or advanced undergrad level, but the chapters are, I am pleased to say, impressive enough to also be of real value for scholars. The book is designed as I would teach a journalism ethics class, but one could easily move chapters around to fit one's needs—with the exception of Deni Elliott and David Ozar's opening chapter. One should begin there, since they provide an ethics decision-making model that later authors use or expand upon.

A last point about the contributors: they represent the best in the field and are a mix of journalism, communication, and philosophy scholars, most of whom also have a background as reporters. They worked diligently on their chapters, typically with multiple rewrites, striving to make difficult and complex issues both well reasoned and accessible. The results are remarkable and worthy of your careful read and reflection. Upon completion of the book, you should have a far richer understanding of the nature, value, and purpose of journalism and of how to be an ethical practitioner. Enjoy.

Notes

1. In addition to my background in journalism and journalism ethics, I am the clinical ethicist at three area hospitals and I've worked extensively with government agencies and the legal community.

2. Blair was a *New York Times* reporter whose stories were found to be fabricated (2003); Cooke won a Pulitzer Prize for her gripping but, it turned out, fictitious account of an eight-year-old heroin addict in the *Washington Post* (1980); Kelley asked friends to pretend to be sources for his *USA Today* stories, many of which he had been making up for at least a dozen years (2004); and *Dateline NBC* did an investigative report on the propensity of certain General Motors vehicles to explode upon impact but used a hidden incendiary device to produce the explosion on tape. In each of these cases, further investigation revealed a newsroom culture of pressure, fear, and a willingness to look the other way while hotshot reporters came up with suspiciously good stories.

3. Hersh had been working on the story for some time when *60 Minutes II* broke it on April 28, 2004. Two days later, Hersh posted an initial version of his account in the online version of the *New Yorker*, with the full story coming out in print on May 10.

4. The weekend I wrote this, CBS's *60 Minutes* broadcast what was, for them, a routine show, with each segment being first-rate journalism—challenging of power, warning of threats, educating, enlightening, and humanizing. The next morning, however, the same network's *Early Show* pandered to the lowest common denominator, showing an Internet clip of a teen suicide.

5. For a fuller discussion of the role of moral intuitions, see chapter 22, by Julie Newton and Rick Williams.

6. *A Practical Guide to Clinical Ethics Consulting: Expertise, Ethos and Power* (Lanham, MD: Rowman & Littlefield, 2007), esp. chap. 1.

7. See chapter 9, by Stephen J. A. Ward, and chapter 10, by Carrie Figdor.

Acknowledgments

I am grateful, first and foremost, to the book's contributors. The quality of the book is wholly due to their hard work and great thinking.

Thanks also to Jolene Coombs, journalism teacher extraordinaire, for awakening in me a passion for news and its ethical foundations. Similar appreciation is owed to Jay Black for his many years of inspiring work in media ethics and for keeping me connected to associated ideas and the terrific scholars behind them.

I would also like to thank all those journalists who make ethics a high priority; they set the standard for their colleagues and provide a guidepost for many of the ideas to follow.

Special thanks to Brent Kennedy and the gals at Looney Bean, for keeping me fully caffeinated, and to Joe Contaldi, and the rest of the Performance Anglers, for reminding me that chasing an 18-inch brown is at least as valuable as chasing just the right sentence structure.

Contents

Contributors

Jacqui Banaszynski is the Knight Chair Professor, the Missouri School of Journalism, University of Missouri, Columbia, and an editing fellow at the Poynter Institute. She has worked for a number of newspapers and won the 1988 Pulitzer Prize in feature writing, having also been a finalist for the 1986 Pulitzer for international reporting.

Jay Black is a professor emeritus at the University of South Florida, St. Petersburg, where he held an endowed chair in media ethics and directed the Program for Ethics in Education and Community. He edited the *Journal of Mass Media Ethics* 1984–2008. He has coauthored or edited ten books, and presented five hundred papers and workshops, primarily on media and society and media ethics. In 1997 he was awarded the Freedom Forum's inaugural national Journalism Professor of the Year prize.

Sandra L. Borden is an associate professor of communication at Western Michigan University (WMU), having received her doctorate in mass communications from Indiana University in Bloomington. She is also a codirector of WMU's Center for the Study of Ethics in Society. Her chapter in this volume is based on her 2007 book, *Journalism as Practice: MacIntyre and the Press*. She has contributed chapters to a number of books, including Lee Wilkins and Clifford Christians's *Handbook of Media Ethics*. She has also published in a number of refereed journals, including the *Journal of Mass Media Ethics*, *Communication Monographs*, the *International Journal of Applied Philosophy*, and the *Journal of Communication Inquiry*.

Clifford Christians is the Charles H. Sandage Distinguished Professor and Research Professor of Communications at the University of Illinois–Urbana, with joint appointments in Journalism and Media Studies. He has written widely on media ethics, taught it for two decades, and served as the president of UNESCO's Privacy Protection Network, based in Seoul, Korea.

Renita Coleman is the coauthor of a book on moral development and journalists, *The Moral Media: How Journalists Reason about Ethics* (2005). She has conducted numerous studies of moral development, the results of which appeared in, among other places, *Journalism & Mass Communication Quarterly*. She received her PhD from the University of Missouri in 2001, after a fifteen-year career as a newspaper journalist, and now teaches journalism ethics at the University of Texas–Austin.

Stephanie Craft is an associate professor at the Missouri School of Journalism. Before earning a doctorate in communication from Stanford University, she worked as a newspaper journalist in California, Arkansas, and Washington. Her work has appeared in a number of refereed journals, including the *Journalism & Mass Communication Quarterly*, the *Journal of Mass Media Ethics*, *Mass Communication & Society*, *Communication Law & Policy*, the *Howard Journal of Communication*, and the *International Journal of Public Opinion Research*.

Michael Davis is a senior fellow at the Center for the Study of Ethics in the Professions and a professor of Philosophy at the Illinois Institute of Technology in Chicago. Among his recent publications are *Thinking Like an Engineer* (Oxford, 1998), *Ethics and the University* (1999), *Profession, Code, and Ethics* (2002), *Actual Social Contract and Political Obligation* (2002), and *Engineering Ethics* (2005). He has also coedited (with Andrew Stark) *Conflict of Interest in the Professions* (2001).

Rick Edmonds is a media business analyst for the Poynter Institute, where he has done research and writing for the last nine years. Since December 2007, his commentary on the industry has appeared in the Biz Blog on Poynter Online. He has also coauthored the newspaper chapter of the Project for Excellence in Journalism's State of the News Media report 2004–2009. He was a coauthor of Poynter's *Eyetrack 2007*, has contributed to Best Newspaper Writing anthologies, and regularly speaks at national and international conferences. His background includes eleven years with the *St. Petersburg Times* in various editor and publisher roles, including two years as the managing editor of the paper's Tampa edition. He was also James Reston's assistant at the *New York Times* and a reporter at the *Philadelphia Inquirer*, where he was a finalist for the Pulitzer Prize in national reporting in 1982.

Deni Elliott is a professor of philosophy and holds the Poynter Jamison Chair in media ethics and press policy at the University of South Florida in St. Petersburg. She also serves as the ethics officer for the Metropolitan Water District of Southern California and has published widely on practical and professional ethics.

Carrie Figdor received her doctorate from City University of New York and is an assistant professor of philosophy at the University of Iowa. She is a former journalist with the

Associated Press and other mainstream media and combines this background with her research interests in metaphysics and the philosophy of mind. She has publications in the *Journal of Philosophy, Minds & Machines, Consciousness and Emotion,* and other journals.

Candace Cummins Gauthier has a PhD in philosophy from the University of North Carolina–Chapel Hill. She is a professor of philosophy at the University of North Carolina–Wilmington, where she has been teaching since 1986. She specializes in media ethics and health care ethics and has published numerous articles in applied ethics, including her 2002, "Privacy Invasion by the News Media: Three Ethical Models," *Journal of Mass Media Ethics.*

Paul Martin Lester is professor of Communications at California State University–Fullerton. Lester received a master's degree from the University of Minnesota and a PhD from Indiana University in mass communications, after working as a photojournalist for the *Times-Picayune* in New Orleans. He is the author or editor of several books and has published numerous articles in major communications' journals. He also wrote a monthly column, "Ethics Matters" with Deni Elliott, for *News Photographer* magazine for the National Press Photographers Association.

Christopher Meyers is a professor of philosophy at California State University–Bakersfield, and director of the Kegley Institute of Ethics. He has authored numerous essays on practical and professional ethics and wrote *Expertise, Ethos and Power: A Guide for Clinical Ethics Consultants* (2007). He is also on the medical staff at Kern Medical Center and has conducted multiyear participant–observer studies in television and newspaper newsrooms.

Julianne H. Newton is professor of visual communication and associate dean for undergraduate affairs, University of Oregon School of Journalism and Communication, author of *The Burden of Visual Truth: The Role of Photojournalism is Mediating Reality,* and editor of *Visual Communication Quarterly* 2001–2006. Her publications on visual ethics span scholarly and public forums, and her documentary photographs have been shown in more than 50 exhibitions. She has worked as a professional word and visual journalist in newspapers, magazines, radio, and television. *Visual Communication: Integrating Media, Art and Science,* which she co-authored with Rick Williams, won the 2009 Marshall McLuhan Award for Best Book in Media Ecology.

David Ozar is a professor and codirector of graduate studies in health care ethics in the Department of Philosophy at Loyola University in Chicago. He served as the director of Loyola's Center for Ethics from 1993 to 2006 and has served as a founding codirector of the Ethics AdviceLine for Journalists since 2000. He is also an adjunct professor of medical humanities in Loyola's Stritch School of Medicine. He has published more than ninety articles and book chapters in professional journals and has coedited a book on human rights and coauthored a book on professional ethics.

Patrick Lee Plaisance is an associate professor in the Department of Journalism and Technical Communication at Colorado State University. He received his doctorate from Syracuse University and has worked as a journalist at various newspapers around the country. His work focuses both on the application of philosophical ethics to media practice and on social science research into decision-making and journalistic behavior. He has authored multiple publications, including *Media Ethics: Key Principles for Responsible Practice* (2008), and has contributed to several books and academic journals, such as *Communication Theory, Journalism & Mass Communication Quarterly,* the *Journal of Mass Media Ethics,* and the *International Journal of Applied Philosophy.*

Aaron Quinn is an assistant professor of journalism at California State University–Chico. His work has appeared in such publications as *Journal of Mass Media Ethics, International Journal of Applied Philosophy,* and numerous other academic journals and books. He was the managing editor of the *Pinellas News,* a weekly newspaper in St. Petersburg, Florida; covered public safety for the *Bradenton Herald,* a daily newspaper in Bradenton, Florida; and was a freelance photographer who shot for the National Football League, National Hockey League, and other news and sporting publications.

Ian Richards is a professor and director of the postgraduate journalism program at the University of South Australia in Adelaide. He is also the chair of the university's Human Research Ethics Committee and the editor of *Australian Journalism Review,* Australia's leading refereed journal in the academic field of journalism. A former newspaper journalist, he received his doctorate from the University of South Australia. His publications include *Quagmires and Quandaries: Exploring Journalism Ethics* (2005).

Jane B. Singer is the Johnston Press Chair in digital journalism at the University of Central Lancashire (UK). Her research explores digital journalism, including changing roles, perceptions, and practices. Before earning a PhD in journalism from the University of Missouri, she was the first news manager of Prodigy Interactive Services. She also worked as a newspaper reporter and editor. Jane serves on the editorial boards of several academic journals, including the *Journal of Mass Media Ethics,* and is president of Kappa Tau Alpha, the national U.S. journalism honor society. She is on leave from the University of Iowa School of Journalism and Mass Communication, where she is an associate professor.

Martha (Marty) Steffens is the SABEW endowed chair in business and financial journalism at the University of Missouri School of Journalism. She spent thirty years in the newspaper business, including as executive editor of the *San Francisco Examiner* and the *Binghamton Press* and *Sun-Bulletin.* She was also an editor for the *Los Angeles Times, Minneapolis Star, Dayton* (Ohio) *Daily News,* and *St. Paul Pioneer Press.* She often lectures in China and the Middle East.

Stephen J. A. Ward is the James E. Burgess Professor of Journalism Ethics at the University of Wisconsin–Madison. He received his doctorate from University of Waterloo and is the author of *The Invention of Journalism Ethics: The Path to Objectivity and Beyond* (2005). He is the director of www.journalismethics.info, a comprehensive Web site devoted to journalism ethics.

Edward Wasserman is the John S. and James L. Knight Foundation professor of journalism ethics at Washington and Lee University in Lexington, Virginia. Since 2001 he has written a biweekly column on the media for the *Miami Herald* and the *Palm Beach Post*, which is distributed nationally by the McClatchy–Tribune News Service. Wasserman joined Washington and Lee in 2003 after a career in journalism that began in 1972 and included working for news organizations in Maryland, Wyoming, Florida, and New York. Among other positions, he was the CEO and editor-in-chief of American Lawyer Media's Miami-based Daily Business Review newspaper chain, executive business editor of the *Miami Herald*, city editor of the Casper (Wyo.) *Star-Tribune*, and editorial director of Primedia's 140-publication Media Central division in New York. Wasserman received a bachelor of arts cum laude in politics and economics from Yale, a *licence* in philosophy from the University of Paris, and a PhD from the London School of Economics, where he studied media politics and economics.

Herman Wasserman is a senior lecturer in journalism studies at the University of Sheffield, United Kingdom. He previously taught at the University of Stellenbosch, South Africa, where he still holds a visiting position as associate professor extraordinary. He was a Fulbright fellow at the School of Journalism at Indiana University, and a media ethics colloquium fellow at the University of Missouri. Before joining the academy, he worked as a newspaper journalist in Cape Town. His research interests include global journalism ethics; journalism in emergent democracies; and media, culture, and society in Africa. He edits the journal *Ecquid Novi: African Journalism Studies*.

Lee Wilkins is a Curator's Teaching Professor at the University of Missouri. She is also a professor at the Missouri School of Journalism and an editor of the *Journal of Mass Media Ethics*. Her research includes studies of media coverage of the Midwest flood of 1993; the Bhopal, India, disaster; and global climate change during the late 1980s and early 1990s, the results of which have appeared in leading communications ethics journals and as book chapters. She is also the coauthor of multiple books in media ethics and criticism. Her doctorate is in political science from the University of Oregon; her professional career includes work as both a political reporter and an editor for newspapers in three states.

Rick Williams is an award-winning visual arts communications scholar and documentary photographer and the Chair of the Division of the Arts at Lane Community College. His research includes theoretical and practical explorations in the use of art and visual communication as pedagogical tools that help students integrate rational and intuitive intelligences to enhance creativity, intelligence, problem solving, decision making, and performance across academic and professional disciplines and life practices. His books include an ethnographic/photographic study, *Working Hands* and *Visual Communication: Integrating Media, Art and Science* with co-author Julianne Newton. *Visual Communication* won the 2007 AEJMC Creative Projects Award, NCA Outstanding Achievement in Visual Communication Research Award, and the 2009 Marshall McLuhan Award.

Wendy N. Wyatt received her doctorate from the University of Oregon and is an associate professor of media ethics in the Department of Communication and Journalism at the University of St. Thomas. In addition to interests in media and democracy and media literacy, she has developed a theoretical perspective on press criticism that is introduced in her book, *Critical Conversations: A Theory of Press Criticism* (2007).

Theoretical and Conceptual Foundations

PART I

Ethics Theory and Decision Making

Introduction

Imagine you are the mayor of a small town in Greece during World War II.[1] You've had generally good relations with the occupying German forces, mostly Austrians, but then the peace is shattered when a small group of Greek guerilla fighters kills four German soldiers as they lounged on the beach. The guerillas, all from different islands than yours, are frustrated with their compatriots' complacency toward their occupiers and are trying to motivate a wider resistance movement. They are eventually captured and tortured, but the SS officer who has come to oversee the interrogation reminds you of the standing policy: for every German death, twenty Greeks will be killed. Thus, you are brought to the town square—where eighty islanders have been gathered—and given a choice. If you kill—beat to death, it turns out—the three guerillas who survived the torture, the eighty will be spared and only sent to a labor camp for the duration of the war.

What should you do?

If you are like the hundreds of students to whom I've presented this scenario, and if you think it through with even a bit of care, your reaction probably is, indeed probably should be, "How can I possibly know the morally right choice?" You might have considered eighty lives versus three and decided to whack away. But it doesn't take much pushing to see how that choice is at least problematic: Should we ever become direct participants in evil? Is that the kind of legacy you want attached to your name and memory? What is your relationship with the eighty hostages, or with the guerillas, and how should that affect your choice? Is killing them consistent with any reasonable standard of justice? Does your role as mayor bring special moral duties?

In short, while your initial analysis may have been deeply thoughtful, even insightful, it was nonetheless probably ad hoc, based on gut reactions rooted in upbringing or religion (or in evolutionarily determined brain structure—see Julie Newton and Rick Williams's essay in chapter 22). Or, once you're pushed by questions like those above, you may fall back on some form of relativism: "Who am I to judge anyone else's answer, since there are no right answers in ethics?"

In a ten-week college quarter, I proceed to show students, first, why such relativism, at least in its simplest forms, is false, and, second, how the great theorists have attempted both to explain the nature of ethics and to provide a method for ethics decision-making.[2] And those ten weeks barely scratch the surface.

In a practical ethics course, like journalism ethics, you obviously don't have that luxury. You need a brief introduction to the nature of ethics and a good method for working out tough problems. Most practical ethics books have addressed these needs by providing excerpts or summaries of the classical theorists—for example, Aristotle, Kant, Mill, Ross, Rawls, Gilligan—along with brief editorial explanations and criticisms. Students are then told to work their way through the arguments, often from dense original sources, and to somehow conclude from this how to better manage ethics decision-making.

For years I taught this way, in large part because that's how I had been taught and because existing books did not provide a good alternative. Students undoubtedly benefited from being exposed to some of history's great minds and from being forced to think deeply about such moral concerns as duty, consequences, character, justice, and relationships. In my experience, though, two things typically happened. First, those students who took the task seriously inevitably rode the "he's right, no *he's* right, no . . ." roller coaster; that is, they read Aristotle and were convinced his is the best theory. Until they read Kant, when they became convinced anew. And then Mill. . . .

That reaction reveals why students should have at least some exposure to these theories: despite their respective problems, these great thinkers draw attention to fundamental human insights.

But insights don't, as the saying goes, pay the bills.

In the, at best, two weeks typically devoted to ethics theory and method in a practical ethics course, one hopes the students learn what's interesting and important in ethics—those "impressive insights," particularly as they relate to concerns like duty, consequences, character, justice, and relationships. But as faculty, we must realize they haven't learned *how* to apply ethics, even if they become truly convinced by any of the theorists. Part of the reason they don't know how to apply ethics is that such a brief overview just cannot provide the necessary details and nuance. For example, how would Kant distinguish (always prohibited) lying from (sometimes allowable) withholding of information? How does Mill try to solve the problem of justice? Are there guiding principles in Aristotle's virtue theory? Is Rawls's Original Position a real thing or just a heuristic device? These are all glorious topics, ones to which moral philosophers devote lifetimes, but they are far beyond the purview of a practical ethics class.

For the student just trying to figure out whether to whack the guerillas, or more realistically, whether it's OK to lie to sources or to invade a politician's privacy, the ambiguity and abstractions get old quick. She needs, instead, a practical method for addressing tough ethical problems.

Largely because of this first reaction, many students simply ignore all the theory as the course moves into the issues section. Exposure to the theorists means students now address problems in a more informed fashion, but in all but rare cases, their approach is still largely ad hoc. Studying the theories was an interesting intellectual exercise, but one quickly forgotten when the course turns to the (in their mind) *real* material. The professor can force students to continue addressing the theorists by creating artificial assignments—"Write a paper explaining what Kant would say about protecting sources and how Mill would respond"—but they truly are artificial; great, maybe, for budding philosophers, but for everyone else too often seen as just another classroom hoop to jump through.

Hence the dilemma: How can one provide a practical method for ethics decision-making without it being hopelessly superficial? As mentioned above, there's a reason we continue to read the classics: their authors recognized sophisticated moral reasoning necessarily entails certain key elements; that is, they teach us that we must acknowledge at least the following:

- The inherent moral force present in key principles such as "respect for persons,"
- The obligation to benefit others,
- The need to develop a virtuous character,
- The special duties attached to personal and professional relationships, and
- The importance of treating others justly.

Thus any ethics method worth its name will retain a sophisticated, philosophically informed discussion of vital moral and metaphysical concepts. And it will do so in a way that is sympathetic to all parts of the canon. If we've learned anything from the last forty years of the practical ethics movement, it is that careful moral reasoning incorporates central points from each of the classical theorists. To see them as necessarily distinct or incompatible, as, again, most practical ethics texts do, is to miss critical subtleties. Take three examples, commonly misrepresented: Kant thought results were critical to ethical choices, just not the defining feature; Mill's rule-utilitarianism is, in practice at least, virtually indistinguishable from some versions of deontology; and Aristotle's virtue theory allows for, probably even demands, a reliance on moral principles.[3] In other words, all the classical theorists accepted variants on all the elements in the list above, even if they strongly stressed individual parts. Thus, any plausible version of an ethics method must incorporate them all, while also realistically assessing the empirical circumstances in which choices reside.

Deni Elliott and David Ozar's essay does just this. Elliott and Ozar, two of the more respected philosophers working in practical ethics today, address ethics decision-making from top-down and bottom-up perspectives. That is, they build upon classical theory but also situate decisions within the realities and options present in journalistic practice, asking "three basic questions": "'Whom do the members of the profession serve?'; 'What good do they do for those they serve?'; and 'What is the ideal relationship between the professional and the person served?'" From this analysis of the purpose of journalism, they then develop clear ethical principles for the working journalist, principles grounded in classical ethical theory. From there they devise a specific method—a "systematic moral analysis" (SMA)—to follow when faced with an ethical problem.

Elliott and Ozar deserve deep thanks and respect for their work. No framework will please everyone—some will stress principles more than outcomes, others character more than individual choices—but their SMA is indeed an impressive start, one that the student or professor should feel free to adjust as needed.

One of the first things the discerning student will notice upon reading Elliott and Ozar's essay is *this stuff is hard*. Despite the cultural norm of too often simplifying complex problems,[4] all one need do is peek under those superficial covers to realize ethics decision-making is fraught with uncertainties—factual, epistemological, and axiological—that demand extensive, and often thorny, analysis.

This does not mean, however, such uncertainty amounts to moral relativism. That *problems* are complex, requiring careful empirical and normative analysis, does not mean there aren't correct *answers*. To the contrary, while each situation brings its array of context-dependent variables, I align with W. D. Ross in believing when one discerns that situation's right answer, it is *the* right answer, the one all persons in morally similar circumstances should adopt.[5] This places, in fact, an even greater duty upon each of us to take ethics decision-making quite seriously; if there are *right* answers, there are also *wrong* ones, ones any moral person should strive mightily to avoid.

Why? Because, Renita Coleman explains, that is what morally mature persons do. Children and nonhuman animals act almost exclusively from self-interest, or at most from clan interest. Building upon Kohlbergian development theory, Coleman explores the social conditions that motivate persons to expand the circle of those whom they feel obliged to treat as moral beings, worthy of respect and decent consideration. She then applies this theoretical construct to specific professions, including journalism, revealing "the most important influences on journalists' quality of ethical reasoning."

One of those influences is their organization's ethical culture. As you read this book and as you think about the myriad ethical dilemmas individual journalists face—and cause—ask yourself whether it is realistic to reduce these problems to independent, autonomous choices. As I type this, banner headlines announce the likely trillion-dollar bailout of the U.S. financial industry, due, as even the current Treasury Secretary Henry Paulson attributed it, to Wall Street "excesses."[6] While such excesses were undoubtedly the result of individual greed and recklessness, it is widely acknowledged the actions occurred within a *culture* of excess, one that not only tolerated such behavior but even valorized it.

As the numerous studies confirm, it is naïve to think each of us is a moral island, able to brush aside powerful organizational influences—for good or ill.[7] One must have a method for ethics decision-making—and Elliott and Ozar's is as good as I've seen—but if the institution creates an ethical culture, an ethos, that encourages, for example, getting the story at all costs or treating sources as mere means, it will take the strongest of characters to consistently act rightly.

For the budding practitioner, this reality is important for three reasons. First, it serves as a warning flag: Be careful about where you go to work and pay close attention to the *real* behavioral norms. Are they paying lip service to high ethical standards while rewarding (with a wink and a nudge) those who bend the rules? Second, know your own standards, know which lines you are not willing to cross.[8] And, finally, develop your character to the point where you can, in fact, stick to those standards, to resist the inevitable temptations to see such lines as merely suggestions.

Understanding the organizational ethos is also important for the professor and scholar. While I may lose my philosopher's card for publicly acknowledging this, the best theory is of little value if it is devoid of a deep understanding of empirical realities. Elsewhere I urge that one employ ethnography as the preferred empirical method,[9] but any method that gets at structural norms and motivations would do. As this book progresses, I will point to examples of professional and organizational ethos, as revealed in the essays and in case studies.

Notes

1. This story is excerpted from John Fowles's wonderful novel *The Magus* (Boston: Little Brown, 1978), chap. 53.

2. Disputing relativism is, in fact, an easy task: It is wrong, absolutely wrong, to torture a child simply for the fun of it. It is wrong, regardless of the place or time period. No sane person thinks this proposition is false and, in fact, I have never met a single person who genuinely believes (i.e., who isn't just playing the academic game) otherwise. Now, *why* relativism is false, that takes a lot more time to explain.

3. On the last point, see Rosalind Hursthouse's discussion of "v-rules" in *On Virtue Ethics* (New York: Oxford University Press, 2002).

4. That "cultural norm" is reinforced by news media's routine characterization of social and political problems in stark, and often extremist, either/or positions.

5. For a fuller explanation of this "universalist contextualism" see my, "Appreciating W. D. Ross: On Duties and Consequences," *Journal of Mass Media Ethics* 18 no. 2 (2003), pp. 1–18.

6. NBC, "Meet the Press," September 21, 2008.

7. The most compelling of these studies are Philip Zimbardo's infamous "Stanford Prison Experiment," detailed in his book, *The Lucifer Effect: Understanding How Good People Turn Evil* (New York: Random House, 2008), and Stanley Milgram's *Obedience to Authority* (London: Pinter & Martin, 2005). Patricia Werhane's *Moral Imagination and Management Decision Making* (New York: Oxford University Press, 1999) is, in my judgment, the best philosophical review of the topic and a must read.

8. See, for example, the film "Broadcast News," in which Jane (played by Holly Hunter) confronts the rising star Tom (played by William Hurt) for on-air deception. She says, "You totally crossed the line between" only to have him interrupt with, "It's hard not to cross it; they keep moving the little sucker, don't they?" The movie also nicely illustrates the range of temptations, from the excitement at getting a great story, to deadline pressures, to awards and promotions.

9. *A Practical Guide to Clinical Ethics Consulting: Expertise, Ethos and Power* (New York: Rowman & Littlefield, 2007), esp. chap. 4.

I

An Explanation and a Method for the Ethics of Journalism

Deni Elliott and David Ozar

The aim of this chapter is to help readers understand their responsibilities as persons and as journalists, and to provide them with a framework for addressing the ethical issues that routinely arise in the practice of journalism. Our approach, which is informed by the basic tenets of Western ethical traditions and which borrows from Ozar's and Elliott's previous works, develops from the abstract to the concrete.[1] That is, we move from a discussion of the purpose of journalism, and the specific values that emerge from that purpose, to ideal relationships and practice rules, and, ultimately, to a recommended method.

In doing this we assume what Michael Davis defends in chapter 6—that journalism is a profession and, thus, that its practitioners assume special role-based duties. Those duties, for journalists as for all professionals, are reflected in but not fully captured by the respective code of ethics of each profession. Codes, as in the one developed by the Society for Professional Journalists,[2] provide a snapshot of a profession's ethical norms. But, given their necessary brevity and the often political process by which they are developed, they cannot provide a complete picture.

Our approach instead is empirical and normative; we explore what journalism does—its historically and politically grounded social function—and then draw from this its core values. We then align these values with classical moral injunctions not to harm and to respect others' rights, from which emerges our recommended method.

We want to stress the importance of the empirical. Most philosophical ethics treatises begin with abstract principles to which, they insist, practice must align. But it is the rare professional who learns their ethical duties in this top-down fashion. Rather, they learn from members of the profession in regular communication with one another about their practice, in their interaction with the people to whom they provide their services, and in the relationships that emerge from all these interactions. New practitioners observe how the members of the profession judge one another's conduct, how the people whom the profession serves judge their conduct, and how the larger society judges and reacts to all of this. And they imitate or avoid the behavior of professional role models, both positive and negative.

This is the most important "classroom" for professional ethics. And it is in this complex, ever-changing blend of interactions and communications, with its commendations and criticisms, that the full details of the ethics of a profession are expressed and acquired. Further, as Christopher Meyers suggests in the introduction to this chapter, the interactions that influence the formation of ethics vary not only by profession but by organization. Thus, the ethics of the *New York Times* will differ, if sometimes only in subtle ways, from those of the *Washington Post* or NBC News.

None of this, though, lends itself to easy articulation. Explaining what one has learned or is learning from the practice of a profession in interaction with those they serve and the larger society depends on having some conceptual tools specifically designed for this purpose. In addition, having conceptual tools, which we call here a method of systematic moral analysis (SMA), brings to consciousness some of the decisions that people generally make based on habit or intuition. Once the method of ethical decision-making is brought to a conscious level, it is much easier to ensure all ethically relevant aspects are considered and, subsequently, to explain and defend the resulting decisions.

Journalists make choices that cause emotional, physical, financial, or reputational harm; such harm is built into journalistic functions. Another way of thinking of this is to note that, since journalism fulfills a vital social function (see the essays by Stephanie Craft and Sandra Borden), journalists have a *duty* to cause harm. Thus, they must be able to effectively evaluate when they can prevent or reduce harm, when such harm is fully justified, and how to explain their choices both to those they harm and to the citizens they serve.

We think the best way to unpack these concerns is to ask three basic questions: "Whom do the members of the profession serve?"; "What good do they do for those they serve?"; and "What is the ideal relationship between the professional and the person served?"[3] The first two get at the purpose of journalism, thereby revealing its core values, which in turn inform the relationship analysis. The first two also, it turns out, are so closely intertwined that neither of them can be answered satisfactorily until a careful answer to the other has been developed. But we need to begin somewhere, and so we start with the first.

Whom Does Journalism Serve?

One obvious answer to the question of who journalism serves would be that journalism—and therefore journalists—serve readers, listeners, and viewers in the journalist's society. That is, they serve the audiences of the various print and electronic media by which journalists communicate. This first effort at an answer suggests that the practice of professional journalism includes anything and everything that one might speak about and is directed at anyone who happens to be listening. But this is not how journalism understands itself and, when we are reflective about it, this is not how the rest of our society expects journalism to be practiced. That is, this is not how the profession of journalism is understood in the ongoing dialogue about journalism and its ethics in our society.

A more informative answer to the question of who journalism comes from journalists themselves: "the public." Admittedly, these words are sometimes used to refer to everyone in the relevant society. But when journalists say they serve the public, they use this expression with a specific connotation that is central to understanding journalism's professional ethics. "The public," in this context, refers, to a geographic *population*, a whole society, the whole group of people living in a particular society at a particular time. Of course, the benefits of journalists' expertise reach other persons as well, that is, people outside that society; and journalists are pleased when their work assists these people. But journalism as it is ordinarily practiced, and especially as it is understood in the dialogue about journalism and ethics in our society, is focused on the people of *our* society.[4] But what the people living in a society have in common, from the point of view of journalism's professional role, is not that they happen to be living in the same geographic location, but that they *interact* with one another. The public that journalists serve is the people of that society, insofar as those people are involved in public matters. This is the same public that we refer to when we use the expression "public affairs." For journalism, the public is the people of the society specifically regarded as engaging in actions that actually or at least potentially *affect other persons* in the society.

By contrast, members of many professions (e.g., doctors, nurses, and counselors) serve primarily individuals, and their expertise benefits principally these people, with other persons only indirectly involved. There are members of other professions, such as elementary and secondary school teachers, who serve small groups of people primarily. But journalism's commitment is to serve "all the people," the society as a whole, and to relate to that society precisely insofar as people's actions actually or potentially affect the lives of others in the society. This is the public that journalism serves.

Some journalists' audiences may in fact be very small, but that is not because journalism as a profession views those it serves only in terms of small groups. Journalism's commitment is to serve the whole population of a society, even when it turns out the audience is a small, specialized subgroup. Although there is no hard and fast line to be drawn, if a person serves a subgroup audience such that the interests of the larger society have no role, this person is more likely to be viewed as an advocacy or public relations specialist rather than as a professional journalist.

In this respect, journalism resembles public administration, which similarly is always serving the whole population of a particular society at a particular time and place (although the ethics of public administrators derive first of all from their role as public servants rather than from their membership in a profession). Thus, for example, if a newspaper published a story that was of no value to the public but served only to please the leaders of a particular company, this would not be a proper use of the professional expertise of the journalists involved, even if the story was completely accurate. For this reason, such an action would rightly be judged unprofessional and would be unethical unless a very good reason could be offered for setting aside, in this particular situation, journalism's professional commitment to serve the whole society.

What Good Does Journalism Do Those It Serves?

Having answered the question, "Whom does journalism serve?" let us turn to the second question, "What good does journalism do for those it serves?" What things of worth, and what harms, does journalism produce? To ask this question more technically, what are the *central values* of journalism? That is, what are the social values journalism is committed to produce and, thus, what are the ethical values journalists must embrace to achieve them?

Two answers leap to mind: *knowledge of the truth* and *information.* But the first of these proves immediately problematic. Even apart from complex philosophical questions about how one might measure truth or assure its delivery, most of what is offered as knowledge in our society is closely connected to very detailed explanations of the evidence for the claim, the methods used to gather and process the evidence, and the reasoning linking the evidence to the conclusion that is offered as knowledge. Journalists, however, rarely have the opportunity to delve into a topic in great depth; and even when they do, it is rare that a journalist can offer the public all the evidence and reasoning that is needed to support a claim that is offered as knowledge. So it seems more accurate to say that one of the central values of journalism that good journalists provide to the public is *information.*

There are many kinds of information, even if we focus narrowly on information for the public, as defined above. Does journalism's ethics hold every kind of information to be of equal value, or do different kinds of information have different levels of ethical priority for the journalist?

Some kinds of information are essential for people to function as a society, and the absence of such information makes it extremely difficult for individuals to work together in groups and for both individuals and groups to give direction to the society and to effect important changes in the society when these are needed. This is the kind of information that both journalists and political theorists have in mind when they talk about journalism as an essential tool for controlling governments' abuses of power and for preserving and growing a democratic society (see Craft's and Borden's essays in part two). And it is people's lack of access to such information that is decried in societies without an independent press. Clearly there is a lot of information about governments and other institutions and centers of power in the society—and about the persons who hold offices or in other ways wield such power—that the people of any society *need* in order to effectively function as a society and pursue their collective or individual goals.

In addition, the information a society needs to function effectively includes information about matters of safety. Of course, some threats to health and physical well-being are recognizable using common sense observation. But, especially in complex societies like ours, there are many threats to health and well-being that are not easily identified. People need such information to protect themselves and to minimize the negative effect of things that are unavoidable, and thereby to be able to interact in dependable and effective ways and to achieve their collective and individual goals.

Further, as societies become more complex, new forms of social and organizational power arise that are not readily recognizable by commonsense observation but that have the potential to harm people, either directly or by limiting their opportunities for change and growth. In such cases, information about the bases of power and the persons who wield it is something people need in order to interact dependably and effectively to achieve their collective and individual goals.

These are three examples of the kind of needed information that journalism is committed to providing to the society it serves.[5] In fact, as we explain in more detail below, it is this role-related responsibility of providing needed information that makes journalism unique.[6] Notice also that, while human societies certainly have characteristics in common, and therefore there are certain categories of information that every society needs, it is also true that societies are significantly different from one another. Therefore, one of the central ethical values to which journalists must be committed is undertaking discerning pursuit and effective dissemination of needed information: they must recognize and distinguish the kinds of information needed by the society being served and ensure that the information is effective and accurate and is heard and read.

In making ethical judgments, journalists are required by their professional ethics to prioritize the discerning communication of needed information. The second-highest priority is to provide information that enables people to respond to their *desires*, specifically to the desires that the members of the society consider to be common to everyone, or almost everyone, in the society. Two fairly obvious examples from U.S. society are the value most people place on learning about the generous and self-sacrificing actions of exceptional individuals, and on hearing or reading about leisure pastimes (sports, cultural pursuits, vacation opportunities, etc.).

These are areas of human life that are widely valued across our whole society and, because of this, are also widely seen as bonds within the society itself. Therefore, when providing this information, it is reasonable for journalism to consider itself to be serving the public, rather than merely a number of individuals. Because journalists should be committed to providing information related to common social desires, they are duty-bound to be sufficiently attuned to society's interests and to clearly, accurately, and effectively convey the desired information.

But the information society *desires*, though its value is widely agreed upon in the society, is *optional* rather than *needed* for societal functioning or for people to pursue their collective and individual goals.[7] This is the reason that, from the point of view of journalism's professional commitments, information related to *needs* outranks information related to *desires*.

There are also many things that people might seek information about that are neither matters of need nor matters of desires but are widely affirmed across the society. These individualized interests can be called "preferences," and include those things we want to know about that do not have a significant effect on the strength of the society; that is, they affect it neither directly nor because they are widely shared and so function to bond us. The expertise of the journalist could be used to serve people's preferences, but that is not the reason a society establishes and supports journalism. That is, providing information about people's preferences is not a central value of journalism.

The fact that information about people's preferences is not a central value of journalism is another reason that, as in the earlier example, it is arguably a misuse of professional expertise to report on something that benefits only a subgroup of society. For in that case, it is the group's preferences rather than the needs of the society or the common desires of the public that are being served.

In addition to providing information the society needs and information about the common desires of the society, there are two other central values that should be mentioned here. The first is *autonomy*. Every profession enables those it serves to overcome aspects of powerlessness, to take (or resume) control of something important in their lives. Many journalists are uncomfortable with a claim they are somehow responsible to empower others, but we see this as an indirect commitment: by doing their jobs well, by accurately reporting on vital information, and by acting as a watchdog of powerful institutions, journalists enhance society members' autonomy.

Autonomy refers to a person's or group's ability to act on the basis of the values and goals that person or group has chosen. It correlates closely with the notion of self-determination, except that the expression "self-determination" does not naturally account for the values and goals that groups strive to act on.

When people lack needed information, good journalism can provide the good of the information they need and can thereby enable people to act more effectively to achieve their goals: providing people with information enhances their autonomy. A great deal of journalism's enhancement of autonomy is achieved by providing needed information. But there are many ways in which an individual's or a group's autonomy can be diminished and, therefore, there are many ways in which autonomy can be enhanced.

For example, many people view themselves as prevented from acting on their chosen values and goals by complex bureaucratic government systems. Reporting about persons who overcame bureaucratic obstacles can help them view themselves as able to handle the challenge rather than passively give up. Similarly, challenging these same systems when they overstep their democratic functions grants power indirectly to individuals and groups who may otherwise feel impotent. In addition, some journalistic organizations have used their power over information, or their more direct social power, to get bureaucracies to respond to individuals or groups that the bureaucracy has been overlooking or ignoring, thereby enhancing those persons' or groups' autonomy.

A fourth central value of journalism is *community building*. In addition to providing the society with information and enabling individuals and groups to act autonomously, it is also part of journalism's appropriate work to build the bonds of the society in other ways. "Human interest" stories are an example of stories that help build community. Consider stories about individuals or groups in the society who go out of their way to help other individuals or groups in need. Such stories contribute to community building in two ways. They reassure the members of the society that, even when they find themselves unable to respond to a need, there are others in the society who might assist them. Even though they may be unable to help themselves, they are not automatically cut off from the concerns of others: they remain, even under difficult circumstances, fellow members of the community. Second, such stories can also motivate other individuals or groups in the community to help others, either by contributing effort or other resources to the same good cause or by acting more energetically in relation to another cause.

A second example of "human interest" stories that contribute to community building is stories of persons suffering misfortune, even if there are no special efforts being made by others to assist them when the story is reported, and stories of the admirable achievements of members of the society. As Jacqui Banaszynski argues in chapter 16 of this volume, stories of other persons' misfortune can elicit empathy for those currently in trouble, and such feelings can bind members of the community together. Similarly, stories of achievement can elicit feelings of admiration or even pride that the person who has succeeded in a particular achievement is a member of one's own society. In this way such stories can contribute to community building even if they do not prompt readers to act in response. In fact, many who read or hear the story may not themselves have the resources or opportunity to help those whose misfortunes are reported or may lack interest in or the opportunity to strive for similar achievements. But eliciting empathy, like eliciting admiration or pride in others' achievements, can enhance the bond that joins people together as a society.

It is very possible, as every journalist knows, to report such stories in a fashion that is maudlin or sensational or merely ego-boosting and voyeuristic, and that therefore puts readers off rather than engaging them. But properly reported, human interest stories of this sort are examples of reporting that can build community and, by doing so, fulfill one of the central values of journalism.

In summary, while other values are undoubtedly important to good journalism (e.g., accuracy, good writing, a deep interest in the world and its people), we conclude these four to be central:

> Making discerning pursuit and effectively disseminating needed information,
>
> Sufficiently attending to society's pulse to clearly and effectively convey common social desires,
>
> Enhancing clients' autonomy by reporting on vital information and acting as a watchdog of powerful institutions, and
>
> Drawing upon and powerfully conveying those human interest stories that serve to build community.

With these values as the core, we will now examine how they best translate into ethically appropriate relationships.

The Ideal Relationship between Journalism and Its Audience

The third category of professional obligation concerns the relationship between journalists and journalistic organizations, on the one hand, and their audience, those who read, hear, or watch the product of their efforts. This relationship might seem to be quite straightforward. Either the audience reads, listens, or watches, or they don't. That is, journalism should consider its audience to be active only in deciding whether to attend to the product that is produced. Once that decision is made, the rest of the audience's role is completely passive, and there is nothing ethically significant to consider except the obligation to employ the central values just examined when producing stories.

This *could* be the relationship between journalists and their audience. But is it not the relationship that is built into the ethics of this profession in our society. The thesis of this part of this essay is that the ideal relationship, the one that journalists are committed to building between themselves and the people they serve is a *collaborative* relationship. Viewing the relationship as one in which the audience is simply passive, once it has chosen to read, listen, or watch, does not represent what journalists in our society are ethically committed to working toward.

We recognize there may be a gap here between what journalism's ethics *ought to* require in our society and what society, in dialogue with the profession, currently *does require*. This essay will propose that a collaborative relationship is the one to which professional journalists in our society are committed.

As the arguments in parts I and III of this book attest, journalism is not just a marketplace activity. Its historical significance and its importance to society and to political institutions (all reflected in its First Amendment protections) show journalism to be, first and foremost, a socially vital enterprise, and only secondarily a profit-making business. Indeed, if this were not the case, journalism ethics would be just another form of business ethics, and there would be no need for books like this one.

Furthermore, as noted above, we agree with Davis's conclusion that journalism is a profession. Consequently, its practitioners have special obligations to their clients, in particular the obligation to make clients' best interest the primary focus.[8] Professional-ethics literature has extensively explored which relationship model best helps journalists fulfill this and other professional obligations; the consensus favors a variant of the collaborative model, which we adopt here: the way to understand the ideal relationship between journalist and audience is to see them as partners in judging what information is needed, what information responds to common social desires, what enhances autonomy, and what builds community.

To focus (for the sake of brevity) on just one of these four, what does striving for a collaborative relationship imply about the information a society needs? It implies that, while the journalist has expertise in gathering data for and weighing the reliability of sources about a given story, the audience should be expected to be playing an active role in determining whether the result is dependable and useful for meeting the society's or a given group's needs. That is, the journalist should assume that the reader is capable, in a non-expert way, of evaluating whether information is needed and whether the means used for gathering it were legitimate and adequate. The journalist, thus, should include in the reporting enough background about the information and its sources that the audience can evaluate these.

The audience should not be viewed as passive in the sense of having no shared interest with the journalist about the well-being of the society (which passivity risks reducing their relationship to a commercial one); neither should the audience be viewed as passive in the sense that the journalist's ability so exceeds that of the audience that the audience should simply accept the journalist's judgment of relevance, dependability, and usefulness. One component of a collaborative relationship in practice is an openness on the part of journalists and journalistic organizations to accept feedback from their audience. But the feedback they actually receive is not necessarily representative of the whole audience. So, of even greater importance is the journalist's efforts to understand the audience in advance and to be responsive to the audience, especially regarding the audience's judgments about the two most important questions about any information: its dependability and its usefulness to the society. Similar arguments can be given for the other three central values.

To put this point differently, striving for a collaborative relationship with one's audience regarding needed information requires that the journalist reflect carefully on how co-investigators can work together to gather facts and interpret meaning. Clearly, one thing that is necessary is attending to the contribution of the other, which means, in practice, that each offers the fruits of his/her research and judgment to the other as, first of all, a hypothesis to be examined by the other, rather than as an already finished product. And this requires that, in presenting his/her conclusions, each provides the other with the sources of information, the reasons for thinking them dependable, and so on, so the other can see why the proposal is plausible as a hypothesis and can evaluate it properly in the light of relevant evidence.

Second, it is necessary that each investigator be open to the possibility that his or her research and judgment are not comprehensive. Third, each investigator must be as explicit as possible about the meanings that she attaches to what has been learned so others can interpret what is offered. These characteristics do not exhaust the characteristics of an ideal collaborative relationship, but they are a solid beginning and are suggestive of other characteristics that will make the relationship as collaborative as possible.

If we have done our job well, we have answered the first three questions critical to a method of ethical decision-making. We have addressed the purpose of journalism by determining whom journalists serve. From this, we discerned four central values, which in turn informed our determination of the ideal journalism–client relationship. Let us now turn to our practice rules and method.

Role-Related Responsibilities as an Ethical Guide for Journalists

Like all other professionals, journalists have a basic obligation to meet the special responsibilities attached to their role.[9] Paramount among these, as it is in nearly all human contexts, is the obligation to avoid causing unjustified harm. Journalists have ample opportunity to violate this principle; their expertise and the social role they fill give them the power to wreak considerable damage.

Of course, professionals sometimes cause harm that is justified. For example, a surgeon who removes the leg of someone with bone cancer is causing a disability but is doing so with the patient's consent and in the hope of saving the patient's life. A lawyer providing an adequate defense to the plaintiff in a libel case may well cause harm to the defendant reporter and news organization that have published defamatory statements. But this harm is justified if it is caused by a practitioner in the course of fulfilling his or her unique role-related responsibility, and if the responsibility cannot be met without causing such harm. So is it also the case for journalism when, for example, news organizations publish the names and details of politicians who have engaged in corruption. The actions of the news agency are within the scope of their unique role-related responsibilities, and they could not fulfill those responsibilities in any other way.

Thus, we need a systematic moral analysis that will help us discern just what the role-related duties are and whether associated harms are ethically justified. From there, we provide four categories of action the practitioner should examine when faced with an ethical challenge.

Two Initial Questions

The SMA begins with a two-part question:

What is the role-related responsibility of the profession or practitioner? If the intended action is among the role-related responsibilities of journalists, will the intended action of the practitioner cause potential emotional, physical, financial, or reputational harm?

If the answer to the second part is "yes," then journalists should consider, or engage in a conversation within their newsroom, to determine if causing such harm is justified because it is the only way for them to fulfill their role-related responsibilities. Sometimes that call is easy, as in the above corrupt-politician example. Or sometimes the call is easy for another reason, such as because withholding the identity of a child who has been sexually abused overrides the public's need to know. It is possible to name an alleged perpetrator (and thus provide an opportunity for others to come forward with additional charges—which, in combination with the goal of protecting other potential victims is the reason the potential harm to the perpetrator is justified) without identifying the children. In almost all cases, news organizations choose to avoid causing that additional harm by identifying the child victim. If causing harm is not directly tied to role-related responsibilities (e.g., the harmful material or embarrassing picture would be included just for the viewer's amusement), then, ethically speaking, the harm is not justified.

Questions to Determine If Causing Harm Is Justified

Two thousand years of thoughtful analysis in the study of moral philosophy have resulted in useful questions for determining when causing harm is justified and when it is not. The classical philosophers Aristotle, Immanuel Kant, and John Stuart Mill are those most often found in journalism casebooks. While these are not the only influential philosophers, their primary concerns and methods resonate with the public and with the social practices of journalism and many other professions. Questions based on those philosophers, and one from the influence of twentieth-century feminist philosophers, follow. Textbooks too often give students a "grab bag" of these theorists' views, typically presenting them as adversaries, and then leave the student to sort out the respective (dis)advantages. We believe, instead, the theorists, in fact, agree on key points, even if they come at them from different angles. We thus bring together their great thoughts to make sure that aspects of an ethical concern are considered, in a process we call "mixed formalism."[10]

If it is determined that a role-related action may cause harm, further analysis is required. Consider the following questions to determine if causing harm is justified:

(1) Does the intended action respect all persons affected? Does it treat all persons in the situation in a consistent and impartial way?

These questions are based on the moral philosophy of Kant, an eighteenth-century German philosopher. Kant taught that all persons were worthy of respect because of their shared humanity. We know a lot about other people, based on a kind of human analogy. I know that other humans are like me in that they generally want to avoid pain and death. If this were not true, torture and terrorism would not be possible.

Bringing Kant into our SMA means that we need to consider every person's right to avoid being caused unjustified harm. However, it is still ethically permitted to sometimes cause people harm. For example, Kant believed strongly in the state's right to punish those who disobeyed the law. Kant argued that people who knowingly disobey the law or intentionally do the wrong thing, actually *choose* the consequences of their action and so deserve those consequences.

Respecting the humanity of *everyone* involved in a situation means that journalists should make choices they can defend no matter who happens to be the victim or beneficiary of their publication. Any harm caused to the story's subject should be justified by the actions that the story's subject brought on himself or herself. If citizens know that anyone in a similar situation would be treated similarly, then journalists are acting impartially.

(2) Is each person getting what he or she is entitled to? Does the intended action promote the aggregate good of the community?

These questions come from the philosophical ethics of John Stuart Mill, a nineteenth-century British philosopher. Like Kant, Mill has great respect for the importance of individual human life, but he also discusses the importance of promoting the good and the growth of the community.

Just as Kant counsels that we need to respect the humanity in every person, Mill says that one should focus primarily on the principles of justice when considering how to treat people.

(2a) Are people getting what they have a legal and moral right to? Are they getting what they deserve, including the outcomes of any promises made to them? Are they being treated impartially?

Only if the answer to all of these questions is "yes" is it ethically permitted for someone who may cause harm to an individual to consider the next question.

(2b) What overall good is promoted by this action? What overall harm will come if the action is not taken?

Notice that the stress in this question is on the *overall* good and the *overall* harm resulting from an action; that is, both good and harm result when we take into account *everyone relevantly affected* by the action. This way of asking the question is associated with Mill and his predecessor in Utilitarian thinking, Jeremy Bentham. These thinkers are often (mis)represented as having taught that the standard of ethical action is "Do the greatest good for the greatest number." But phrasing it this way can lead to the inaccurate conclusion that Mill thought it was okay to sacrifice one individual for the happiness of the majority. Mill and Bentham both argued, however, that actions should promote the aggregate good—the good of the whole, which involves more than tallying how many people are harmed and how many are helped or made happy.

Thus, a profession's role-related responsibilities express how the profession is expected to promote the aggregate good. In the case of journalism, one example of the aggregate good is the information necessary for self-governance that the profession supplies. If the aggregate good is being promoted, then even the person who is being harmed should be able to agree to the publication of the information. For example, no burglar would want to have his actions reported; such reports are likely to make potential victims aware and vigilant. However, the burglar would want to be warned about someone who was a potential threat to him. Reporting thus promotes the overall interest of the burglar in addition to that of the larger society in that, at some point, the burglar might be protected by the journalist's reporting.

However, imagine running a photograph of a mother standing on the street and staring in horror as her house in engulfed in flames with her young children still in it. We can begin to see how applying the principles of justice might protect this woman. It is certainly legal to print such a photo, but one might argue that this woman has a moral right to be treated with respect and not to be objectified in such a moment. The pain caused by publication of that photo is not what she deserves. In addition, it is hard to imagine how publication of this photo would in any way promote the aggregate good. Human interest stories promote human bonding, but human bonding often occurs through the sacrifice of an individual. The harm caused to this individual (assuming that the photo is published without her consent) would not benefit her or people who might find themselves in a similar situation. People do not need to see this excruciating moment in this woman's life to assist in their self-governance.

(3) What would your moral or professional heroes do?

This question is inspired by Aristotle, who said that when we cannot figure out what to do, we should consult a person with practical wisdom. Professionally, as well as personally, it is good to have heroes, to have someone who exemplifies what it means to be a good journalist doing well. Choosing the action that your moral hero might choose leads one to consider what is ethically ideal.

(4) Is each person in the situation getting what he or she needs? How can we devise a solution that addresses each person's needs, and most particularly, the needs of the most vulnerable? Does the intended action promote relationship, and does it promote community? Does it promote trust among people? Is the process of decision-making itself respectful of everyone involved?

Feminist philosophers throughout the ages, and most particularly in the twentieth-century, have reminded us that it is rare that all people in a given situation have equal power. For the most part, there are vulnerable parties and they should be cared for first. Feminist philosophers tell us not to be distracted by the influence of the powerful in society, and urge us to give voice to the voiceless and to make sure that the parts of a community most likely to go unnoticed be given attention.

By carefully examining our actions in terms of these questions and aligning the answers with our role-responsibilities, we can determine into which of the four kinds of action, as noted below, our proposed course of action falls. Doing this carefully, whenever there is a complex ethical decision to be made, is what we mean by systematic moral analysis.

The Goal of SMA: Identifying Four Categories of Actions

Systematic moral analysis is the process by which thoughtful practitioners reason through an ethical concern. Practitioners should have all available facts before they begin, understanding that all analysis is made with some degree of uncertainty. We cannot have all the facts, ever. We cannot know how someone might react to the publication of certain facts; we can only make predictions, based on our own experience and empathy. SMA is not a calculation that results in a good/bad, right/wrong final answer. However, the rational base of this type of moral analysis promotes consistent decision-making that takes all factors into account. Careful reasoning results in four categories of possible actions:

1. Ethically prohibited (It would be just wrong to do x in this case, and here is why.)
2. Ethically required (The practitioner can fulfill role-related responsibilities only by taking one of these potential actions.)
3. Ethically permitted (The group of ethically permitted actions includes only those that fulfill role-related responsibilities without causing unjustified harm; this group of actions includes those considered "ethically required," and also shows why different news organizations might choose different ways of meeting their role-related responsibilities.)
4. Ethically ideal (These actions go beyond doing what is required or permitted in that ideal actions prevent or avoid harms rather than merely not causing them, or they address other harms caused.)

A Professional-Ethical Decision Guide

We believe that everything to this point can be combined into a set of questions to assist journalists in professional ethical decision-making. The resulting decision guide looks like this:

STEP ONE. Identify the courses of action available to the journalist (or the news organization) in the situation. Do not examine only the action presently under consideration; use your moral imagination and the assistance of other persons, if possible, to determine what other courses of action might be undertaken. Then carefully evaluate each of them using the following questions.

1. Does the action fulfill one or more of the professional journalist's role-related responsibilities?
   a. Is the action serving the public, that is, the people of the society in which the journalist practices? Or are the actions serving only the preferences of an individual or subgroup within the society?
   b. Does the action address the central values of journalism? Are there other available actions that would more effectively maximize these values for the public? If several central values are involved, does this action rank information the society needs above the other values?
   c. Does the action employ and facilitate a collaborative relationship between the journalist and the audience? Or does it negate or inhibit such a relationship? Are there other available actions that would do this better?
2. Will the action cause potential emotional, physical, financial or reputational harm?
3. Is causing this harm justified?
   a. Does the intended action respect all persons affected? Does it treat all persons in the situation consistently and impartially?
   b. Is each person getting what he or she is entitled to? Does the intended action promote the good overall? Do the agent's actions promote the aggregate good of the community? Are people getting what they have a legal and moral right to have? Are they getting what they deserve, including the outcomes of any promises made to them? Are they being treated impartially? What overall good is promoted by this action? What overall harm will come if the action is not taken?
   c. What would your moral or professional heroes do?
   d. Is each person in the situation getting what he or she needs? How can we devise a solution that addresses each person's needs, and

most particularly, the needs of the most vulnerable? Does the intended action promote relationship, and does it promote community? Does it promote trust among people? Is the process of decision-making itself respectful of everyone involved?

STEP TWO. Given the answers to the above questions, of which type is this action? The four possible characterizations are:

1. Ethically prohibited (It would be just wrong to do x in this case, and here is why.)
2. Ethically required (Only by taking one of these actions will the practitioner be able to fulfill the role-related responsibilities.)
3. Ethically permitted (This group of actions will overlap some of those in the "ethically required" scope of possibilities; the actions that are ethically permitted are those that fulfill role-related responsibilities without causing unjustified harm.)
4. Ethically ideal (These actions are those that go beyond doing what is required or permitted in that ideal actions prevent harms rather than merely not causing them, or they address other harms caused as well.)

Notes

1. David Ozar, "Professions and Professional Ethics," *Encyclopedia of Bioethics*, 3rd ed., ed. Stephen Post (New York: Thomson/Gale, 2003), 2158–68; Deni Elliott, *Ethics in the First Person: A Guide to Teaching and Learning Practical Ethics* (Lanham, MD: Rowman & Littlefield, 2007).

2. Society of Professional Journalists, *Code of Ethics* (Indianapolis, IN: Society of Professional Journalists, 1996); available online at http://www.spj.org/ethicscode.asp.

3. These are taken from Ozar's fuller analysis in "Professions" (p. 2162) where he includes six additional questions.

4. This focus on a particular society is what at least loosely distinguishes the journalist from the professional scholar, who aims to enlighten *the whole world*.

5. Deni Elliott, *Responsible Journalism* (Beverly Hills, CA: Sage, 1986), and Bill Kovach and Tom Rosensteil, eds., *Elements of Journalism* (New York: Crown, 2001).

6. Deni Elliott, *Ethics*, pp. 90–91.

7. Len Doyal and Ian Gough, *A Theory of Human Need* (New York, Guilford, 1991).

8. Identifying journalism's "client" is one of the sticking points to classifying it as a profession. However, we find Davis's arguments (below) compelling.

9. Elliott, *Ethics*, pp. 90–91.

10. Elliot, *Ethics*, p. 58.

2

Moral Development and Journalism

Renita Coleman

J ournalists don't start to learn about their ethical duties the day they walk into their first newsroom or journalism class. While new journalists do learn specifically about the ethics of their profession by watching other journalists, taking courses, and studying ethics codes, they hardly arrive at the industry as blank slates. Even the most neophyte journalists have had at least eighteen years to acquire, grow, and fine-tune the general moral compass they bring into the profession. Parents, friends, relatives, teachers, clergy, and others all have the potential to make a lasting impression on the new practitioner's future moral decisions. Questions such as whether and under what circumstances it is OK to deceive another, if one should keep the change that was returned in error, and how one justifies a lie are all based upon moral codes that are formed in early childhood and continue to develop as we learn and age. Those early ethical encounters provide the foundation for the kinds of moral decisions a journalist—or anyone in a professional capacity—will make. So do certain individual characteristics, such as how much education one has and the political ideology one subscribes to.

This chapter looks at how people develop into ethical beings, with special emphasis on Lawrence Kohlberg's moral-development theory. It then explores ethical development in the professions, including journalism. Just as medical professionals develop proficiency in areas unique to their work, such as ensuring patient confidentiality and avoiding harm, journalists develop special expertise in such topics as ensuring privacy, avoiding plagiarism and deception, and keeping promises. New journalists find that organizations, codes, and colleagues continue to shape their moral fiber. This chapter also examines the current research on the most important influences on journalists' quality of ethical reasoning. Above and beyond things such as religion and education, moral development for journalists is influenced by factors such as professional autonomy and experience with investigative reporting.[1]

Moral Development

The roots of moral-development theory, as a branch of psychology, extend back to the respected Swiss psychologist Jean Piaget.[2] Piaget set the wheels in motion for the systematic study of moral development when he mapped the stages of moral growth in young boys. From this work, he determined that moral reasoning is a set of cognitive operations characterized at the higher stages by the ability to consider more things in the mind at once and in more complex ways.[3] Erik Erikson extended Piaget's work in development beyond puberty into old age.[4] In his book *Childhood and Society*, Erikson theorized eight stages from birth to death, seeing growth as something that occurred throughout a person's life and that resulted from a conflict or crisis. When a person successfully resolved a significant internal struggle or challenge, he moved into the next higher stage of the life cycle.

Piaget and Erikson laid the groundwork for Kohlberg's theory of development specifically focused on morality. Kohlberg is best known for his six-stage theory, one of the more widely used today in research.[5] Kohlberg took the psychological idea of human development occurring in stages and combined it with ethical philosophy to propose how people progress ethically as they go through life. Kohlberg focused on how people chose what was right, and the cognitive processes, or kinds of reasoning, they used to justify their ethical decisions.

Key to Kohlberg's theory is the idea that ethical development is hierarchical: people improve at making good ethical decisions.[6] His theory rests on the assumption that some reasons used to make ethical decisions are better than others. The better reasons for choosing a course of action represent more comprehensive, coherent, elaborated, or developed ideas, and he described the course of moral development as evolving from simpler ideas to more complex ones. In Kohlberg's theory, the higher stages represent better reasoning. For a definition of what was "good" or "better," he looked to the ethical theorists from philosophy; that is, unique among moral-development theorists, Kohlberg embraced philosophy as important in the definition of what is moral.[7] For example, foundational principles, such as Mill's greatest aggregate good, or Kant's categorical imperative, are evident in Kohlberg's highest stage of ethical development.

Kohlberg relied most heavily on John Rawls's ethical and political theory.[8] Rawls proposed that the concept of justice originates from an "original position" in which the person making the ethical decision was ignorant of both her own station in life and that of others. She would not know whether she was an African American janitor with five children to support, or the white CEO of a corporation with a golden parachute. Those making ethical decisions would assume this original position in a hypothetical exercise behind what Rawls termed a "veil of ignorance." Kohlberg called it "moral musical chairs." Basically, it involved the ethical decision-maker's systematically taking the position of all participants in a dilemma and analyzing the situation from each person's, or no specific person's, viewpoint. If decision-makers did their reasoning behind a veil, Rawls concluded, it would result in all people being afforded equal dignity and respect. Thus, Rawls's model is emblematic of Kohlberg's highest level of reasoning—complex, abstract, and rule-driven.

Another similarity between Kohlberg's theory and Rawls's is in the moral problems they address. Both are macromoral theories, concerned with problems in society among strangers, competitors, and social institutions, not with special relationships among family, friends, and the groups one belongs to.[9] It is about the way fundamental rights and duties are distributed, with justice as the overriding ethical goal. Kohlberg's emphasis on justice is also more political than private, as is that of Rawls. Based more on the concept of what is right and good in a broader, social sense and less on individual standards, it is about impartial, generalizable norms, and a fair playing field for diverse people. While this is a limitation of the theory in that it does not include micromoral issues, it is also a strength in that it does not try to explain all ethical reasoning in every context. Kohlberg defended his choice to focus on macromorality by saying that it was important to understand ethical judgments that affected a broad range of people rather than those that affected only a few.[10] It is also a good orientation for ethics in professional settings, such as law, medicine, or journalism.

The Stages of Moral Development

Kohlberg believed people did not regress; that is, once a higher stage was achieved, the person never slipped back. Since Kohlberg's death, however, his students have modified that stance to say that people do use reasons from more than one stage at one time. They can regress and use lower stages at the same time they use the higher ones; however, generally, people are likely to use the higher stages more often as they grow and develop.[11] Each higher stage represents a more complex set of ethical considerations.

While Erikson proposed that a person goes through eight stages to develop an identity, Kohlberg narrowed the development of morals to six stages, which are in turn subsumed under three major levels, with two stages in each (his pupils have since combined the last level's stages into one). The three major levels are called Pre-conventional, Conventional, and Post-conventional, in ascending order of ethical quality.[12]

The Pre-conventional level represents the two lowest stages of ethical reasoning. As Piaget discovered, this type of thinking is found most often in children, who see that rules are made by authority figures and cannot be broken.

Breaking the rules results in punishment, and the reason one obeys the rules is either to avoid punishment or to gain rewards. In the first stage of this level, people tend to view what is ethically right as that which requires obedience to authority; obeying is right, disobeying is wrong. The second stage is defined by a concern with one's own welfare. Doing things that make you happy are "right." People using this level of morality make decisions based on self-interest; for example, they may choose to run a story because it might help their career. At this stage, people also realize that other people are self-interested. Here, reciprocity and fairness begin to emerge in a self-serving way. For example, if everyone is self-interested, people can make deals with each other, exchanging favors and cooperating so that everyone gets some measure of happiness.

The second level encompasses the two stages of Conventional reasoning. This is where rules begin to be respected for their own sake and are eventually seen as serving society. Those who have achieved this level of moral development see the rules as necessary for maintaining social order and as subject to change if there is a consensus for doing so. This level is defined by conformity to the expectations of society. Helping others and gaining their approval drives an individual's actions; moral reasoning is dominated by doing one's duty and maintaining social order for its own sake. At this stage, people expand on the idea of cooperating with others beyond the short term, and they realize that people establish enduring relationships that require long-term cooperation. Authority here is vested in the social groups to which the individual belongs. The notion of social systems is important, as is conformity, or doing what others expect. In the lower stage of this level, the social relationships that are valued are limited to friends, family, and people one knows. In the higher stage, they include strangers and even competitors and enemies, and cooperation is achieved through laws. Laws allow us to count on even those we don't know to behave in certain ways. In stages three and four, what is morally right is what the law says. Research suggests that most adults operate at this level of moral development most of the time.

Kohlberg's highest level is the Post-conventional.[13] At this level, laws and rules are respected only if they appeal to universal ethical principles. Rules are the result of intellectual reasoning, and they should achieve full and impartial reciprocity—that is, the rules themselves should not favor one group over another. Right and wrong, and the value of rules and law, are determined by their appeal to mutuality and universality. For example, even the ancient Egyptians' social system of slaves would be considered morally defensible by the standards of the Conventional level; rules and laws existed and were obeyed by all for the sake of maintaining social order. However, the idea that the happiness of some people (those served by the slaves) was more important than that of others (the slaves), would not meet the test of universality and reciprocity inherent in the Post-conventional level.

Individual principles of conscience define morality at this level. People who use this type of reasoning are concerned about the reason for the rules and are willing to challenge both social norms and self-interest for a more universal understanding. At this level, there is an awareness of both the process by which rules are arrived at and the content of the rules; shared ideals are open to debate and tests of logical consistency. People are aware of concepts such as a social contract that demands citizens uphold laws even if they are not in the individual's best interest. It also includes an understanding that some rights are beyond debate, for example, life and liberty. This most advanced form of ethical reasoning, Kohlberg says, involves an individual's cognitions and an ability to reflect independently, apart from others involved.

Moral Development in a Professional Setting

The person most associated with applying Kohlberg's theory to specific professions is James Rest.[14] Starting with nurses and dentists, the list of professionals whose moral development has been studied now includes veterinarians, doctors, social workers, and journalists, among others.[15] Rest and his colleagues also are known for creating a survey in a paper-and-pencil format that made it fast and easy to give to busy professionals. Called the Defining Issues Test (DIT), the survey is based on Kohlberg's theory. Scoring allots more "points" to a person who uses the higher stages more often in making ethical decisions.[16] The resultant score, called the "P score"("principled" score) is roughly the percentage of the time a person uses post-conventional considerations in his or her ethical thinking. The average adult scores about 40, meaning that 40 percent of the time, he or she considers the highest stage principles. The DIT has been used for more than thirty years in hundreds of studies, allowing us to see where certain professionals rank and how they compare with one another. In three studies of journalists, these professionals have ranked fourth, behind seminarians and philosophers, medical students, and physicians, but above dental students, nurses, graduate students, undergraduate college students, veterinary students, and adults in general.[17] (See Table 2.1 for a comparison of professions.)

The interest in ranking specific professions on the moral-development scale is not about "bragging rights" but rather about discerning what things predict higher level ethical reasoning, so that those things can be taught and encouraged. To that end, more than four hundred studies of moral development have identified three predictors of high moral reasoning that appear to cross professional boundaries.[18]

Influences on Moral Development

Any theory that claims to be "developmental" implies that people change as they age.[19] While age is generally implied in development theory, the first fundamental influence is education. Longitudinal studies have found a stage progression, as predicted by the theory, from high school into adulthood, with moral development leveling off when formal education stops. Furthermore, the key factors about age that foster moral development are life experiences involving intellectual stimulation, supported learning, and a life that includes energizing friends and family.[20] Many possible reasons that education improves moral development have been proposed, including the fact that college aims to develop critical-thinking skills and that professors expect students to give evidence for opinions and to think for themselves. Also, the social experience of college exposes students to a diversity of facts, ideas, people, and cultures. As well, the people who choose to go to college may be more interested in their own intellectual development than those not pursuing college, and college stimulates such development. Kohlberg thought it was learning to see things from other people's points of view that provided the key to growth in moral judgment.

Although fewer than 10 percent of all journalists have a graduate degree, enrollment in master's programs is growing by about 5 percent a year, a positive sign.[21] In a study of journalists, education was nearly significant in a statistical sense in predicting higher moral development; that is, those journalists with more education were more likely to score higher on the DIT than those with less education.[22] Furthermore, journalists are getting older; the median age was forty-one in the latest study—five years older than a decade ago.[23] Both of these changes bode well for improvement in journalists' ethical reasoning.

Interestingly, some forms of religious beliefs have a negative effect on moral development.[24] More fundamental or conservative religious beliefs consistently correlate with lower levels of moral development. This effect is seen only in those who believe in a literal interpretation of religious texts, as opposed to those who merely claim a religious affiliation. While there is debate over why this is the case, one plausible explanation is that some religions believe it is improper and sinful to question, critique, or scrutinize the church or divine authority. Furthermore, orthodox Christian beliefs are highly correlated with social intolerance and a greater disregard for others' rights.[25]

The final powerful predictor of moral development is political ideology.[26] Typically, conservative attitudes are more supportive of authority and established practices—consistent with the Conventional level of moral development. Political positions that encourage freedom of thought are more attuned to Post-conventional thinking. This correlation, encouragingly, did not appear in journalists. Affirming their long-claimed stance, journalists appear able to separate their political biases from their ethical reasoning.[27]

Journalism-specific Factors

Studies of journalists' ethical reasoning revealed two important influences—investigative reporting and increased professional autonomy—that led to higher quality ethical reasoning.[28]

Investigative reporting entails making moral judgments and wrestling with ethical issues as part of the reporting process more often than beat reporting does.[29] Thus, it makes sense that investigative reporters who regularly practice and refine their ethical skills would be likely to do better on tests of ethical reasoning. This finding does raise an important chicken-and-egg-type question: Which came first? Does investigative reporting attract better ethical thinkers or does it make them?

Professional autonomy, as defined by independence on the job, choices of assignments, and decision-making authority, was also a significant predictor of better ethical reasoning.[30] The good news is newsroom managers should find it easier to give their reporters such autonomy than to ensure that reporters are older, have higher education, or have investigative-reporting experience. Furthermore, as Christopher Meyers suggests in the introduction to this chapter, granting autonomy is just one of the many ways organizations affect employees' ethical reasoning and behavior. In short, newsroom managers who model good ethical behavior and who inspire independent, autonomous thinking in their employees will enhance those employees' ethical reasoning. They will also encourage a greater number of ethical organizations and the overall ethical quality of journalism. In this way, the industry can do its part in upholding proper ethical standards.

TABLE 2.1. Mean "P Scores" of Various Professions

Seminarians/philosophers	65.1
Medical students	50.2
Practicing physicians	49.2
Journalists	48.1–48.68
Dental students	47.6
Public relations professionals	46.2
Nurses	46.3
Lawyers	46
Graduate students	44.9
Undergraduate students	43.2
Pharmacy students	42.8
Veterinary students	42.2
Navy enlisted sailors	41.6
Orthopedic surgeons	41
Adults in general	40
Business professionals	38.13
Accounting undergraduates	34.8
Accounting auditors	32.5
Business students	31.35–37.4
Advertising professionals	31.64
Public relations students	31.18
High school students	31
Prison inmates	23.7
Junior high students	20

Compiled by the authors from individual published studies and data supplied by the Center for the Study of Ethical Development.

Notes

1. Renita Coleman and Lee Wilkins, "The Moral Development of Journalists: A Comparison with Other Professions and a Model for Predicting High Quality Ethical Reasoning," *Journalism & Mass Communication Quarterly* 81, no. 3 (2004), 511–527.

2. Jean Piaget, *The Moral Judgment of the Child* (New York: Free Press, 1965).

3. Piaget, *Moral Judgment.*

4. Erik H. Erikson, *Childhood and Society* (New York: Norton, 1964).

5. Lawrence Kohlberg, *The Philosophy of Moral Development: Moral Stages and the Idea of Justice* (Cambridge, MA: Harper & Row, 1981); Lawrence Kohlberg, *The Psychology of Moral Development: The Nature and Validity of Moral Stages* (San Francisco: Harper & Row, 1984).

6. *Kohlberg, Philosophy of Moral Development; Kohlberg, Psychology of Moral Development.*

7. Kit-Tai Hau and William J. F. Lew, "Moral Development of Chinese Students in Hong Kong," *International Journal of Psychology* 24 (1989).

8. John Rawls, *A Theory of Justice* (Cambridge, MA: Belknap, 1971).

9. James R. Rest et al., *Postconventional Moral Thinking: A Neo-Kohlbergian Approach* (Mahwah, NJ: Lawrence Erlbaum, 1999).

10. Rest et al., *Postconventional.*

11. Rest et al., *Postconventional.*

12. Lawrence Kohlberg, "State and Sequence: The Cognitive-Developmental Approach to Socialization," in *Handbook of Socialization: Theory and Research,* ed. E. Goslin (Chicago: Rand McNally, 1969).

13. Kohlberg originally divided this into two stages. His followers have found the separation confusing and unnecessary and I stick with that reading here.

14. James R. Rest, *Moral Development: Advances in Research and Theory* (New York: Praeger, 1986); James. R. Rest, "Morality," in *Handbook of Child Psychology, Vol. 3 Cognitive Development,* ed. P. H. Mussen (New York: John Wiley & Sons, 1983).

15. J. R. Rest and Darcia Narvaez, eds., *Moral Development in the Professions: Psychology and Applied Ethics* (Hillsdale, NJ: Lawrence Erlbaum, 1994).

16. For details about the DIT and how it is scored, please see R. Coleman and L. Wilkins "Moral Development: A Psychological Approach to Understanding Ethical Judgment," in *Handbook of Mass Media Ethics,* ed. Lee Wilkins and Clifford G. Christians (Mahwah, NJ: Lawrence Erlbaum, 2008), 40–54.

17. Coleman and Wilkins, "Moral Development of Journalists"; Renita Coleman and Lee Wilkins, "Searching for the Ethical Journalist: An Exploratory Study of the Ethical Development of News Workers," *Journal of Mass Media Ethics* 17, no. 3 (2002); Thomas L. Westbrook, "The Cognitive Moral Development of Journalists: Distribution and Implications for News Production" (Austin: University of Texas, 1995).

18. *Rest et al., Postconventional.*

19. Rest et al., *Postconventional.*

20. D. Deemer, "Moral Judgment and Life Experience," *Moral Education Forum* 14, no. 2 (1989).

21. David Weaver et al., *The American Journalist in the 21st Century* (Mahwah, NJ: Lawrence Erlbaum, 2006); Jarrett Renshaw, "Glass Half Full: While Journalism's Job Pool Shrinks, J-School Enrollments Expand," *Columbia Journalism Review* (Sept./Oct. 2007), http://www.cjr.org/short_takes/glass_half_full.php (accessed June 3, 2008).

22. Coleman and Wilkins, "Moral Development of Journalists."

23. *Weaver et al., American Journalist in the 21st Century.*

24. *Rest et al., Postconventional Moral Thinking: A Neo-Kohlbergian Approach.*

25. Radha J. Parker, "The Relationship between Dogmatism, Orthodox Christian Beliefs, and Ethical Judgment," *Counseling and Values* 34, no. 3 (1990); Albert Ellis, "Fanaticism That May Lead to a Nuclear Holocaust: The Contributions of Scientific Counseling and Psychotherapy," *Journal of Counseling and Development* 65, no. 3 (1986).

26. *Rest and Narvaez, Moral Development in the Professions.*

27. Coleman and Wilkins, "Moral Development of Journalists."

28. Coleman and Wilkins, "Moral Development of Journalists."

29. James S. Ettema and Theodore L. Glasser, *Custodians of Conscience: Investigative Journalism and Public Virtue* (New York: Columbia University Press, 1988).

30. Coleman and Wilkins, "Moral Development of Journalists."

PART II

History and Justification

Introduction

Quick, name all the businesses that have explicit U.S. Constitutional protection. It's a pretty short list: "the press."

Congress shall make no law . . . abridging the freedom of speech, or of the press. . . .

Simple words and powerful—unique—protections, both of which the courts have been trying to interpret for the last two hundred–plus years. Just what does it *mean* to have a free press, and how far should the protections extend? For example, while they have been expanded to include publishing generally, including the Internet, such protections do not extend to other news media. The courts long ago determined that because television and radio rely on limited publicly owned airspace, their activities are regulated by the federal government. Broadcast stations are required to have a federally granted license to operate, one that must be periodically renewed and that, in theory at least, can be withheld if the station does not meet its public-service requirements. Try to imagine the uproar if the government attempted to impose a public-service duty upon newspapers, let alone insisted upon licensing.

While persons in the United States take these press protections for granted, they are in fact extraordinary—rare among nations, both contemporary and historical. They are also a pretty good deal for newspapers. You could start a newspaper tomorrow that prints nothing but hourly updates on, say, Lindsay Lohan, and the Constitution would prevent the government from interfering in or regulating your activities.[1] Surely such tripe isn't what the Founders had in mind when they penned the Bill of Rights. They envisioned soaring ideas, grand debates, powerful intellectualism, along the lines of the Federalist and Anti-Federalist Papers, right?

Well, they certainly may have hoped for that, but they also knew that guarantees of freedom would unavoidably extend to drivel. They knew this because there was plenty of it in their day—commentary and, especially, cartoons that would make even our cable talk jocks blush. So if they knew grand paeans to democracy would reside alongside smut, why did the Founders give press freedom such a privileged Constitutional status? Because they also knew, or at least believed, modern democracy could not otherwise survive.

I use the "believed" qualifier because, remember, democracy was still very much an experiment, one no Western nation had attempted since the ancient Greeks. The Founders appealed to powerful but mainly theoretical arguments from the likes of Milton and Rousseau, but they had no sustained empirical evidence those arguments were right.

Were they? Stephanie Craft and Sandra Borden think so. Both believe that contemporary journalism could—should—do a far better job of responsibly informing and involving the citizenry and they also conclude a free press is vital to democracy. But, importantly, neither defends the dominant view of absolutist libertarianism that any direct government involvement in press activities is prohibited. Neither does Herman Wasserman, whose primary task is to provide an overview of contemporary global journalism as it has adopted, rejected, or transformed notions of freedom dominant in Western press values. He notes, in particular, the potential disconnect between press rights premised on individual liberty and the realities—political and moral—of some African contexts.

For Craft—who also provides a succinct and informative history of press rights, including discussion of key U.S. Supreme Court cases—press freedom is "the vanguard of all liberties," through its dual role as informer and watchdog. As a constitutionally protected Fourth Estate, news media alone have the standing to effectively challenge those who wield social, economic, and political power; they alone can "comfort the afflicted and afflict the comfortable."[2] "News media," of course, are not restricted to so-called mainstream media (MSM). Bloggers play an increasingly important watchdog role and are slowly also becoming genuine informers (i.e., not just aggregators of MSM news).

Craft, though, also concludes that with press freedoms come duties, for individual journalists and for news organizations. And if they shirk those duties, she argues, it would not be a First Amendment violation for the government to provide at least positive incentives for a more responsible press. She points to Finland, where the government provides "direct grants to newspapers and funds to political party presses" and yet has been judged as having significantly greater press freedoms than do U.S. papers.

Key to this part of her argument—one extended considerably in the essays by Ian Richards, Rick Edmonds, and Marty Steffens in part 5—is the recognition that government is only one threat, and probably not the greatest. For that, one must look at the marketplace, at how economic forces motivate and constrain press activities. It is also unclear which duties would apply to new media and how one might enforce them.[3]

Although she comes at the issues from a different theoretical starting point, Borden calls upon journalists to move beyond minimalist First Amendment rights and instead to embrace socially and professionally situated virtues. She argues the purpose of the press, and ultimately its social value, is found in its *communitarian* role. She writes, "Liberalism's conception of liberty as consisting primarily in the preservation of personal prerogative does not give enough attention to positive rights and their link to the common good. . . . This essay [argues] an occupation's purpose provides it with moral justification if it can be integrated into a broader conception of the human *telos,* or natural purpose."

In classically Aristotelian language, Borden implies the justification for press freedom is found not in its ability to sustain individual rights or preferences, but in its promotion of human excellence—individual and social. She gives considerable attention to liberalism's shortcomings, showing how a communitarian approach is superior. She then demonstrates how, from this perspective, the press's role extends beyond being a watchdog, to helping provide the conditions for a truly participatory democracy, a role that "embraces the more morally ambitious goal of helping citizens to live a good life."

While I am not comfortable with some communitarians' characterization of the liberal rights tradition, Borden is careful not to overstate the criticism. And even if one is more sympathetic to liberalism, as most students are, communitarians provide a powerful challenge: is the negative right of free expression adequate to justify a morally grounded journalism?[4] That is, regardless of constitutional protections, shouldn't news media strive for more than the moral minimum? Shouldn't the public good be at least as important a driving value, particularly given contemporary market forces? If, like any other business, they're simply in it for the money, why should they alone be exempt from regulation?

The clearly dominant journalistic mindset, however, would find these conclusions anathema. While some version of the public-benefit—even of the "with liberties come duties"—view is present in the public-journalism movement, the typical street reporter would howl at the prospect of partnering with government or, heaven forbid, being regulated. Acknowledging a duty to the public, however, by no means entails government involvement, and both Craft and Borden would certainly prefer journalism meet its duties independent of government involvement. Is this possible, especially given market forces?

For Wasserman, these noninterference concerns are interesting enough but typically not immediately relevant to journalists in emerging nations: "While developed countries are seeing an ongoing reshaping of what counts as journalism or a journalist, developing regions often struggle just to establish a journalistic presence." And as that presence emerges, it often looks very different from journalism in the United States. Western, liberal values often have a limited place; in Wasserman's words, "different cultural and social formations also play a role in what we may consider the ideal role for journalism in society. In many African countries, for example, the way people interact with journalism and media should be understood in terms of the way they negotiate between different roles in society. While they perform the roles of individual citizens in ways similar to that of liberal democracies in the developed world, they are also subjects, bound by loyalties to ethnic, cultural or religious groups."

The questions these authors raise are among the most important in this book: is journalism, *real* journalism—investigative, informative, watchful, promoting of human excellence, appropriately responsive to the circumstances of its community—still possible? As noted in the introduction, we would all be far worse off without good news media. So what do we need to do to sustain it? Can you, as future practitioners, fulfill all the noted roles?

The rest of this book is intended to help answer these questions in the affirmative. Those answers, though, require theory and practice, conceptual analysis and real-world problems, all nicely provided by our authors in this chapter.

Notes

1. Lest you think there could be no market for Lindsay Lohan news, when I did a Google search on the correct spelling of Lohan's name, the top entry was only three hours old and was one of millions of hits. Regarding government regulation, exceptions are libel (a civil action with such high standards—knowledge of falsehood and intent to harm—it is very difficult to successfully sue) and obscenity, which requires only that publications must not violate community standards and must not be in view of children.

2. For a more hesitant take on this famous phrase, see the Project for Excellence in Journalism's commentary on the Committee of Concerned Journalists' Web site: http://www.concernedjournalists.org/watchdog-misunderstood. Accessed October 1, 2008.

3. See Jane Singer's essay (chapter 8 of this volume) for one answer to that question.

4. In *On Liberty*, John Stuart Mill makes a kind of "invisible hand" case that free expression enhances the emergence of truth, by which society as a whole benefits (New York: Bobbs-Merrill, 1956). Even Adam Smith, though, assumed the invisible hand would be guided by a virtuous character, one that had social advantage as a primary motive. (See Mark Evans, "Virtues, Ethics, and the Introductory Economics Course," and Steven Gamboa, "Economics and Ethics: A Tale of Mutual Dependence," both available at http://www.cs.csub.edu/~donna/kie/research.html.)

3

Press Freedom and Responsibility

Stephanie Craft

Freedom House, an organization that promotes democratic values around the world, annually ranks nations by the amount of freedom they accord to the press. Perhaps surprisingly, the United States does not appear in the top ten of recent rankings. Despite the First Amendment to the U.S. Constitution, which prohibits laws that would abridge free press rights, and widespread agreement that the United States is among the most democratic nations in the world, the United States shares the number-sixteen ranking with Estonia, Ireland, Germany, Monaco, and St. Lucia.[1]

In North Korea, the nation with the least press freedom in the world, the constitution includes a guarantee of freedom of speech, but expression that does not align with the "collective spirit" is not permitted. In Iceland, which, along with Finland, has the greatest press freedom, speech and press freedom are constitutionally guaranteed, but a person who denigrates the doctrines of religious groups faces fines and imprisonment. And in Finland the government has provided direct grants to newspapers and funds to political party presses in its autonomous territory, Aland Island.

But wait, you might say. The governments of North Korea and Iceland both place limits on the press, so why is North Korea considered the worst? And why is Iceland considered to have greater press freedom than the United States, where the Constitution not only guarantees freedom of speech and the press but does so without limits on expression about religious or other groups? Moreover, doesn't the Finnish government's financial support for journalism put the news outlets' independence at risk? If the government intervenes in free expression—whether by exercising strict control over all speech, prohibiting certain kinds of press content, or even promoting the political press—then what does it mean for the press to be free?[2]

The answer to that question depends, first of all, on what one believes the function of the press to be. Is it to support—and build citizen support for—the regime? Such would seem to be the case in North Korea, where press freedom is construed as freedom to promote what the regime deems the interests of the collective. Or is the function of the press to aid citizens in their individual efforts to be self-governing, particularly as that involves making sure the government acts in the public interest?

These examples, then, demonstrate how important it is to be clear about what we mean by "freedom" of the press; what, if any, legitimate role the government can or ought to play in promoting it; and what the press is supposed to do with the freedom it is guaranteed. The experience of these countries with vastly different levels of freedom suggests that independence from government control, the kind of independence enjoyed by the U.S. press, may not be the only, or even the most important, kind of freedom the press needs to perform its function in democracy. The rankings by Freedom House reflect this understanding, as they are based on evaluations of the economic and political environments in which the press operates, in addition to the legal circumstances, such as constitutional guarantees of freedom.

This essay proceeds from an American point of view, though many of the issues apply to democratic systems more broadly.[3] First, I explore what democracy needs from the press, what the press requires to meet those needs, and whether, in the United States, the press and democracy are getting what they need. Next, I focus on the kinds of moral obligations the press might have, given the essential democratic role it plays and the freedom it has to do so. Finally, I consider the future of press freedom and responsibilities in the face of old constraints and new technological realities.

What Does Democracy Need from the Press?

Free expression, including criticism of government policies and actions, is among the key markers of a democracy. The system through which such expression occurs differs among the world's democracies, but for our purposes, the central issue is that the press, in whatever form, plays a role in sustaining democratic life.

Eloquent statements about this essential role abound in the writings of Thomas Jefferson, James Madison, and their fellow Founders; and in U.S. Supreme Court rulings, the columns of journalists, and the proceedings of blue-ribbon panels, such as the 1947 Commission on Freedom of the Press:

> Freedom of the press is essential to political liberty. Where men
> cannot freely convey their thoughts to one another, no freedom is
> secure. Where freedom of expression exists, the beginnings of a free
> society and a means for every extension of liberty are already present.

Free expression is therefore unique among liberties: it promotes and protects all the rest.[4]

This notion of press freedom as the vanguard of all liberties finds support in the common observation that "only the press . . . has the capacity to do business on an equal footing with the government, to inform the public, and to facilitate the exchange of public opinion."[5]

Timothy Cook, summarizing James Curran, identifies five specific needs of democracy that the news media system can (and should) fulfill: representation, deliberation, conflict resolution, accountability, and information dissemination.[6] The first three functions together refer to the forum that news media provide for civil society's groups and organizations to make themselves heard or represented in public life, to communicate with one another and with the government about issues affecting them, and to seek ways of resolving disagreements. This public-forum role highlights the importance of the press in building civic culture, a topic Sandra Borden takes up in more depth in the next chapter. The last two functions, accountability and information dissemination, refer to the press's role in monitoring those in power and giving citizens the information they need to participate effectively in decision-making about public affairs. These functions are often expressed in terms of two distinct but related metaphors: the marketplace of ideas and the watchdog.

The "marketplace of ideas" metaphor is generally traced to John Milton's 1644 treatise on freedom, *Areopagitica*, in which he asked, "Who ever knew Truth put to the worse, in a free and open encounter?"—a question similar to that found in the writings of a number of Enlightenment scholars, including Jean-Jacques Rousseau and John Stuart Mill. Not all these thinkers fully embraced the idea that the truth is found through free and open encounters (e.g., Milton worried that the unfettered and uneducated masses would choose the wrong ideas), and others have been uncomfortable with the implied commodification of ideas (e.g., Thomas Jefferson "never appeared to have conceived of public discourse as a marketplace. Instead, he seemed to think of it as a town meeting"[7]). Nonetheless, the metaphor has had significant rhetorical power in scholarship and judicial opinions. Supreme Court Justice Oliver Wendell Holmes's dissent, in *Abrams v. United States*, a case in which several men were convicted of violating the Espionage Act of 1917, is perhaps the best-known example. In criticizing the conviction of Abrams (and others) for distributing leaflets supporting the Russian Revolution, Holmes wrote:

> When men have realized that time has upset many fighting faiths,
> they may come to believe even more than they believe the very
> foundations of their own conduct that the ultimate good desired is
> better reached by a free trade in ideas—that the best test of truth is
> the power of the thought to get itself accepted in the competition of
> the market.

In the U.S. Supreme Court's landmark 1964 decision in *New York Times v. Sullivan*, the marketplace metaphor transforms from rhetorical device to rationale. The case began with a full-page advertisement published in the *Times* seeking funds to help the Rev. Martin Luther King Jr. pay legal fees. The ad, which was signed by a number of religious and civil rights leaders, described the harassment that African Americans were facing in their struggle for civil rights and included details of abuses by Montgomery, Alabama, police. L. B. Sullivan, an elected commissioner in Montgomery, sued the *Times* for libel, claiming the ad contained several factual errors. Sullivan won in the Alabama courts, but the U.S. Supreme Court reversed the judgment.[8]

In the majority opinion, Justice William Brennan acknowledged the factual errors but also noted that Sullivan was a public official. If those who would criticize public officials could be held liable for minor mistakes, Brennan argued, then the potential for self-censorship was great. As Timothy Cook notes, "Brennan's bugaboo was the era of the 1790s, when, under the Alien and Sedition Acts, President John Adams's administration prosecuted editors in the opposition camp for 'seditious libel' that it alleged brought the government into disrepute and thereby undermined authority."[9] Brennan's remedy was to limit public officials' ability to win libel cases unless they can show "actual malice." The rationale in his opinion, Cook notes, was firmly grounded in marketplace thinking: "Thus we consider this case against the background of a profound national commitment to the principle that debate on public issues should be uninhibited, robust and wide-open, and that it may well include vehement, caustic, and sometimes unpleasantly sharp attacks on government and public officials."[10]

While the "marketplace of ideas" language sees the press as the locus and even promoter of democratic discussion, unrestrained by state or religious authority and offering the widest possible range of opinions, the watchdog metaphor demands even more from the press. In the watchdog role, the press plays an active part as a check on those in power. The fact that the press is the only entity with such capacity is part of the influential view of the press as an institution—the Fourth Estate—"an entity serving," Bollinger explains, "a critical, quasi-official function in the political system. It elevates the press to the highest rung on society's organizational chart and anoints it as the public's representative."[11]

The watchdog role relies on one basic assumption: Those with power, especially governments, tend to abuse it. The watchdog is supposed to start barking when they do. W. Lance Bennett and William Serrin define journalism in the watchdog vein as "(1) independent scrutiny by the press of the activities of government, business, and other public institutions, with an aim toward (2) documenting, questioning, and investigating those activities, in order to (3) provide publics and officials with timely information on issues of public concern."[12]

The watchdog role is among the most "hallowed" in U.S. journalism, and it is, indeed, difficult to match the fiery and inspirational rhetoric it has produced.[13] The nineteenth-century publisher Joseph Pulitzer famously contended that "more crime, immorality and rascality is prevented by the fear of exposure in the newspapers than by all the laws, moral and statute ever devised."[14] Fast forward 150 years or so and Charles Lewis, the founder of the Center for Public Integrity, a nonprofit investigative-reporting organization, echoes just this view: "Serious journalism, public interest, energy and sometimes outrage—all happening together and at once—have often brought out the best in our leaders. Indeed, independent, investigative journalism about the uses and abuses of power have positively influenced the course of U.S. history on many momentous occasions."[15]

Justice Potter Stewart considered the watchdog role unique to the press and one accorded special constitutional status. Speaking at Yale Law School in 1974, Stewart emphasized that the founders made a distinction between free speech and the free press and argued they would not have done so if they did not see the press as playing some sort of unique, institutional role. "The publishing business is, in short, the only organized private business that is given explicit constitutional protection," he concluded. The founders distinguished the press in this way because they intended it "to create a fourth institution outside Government as an additional check on the three official branches." The press was intended to provide "expert scrutiny" of government.[16]

While the concept of special status for the press has never received the sort of judicial support for which Stewart argued—for example, the Court has refused to recognize a right of the press to refuse to reveal sources—it remains a potent part of journalists' self-identity and of dominant popular notions of the press in society. Even so, it highlights a tension in First Amendment thinking, as I will explain in the next section. For now, we have a basic answer to the first question I posed: democracy requires a press that is both open to the voices of the public and powerful enough to hold government to account.

What Does the Press Need to Perform Its Democratic Functions?

If government is prone to overstep its authority and the press is the only entity capable of standing up to it, and if wide-open debate is essential to democracy and the press is uniquely qualified to foster that debate, then what must be true of the circumstances in which the press operates? That is, what permits the press to do its job? The answer to these questions appears at first glance to be tautological: the press requires freedom to do the things a free state requires of it. A complete response, however, must offer some account of what we mean by "freedom." Freedom from what? Freedom for what?

The First Amendment to the U.S. Constitution offers a direct answer, in its prohibition of government interference in free expression. The amendment reads, in part: "Congress shall make no law . . . abridging the freedom of speech, or of the press." The absolutist, and highly influential, view in First Amendment jurisprudence and among journalists has been that "no law" means *no* law. Any action by the government to suppress or punish the press is seen as contrary to the Constitution.[17] It is a commonsense connection: If the government intrudes in the activities of the press, then the press cannot really be said to be free, the public cannot receive the information it needs, and democratic values are undermined. Bollinger calls this the "central image of the American ideal of freedom of the press," which found its fullest expression in the 1964 *New York Times v. Sullivan* decision.[18]

Bollinger argues that *Sullivan*, though fairly recent in historical terms, has contributed more to societal understanding of press freedom than has any other case; it articulates an intellectual framework in which "the press is the public's representative, its agent, helping stand guard against the atavistic tendencies of the state and serving as a forum for public discussion."[19] In such a framework, the press is and must remain autonomous. While not all Court decisions subsequent to *Sullivan* have favored the press, the autonomy model has become the default position. It is difficult to overstate the power of this line of reasoning among journalists. As Frederick Schauer describes:

> For most journalists, especially American ones, belief in the "chilling effect" is a central feature of their professional ideology. Concern over the deterrent effect of potential legal liability is an omnipresent feature of journalistic discourse, and the view is widespread that the press is better when it is more free, that it is more free when there is less law, and that when there is less law the press is more able to perform its functions in a democracy.[20]

Notice that the government is the primary potential foe of freedom in this account. Certainly, government action would have been the chief concern of Madison and the other Framers, who in drafting the Constitution and Bill of Rights were reacting to aspects of English law that they found particularly irksome, such as licensing and the exercise of prior restraint. And, of course, these founding documents were intended to elucidate the nature of the relationship between the people and the government they elect to serve them, so it is logical that they saw the government as the key threat.

The press, then, needs freedom *from* government *for* the purpose of giving the people access to diverse information and ideas and holding the government accountable. This answer, however, is still incomplete, as any account of press freedom must define who or what counts as the press. Here, what Cook describes as a duality in First Amendment thinking becomes clear: In guaranteeing press freedom, were the framers protecting individual or institutional rights?[21] The answer has implications for any proposed policies to enhance press freedom and for understanding the kinds of responsibilities we might rightly assign to the press.

The duality is evident in the "marketplace" and "watchdog" rationales for press freedom, going back to the Revolutionary period and resonating well into the present. The Pennsylvania Constitution of 1776, for example, included two separate clauses regarding press freedom: first, "the people have a right to freedom of speech, and of writing, and publishing their sentiments; therefore, the freedom of the press ought not to be restrained"; and second, "the printing presses shall be free to every person who undertakes to examine the proceeding of the legislature, or any part of government."[22] In the *Red Lion* case in 1969, the U.S. Supreme Court likewise focused on individual rights to receive information over media rights to disseminate it.[23] In both examples, then, press freedom is seen as belonging to citizens as much as, if not more than, to media institutions. Even *Sullivan*, the case so important to our conception of press freedom, emphasized the importance of citizens' ability to voice their views without fear of legal consequences.

In the next sections, this duality will be explored further, as it relates to the sources of interference and pressure on news media and the corresponding duties these metaphors and models seem to suggest the press has.

Does the Press Have What It Needs? Is It Free?

Just 38 percent of the world's nations have a free press, according to Freedom House's analysis. And, as I've already noted, the United States is not at the top of the list, even though it is clear from the preceding discussion that such freedom is a cornerstone of U.S. democracy, that specific protections were created to ensure it, and, as I'll discuss below, that certain responsibilities accrue from it. Press protection, though, is aimed almost entirely at preventing the government from squelching expression. The First Amendment does not address the kinds of control that economic, social, and political pressures can exert on the press, inhibiting its ability to act independently, make its own judgments, and, ultimately, perform its functions as a marketplace of ideas and as a watchdog. Particularly in the realm of political news, these pressures, Bartholomew Sparrow contends, create an environment in which news media often "violate their own ethical standards and, indeed, the norms of democratic government."[24]

Economic pressures arise from the fact that the U.S. press consists almost entirely of commercial enterprises that need to make a profit. Advertising subsidizes journalism, and news outlets are increasingly owned by public (i.e., stock-issuing) companies, both of which mean that the public is not the only stakeholder the press must satisfy. It is entirely possible, and all too common, for the interests of advertisers and stockholders to conflict with the interests of citizens. The temptation is to treat the public as an audience and journalism as any other product and, therefore, to focus on satisfying audience wants over citizen needs. The result is a conflation of the marketplace of ideas with an actual marketplace in which goods are bought and sold. Where Milton believed ideas with greater truth would win in the marketplace, ideas with greater ability to generate profit, regardless of their truth value, are considered marketplace winners. Blogs, news aggregators, and other new media sources for news have intensified economic pressures, particularly on newspapers. Much of the work traditional news organizations produce at considerable expense is available for free via these Internet news and opinion outlets. (Ian Richards and Marty Steffens address the business of journalism in more depth in chapters 11 and 13.)

Social and political pressures, and even journalistic competition, also inhibit press freedom. For example, efforts to diminish public accusations of media bias can contribute to the production of less hard-hitting or controversial news, as evidenced in news coverage in the run-up to the Iraq War. Also, the national press is dependent on the very political actors it is supposed to be monitoring in its watchdog role. A heavy reliance on official sources in reporting means that journalists may not feel—or really be—free to pursue stories that might alienate those sources.

This analysis treats "the press" as a single entity even though it is made up of thousands of individual journalists working for many news organizations. That is not a mistake. The results of individual journalists' work are strikingly uniform, in part because they face uniform external constraints. While not working in concert in a conspiratorial sort of way, news media tend to act in concert, covering the same stories in much the same way. This interplay of forces points to the layered quality of press freedom:

> In terms of the day-to-day operation of the newsroom, journalists
> retain a remarkable degree of control and autonomy; they and they
> alone decide how to write their stories, which sources to contact,
> what quotes to use, and so on. But power at this level differs in kind,
> and pales in comparison to, the power associated with the allocative
> decisions that determine basic policies, long-term goals, and the
> general disposition of resources.[25]

While individual journalists control technical aspects of their work, they do not control the more substantial components of news gathering. And even the news organizations whose control is more substantive are bound by economic, political, and social forces. Institutionally speaking, then, the U.S. press is not, in fact, entirely free, and *institutionally* is what matters most, if the press is to perform its marketplace and watchdog roles effectively. Also, institutional independence is what people likely have in mind when they criticize the performance of "the media."

What I am calling the layered quality of independence here brings us back to the duality in First Amendment thinking—the tension between individual and institutional conceptions of press freedom—mentioned earlier. As an institution, the press is generally free from government intrusion (though broadcasters face greater regulation than do print media), but constrained by economic and political forces. This circumstance is hardly new. The Commission on Freedom of the Press (known as the Hutchins Commission) was already, in 1947, sounding the alarm about ownership concentration and economic pressures on the performance of news media. But here's the rub: the First Amendment is routinely invoked, at least by journalists, not just to protect the press from government restriction but also to shield it from government attempts to mitigate the negative impact of other external pressures on the press. That is, almost every law regarding the press is seen as abridging freedom, to use First Amendment language, not as potentially enhancing it. To offer one example, the challenge to the Fairness Doctrine, which was the basis of the *Red Lion* case, alleged that such a government mandate to broadcast certain content amounted to a violation of broadcasters' First Amendment rights. Contrast this with the Finnish government's direct financial support of some press outlets.

Meanwhile, individual access to the public forum is largely unrestricted. In fact, thanks to the Internet, citizens' opportunity to speak and be heard may be greater now than in previous generations. So the press is both *more* and *less* free, depending on where one looks.

Our next step is to consider whether obligations are attached to press freedom and what can be done if the press is too constrained to act on them.

Does Press Freedom Entail Responsibility?

It is difficult to imagine any other answer to this question but "yes," given how dependent democratic life is on the accountability and openness a free press promotes and provides. Moreover, if one conceives of the press as having special constitutional status, it is not unreasonable to suggest that the press likewise has special, corresponding duties. For the Hutchins Commission, which saw the problems of the press as "public dangers" and not just "private vagaries," the duties of the press arise directly from its rights: "Its moral right will be conditioned on its acceptance of this accountability. Its legal right will stand unaltered as its moral duty is performed."[26] That sounds a little like a threat, and, in some sense, it was. How far would the Hutchins Commission go to ensure that the press acted on its duty? According to Bollinger, "The commission stopped short of calling for government regulation. But such involvement clearly was not unthinkable. Freedom of the press, it said again and again, ought to be viewed as a 'conditional right,' one extended by society because of the advantages an autonomous press might provide."[27]

There is, however, some discomfort with this notion of duties. That the problems the Hutchins Commission described sixty years ago persist today implies that few of its recommendations took hold. The libertarian bent of much of press theory—for example, the ideas that "no law" means *no* law and that the market is the best arbiter of competing messages—has meant that attempts to assign responsibilities to the press face enormous obstacles. If the talk turns to enforcement, the First Amendment trump card is played and the discussion is over. News media accountability in the United States, then, is voluntary, dependent on the conscience of individual journalists, the civic-mindedness of media owners, and the judgments of the court of public opinion.

That accountability is voluntary does not mean it is empty. Journalists see their independence—and press freedom generally—as not just a right but also an obligation to act in specific ways. A duty to "act independently" can be found in the Society of Professional Journalists code of ethics, which instructs journalists to "be free of obligation to any interest other than the public's right to know." Among the examples of independent action are to "be vigilant and courageous about holding those with power accountable" and to resist advertiser and special-interest influence on news coverage.[28] The code is describing a way in which responsibility is bound up in journalistic practice, a way in which exercising rights and fulfilling obligations are concomitant activities. If that is true, then ensuring press freedom means going beyond merely preventing government interference to overcoming whatever might get in the way of fulfilling responsibilities, whether it be economic or political constraints on the press or a lack of laws mitigating negative influences on it.

Notice that while the Hutchins Commission regards the press as an institution, the Society of Professional Journalists' code of ethics, like most journalism codes, is directed at the behavior of individual journalists. Here we see, again, how the duality in conceptions of press freedom mentioned earlier is echoed in a duality in conceptions of press responsibility. Is institutional or individual behavior the appropriate focus? Even though both are clearly important, there is a sense in which we tend to treat the press as an institution when considering what the press must do for democracy, but focus on individual journalists or news organizations when it come to evaluating press performance.[29] If poor individual behavior were at the root of news media's difficulties in fulfilling their democratic duties, then such reasoning would make sense. What seems to be true, however, is that external pressures on the institutional news media pose the greater obstacle.

Attempts to bolster both press freedom and press responsibility create an apparent paradox: Could the press be more free (and, therefore, better able to meet its obligations) if the media *system* were more restricted? I argue that it is possible, and many scholars agree. C. Edwin Baker, for example, asserts that in a complex democracy the press clause of the First Amendment "should be read to allow the government to promote a press that, in its best judgment, democracy needs but that the market fails to provide. The Constitution should only be invoked in cases of obvious governmental abuse—when the government engages in censorship or undermines the integrity of media entities."[30] So the answer that began this section—yes, freedom does entail responsibility—is correct, as long as we recognize that such responsibility falls not only on individual journalists but also on media owners, policymakers, and perhaps even citizens, who create the conditions under which journalism plays its watchdog and marketplace roles.[31]

The Future of Press Freedom

It is easy to become disheartened about the threats to press freedom posed by economic and political pressures or, in the post-9/11 era, by legislation such as the USA PATRIOT Act, which aimed at thwarting terrorists by, among other things, restricting the information available to the public. Also disconcerting are the annual "State of the First Amendment" surveys conducted by the Freedom Forum, which reveal a public whose appreciation for the press is limited at best.[32] One-third of the respondents in 2007 said the press has too much freedom. The good news—and maybe the bad news—is that things change.

Certainly, the Internet, as Jane Singer argues in chapter 8, holds great potential for widening the marketplace of ideas and dramatically increasing the number of potential watchdogs and, thereby, changing how we think about press freedom. In fact, the Internet, in many ways, looks more like the press of Jefferson's day than what we now call "mainstream media" does, taking us, in some sense, back to the future. The proliferation of news sites, blogs, and other online information resources means that the institutional press no longer has a monopoly on information, nor is it the only forum for airing and discussing diverse issues in public life. Freedom of the press, therefore, seems to have been enhanced.

I wonder, however, whether the sheer number and variety of information sources is on its own sufficient to perform all the functions democracy requires of its news media, or even whether taking on such responsibilities is something these recent entrants to the news media care to do. In its current state, the Internet is stronger on the marketplace front (the disseminating and discussing of opinions) than on the watchdog front (the gathering and verifying of information), which requires significant financial resources to undertake. That, too, can, and likely will, change.

In the meantime, it is worth considering what kind of news media system—what arrangement of new and old media; citizens, bloggers, and professional journalists; and commercial and nonprofit media—can best provide the public goods the First Amendment guarantee of freedom is meant to promote. It is also well past time to take calls for media reform seriously, to consider whether and how regulations, incentives, support for nonprofit and grassroots media, or, most likely, some combination of initiatives could work to enhance, and not abridge, press freedom. Even staunch First Amendment defenders like me, whose default position is skepticism about any government action relating to the news media, recognize that our press—though among the world's most free—is still not free enough to provide all the goods that our nation's founders wanted for us and that our democracy requires.

Notes

1. For details on the methodology Freedom House employs in creating the rankings, see http://freedomhouse.org/template.cfm?page=251&year=2007. Accessed August 15, 2008.

2. Note that I am using "expression" as the broader category encompassing both speech and the press. While the First Amendment to the U.S. Constitution lists speech and press individually, in practice, the U.S. Supreme Court has largely treated expression, whether via individual speech or the press, the same way.

3. For a comparison, see Herman Wasserman's essay in this volume.

4. Commission on Freedom of the Press, *A Free and Responsible Press; A General Report on Mass Communication: Newspapers, Radio, Motion Pictures, Magazines, and Books* (Chicago: University of Chicago Press, 1947), 6.

5. Lee C. Bollinger, *Images of a Free Press* (Chicago: University of Chicago Press, 1991), 20.

6. Timothy Cook, "The Functions of the Press in Democracy," in *The Press*, ed. Geneva Overholser and Kathleen Hall Jamieson, 115–119. Cambridge: Oxford University Press, 2005. Also James Curran, "What Democracy Requires of the Media," in *The Press*, ed. Geneva Overholser and Kathleen Hall Jamieson, 120–40. Cambridge: Oxford University Press, 2005.

7. John C. Nerone, *Last Rights: Revisiting Four Theories of the Press* (Urbana: University of Illinois Press, 1991), 46.

8. For an excellent overview of the *Sullivan* case, see Bollinger, *Images of a Free Press*, 2–8.

9. Timothy E. Cook, "Freeing the Presses: An Introductory Essay," in *Freeing the Presses: The First Amendment in Action* (Baton Rouge: Louisiana State University Press, 1999), 4. Scholars see the Alien and Sedition Acts as marking the point when the First Amendment began to be seen as expressing not just states' rights but the rights of individuals and the press. See Michael Schudson and Susan E. Tifft, "American Journalism ini Historical Perspective," in *The Press*, 20.

10. Cook, *Freeing the Presses*, 4.

11. Bollinger, *Images of a Free Press*, 57–58.

12. W. Lance Bennett and William Serrin, "The Watchdog Role," in *The Press*, 169.

13. Bennett and Serrin, "The Watchdog Role," 169.

14. As quoted in Bennett and Serrin, "The Watchdog Role," 172.

15. Charles Lewis, *A Letter from Charles Lewis*, http://www.tfij.org/about/why (accessed August 15, 2008).

16. Cook, *Freeing the Presses*, 5. Historians have questioned aspects of Stewart's view, pointing out that the press of the founders' day could not accurately be considered expert or autonomous in the way Stewart describes. Indeed, the pre-Revolutionary U.S. press had only recently taken on a collective identity as "the press," its autonomy was limited by a number of political and other pressures, and any organized, expert scrutiny of government was still in the press's future. See Charles E. Clark, "The Press the Founders Knew," in *Freeing the Presses*, 33–50.

17. In practice, of course, there are laws limiting speech and the press. National security concerns put certain kinds of speech at certain times off limits, obscene speech enjoys no constitutional protection, and the protection of journalists' sources is spotty and currently under siege. Broadcast journalists, of course, are subject to more restrictions, given that television and radio stations must have government-issued licenses to broadcast. The rationale for such restrictions originally focused on the scarcity of the airwaves, considered public property, which broadcasters use to transmit programming.

18. Bollinger, *Images of a Free Press*, 1–2.

19. Bollinger, *Images of a Free Press*, 20.

20. Frederick Schauer, "On the Relationship between Press Law and Press Content," in *Freeing the Presses*, 51–68.

21. Timothy E. Cook, *Governing with the News: The News Media as a Political Institution* (Chicago: University of Chicago Press, 2005), 177.

22. Quoted in Cook, *Governing with the News*, 177. Cook's summary of earlier work by David Anderson and his general discussion of First Amendment duality is particularly useful.

23. The Fairness Doctrine required broadcasters to give reply time to political candidates and others who had been attacked on the air. It was abolished in a wave of deregulation in 1987.

24. Bartholomew Sparrow, *Uncertain Guardians: The News Media as a Political Institution* (Baltimore: Johns Hopkins University Press, 1999), 5.

25. Theodore L. Glasser and Marc Gunther, "The Legacy of Autonomy in American Journalism," in *The Press*, 390.

26. Commission on the Freedom of the Press, *A Free and Responsible Press*, 18–19.

27. Bollinger, *Images of a Free Press*, 32.

28. The Society of Professional Journalists is a leading association of journalists, with membership numbering 10,000. Its code of ethics can be found at http://www.spj.org/ethicscode.asp.

29. See Charles N. Davis and Stephanie Craft, "New Media Synergy and the Emergence of Institutional Conflicts of Interest," *Journal of Mass Media Ethics* 15 (2000): 219–31.

30. C. Edwin Baker, *Media, Markets, and Democracy* (New York: Oxford University Press, 2002), 213. In addition to Baker, see the Commission on the Freedom of the Press; W. Lance Bennett, Regina Lawrence, and Steven Livingston, *When the Press Fails: Political Power and the News Media from Iraq to Katrina* (Chicago: University of Chicago Press, 2007); Bollinger; and Cook for discussion of a number of media-policy alternatives.

31. See Wendy Wyatt's essay in this volume.

32. The Freedom Forum is "a nonprofit foundation dedicated to free press, free speech and free spirit for all people." See http://www.freedomforum.org.

4

The Moral Justification
for Journalism

Sandra L. Borden

As Lee Wilkins argues in her article in this collection, journalism seems to come into its own during natural disasters. The sheer drama of such events makes for great storytelling and provides a national showcase for the talents of local reporters. This was illustrated again in 2005 when the great flood caused by Hurricane Katrina overcame New Orleans and chased out the staff of the *Times-Picayune*. At first, the paper was unable to issue a print edition and instead published on its affiliated Nola.com Web site. HELP US, PLEASE was the headline read by millions around the country and around the world. When the *Picayune* finally was able to produce a print edition, staffers gave it out for free at the Convention Center, where thousands of trapped survivors eagerly sought copies. Summing up the significance of what these journalists did, the *Columbia Journalism Review* contributor Douglas McCollam wrote:

> Living mostly in borrowed houses, often separated from friends and family, wearing donated clothes, and working with hand-me-down equipment and donated office space, the paper managed to produce coverage of the disaster that serves to remind us all of just how deep is the connection between a city and its newspaper, how much they need each other.[1]

There seems to be more to the *Picayune*'s actions than the thrill of what-a-story or the calculations of career climbing. Indeed, whether it is Los Angeles during the 1994 earthquake, or Grand Forks, North Dakota, during the 1997 flood, journalists often set aside competitive considerations to help their colleagues and endure extreme personal hardships to give communities the news they need. So what else is going on here? To find the deeper meaning of journalistic work, we need to understand *why* journalism exists as a moral practice in the first place. It is an occupation's larger purpose that lends it moral coherence.[2]

Many theorists use a rights approach, grounded in a liberal interpretation of the First Amendment, to justify journalism's activity. Rights are thus an important component of the analysis, and liberalism resonates with the democratic tradition in the United States. However, liberalism's conception of liberty as consisting primarily in the preservation of personal prerogative does not give enough attention to positive rights and their link to the common good. These elements, also part of the democratic tradition, are given more weight in a view called "communitarianism." This essay proceeds from a variant on communitarianism rooted in Aristotelian virtue theory. From this "virtue" perspective, an occupation's purpose provides it with moral justification if it can be integrated into a broader conception of the human telos, or natural purpose. Aristotle understood the human telos as eudaimonia, the good of a whole virtuous life, which includes doing one's role-related work well and promoting the common good. The good society, in essence, becomes the context for achieving not only individual but also common excellence. I suggest journalism's role is to help citizens discover the common good as intellectually responsible participants in a diverse political community.

Journalism's ultimate purpose, then, is more basic and more demanding than the watchdog function typically attributed to it within the liberal framework. By situating journalism within a communitarian account of participatory citizenship and linking it to the notion of virtue, we arrive at an expansive conception of journalism's purpose. This purpose highlights journalism as a practice that is called to go beyond simply warning citizens about abuses of power—the minimum required by moral obligation—and instead embraces the more morally ambitious goal of helping citizens to live a good life.[3] When done well, then, journalism is a moral calling vital to us all.

The essay will proceed in four parts. The first section will address the liberal assumptions of the First Amendment and how these contribute to moral minimalism in journalism. The second section will discuss various conceptions of citizenship and relate these to a communitarian framework for understanding civic participation. The third section will explain how journalism can contribute to the common good by exercising and promoting epistemic responsibility. The fourth section will discuss the implications of this argument for what counts as excellent news, which journalists are responsible for offering to citizens to aid their flourishing. I limit my argument to U.S. journalism, since that is what I know, but I think the ideas presented here can be useful for analyzing other journalistic traditions as well, as suggested by Herman Wasserman in the following chapter.

Looking beyond the First Amendment

Those who stress the First Amendment and its liberal tradition see the associated rights as giving the press a mandate to protect citizens from government intrusion, government secrecy, and official wrongdoing.[4] In fact, the First Amendment is practically journalism's sacred scripture.[5] But does the First Amendment provide sufficient reason to believe that journalism is a fundamentally moral activity? I will argue, in fact, it provides only a partial normative rationale for U.S. journalism, because its liberal assumptions encourage moral minimalism.

Liberalism's Legacy of Individual Rights

The First Amendment and the rest of the Bill of Rights reflect classic liberalism, a political philosophy linked to the Enlightenment project of promoting tolerance and social order by grounding knowledge in reason rather than revelation, authority, or tradition. One result of this emphasis is a focus on individual rights instead of collective rights. Individual rights (such as the rights to life, liberty, and property) stress individual independence, individual choice, and individual self-reliance over and above any rights that the community as such might claim. The government is supposed to keep its hands off—and so are other individuals who might want to limit someone's prerogatives. Public virtue, in this view, becomes mostly a procedural matter, consisting of respect for individual rights and the means for safeguarding them (such as ensuring free elections).

Collective rights, by comparison, are attributed to groups and peoples. As *The Stanford Encyclopedia of Philosophy* details, "The Convention against Genocide, for example, forbids actions intending to destroy any national, ethnic, racial or religious group; and the Covenant on Economic, Social, and Cultural rights ascribes to peoples the right to self-determination."[6] Earlier conceptions of public virtue held that citizens should set aside their own individual interests, when necessary, to serve common ends.[7] Communitarians question the subordinate status of collective rights in liberalism.

Liberalism had important implications for how U.S. journalists came to understand their role. At first, the press focused almost exclusively on its own rights (or, more accurately, the rights of press owners). With the 1947 Hutchins Commission report, the press began to accept formal responsibility for advocating the public's "right to know."[8] Although journalists have not articulated this right with moral clarity,[9] it has come to legitimize a belief in the press's power to foster democracy by agitating for government openness and by criticizing officials in the name of the people—the familiar watchdog role epitomized by Robert Woodward and Carl Bernstein's Watergate investigation in the early 1970s. Watergate, in fact, is a prominent chapter in the legal saga associated with the watchdog heritage in U.S. journalism.[10]

The Watchdog Press and the Monitorial Citizen

Competent performance of the watchdog role seems sufficient for the purposes of good citizenship, if being a good citizen consists primarily of safeguarding individual rights. Citizenship in this "monitorial" mode means keeping tabs on the public sphere just enough to avert threats to our personal well-being and to make sure that we can exercise our rights.[11] This alone can be quite a bit of work: We live in a complex society increasingly defined by the power and abundance of information. Therefore, we are dependent on news media to orient ourselves to the world. At the most basic level of human need, we must "understand the emerging environment" so we can look out for our safety and general well-being.[12] As individual moral agents, we need to understand our world so that we can exercise autonomous choice. As social beings, we need information about others for "creating community, making human connections"—a need so intense that news binds people together even in tyrannical societies.[13] In response to this vulnerability, journalism is indeed responsible for assisting citizens to scrutinize their government. The surveillance function of news consists of monitoring people, events, and sources of power. The practice has further obligated itself to perform this function through explicit and implicit promises in ethics codes and other public statements. For example, the American Society of Newspaper Editors ethics code states: "The American press was made free not just to inform or just to serve as a forum for debate but also to bring an independent scrutiny to bear on the forces of power in the society, including the conduct of official power at all levels of government."[14] The Society of Professional Journalists also urges journalists to "be vigilant and courageous about holding those with power accountable."[15]

Journalism is arguably pretty good at the watchdog role, especially considering that news media are structured primarily around the profit motive and that most people do not dutifully attend to the news. News media look even better, the political scientist Doris Graber assures, if we do not judge them based on the needs of some idealized citizen—one who does not exist and probably never will.[16] Graber reached this conclusion after considering Michael Schudson's historical analysis of U.S. citizenship, in which he argued that the original model of the U.S. citizen was the deferential citizen of the colonial period, still evident in the Founding Fathers' decision to make the electoral college decisive in presidential elections.[17] The emphasis on democracy mediated by trusted local leaders and, later, political parties, gradually gave way to an emphasis on the rational individual directly connected to the state via the ballot box. The "informed citizen" emerged in the Progressive era in the context of that movement's faith in knowledge, democracy, and the common man,[18] when "voting changed from a social and public duty to a private right, from a social obligation to party enforceable by social pressure to a civic obligation or abstract loyalty, enforceable only by private conscience."[19]

The Progressive era has had an enduring influence on journalistic values.[20] For example, Stuart Adam waxes poetic about journalism as a "democratic art," seemingly inspired by the Progressive ideal of a participatory democracy, "where politically well-informed citizens play an active role in government."[21] However, our ideas about citizenship fundamentally changed again in the 1960s as a result of rights expansions won by social movements and court victories. In acknowledgment of this "rights-bearing citizen," Schudson proposed the monitorial citizen as a more realistic model that fits our times. However, he suggested that this model should coexist with earlier ideas about citizenship to have a healthy civic imagination that is "informed but not imprisoned by the past."[22]

Civic Participation and the Common Good

Although liberalism has successfully expanded individual rights and established a healthy "institutionalized distrust" necessary to avoid state domination,[23] its moral model is minimalist. In Philip Zelznick's terms:

> As a philosophy of liberation, liberalism is understandably preoccupied with individual, person-centered rights. This preoccupation has great merit, but it tends to create a rights-centered morality and a rights-centered politics. In the process, rights are divorced from discipline and duty. They become abstract, unsituated, and absolute.[24]

One result is that liberalism does not actually hold citizens responsible for participating in public life—though they certainly have the right to participate if they choose. In contrast, Aristotle viewed humans as inherently social beings who flourish by participating in the political community—and who, in fact, cannot flourish without such participation. Neither can their communities. Therefore, citizens are *responsible* for participating in public life as an expression of individual and common excellence.

Various forms of participation are acceptable. In this regard, it is useful to remember that voting is only one (formal) way of participating. Involvement in community associations and even lawsuits can be forms of civic participation.[25] However they participate, citizens are expected to do so generously within the context of their roles and positions.[26] This expectation refers not only to the *amount* of participation, but also the *kind* of participation. Because communitarianism stresses the continuities between self and society, it envisions high-stakes participation in two senses. First, participation in public life implicates persons and groups at the level of their being. Community is "not just what they *have* as fellow citizens but also what they *are*, not a relationship they choose (as in a voluntary association) but an attachment they discover, not merely an attribute but a constituent of their identity."[27] Monitoring is the bare minimum required.

Another important difference between liberalism and communitarianism is the *point* of civic participation. For liberals, civic participation is a way to make sure individual rights are protected; it is procedural (although individual citizens may enjoy public life more as a result). For communitarians, civic participation is goal-directed: it aims to promote the common good. What is the common good? It consists of those social conditions that allow both communities and individuals to flourish. Surely, promoting individual fulfillment should be included in any conception of the common good—but that requires paying attention to what every person needs to *flourish*. This includes three main elements: respect for the person as such; the social well-being and development of the community; and peace, to ensure stability to sustain the common good.[28]

It should be clear by now that communitarianism places as much value on positive rights as it does on negative rights. Negative rights focus on what we are entitled to do or to have without interference from others (e.g., choose a doctor, or even forgo medical treatment if we wish), rather than on activities and provisions we are entitled to claim for ourselves (e.g., guaranteed access to health care of sufficient quality to lead "a truly human life"[29]). Liberalism's tendency to prioritize negative rights, like its ordering of individual rights over collective rights, owes much to that tradition's experience struggling to defend civil liberties. Even welfare liberals such as John Rawls remain uncertain about "individual *obligations*, as distinct from individual *rights*" and about the desirability of "formulat[ing] and embrac[ing] positive conceptions of the common good."[30] In a way, liberalism has been concerned for the *survival* of individuals in society. Communitarianism, on the other hand, is concerned for the *flourishing* of persons in society—and that requires respect for both positive and negative rights, both collective and individual rights.

Human flourishing in society requires a deep sense of the link that exists between our own well-being and that of others. We need to feel connected to others on the basis of solidarity, not just tolerance. We need, as the philosopher William May put it, to cultivate our "civic self," who "understands and accepts itself as limited and amplified by others . . . [and] recognizes that it enjoys an expansion of its life in and through its participation in community."[31] And sometimes this means one must give up some individual advantage in order for everyone to have the goods that are mutually acknowledged as necessary for human flourishing. Liberalism regards this choice as an optional form of self-sacrifice. As a matter of solidarity, communitarianism does not allow me to enjoy nutrition, shelter, and so on as a good for me unless others also have these things. However, it does not follow that communitarianism prioritizes communities over the individual; rather, it claims that individuals cannot be fully realized except as members of communities. Put another way, social responsibility is not a matter of "me versus community" but rather is two different "aspects of our own nature: our self-interest as individuals and our self-interest as members of a community."[32] Individual action is empowered in the communitarian framework—"a common life is not a *fused* life"—but so are the connections between individuals and the communities of which they are members.[33]

There is no denying, of course, that what individuals consider to be good and desirable can vary widely. Indeed, a healthy community, as Aristotle noted, presumes diversity.[34] However, it does not follow that we cannot devise some way of assessing the relative importance of these goods and the degree to which they may be compatible with the common good. Larry May suggests we think of community as a "social web of relationships," in which competing conceptions of the good can coexist: "The challenge of living among diversity is to construe morality in such a way that it is flexible enough to accommodate very diverse circumstances and life-styles, but not yet to give up on a vision of a shared conception of the good life."[35] By balancing autonomy with other values important to both individuals and communities, communitarianism promotes the kind of public soul searching that is difficult, but necessary, if we are to structure institutions around social goals that "exhibit enough coherence to sustain the foundations of a common life."[36] When civic participation is construed in this richer sense, it is clear that journalism has a moral reason for being beyond surveillance, as it becomes a vehicle for responsible civic participation.

The Informed Citizen in an Information Society

The transition to an information society gives reason to hope that journalists can perform this more expansive role. Mark Bovens describes an information society as one in which geographical boundaries are becoming less relevant, new technologies are developing at an unpredictable pace, corporations and governments are being overshadowed by markets and networks, and data processing is becoming the primary mode of production. These conditions, Bovens says, have the potential to bring "the classic republican ideal of politics as a debate between well-informed citizens into the realm of reality."[37] However, the public sphere is, if anything, more complex to negotiate than ever. This complexity is the single most relevant context for news,[38] more so than any specific political or economic system. It is this fact that makes knowing *well* so challenging—and so relevant to flourishing. We are not there yet, but new technologies that allow citizens to leverage information have definitely increased their capacity to act collectively and to challenge entrenched power structures. The Internet has made it possible for interested citizens to easily research people, issues, and institutions; to communicate their ideas with millions of other interested citizens in an instant; to mount grassroots movements;

to mobilize public opinion; and even to produce their own alternative media messages.

The press has not escaped the scrutiny of this new generation of empowered citizens. In a 2004 Internet survey of more than twenty-five hundred wired newspaper readers from around the United States, the Associated Press Managing Editors' National Credibility Roundtables Project reported that those who consider blogs especially useful cited the new online journals' willingness to question the mainstream media as a major aspect of their appeal. Such questioning was apparent in bloggers' reaction to the "Memogate" press scandal of 2004. The *60 Minutes Wednesday* election-year story about President George W. Bush's National Guard service suggested that Bush had not fulfilled his service commitment during the Vietnam War. It was based partly on documents that CBS said were written by one of Bush's former commanders. The documents said Bush had been ordered to take a medical exam and suggested that one of his commanders felt pressured to take it easy on him. Before the piece had even finished airing, however, bloggers started questioning whether the fonts on the documents could have been made by typewriters typically used by the Texas Air National Guard at that time. Later, it turned out that the person who gave producer Mary Mapes the documents was of questionable reliability and that, contrary to claims, the documents had not been properly authenticated by experts.[39] Dan Rather—who narrated the segment—apologized for the mistakes and announced his retirement from the anchor's desk of the *CBS Evening News* (though he did not directly link his decision to the controversy).

Journalism as Civic Inquiry

As the CBS example illustrates, new technologies both complicate the public sphere and open the door to joint civic inquiry by journalists and citizens. Lorraine Code's notion of *epistemic responsibility* highlights the moral significance of the investigative processes *both* journalists and citizens use to make sense of the world. She says moral reasoning typically proceeds "from epistemic to ethical (from what I know to what I do)"[40] and both the epistemic efforts involved in such reasoning and the ethical action ultimately taken on the basis of those efforts can be criticized. Thus, contrary to the tolerance-driven cliché, we are not justified in believing whatever we wish; many beliefs lead to significant actions and thus ethically demand epistemic care.[41] The *60 Minutes Wednesday* team that produced the segment on President Bush's National Guard service can, therefore, be faulted *both* for the shoddy verification processes that undercut the story's reliability *and* for the decision to rush the story to air despite having reasons to question the source and the authenticity of key documents.

Thomas Cooper underlines the relevance of epistemic responsibility to journalism, writing:

If the news were perceived as a type of serialized fiction or daily distraction or entertainment "bait" for the advertisers' hook, then perhaps there need be no discussion of the journalists' epistemic responsibility. However, because most consumers treat news as a direct, even if somewhat distorted, conduit of "knowledge"—about an "outside world," about life's unveiling, about a collective reality—a discussion of epistemic responsibility among journalists becomes paramount.[42]

Code suggests that we are *all* responsible for using sound investigatory strategies when we want to know something. Within the constraints of the "nature of the world and of human cognitive capacity," there is much freedom but also a limit to "what kinds of sense can *responsibly* be made of the world."[43] The concept of epistemic responsibility underscores journalism's commitment to truth and the important role that good journalism has to play in an information society. It binds journalists to other citizens.

And Now the News

When news meets the demands of epistemic responsibility, it helps empower citizens to participate responsibly in community life (rather than just to monitor the public sphere for signs of danger). Non-journalists possessing certain skills and resources may also help citizens achieve this goal.[44] But journalism has the rare ability to promote civic participation in ways that are timely (unlike most scholarship), independent (unlike political parties or special-interest groups), and contemporaneously available to nearly all segments of society (unlike classroom discussions or even blogs, which are available only to those with a computer). To best achieve this role, I suggest the news should be guided by the following priorities:

- Address communities instead of audiences,
- Avoid false consensus and social injustice,
- Keep the focus on the common good, and
- Create common knowledge that empowers citizens to act.

Address Communities Instead of Audiences

The media industry tends to address "audiences" rather than communities. "Audiences" are defined by demographic characteristics that predict patterns of private consumption. So the first effect of addressing us as audiences is that we are encouraged to consider happiness only as a private good. The very word *audience*, furthermore, implies we are merely spectators, rather than participants. Excellent news oriented toward a telos of civic participation, oriented to the common good, is *not* information that is primarily directed at audiences defined by individual wants and needs. If I need to find something that affects only me, I can easily enough do a Google search, make a phone call, look through a catalog. "News," on the other hand, is never about just one person. Even human interest stories are properly called "news" only if they shed light on some broader social phenomenon illustrated by an individual case. "News," then, is *inherently communal* in nature.

Journalism's tradition has emphasized localism, or geographically bound communities,[45] but news can also be about an ideological community, a community of shared interests, a community of shared beliefs, and so on.[46] What specifically counts as news for each of these communities will depend on how they have ordered the values that are relevant to *all* communities. It will also depend on how the virtues are embedded in the conception of a given community's way of life. For example, courage would be more prominent in a military community than in an academic one (though courage would still be a virtue in both). Addressing the particularity of communities is the realm of niche journalism. Civic participation is "mediated by membership in subgroups," which need to properly examine their separate interests, in addition to interests they may have in common with others in the larger public sphere. This is especially relevant to subordinate communities, which might not otherwise have a chance to engage in such deliberation.[47]

Avoid False Consensus and Social Injustice

On the other hand, the various communities to which we belong result in relationships that touch more than one interest. For example, I am a scholar, in addition to a teacher, a mother, and a homeowner. Some of my relationships involve more aspects of my social self than do others, but none encompasses them all. Therefore, there is also a need for integration. This makes traditional journalism aimed at the general public extremely valuable for flourishing persons and communities.

News directed at the general public attempts to go beyond the particularities of specific communities and generates the possibility for constructive collective action in the public sphere. General news should strive to promote significant overlap in the knowledge of various communities. The goal is not to gloss over differences, but to reveal and accommodate differences so that it is possible for all citizens to participate meaningfully in the public sphere and to take concerted action on behalf of public concerns.[48] As the sociologist Philip Selznick notes, we do not gain from diversity if we "ask the participants to shed their distinctive identities."[49]

Christians, Ferre, and Fackler (1993) note the common good does not refer to majority opinion or some false consensus but rather to a commitment to transnational human norms that foster good communities, such as truthfulness, justice, and empowerment. Such a universal criterion is consistent with virtue theory's claim that there are objective conditions for human flourishing, and the criterion keeps the common good from being relativistic. It also imposes a requirement for critical reflection that can prevent the worst vices of conventional morality, including hegemonic domination. Excellent news is common knowledge that is inclusive and empowering rather than coercive and subordinating—a "normative pluralism," in the words of Christians et al.[50] No citizen left behind. A healthy news system, then, should include outlets that cater to particular subgroups in addition to ones that speak to the wider political community.

Keep the Focus on the Common Good

Recasting journalism's democratic role in communitarian terms would mean defining and covering news in ways that reflect the kind of knowledge citizens need to jointly discover and achieve the common good. This would mean no more framing issues in the black-and-white rhetoric of warring interest-group leaders, no more reducing public opinion to the aggregation of fleeting individual preferences. Instead, journalists should help citizens assess the relative importance of information and its relevance to the common good. To help citizens perform this function, excellent news meets high standards of reliability and demonstrates independence. In these regards, the traditional journalistic practices of gate-keeping remain pertinent.

Excellent performance of this function also entails a commitment to community service backed up by transparency, self-reflection, self-criticism, and other disciplines rendering journalists accountable for their performance. As far as these standards are concerned, journalism should be more open about how it creates news, providing access to raw materials and explaining the process of verification. Journalists also need to provide citizens with a wide diversity of viewpoints, opportunities to try out ideas, and help in assessing presuppositions. They can help citizens choose materials and access multiple perspectives, rather than offering a singular synthesis of the day's news. To achieve these goals, news stories might fruitfully incorporate an interactive component, such as links to original documents and alternative news sources.[51] This technique, of course, was pioneered by bloggers and now is widely available on news Web sites.

Create Common Knowledge That Empowers Citizens to Act

The news should also help citizens evaluate the *actionability* of specific issues arising in the public sphere; that is, the realistic possibility of citizens influencing them through collective action. To communicate actionability, journalists must know the system and its players and also be familiar with grassroots movements and whether there are enough people concerned about a problem to influence policy. Other ways in which they can help citizens judge actionability is to provide a reliable assessment of risks and benefits, and views on a range of possible approaches and their costs, effectiveness, and durability. This overview should include a thorough analysis of the values at stake in various policy options.

Journalists can also inform citizens of collective action that may be effective, depending on the problem. For example, collective action may consist of "voluntary community intervention" or lobbying "relevant political actors and institutions."[52] Practitioners engaged in public journalism projects have been interested in correcting for journalism's traditional lack of attention to this function of the news by broadening the range of sources they interview, focusing as much on solutions as they do on problems, conducting public surveys, and undertaking other strategies. However, as Renita Coleman has noted, it is important to avoid paternalism when taking on this function.[53]

Conclusion

I have relied on a broad virtue framework to justify journalism as a moral activity, offering a communitarian account of participatory citizenship that binds journalists to other citizens in the pursuit of the common good. Both journalists and citizens, I suggest, should be epistemically responsible as they strive for excellence in the performance of their particular roles. Journalists' ultimate goal as members of a virtuous practice is to help citizens know responsibly in the public sphere. This goal makes journalism an endeavor with a moral mission (as opposed to just a social function or a legal mandate). It also gives us a way to evaluate the excellence of news stories and the epistemic and ethical efforts that went into generating them.

I, like most other communitarians, do not advocate throwing out liberalism's rights tradition altogether, but, rather, favor rethinking it to enhance appreciation for socially constituted selfhood, for positive rights, for the moral status of communities as such, and for socially constructed goods. Shared conceptions of the good can, in fact, incorporate much of what liberals value. I also do not think that excellent news as I have outlined it here requires entirely abandoning the verification and reporting strategies associated with objectivity (although I see no reason that excellent journalism cannot take other forms as well). Neither objective reporting nor civic engagement precludes epistemic responsibility—in fact, they demand it. On the other hand, journalists should be disciplined when it comes to emotions that can interfere with the skepticism and larger perspective that characterize virtuous reporting.[54] This is one reason that journalism's *discipline of verification* continues to be critical to exercising epistemic responsibility.

Nevertheless, a new *discipline of confirmation*, consisting of consultation with non-journalists after the news is disseminated, could help journalists take epistemic responsibility a step further. By enlisting fellow citizens to confirm the reliability of the news—or to modify knowledge claims, when warranted—journalists would give up some of their advantage in the public sphere. Unlike the internal, collegial process that characterizes journalistic verification, journalistic confirmation would be an external, participative process. This discipline should be characterized by accessibility, transparency, and tentativeness, in the spirit of shared inquiry—modeling the dispositions needed to engage in a virtuous quest for the good life.

Notes

This essay is a condensation of Sandra L. Borden, *Journalism as Practice: MacIntyre, Virtue Ethics and the Press* (Ashgate, 2007). Published with permission from Ashgate Publishing.

1. Douglas McCollam, "Uncharted Waters," *Columbia Journalism Review* (November/December 2005), para. 4, http://www.cjr.org (accessed November 17, 2005).

2. James A. Donahue, "The Use of Virtue and Character in Applied Ethics," *Horizons* 17, no. 2 (1990): 228–43.

3. I am using "practice" in Alasdair MacIntyre's sense of a cooperative endeavor that gives meaning to moral action. See MacIntyre, *After Virtue*, 3rd ed. (Notre Dame, IN: University of Notre Dame Press, 2007), 187.

4. G. Stuart Adam, Stephanie Craft, and Elliot D. Cohen, "Three Essays on Journalism and Virtue," *Journal of Mass Media Ethics* 19, no. 3–4 (2004): 247–75; Louis W. Hodges, "Defining Press Responsibility: A Functional Approach," in *Responsible Journalism*, ed. Deni Elliott, 13–31 (Beverly Hills, CA: Sage, 1986); William May, *Beleaguered Rulers: The Public Obligation of the Professional* (Louisville, KY: Westminster John Knox Press, 2001), 198.

5. Jay Rosen, "Journalism Is Itself a Religion: Special Essay on Launch of *The Revealer*," *PRESSthink*, January 7, 2004, http://journalism.nyu.edu/pubzone/Weblogs/pressthink/2004/01/07/press_religion.html (accessed January 27, 2005); John C. Watson, "Civic Responsibility: A Casualty of Ethical Principle" (paper presented at the meeting of the Association for Education in Journalism and Mass Communication, San Antonio, August 2005), 20.

6. "Rights," in the *Stanford Encyclopedia of Philosophy*, http://plato.staford.edu/entries/rights/#1 (accessed July 30, 2008), section 7.1 "Critiques of Rights Doctrine," para. 6.

7. Eric Lane and Michael Oreskes, *The Genius of America: How the Constitution Saved Our Country and Why It Can Do It Again* (New York, Bloomsbury, 2007), 23–25.

8. François Demers, "Journalistic Ethics: The Rise of the 'Good Employee's Model': A Threat for Professionalism?" *Canadian Journal of Communication* 14, no. 2 (1989): 15–27.

9. Sissela Bok, *Secrets: On the Ethics of Concealment and Revelation* (New York: Vintage, 1989), 254–58.

10. Rosen, "Journalism Is Itself a Religion."

11. Jurgen Habermas, *The Structural Transformation of the Public Sphere: An Inquiry into a Category of Bourgeois Society*, trans. Thomas Burger, with Frederick Lawrence (Cambridge, MA: MIT Press, 1989), 4–6, 30–31. The public sphere is that "space" outside of government, Big Business, and the family where private individuals come together through various civic institutions and associations to constitute a "public" that can effectively assert the interests of the political community. Although not everything from Habermas translates well into this communitarian framework, his concept of a public sphere provides a useful starting point within journalistic tradition for understanding the integrative function of political discussion. My view, however, is different from those who theorize the public sphere as a procedural mechanism for promoting civic discourse without the goal of helping citizens discover what actually constitutes the common good. For example, see Wendy Wyatt, *Critical Conversations: A Theory of Press Criticism* (Cresskill, NJ: Hampton, 2007), 122; and Patrick Lee Plaisance, "The Mass Media as Discursive Network: Building on the Implications of Libertarian and Communitarian Claims for News Media Ethics Theory," *Communication Theory* 15, no. 3 (2005): 292–313.

12. Wendy Barger and Ralph Barney, "Media–Citizen Reciprocity as a Moral Mandate," *Journal of Mass Media Ethics* 19, nos. 3–4 (2004): 201.

13. Bill Kovach and Tom Rosenstiel, *The Elements of Journalism: What Newspeople Should Know and the Public Should Expect* (New York: Three Rivers, 2001), 21.

14. "ASNE's Statement of Principles," the American Society of Newspaper Editors Web site (August 1, 2008), http://www.asne.org/article_view/smid/370/articleid/325/reftab/132/t/asnes-statement-of-principles.aspx.

15. www.spj.org/ethicscode.asp, accessed July 1, 2008.

16. Doris Graber, "The Media and Democracy: Beyond Myths and Stereotypes," *Annual Review of Political Science* 6 (2003): 148.

17. Michael Schudson, *The Good Citizen: A History of American Civic Life* (New York: Free Press, 1998), 308–10.

18. Michael Schudson, *Good Citizens & Bad History: Today's Political Ideals in Historical Perspective* (Murfreesboro: John Seigenthaler Chair of Excellence in First Amendment Studies, Middle Tennessee State University, 1999), 9–10; J. Hebert Altschull, *From Milton to McLuhan: The Ideas behind American Journalism* (New York: Longman, 1990), 248–53.

19. Schudson, *Good Citizens & Bad History*, 11–12.

20. Herbert J. Gans, *Deciding What's News: A Study of CBS Evening News, NBC Nightly News, Newsweek and Time* (New York: Vintage, 1980), 68–69.

21. Adam, Craft, and Cohen, "Three Essays," 143, 249.

22. Schudson, *Good Citizens & Bad History*, 12–15, 24.

23. Schudson, *Good Citizen*, 301, 310.

24. Philip Selznick, *The Moral Commonwealth: Social Theory and the Promise of Community* (Berkeley and Los Angeles: University of California Press, 1992), 378–79.

25. Schudson, *Good Citizens & Bad History*, 12, 18.

26. As with any other Aristotelian virtue, this precludes extremes, such as being disposed to participate in public life to such an extent that one fails to fulfill his personal responsibilities at work and at home. In fact, excellence in the performance of one's private roles also contributes to the common good.

27. Michael J. Sandel, *Liberalism and the Limits of Justice* (Cambridge: Cambridge University Press, 1982), 150.

28. United States Catholic Conference—Libreria Editrice Vaticana, *Catechism of the Catholic Church in the United States* (Liguori, MO: Liguori, 1994), 465.

29. U.S. Catholic Conference, *Catechism of the Catholic Church*, 465.

30. Selznick, *Moral Commonwealth*, 376–77.

31. May, *Beleaguered Rulers*, 188–89.

32. William J. Prior, "*Eudaimonism* and Virtue," *Journal of Value Inquiry* 35 (2001): 331.

33. Selznick, *Moral Commonwealth*, 369.

34. John Hendry (*Between Enterprise and Ethics: Business and Management in a Bimoral Society* [Oxford: Oxford University Press, 2004], 170) points out that identifying strictly with others who are similar (e.g., those who share the same "lifestyle") unduly narrows the moral focus of individuals, compared with the moral demands of "traditional communities of diversity." Also see Selznick, *Moral Commonwealth*, 360–65, for a discussion of the elements of flourishing communities, and 368–71 for understanding diversity in community as a "unity of unities."

35. Larry May, *The Socially Responsive Self: Social Theory and Professional Ethics* (Chicago: University of Chicago Press, 1996), 104.

36. Selznick, *Moral Commonwealth*, 364. Communitarianism, furthermore, does not construe autonomy as "equivalent to unconditional opportunity and choice" but, rather, as "an attribute of selfhood and self-affirmation," a matter of "commitment as well as choice" (363).

37. Mark Bovens, "Information Rights: Citizenship in the Information Society," *Journal of Political Philosophy* 10 (Sept. 2002): 320, 325.

38. Jay Rosen, "BloggerCon: Discussion Notes for 'What Is Journalism? And What Can Weblogs Do about It?'" *PRESSthink*, March 25, 2004, http://journalism. nyu.edu/pubzone/weblogs/pressthink/2004/03/25/con_prep.html (accessed May 20, 2005), at "The Professionals Set a Standard," para. 2.

39. Associated Press, "CBS Ousts Four in Wake of National Guard Story Flap," *USA TODAY*, January 10, 2005; also online: http://www.usatoday.com (accessed January 19, 2005), paras. 7–8.

40. Lorraine Code (*Epistemic Responsibility* [Hanover, NH: Brown University Press, 1987], 79) notes, however, that sometimes "ethical considerations are permitted to create epistemic constraints." A journalistic example might be a reporting team that stops digging for information that would invade someone's privacy, even though truncating the investigation in this way means it will not arrive at the best possible approximation of the truth.

41. See William Clifford, "The Ethics of Belief," originally published in *Contemporary Review* and now widely available in print and on the Web at www.infidels.org/ library/historical/w_k_clifford/ethics_of_belief.html.

42. Thomas Cooper, "Lorraine Code's 'Epistemic Responsibility,' Journalism, and the Charles Stuart Case," *Business and Professional Ethics Journal* 12, no. 3 (1993): 95.

43. Code, *Epistemic Responsibility*, 9.

44. See Wendy Wyatt's essay in this volume.

45. Altschull, *From Milton to McLuhan*, 212–17.

46. On the other hand, not all groups have a broad enough range of activities, or a comprehensive enough framework of shared values, or a strong enough claim on members' identities to be considered communities (Selznick, *Moral Commonwealth*, 358).

47. Selznick, *Moral Commonwealth*, 370. Tanni Haas and Linda Steiner, "Public Journalism as a Journalism of Publics: Implications of the Habermas–Fraser Debate for Public Journalism," *Journalism* 2, no. 2 (2001): 123–47.

48. Rob Anderson, Robert Dardenne, and George M. Killenberg, "The American Newspaper as the Public Conversational Commons," in *Mixed News: The Public/Civic/Communitarian Journalism Debate*, ed. Jay Black, 109–12 (Mahwah, NJ: Lawrence Erlbaum, 1997); Haas and Steiner, "Public Journalism," 123–47.

49. Selznick, *Moral Commonwealth*, 399.

50. Clifford G. Christians, John P. Ferre, and P. Mark Fackler, *Good News: Social Ethics & the Press* (New York: Oxford University Press, 1993), 194.

51. Donald Matheson, "Weblogs and the Epistemology of News: Some Trends in Online Journalism," *New Media & Society* 6, no.4 (2004): 443–68.

52. Haas and Steiner, "Public Journalism," 137.

53. Renita Coleman, "The Ethical Context for Public Journalism: As an Ethical Foundation for Public Journalism, Communitarian Philosophy Provides Principles for Practitioners to Apply to Real-World Problems," *Journal of Communication Inquiry* 24, no. 1 (2000): 54.

54. Katie O'Keefe, "Ethical Firestorm: A Month after One of the Greatest Natural Disasters in American History, Experts Grade the Media on Their Coverage of Hurricane Katrina," *Quill Online*, December 1, 2005, http://www.spj.org/quill_list.asp, para. 4 (accessed December 1, 2005).

5

The Search for Global Media Ethics

Herman Wasserman

G lobal news media have contributed to a world where we are confronted
with the faces of Others we will never meet. Although the interconnections between people in a globalized world are often overstated, it is hard not to
agree with Zygmunt Bauman when he speaks of "being aware of the pain, misery and suffering of countless people whom we will never meet in person."[1] In
today's globalized world, news media have brought distant people closer, and
the media confront us with a moral responsibility for how we will represent
and relate to those faraway others.

News media are all around us—they have become "environmental" in the
contemporary world, as Roger Silverstone argues.[2] This certainly is true for
societies in the developed world, where news media have saturated almost
every part of individual and community life. But the global reach of journalism
can also be exaggerated. While societies in the developed world are awash with
news media in an ever-increasing range of formats and shapes, many areas of
the developing world do not enjoy the same level of access to news media.
There are many reasons for this lack, including poor infrastructure, illiteracy,
authoritarian governments, and poverty. However, even for societies where
media are not as pervasive, the *implications* of forming part of a world that is
hyper-mediated remain important. These implications are even more significant for those who live on the outskirts of the mediated world-city—or the
"mediapolis" as Silverstone calls it[3]—because they are affected by, but do not
participate in casting, the global media gaze.

The role journalism plays in this media-saturated world also varies considerably. While developed countries are seeing an ongoing reshaping of what
counts as journalism or a journalist, developing regions often struggle just to
establish a journalistic presence.

Cultural and Social Formations

Various cultural and social formations also have a function in what we may consider the ideal role for journalism in society. In many African countries, for example, the way people interact with journalism and media should be understood in terms of the way people negotiate their various roles in society. While they perform the roles of individual citizens much like citizens in liberal democracies in the developed world, they are also subject to social hierarchies, and bound by loyalties to ethnic, cultural, or religious groups.[4] These loyalties may affect the ethical roles journalism is expected to play, with alternative frameworks competing for validity against the dominant Western, liberal, democratic vision.[5] Normative frameworks from the developed North have sometimes met with resistance or have undergone reframing to adapt to local realities.[6]

Three major trends can be identified in the recent development of global news media. Majid Tehranian categorizes these as transnationalization, tribalization, and democratization.[7] "Transnationalization" means the disembedding and re-embedding of cultural content across national borders.[8] Examples of transnationalization include global media networks like CNN and Al-Jazeera, and the appropriation (and adaptation) of U.S. popular culture in other regions of the world.

"Tribalization" is a reaction to transnationalization and takes the form of a reassertion of localized cultural identity, sometimes involving essentialist claims to origins and roots, or the development of local media to counter the dominance of U.S. or European media content. Localization can also be driven, unfortunately, by global media conglomerates that, in order to maximize profits, merely repackage content for local markets, thereby undercutting the progressive goal of giving local communities a voice.

By "democratization" we mean the potential for media, especially new media, to foster global civil society, amplify resistance efforts, and open new channels of communication.[9] The global trend of "citizen journalism" can be seen to form part of this perspective on global media.

These three trends can all be seen as reactions to the key issue of *difference*. In an era where global journalism reaches into varied cultural and social settings, audiences are confronted with information and images about people, cultures, and worldviews that differ from theirs. How journalism deals with this difference and the power imbalances linked to them has become a major ethical question. How can a globalized journalism guide us to live well together in a post-millennial world marked by persistent ethnic and religious conflict, terror on a global scale, looming shortages of food and natural resources, and even the potential destruction of our planet?

Faced with these global crises, journalism's responsibility cannot be confined to localities or nations, it is now transnational. This does not mean the specificity of localities has completely given way to the forces of global electronic empires. On the contrary, the tensions and fissures between the local and the global have in recent years been brought to the fore, in stark relief. September 11 and its continuing bloody aftermath have put the lie to any simplistic notions of a global village. That day and the subsequent years of the so-called war on terror have made it clear that the global village we live in is an increasingly "interdependent and fragile" one.[10] Thinking about journalists' roles and responsibilities in *global* terms also means recognizing and addressing news media's effect on *local* settings. A journalism ethic has to be found that can provide a framework within which journalism can operate globally yet also allow for the contextual specificities of localities. While the search for a global journalism means finding values that resonate even in disparate societies, such an ethic should also account for the problematic nature of "universals." Hegemonic values can claim universality in order to assert their dominance, as has historically been the case when Western cultural and knowledge frameworks masqueraded as universal values to serve the exercise of colonial power.

What complicates matters further is the fact that even if certain values can be identified as having universal resonance, their interpretation and relative value may differ vastly depending on context. The worldwide outcry following the controversial publication of cartoons depicting the prophet Muhammed in the Danish newspaper *Jyllands-Posten* in September 2005 is a clear example of how the interpretation of journalistic values like freedom of speech and social responsibility are understood differently in different places. These values came to be refracted through the lens of geopolitical power struggles. The outcry following the publication of the cartoons was a clear indication that news media are on the cusp of struggles between sameness and difference, between inclusion and exclusion, between recognition and marginalization.

The unstable interdependence of the globalized, twenty-first-century world brings with it a pressing moral question: How should journalism help us find our place in the world and in relation to the Other, where our ethical responsibilities can no longer be seen as limited to a nation or society but are instead recognized as having global implications? How should journalism's ethical responsibility toward a global community be reconciled with claims to specificity and difference? How should journalism conceive of its ethical role, globally, in terms of vast material inequalities, power struggles, and cultural politics? Put simply—what should journalism do to contribute to the good life on a global scale?

Varied Approaches

To date, scholarly debate about global journalism ethics has produced several perspectives, all facing the central challenge of how to approach the normative framework for global journalism from a transnational perspective. Ethical guidelines for media will have to include various points of view, culturally, and be applicable to the diverse contexts and lived experiences of journalists world-wide. A consensus on such a framework, however, still eludes scholars. The "misunderstandings and disagreement on fundamental theoretical issues" center around the nature of "universals" in journalism ethics, and what type of theory might provide a framework within which an inclusive and broadly acceptable notion of universals could be couched.[11]

The first step is for scholars to recognize that their perspectives on journal-ism ethics are never neutral or value-free but always located within particular histories, cultural backgrounds, and political positions.[12] Deni Elliott and David Ozar (in chapter 1 of this volume) seem to acknowledge the grounded nature of journalism in their approach to journalism ethics. They set out to locate the function of journalism historically and politically and then extrapolate its core values while aligning them with moral injunctions extant in a broader social sphere (such as the obligation not to harm others but rather to respect their rights). The latter part of their model—the "classical moral injunctions" they use as guiding principles—is where the challenge for an approach to global journalism ethics lies. An inductive approach to journalism ethics—one start-ing "from the ground up," with empirical facts rather moral values imposed from above—would have to be globally inclusive. The empirical basis for jour-nalism ethics would have to incorporate contextual facts from around the world to lay claim to universality. Moreover, it would not be enough to describe jour-nalism in various global settings and derive ethical norms from these contexts in isolation—the power asymmetries between and among these various set-tings would also have to be taken into account. Journalistic practices, norms, and values have to be situated historically and politically. In other words, it is insufficient to derive an ethical norm from a set of practices in a particular lo-cale if an attempt is not also made to understand the historical processes that led to that particular set of practices and norms. For instance, avoiding the use of racial signifiers in South African journalism (and the codification of that restraint) should be understood in terms of the history of apartheid. That his-tory, in turn, is the result of centuries of white supremacy, including that exhib-ited in a colonial era, where values imported from the West masqueraded as "universal" standards of "civilization," leading to the suppression and denigra-tion of indigenous knowledge frameworks. Therefore, when a South African newspaper (City Press) proclaims to be "Distinctly African," one can assume that it would, in its journalistic practices and norms, be in line with the call of that country's (then) president, Thabo Mbeki, who (perhaps problematically) encouraged journalists to "report Africa to the Africans, carrying out this responsibility as Africans,"[13] and attempt to re-inscribe a previously suppressed African identity and perspective into journalistic discourse. These values are shaped by histories and power struggles, and when viewed in relation to the historical imposition of Western values on non-Western contexts, have implications for notions of "truth" and "universality" as well. When norms in different local settings are taken seriously using an approach such as the one advocated by Elliott and Ozar, it may lead to a questioning of dominant ethical values and norms, or at least a questioning of their interpretation in various contexts.

Important as the empirical realities of local contexts are, care should be taken not to lapse into a relativism where ethics vary so much between journalistic organizations, cultures, and regions that, in the end, it becomes impossible to agree on a normative framework that should again guide practice. In a globalized world, attention to localities are important to avoid cultural imperialism by powerful interests; yet, in a globalized world we are more interconnected than ever before and therefore cannot be content with viewing journalism's obligations only in terms of the journalist's own society. Finding the correct balance between the local and the global, the particular and the universal—that is the major challenge for global journalism ethics. Elliott and Ozar are right, however, when they say different kinds of societies need different specific kinds of information; and in the search for a global journalism ethics, it is important that this difference be respected.

Historically, "universal" values have often been Western values in disguise— values either implicitly or explicitly imposed upon non-Western contexts. The notion of universal ethics is fraught with problems because the concept of universality needs to be scrutinized. The idea of universal values has its roots in Western rationalist thought, as Cliff Christians has shown.[14] Traditionally, it was the "logical structure" of moral prescriptions, not their context, that ensured their legitimacy.[15] In the late twentieth century, however, the "paradigm of immutable and universal morality" has been widely challenged as belonging to the dominant gender and class.[16] This does not mean the universalist project is necessarily doomed; arguments for universal values, rights, and responsibilities continue to be made and contextualized within a new, globalized environment.

Universalist claims have also been contentious in journalism ethics scholarship. The classic liberal commitment to "individual rights and personal decision-making" has dominated journalism ethics frameworks for decades, with occasional challenges from communitarianism, and feminist and care ethics.[17] While still peripheral, these challenges have opened some new theoretical lines of inquiry, including an ontological approach to global journalism ethics, a theory of invention, a neo-Aristotelianism, and a postcolonial critique of uni versalism. These approaches will be summarized below.[18]

Ontological Ethics

In his approach to universal values, Christians argues against the modernist version of universal values based in Enlightenment rationalism, contending, instead, that universal values can be found only by recognizing that humans always stand in relation to one another.[19] Normativity is understood in terms of the wholeness of human beings, and universal values are those that are rooted in ontology—in what we have in common as humans, across cultures:

> An ethics of universal being is an alternative. It enables us to start over intellectually with the holistic notion of humans as humans-in-relation, rather than with a truncated notion of humans as rational individuals. It speaks against the claims of both philosophical and cultural relativism. It is held together by a pretheoretical commitment to the purposiveness of life in nature, defined in human terms as the sacredness of life. In our systematic reflection on this underlying perspective, three ethical principles emerge as entailed by it—human dignity, truth-telling, and non-violence. Instead of the individual autonomy of ethical rationalism, ethics begins with its opposite—universal human solidarity. And from that starting point, we enter our own communities and work professions with standards to guide our decisions and behavior.[20]

From this point of view, there are certain core values that people share around the world and across cultures, as these values are rooted in the human condition. The sacredness of life as the fundamental "protonorm," Christians argues, is universal to humans and binds us together beyond culture, ethnicity, or location. As the protonorm, it underlies the more specific principles of human dignity, truth, and nonviolence. Using these guidelines, media ethics codes can be critiqued and constructed to have universal resonance, so they can be grounded in that which is fundamental to being human.[21]

Since Christians's approach allows for inclusivity and diversity in the rich spectrum of human life, it provides a way to include cultural diversity without assuming that people from diverse backgrounds, knowledge frameworks, and belief systems must reach rational consensus about specific norms. It insists only upon respect for life, dignity, truth, and nonviolence. In doing this, it also enriches what it means to be human, beyond rationality and inclusive of a full spectrum of beliefs, emotions, and relationships.

Christians does not, however, fully explain how these principles will be interpreted around the world. Even if we acknowledge and accept his fundamental principles, they may obtain different meanings as they are applied in different settings. The protonorm of "respect for life" may be foundational to our being human, but how this respect is expressed in various settings might result in global/local tensions. Another problem lies in determining how our humanness finds expression within the material conditions and among the power relations that shape human existence in other parts of the world. Accepting these norms should also go further than agreeing to them in the abstract—the search for global journalism ethics should include engaging with the material (including historical and political) factors that affect their use in an ethical framework by media practitioners worldwide.[22] This attempt to ground protonorms in material contexts and within the lived experience of journalists is part of the ongoing project of global journalism ethics.

Global Ethics as Contract and Invention

Another way of seeing global ethics is as a framework that emerges from the contract between journalism and global society. This contract is constructed through rational deliberation among members of that society and would come into being through an inclusive and cosmopolitan dialogue about the duties of journalism. This way, journalism enjoys freedom in return for its services to democracy and the public interest. However, tensions might ensue between the journalist's role as a journalist and his or her role as a citizen. For instance, it is the duty of citizens to testify in court when requested to do so, in the interest of serving justice. When a journalist is subpoenaed to testify in court about his or her sources for a news story, the duty of serving justice can be seen as conflicting with the journalist's right to protect the sources who supplied information in the public interest. Another example of tensions between roles would be the citizen's duty to be patriotic and loyal in times of war, whereas a journalist might want to question, on moral grounds, his or her country's involvement in a particular war. For Stephen J. A. Ward, a journalist's sense of patriotic duty does not preclude the same journalist meeting his or her duties toward the global society.[23] Since, from this point of view, ethical norms are invented rather than found, they can change over time according to context.[24]

Hence, the journalist's attachments and loyalties can also vary from context to context.[25] The challenge, therefore, would be to ensure that participants in the contract truly represent diverse cultural, social, and belief systems. While there may be disagreement on some ethical values, Ward suggests that journalists they would likely agree on certain key values:

> We should not be surprised by the existence of both agreement and disagreement on ethical values. We should expect humans as a species to share some values because they live in common world, face similar physical, social and ethical problems, share cognitive and emotive capacities, and share a genetic inheritance. Given this commonality, it is likely that humans in different cultures will agree on ways of responding ethically to situations and of organizing society, such as agreement on the value of human life, prohibitions against lying, and praise for promise keeping. However,

differences in culture and other conditions also lead us to expect differences.[26]

Ward is optimistic that a global journalism ethics that strikes a balance between the general and the particular, between loyalties to one's own group or community and a sense of global responsibility, could be invented:

> If we adopt a cosmopolitan attitude in journalism, we change the aims and principles of journalism ethics, and we alter our conception of democratic journalism. The object of democratic journalism becomes not only the promotion of national democratic community but also global democratic community. Cosmopolitan journalists are 'global patriots' with a special affection for humanity and its flourishing. The claim of humanity extends the journalist's loyalty from the public of her hometown and country to humanity at large.[27]

One advantage of this approach to global journalism ethics is its flexibility. While it identifies key duties for journalism in democratic societies, these duties remain open to negotiation and change according to circumstances.

A disadvantage of this approach to global journalism ethics is that it is steeped in the tradition of democratic liberalism, which is associated with Western political thinking and individual rights. Therefore, it may be treated—rightly or wrongly—with skepticism by critical scholars who aim to de-Westernize ethical thinking.

More importantly, Ward's approach does not make sufficient allowance for global power struggles around the invention of a global journalism ethics. One must ask how radically different viewpoints about journalistic duties will be resolved when conflict ensues, and how consensus can ever be reached among participants representing a wide variety of often radically conflicting religious, social, and cultural frameworks.[28] Habermasians suggest a proper discourse structure can overcome such conflicts, but global power struggles are not always based on cultural misunderstandings that can be cleared away through gestures of inclusivity; they are instead often rooted in material conditions. The novelist Amos Oz pointed this out with regard to the Israel–Palestine conflict, deriding the "widespread sentimental European idea that every conflict is essentially no more than a misunderstanding": "A little group therapy, a touch of family counseling, and everyone will live happily ever after. Well, first, I have bad news for you: Some conflicts are very real; they are much worse than a mere misunderstanding."[29]

It might be argued that solving these types of conflicts is beyond the scope of the democratic functions of journalism. A journalism ethics that claims to contribute to the vibrancy of democracy and human flourishing globally would, however, have to consider the extent to which disagreements about the news media's role in democratic societies are linked to historical power struggles. This is related to the postcolonial critique of global journalism ethics, to which we will turn shortly.

Neo-Aristotelian Global Ethics

New media technologies, with their capability for higher interactivity, have produced radical change in global news media. The line between news producers and consumers has become so blurred as to motivate Jay Rosen to refer to "the people formerly known as the audience."[30] Against this background, Nick Couldry has argued that journalism ethics codes should no longer be constructed from the point of view of the producers of media, but that an inclusive framework has to be found that would more thoroughly embrace the concerns of all the participants in the mediation process.[31] Like Ward, Couldry stresses dialogue but rejects the existence of global consensus on moral values.[32] Thus, Couldry suggests starting the search for a global media ethic not from the point of view of purported universal principles but from the "minimal premises" of neo-Aristotelian virtue ethics, thereby parting ways with both Christians's ontological communitarianism and Ward's rational contractualism. He instead chooses the Aristotelian emphasis on the "good" (i.e., virtue) above the Kantian deontology of the "right" (i.e., duty) because of his preference for "open-ended and quite general principles . . . on which human beings at a particular time and place *might* come to agree" above a "comprehensive and systematic specification of moral rules for media practice that any rational being anywhere *must* find compelling."[33] The neo-Aristotelian focus on "certain shared questions and shared facts" about the good and how media can contribute to it is, for Couldry, a more viable approach to finding a global media ethical framework in a world marked by vast diversity than an approach that insists on fixed rules and guidelines would be.[34]

Couldry recommends a media ethics, facilitated by global media, that focuses on the virtues, the dispositions to act, that we should strive for so that we may live well together: "'Virtues' are the means by which stable dispositions to act well are specified, but the reference points by which virtues are specified are not particular 'values,' but precisely those facts about shared human life on which potentially we can come to agree."[35]

A challenge for virtue ethics is how to be specific about the virtues so as to respond ethically to shared problems—even, in fact, to establish what shared problems can be agreed upon in the first place.[36] Such agreement might be jeopardized by the problem of having to decide among conflicting virtues, especially in transnational settings involving countries with different priorities. The advantage of this approach is that it is based on practical wisdom (*phronesis*, in Aristotelian terms), which requires an immersion in the lived experience of journalists and their audiences rather than the imposition from above of ethical norms. Couldry suggests two main aims that could orient media virtues: (1) to circulate information that could contribute to successful individual and collective life; and (2) to provide opportunities for the expression of opinion and voice that would help sustain a peaceable life together for humans globally, regardless of "conflicting values, interests and understandings."[37]

Given the new hyper-mediated world, Couldry argues, communicative virtues must exist within media producers *and* in consumers (or consumer–producers). The return to virtue theory, a relatively recent move in journalism ethics, presents potentially useful opportunities for a global approach, since virtues emerge from practice and the corresponding needs of community members.

Postcolonial Global Ethics

Another recent critical challenge to the search for global journalism ethics has been posed by scholars approaching the field from the perspective of postcolonial theory.[38] Postcolonial critics have argued that more theoretical work from non-Western perspectives needs to enter the debate, which according to them has been dominated by theoretical frameworks emanating from the West.[39] For these critics, notions of universalism have to be critically examined against the background of the history of colonialism, where Western frameworks masqueraded as "universal," and where indigenous knowledge frameworks were marginalized. This discourse of universality historically served to legitimize the exercise of Western power over the non-Western Other. Postcolonial critics thus argue that attempts to construct a global framework for journalism ethics might be viewed by journalists in non-Western contexts as yet another attempt to impose Western hegemonic values.[40]

Postcolonial theory is critical of all master narratives and is more interested in describing a "politics of location" than in constructing overarching global structures.[41] However, postcolonial criticism does have an ethical dimension, one that is concerned with global conditions and relations. Divya McMillin points to the "activist and ethical component" of postcolonial studies that demands a "rethinking of peoples and cultures by the experiences that bind them, not just by ethnicity or nationality."[42] Such an approach to global journalism ethics would place purported universals against the shared experience of those large sections of the world still experiencing colonialism's lingering effects.

The role of news media in reproducing unequal global power relations has long been a topic of critical study.[43] Further, the renewed focus on news media's role in economic and capital globalization has brought increased attention to the ways in which contemporary global power relations resemble those of colonialism.[44]

A postcolonial approach to journalism ethics would view ethical frameworks from the perspective of the lived experience of the producers and consumers of media in settings outside the dominant West. It would establish what central normative concepts such as "respect for life," "freedom," "truth telling," or "human dignity" would mean in non-Western contexts, meanings that might differ or conflict with Western ones.[45] Postcolonial theory brings a critical edge to the search for global journalism ethics and serves as a reminder that the quest for universals in journalism ethics has problematic historical and political implications.

Postcolonial criticism also has its disadvantages. The exploration of local knowledge can lead to a romantic idealization of a supposedly pristine postcolonial situation, where local values and epistemologies exist free of outside influence. Crude invocations of postcolonial values, and attempts to impose "indigenous values" on media, can also create new forms of exclusion. This might entail the view that only certain sections of the postcolonial society have the right to criticize the government, for example, or that certain subjects are considered taboo, that open and frank debate belongs to a foreign culture, or that there is only one valid and essential postcolonial cultural identity.[46] Ultimately, one could also ask whether postcolonial theory could contribute to the construction of a global journalism ethics or whether it would remain in the critical mode, merely highlighting the weaknesses in other theories.

Conclusion

From the above discussion it should be clear there is not yet consensus about which theoretical framework(s) would form the best basis for the construction of a global journalism ethics. Various philosophical approaches offer competing understandings of what such an ethics would look like and even whether such an ethics is possible or desirable. Tensions between global and local understandings of what journalism is, and what its role in society should be, complicate the search.

Despite such tensions, it is worthwhile to proceed with further theoretical explorations.

A global journalism ethics that claims to be a comprehensive, final, and authoritative account of journalism's proper role in the attainment of the good will likely fail. The critical scholarship of postmodernism and postcolonialism has quite compellingly suggested that the time for such grand and totalizing schemes is over. We find ourselves in an uncertain age, faced with global crises and conflicts and increasingly complex factors shaping our lives together. An ethics for journalism in this world will have difficulty claiming to offer fixed answers. Instead, a global ethics could insist upon the unremitting reinscription of Otherness and difference into global media narratives. Journalism in this era should constantly confront us with other views, other perspectives, other ways of making sense of the complex and changing world we live in. The recognition of difference is an ethical imperative in a world that is interconnected and interdependent. On a theoretical level, this might mean an eclectic approach to journalism ethics that draws on the strengths of various scholarly traditions and allows them to enter into a critical dialectic with each other.

A journalism ethics for contemporary global society, one that takes into account the vigorous contestations about central moral concepts and rights, one that sees journalism not as a static and closed-off profession but as a dynamic endeavor that changes with societal shifts, cannot but be provisional and inclusive.

The search for a global journalism ethics must be open-ended.

Notes

1. Terhi Rantanen, *Media and Globalization* (London: Sage, 2005), 123.

2. Roger Silverstone, *Media and Morality: On the Rise of the Metropolis* (Cambridge, UK: Polity, 2007).

3. Silverstone, *Media and Morality*, 25.

4. These loyalties to ethnicities and clans were often imposed by colonial authorities as a way of exercising indirect rule. See M. Mamdani, *Citizen and Subject—Contemporary Africa and the Legacy of Late Colonialism* (Princeton, NJ: Princeton University Press, 1996).

5. Francis Nyamnjoh, *Africa's Media—Democracy & the Politics of Belonging* (London: Zed Books, 2005).

6. Nyamnjoh, *Africa's Media*, 21.

7. Majid Tehranian, "Peace Journalism: Negotiating Global Media Ethics," *Harvard International Journal of Press/Politics* 7, no. 2 (2002): 58–83.

8. John Tomlinson, *Globalization and Culture* (Cambridge, UK: Polity, 1997)

9. Tehranian, "Peace Journalism."

10. Tehranian, "Peace Journalism," 59.

11. Clifford G. Christians, Shakuntala Rao, Stephen J. Ward, and Herman Wasserman, "Towards a Global Media Ethics: Exploring New Perspectives," *Ecquid Novi: African Journalism Studies* 29, no. 2, (2008).

12. Stephen J.A. Ward and Herman Wasserman, eds., *Media Ethics beyond Borders* (Johannesburg: Heinemann, 2008), 1–4.

13. Thabo Mbeki, Address at the South African National Editors' Forum on the Media, AU, Nepad and Democracy, Johannesburg, April 12, 2003, http://www.dfa.gov.za/docs/speeches/2003/mbeko412.htm (accessed August 8, 2008).

14. Clifford G. Christians, "The Ethics of Being in a Communications Context," in *Communication Ethics and Universal Values*, ed. C. Christians and M. Traber (London: Sage, 1997), 3–23.

15. Christians, "Ethics of Being" (1997), 3.

16. Christians, "Ethics of Being" (1997), 4.

17. Clifford G. Christians, "Social Ethics and Mass Media Practice," in Josin A.M. Makau and Ronald C. Arnett, eds., *Communication Ethics in an Age of Diversity*,

(Urbana: University of Illinois Press, 1997), 198; for communitarianism, see Clifford G. Christians, John P. Ferré, and P. Mark Fackler, eds., *Good News: Social Ethics and the Press* (New York: Oxford University Press, 1993). For care ethics, see Carol Gilligan, *In a Different Voice: Psychological Theory and Women's Development* (Cambridge, MA: Harvard University Press, 1982).

18. In this summary, I am drawing largely on Ward and Wasserman, eds., *Media Ethics beyond Borders* (2008), and Christians et al. *Towards a Global Media Ethics* (2008).

19. Clifford G. Christians, "The Ethics of Universal Being," in *Media Ethics beyond Borders* (2008), ed. Ward and Wasserman, 6–23.

20. Christians, "Ethics of Universal Being" (2008), 7.

21. Christians, "Ethics of Universal Being" (2008), 18.

22. For a discussion of how one of these values, "human dignity," could be interpreted and applied in a postcolonial setting, see Herman Wasserman, "Media Ethics and Human Dignity in the Postcolony," in *Media Ethics beyond Borders*, 74–89.

23. Stephen J. A. Ward, "A Theory of Patriotism for Journalism," in *Media Ethics beyond Borders*, 42–58.

24. The title of Ward's book *The Invention of Journalism Ethics* (Montreal: McGill-Queens University Press, 2004), which is also used in Christians et al. (2008), encapsulates the stance that journalism ethics emerges out of the lived experience of humans rather than being a set of a priori principles imposed "from above" by a purely rational mind. The norms for journalists emerge in the relationship between journalists and their publics and undergo change over time.

25. Ward, "Theory of Patriotism for Journalism," 42–58.

26. Christians, Rao, Ward, and Wasserman, "Towards a Global Media Ethics."

27. Ward, "Theory of Patriotism for Journalism," 55.

28. Nick Couldry, "Towards a Framework for Media Producers and Media Consumers," in *Media Ethics beyond Borders*, 61.

29. Amos Oz, *How to Cure a Fanatic* (Princeton, NJ: Princeton University Press, 2006), 6–7.

30. Jay Rosen, "The People Formerly Known as the Audience," *PRESSthink*, June 27, 2006,http://journalism.nyu.edu/pubzone/weblogs/pressthink/2006/06/27/ppl_frmr.html (accessed January 3, 2008).

31. Couldry, "Towards a Framework for Media."

32. Couldry, "Towards a Framework for Media," 60.

33. Couldry, "Towards a Framework for Media," 63.

34. Couldry, "Towards a Framework for Media," 64.

35. Couldry, "Towards a Framework for Media," 66.

36. Rosalind Hursthouse provides a promising approach in her discussion of "V-Rules." See her book *On Virtue Ethics* (New York: Oxford University Press, 2002), esp. chap. 1 and 2. See also Aaron Quinn, "Moral Virtues for Journalists," *Journal of Mass Media Ethics* 22, no. 2 (2007): 168–86, which illustrates what virtue ethics would mean in a journalistic context. Quinn also points to the problem of conflicting virtues, which might be a particularly difficult question when journalists in different global settings decide which virtues should enjoy priority.

37. Couldry, "Towards a Framework for Media," 68.

38. One of the first and significant interventions from postcolonial theory in the field of communications was the article by Raka Shome and Radha Hegde, "Postcolonial Approaches to Communications: Charting the Terrain, Engaging the Intersections," *Communication Theory* 12, no. 3 (2002): 249–70.

39. Shakuntala Rao and Herman Wasserman, "Global Media Ethics Revisited: A Postcolonial Critique," *Global Media and Communication* 3, no. 1 (2007): 29–50.

40. Shakuntala Rao and Seow-Ting Lee, "Globalizing Media Ethics? An Assessment of Universal Ethics among International Political Journalists," *Journal of Mass Media Ethics* 20, nos. 2–3 (2005): 99–120.

41. Arif Dirlik, "The Postcolonial Aura: Third World Criticism in the Age of Global Capitalism," *Critical Inquiry* 20 (1994): 328–55.

42. Divya McMillin, *International Media Studies* (Malden, MA: Blackwell, 2007), 57.

43. The debates around the New World Information and Communication Order and the Dependency/Cultural Imperialism paradigm exemplify this criticism. See, e.g., Jan Servaes, *Communication for Development: One World, Multiple Cultures* (Creskill, NJ: Hampton, 1999), or Colin Sparks, *Globalization, Development and the Mass Media* (London: Sage, 2007).

44. McMillin, *International Media Studies*, 55, 60.

45. Rao and Wasserman, "Global Media Ethics Revisited" (2007); Wasserman, "Media Ethics and Human Dignity in the Postcolony," in *Media Ethics beyond Borders*, 74–89.

46. For a critique of postcolonial discourse in media studies, see Pieter J. Fourie, "Moral Philosophy as a Threat to Freedom of Expression: From Christian-Nationalism to *Ubuntuism* as a Normative Framework for Media Regulation and Practice in South Africa," *Communications: European Journal of Communication Research* no. 2(2007): 1–29; and Keyan G. Tomaselli, "'Our Culture' vs. 'Foreign Culture.' An Essay on Ontological and Professional Issues in African Journalism," *Gazette* 65, no. 6 (2003): 427–41.

References

Bauman, Zygmunt. "Quality and inequality." *The Guardian*, December 29, 2001, http://www.guardian.co.uk/print/0, 4326548–103418,00.html (accessed August 21, 2007).

Christians, Clifford G. "Social Ethics and Mass Media Practice." In Josin M. Makau, and Ronald. C. Arnett, eds. *Communication Ethics in an Age of Diversity* (Urbana: University of Illinois Press, 1997), 198.

Christians, Clifford G. "The Ethics of Being in a Communications Context." In C. Christians and M. Traber, eds. *Communication Ethics and Universal Values* (London: Sage, 1997), 3–23.

Christians, Clifford G., John P. Ferre, and Mark Fackler, eds. *Good News: Social Ethics and the Press* (New York: Oxford University Press, 1993).

Christians, Clifford G., Shakuntala Rao, Stephen J. Ward, and Herman Wasserman, "Towards a Global Media Ethics: Exploring New Perspectives," *Ecquid Novi: African Journalism Studies* 29, no. 2., (2008).

Couldry, Nick. "Towards a Framework for Media Producers and Media Consumers," in *Media Ethics Beyond Borders*, ed. Stephen Ward and Herman Wasserman (Johannesburg, RSA: Heinemann, 2008), 61.

Dirlik, Arif. "The Postcolonial Aura: Third World Criticism in the Age of Global Capitalism," *Critical Inquiry* 20 (1994): 328–55.

Gilligan, Carol. *In a Different Voice: Psychological Theory and Women's Development* (Cambridge, MA: Harvard University Press, 1982).

Mamdani, M. (1996) *Citizen and Subject—Contemporary Africa and the Legacy of Late Colonialism*. Princeton, NJ: Princeton University Press, 1996.

McMillin, Divya. *International Media Studies*. (Malden, MA: Blackwell, 2007).

Nyamnjoh, Francis *Africa's Media—Democracy & the Politics of Belonging*. (London: Zed Books, 2005).

Oz, Amos. *How to Cure a Fanatic* (Princeton, NJ: Princeton University Press, 2006), 6–7.

Rantanen, Terhi. *Media and Globalization* (London: Sage, 2005), 123.

Rao, Shakuntala, and Seow-Ting Lee. "Globalizing Media Ethics? An Assessment of Universal Ethics among International Political Journalists," *Journal of Mass Media Ethics* 20, nos. 2 & 3 (2005), 99–120.

Rao, Shakuntala, and Herman Wasserman, "Global Media Ethics Revisited: A Postcolonial Critique," *Global Media and Communication* 3, no. 1 (2007), 29–50.

Rosen, Jay. "The People Formerly Known as the Audience," *PRESSthink*, 2006, http://journalism.nyu.edu/pubzone/weblogs/pressthink/2006/06/27/ppl_frmr.html (accessed January 3, 2008).

Shome, Raka, and Radha Hegde. "Postcolonial Approaches to Communications: Charting the Terrain, Engaging the Intersections." *Communication Theory* 12, no. 3 (2002), 249–70.

Silverstone, Roger. *Media and Morality: On the Rise of the Metropolis* (Cambridge,UK: Polity, 2007).

Tehranian, Majid. "Peace Journalism: Negotiating Global Media Ethics." *Harvard International Journal of Press/Politics* 7, no. 2 (2002), 58–83.

Tomlinson, John. *Globalization and Culture*. (Cambridge,UK: Polity, 1997).

Ward, Stephen J.A. "A Theory of Patriotism for Journalism," In *Media Ethics Beyond Borders*, ed. Stephen Ward and Herman Wasserman (Johannesburg, RSA: Heinemann, 2008), 42–58.

Ward, Stephen J.A., and Herman Wasserman, eds. *Media Ethics beyond Borders* (Johannesburg, RSA: Heinemann, 2008).

PART III

What Is Journalism?
Who Is a Journalist?

Introduction

As I was narrowing down the topics for this book, "What is journalism?" received a very early "can't cut" designation. The *Journal of Mass Media Ethics* was hosting its colloquium, "Who is a journalist?";[1] debate was raging over whether to establish a Federal Shield Law, with much of the disagreement centering on to whom it would apply; and some of the most interesting commentary was coming from such online sources as Slate and Salon. So of course we had to address the topic, and it became quickly apparent that it would be one of the more vexing ones of the book.

But take a look at journalism ethics books from before 1990 or so. You'll notice they don't much worry about the problem of "what" journalism was: it was what outlets like the *New York Times* and CBS News did, and journalists were the people who worked at those places. The books did worry quite a bit, just as we do, about the *degradation* of real news, about news increasingly becoming mere entertainment or salacious gossip. The concern, though, was more that news was acting like *Entertainment Tonight* or the *National Enquirer* than that those sources were themselves considered news outlets.

Then came an explosion of alternative sources, ranging from the Internet to cable political talk shows to talk radio. Maybe the first person to really challenge the standard view was Matt Drudge, whose online "Report" broke the Bill Clinton–Monica Lewinsky story.[2] We can certainly debate whether the affair was an impeachable offense, but, given contemporary social mores and journalistic culture, it was unquestionably a newsworthy story.[3] So did that make Drudge a reporter? The vast majority of his reports were, and are, little more than unsubstantiated political rumor or news aggregated from traditional sources. Yet he was the first to report on what turned out to be one of the more important stories of the last quarter century.

And what of cable talk show hosts such as Bill O'Reilly, Glenn Beck, Nancy Grace, and Sean Hannity? Or the array of blather on talk radio? Surely they are not really journalists, right? Well, they might be, or some of them might sometimes be. Hence the problem: if we don't know what we're looking for, if we don't have some criteria, some standards, then it is impossible to distinguish journalism from all other activities.

As Jay Black stresses from the beginning of his essay, the issue is more than merely rhetorical or of interest to academics only: "It is a pragmatic one, with serious ethical, legal, and craft ramifications." He thus directly takes on the "standards" task, considering the question from various perspectives, including "historical, legal, ethical, technological, and performative." He strives to avoid both a "dogmatic" approach, one that produces a definition so narrow as to include only a "few highly moral professionals while de-pressing or ex-communicating everyone else," and an overly broad one that means "everyone qualifies."

Black's conclusion: whether one is a journalist "should not center on *where* one works, but on *how* one works." He adds, "I believe we should protect those who act as stewards of the public interest, in whatever media or for however much money they function." For Black, that "how" includes an adoption of the traditional journalistic ethos: "If they have inculcated professional ethics while eschewing sleazeball behaviors and violations of the public trust, they should have an easier time convincing legislators and jurors that they deserve the protective mantle."

Michael Davis reaches a similar conclusion, arguing that journalists are "professionals." As he notes, many (including me) have hesitated to grant journalism professional status, since it doesn't meet the traditional criteria. Again, the issue is one of drawing distinctions; professionals have historically been designated by such criteria as their training, the importance of their task, licensing, and, to my mind the most important, their commitment to clients' well-being.

While our lexicon has become quite loose, with everyone and their cousin—hairdressers, used-car dealers, realtors—calling themselves "professionals," the designation has traditionally served an important purpose: professionals are granted higher social status (and, usually, income) in return for a commitment to self-regulation through high ethical principles. Professionals have historically seen their task as a kind of "calling," something beyond a mere money-making occupation.

Journalism, thus, has been a tough nut: most of its practitioners see their work as a calling (they're surely not in it for the money!), and they are undoubtedly engaged in a socially critical enterprise.[4] But most have also shuddered at the prospect of regulation—whether self- or externally imposed—let alone of licensing.[5] Hence many have preferred "craft" language, in which reporters are expected to act professionally, without the constraints associated with being a formal profession.[6]

Davis quite convincingly challenges that approach, concluding, "Journalism is a profession; . . . journalists are something more than *mere* newsmen, editors, media employees, or the like. And that is why they have a future even if mere newsmen, editors, writers, and the like do not." The latter optimism is based, in part, on his use of a "Socratic" approach to (re)define "profession," arguing "a good definition . . . can give us some reason to hope that journalism will remain a profession even if the world changes in most of the ways we now fear." Davis therefore determines, like Black, that what makes for more than "mere newsmen" is the commitment to a higher standard: "Journalists differ from other members of the same occupation (e.g., bloggers) in that they hold themselves to this higher standard, a standard beyond that set by law, market, morality, or public opinion." That standard includes a range of duties, such as accuracy, diligence in seeking information, fairness, and transparency, among many others.

Hence what makes one a professional journalist is, again, *how* one does one's job. Jane Singer agrees but extends the conversation to how online journalism best does *its* job. She addresses the "gatekeeper" role of traditional journalism and observes, "Professional norms are a way to articulate and safeguard the role. They identify responsibilities both to the people on the other side of the gate, the audience, and to other gate-keepers, including employers and colleagues. Journalists fulfill their ethical obligations by providing information of a particular kind (accurate, credible, fair, and so on) that has been gathered in a particular way (honestly and independently, for example)."

But, she notes, those norms have typically included "objectivity" and "distance." The new media world challenges both: "The observers are [now] also the observed, and many journalists have been startled by the scrutiny—and by the fact that most of those doing the scrutinizing reject their claims of objectivity and instead see media professionals as active and self-interested participants in the construction of news." She adds, "Journalists in this environment are necessarily closer to all sorts of people they have not felt close to before. The emergence of blogs was especially eye-opening, with their emphasis on communication not just *to* but also *with* the public, not to mention their more-than-willingness to both attack and traverse the boundaries that journalists have erected over the past 150 years."

This reality calls for a new set of norms, at least for online journalists and maybe for traditional ones as well. It is time, she argues, for journalism to evolve from an ethic of autonomous gatekeepers to one rooted instead in relationships and transparency, where credibility and authority are established not by one's position or role but by how one "networks" one's reporting.

Singer's essay is one of my favorite in the book—wonderfully written and theoretically compelling, with a final section in which she applies that theory to a real case, looking at how journalists at Britain's *Guardian* newspaper are managing this new reality. I worry, though, that she places too much faith in the "Wiki" method,[7] for example, when, she says, "Bloggers embody the idea that democratic power is essentially distributed and that the pursuit of truth works best as a collective enterprise. They personify the marketplace of ideas with a vengeance: Put it all out there, and the truth will emerge. . . . That is what happens when there are no gates and no gate-keepers." Why should we conclude truth will emerge, as opposed to merely the ideas of whomever has the loudest voice or the deepest pockets?

"Professionalism" has, in recent years, not only faced a series of redefinitions, of the sort Davis provides, but has also taken a beating as a social norm. The 1960s call to "question authority" has gradually resulted in a democratization of the professions, with real power shifts. Even those long recognized and respected—law, medicine, the academy—have seen their social power significantly reduced as they have also faced increasing external scrutiny and regulation. Some of these changes have undoubtedly been beneficial: one no longer needs an attorney for simple legal procedures (e.g., writing a will, filing for an uncontested divorce, drafting an advance directive), patients have greater autonomy and input in their medical care, and professors are now expected to focus more on *learning* than on *teaching*.[8]

But . . . can we really do without gatekeepers? Isn't there genuine expertise attached to extensive education, experience, judgment, and character—all traits expected of professionals, or in this case, *editors*? Doesn't the often chaotic and truly nasty nature of blogging or cable talk shows cry out for good oversight?

You are presented with two challenges. First, have our authors correctly characterized what it means to be a journalist, to practice one's skill in alignment with established standards? If so, have they also correctly established those standards? If not, can you provide a better characterization?

Second, whatever standards you adopt must account for some secondary questions; namely, is there a way to sustain journalistic professionalism without the associated distancing and snobbery? Can online journalism, or traditional for that matter, achieve real democratic, transparent, collaboration? Or was Plato right—direct democracy is doomed to collapse into mob rule?[9] The Internet, the driving force behind the problems addressed in this chapter presents both an opportunity and a threat: the opportunity to break down elitism and power asymmetries, and the threat that the journalistic standards all three of our authors so cherish will be drowned out by unregulated noise.

Where does the proper balance lie?

Notes

1. The colloquium is described in Jay Black's essay (chapter 7, this volume).

2. *Newsweek*'s Michael Isikoff evidently had the same information, but the magazine held it.

3. As compared to news media's non-coverage of, for example, President John Kennedy's affairs, apparently widely known among White House reporters.

4. See Stephanie Craft's and Sandra Borden's essays, chaps. 3 and 4 in this volume.

5. See Aaron Quinn's contrary view, in chap. 18 of this volume.

6. Cf., G. Stuart Adam and Roy Peter Clark, *Journalism: The Democratic Craft* (New York: Oxford University Press, 2005).

7. Wikipedia's project relies on collaborative, public editing, rather than on editorial oversight. See http://en.wikipedia.org/wiki/Wikipedia:What_Wikipedia_is_not.

8. It is an open question, however, whether power has truly shifted from professionals to clients, or just to bean counters. For example, I can be fully engaged in medical decision making, but in the end it is my insurance company's utilization reviewers who determine actual treatment options.

9. See Book VIII of *The Republic*.

6

Why Journalism Is a Profession

Michael Davis

Journalism is often said not to be a profession for one or more of the following reasons: (1) journalists are not licensed, (2) journalism lacks a body of theoretical knowledge, (3) journalism has no required curriculum through which all (or even most) journalists must pass, (4) journalists cannot exclude non-journalists (stringers, bloggers, and so on) from reporting news, (5) (most) journalist are not independent consultants but employees (and therefore lack "professional autonomy"), (6) journalists do not serve clients (only employers or the public), (7) most journalists are not members of any professional organization (such as the Society of Professional Journalists), and (8) journalists as such do not have high status or high income (though a few do). Just seeing all these reasons together may seem enough to settle the question of journalism's status as a profession. Clearly, journalism is neither a profession nor even a quasi-profession, proto-profession, or anything close.

And yet, many of us, perhaps even most journalists, feel that journalism is a profession—or, at least, much more like nursing, teaching, or engineering than like selling cars, managing a McDonald's, or even writing novels. Our worry is not whether journalism is now a profession, but whether it can remain a profession in a world where commerce, politics, and technology seem to be working against journalism as we have known it. The great media empires now treat news as a way of getting attention for their advertisements, not as a public service. Governments around the world, including our own, have come increasingly to consider journalists a nuisance rather than the Fourth Estate. And the Internet seems to be making news organizations, including their journalists, unnecessary. The future seems to belong to the bloggers.

What I shall argue here is that journalism is a profession, that our doubts about its status as a profession tell us more about a mistake we make when defining the concept of profession than about journalism itself, and that a good definition of profession can give us some reason to hope that journalism will remain a profession even if the world changes in most of the ways we now fear it will. Journalists are something more than *mere* news reporters, editors, media employees, or the like. And that is why they have a future even if mere reporters, editors, writers, and the like do not.

Some Senses of "Profession"

"Profession" clearly has several senses in English. It can be a mere synonym for "occupation," an occupation being any typically full-time activity defined in part by an easily recognizable body of knowledge, skill, and judgment, a "discipline" by which one can and people typically do earn a living. It is in this sense that we may, without irony or metaphor, speak of someone being a "professional thief," "professional beggar," "professional athlete," and so on, provided the person in question makes a living by the activity in question. Journalism is certainly a profession in this sense, but just as certainly this is not the sense we are interested in. When we talk about journalism as a profession, we are not interested in comparing journalists with thieves or even beggars.

"Profession" can instead be limited to *honest* occupations: "Plumbing is a profession; stealing is not." This is another sense that does not seem relevant here. While journalists seem to agree that journalism is a "craft," most journalists still seem to want to distinguish journalism from (some of the) other crafts, even honest ones, such as plumbing.

"Profession" can also identify a special kind of honest occupation, for example, "white-collar work": "Law is a profession; plumbing is not." This seems closer to the sense of profession in which we are interested. Unfortunately, there are at least two approaches to defining profession in this special-kind-of-honest-occupation sense. One, what we may call "the sociological," has its origin in the social sciences. The other is philosophical. We shall have to decide which to use before we can say anything helpful about what a profession is.

Sociological Approaches

The sociological approach tends to be statistical—or at least to sound empirical. Its statement of what a profession is, a definition of sorts, does not purport to give necessary or sufficient conditions for some occupation to be a profession but merely to state what is true of "most professions," "the most important professions," "the most developed professions," or the like. Sociologists derive their definition from a list of professions they themselves assemble. There is no canonical list of any consequence. Each sociologist studying professions develops his or her own. Law and medicine are always on the list; the clergy, often; and other occupations commonly acknowledged as professions, such as architecture, engineering, the military, nursing, or social work, sometimes.[1] Journalism appears on some of these lists.[2] What explains these different lists? Why doesn't sociology speak with one voice?

We may distinguish three traditions in the sociology of professions: the economic, the political, and the anthropological. Though individual sociologists often mix their elements, distinguishing them as "ideal types" should help us think about them more clearly, even in their less ideal (that is, mixed) forms.

The economic tradition interprets professions as primarily a means of controlling market forces for the benefit of the professionals themselves, that is, as a form of monopoly, guild, or labor union. The economic tradition has two branches: Marxist and free-market. Among recent sociologists in the Marxist tradition, the best is Magali Sarfatti Larson (*The Rise of Professionalism*, 1977); among sociologists in the free-market tradition, Andrew Abbott (*The System of Professions*, 1988) is a good example. For sociologists in the economic tradition, whether Marxist or free-market, it is the would-be members of a profession who, by acting together under favorable conditions, create their monopoly. Successful professions have high income, workplace autonomy, control of who can join, and so on; less successful professions lack some or most of these powers (more or less). Morality, if relevant at all, is relevant merely as a means to monopoly, a way of making a "trademark" (the profession's name) more attractive to potential employers. In this tradition, journalism—in the United States, at least—can, at best, be considered a failed profession. Not only has it never had anything like a monopoly over covering the news, its employers, the media, have always controlled who would report the news.

For the political tradition, however, journalism is plainly a profession in some countries but not others. Often associated with Max Weber, the political tradition interprets profession as primarily a legal condition, a matter of reasonably effective laws that set standards of advanced education, require a license to practice, and impose discipline upon practitioners through formal, governmental structures. "Professional ethics"—and, indeed, even ordinary moral standards—are, if distinguished at all, treated as just another form of regulation. To be a profession is to be an occupation bureaucratized in a certain way. For the political approach, it is the society (the government) that creates professions out of occupations, and the society (the public) that benefits (regardless of who else may benefit). The political approach substitutes the society's very visible hands for the invisible hand of economics. The members of the profession have little or no part in making their profession.[3] According to this tradition, journalism can never be a profession in the United States so long as the First Amendment bars licensure of journalists, but journalism in Russia or India, where journalists are licensed, is a profession (consisting of those journalists who are licensed). Given this understanding of profession, it is easy to see why some U.S. journalists have denied that the journalism they practice is a profession—and, indeed, insist that it should not be.

The anthropological tradition, often associated with Emile Durkheim or Talcott Parsons, interprets professions as primarily cultural facts, the natural expression of a certain social function under certain conditions. Neither the members of the profession nor society can have much to say about whether a certain occupation will be a profession. Professions are a function of special knowledge used in a certain way, a community created by a common occupation requiring advanced study. Among recent sociologists, the best of those working in the anthropological tradition is Eliot Freidson.[4]

Distinguishing these three sociological traditions helps make the point that the sociological approach has not yet yielded a single definition of "profession" and, more importantly, is unlikely to. Sociology's way of developing a definition—abstracting from a list of clear cases something common to most or all—is unlikely to yield a single definition or, at least, is unlikely to until sociologists agree on a list of clear cases that is sufficiently long to exclude most candidate definitions. Today, only two professions appear on all sociological lists (law and medicine). That is too few to derive a widely accepted definition. Whatever the utility of a particular sociological definition for a particular research program, no such definition is likely to seem definitive to more than a minority of sociologists.

The sociological approach offers a wilderness of possibilities, but little help choosing among them. That, I think, is enough to make clear how unattractive the sociological approach should be, even though it continues to dominate discussion of professions.

A Philosophical Approach

Philosophical approaches typically offer necessary and sufficient conditions for an occupation to count as a profession. While a philosophical definition may leave the status of a small number of would-be professions unsettled, it should at least be able to explain (in a satisfying way) why those would-be professions are neither clearly professions nor clearly not professions. Philosophical definitions are sensitive to counter-example in a way sociological definitions are not. Philosophers (and journalists thinking like philosophers) cannot use the standard defense of sociologists confronted with a counter-example: "I said 'most,' not 'all.'"

Of the various philosophical approaches to defining "profession," the best is Socratic.[5] It answers the question, "What do we—professionals and philosophers—'really' think a profession is?" A Socratic definition must be worked out through a conversation: members of various professions say what they mean by "profession," including its necessary and sufficient conditions.

Philosophers, or members of professions, test those definitions with counter-examples and otherwise consider the consequences of adopting the definition. Any problem so discovered should be fixed by revising the definition in a way that seems to resolve the problem. The definition is again examined. And so the process continues until everyone participating in the conversation is satisfied that no problem remains. It is this critical conversation that underwrites the claim that the resulting definition is "what we *really* think a profession is," that is, what we think it is after enough reflection. The conversation need not end with everyone who started out thinking they belonged to a profession ending up with a definition that puts them in a profession. Some participants, for example, "professional managers" or "professional athletes," may instead come to see that they are not members of a profession in any interesting sense of the term or at least not in the sense they are in fact interested in.

The Socratic approach, unlike the sociological, provides a procedure for resolving disputes. Individual insights must be incorporated into a single definition on which everyone agrees. The Socratic procedure concludes only when there is no live alternative to its preferred definition, a definition that necessarily excludes individual mistakes and even widespread but indefensible prejudices. In this respect, the resulting definition is a product of reason rather than of social psychology.

A Socratic Definition

After many years of applying the Socratic method to professions, I have devised the following definition:

> A profession is a number of individuals in the same occupation
> voluntarily organized to earn a living by openly serving a moral ideal
> in a morally permissible way, beyond what law, market, morality, and
> public opinion would otherwise require.

According to this definition, a profession is a group undertaking. This is one respect in which members of professions differ from mere experts, craftspeople, or artists. Experts, craftspeople, and artists can be one of a kind, but members of a profession cannot be, just as citizens, soldiers, and members of a family cannot. There can no more be a profession of one than a citizenry, army, or family of one.

According to the Socratic definition, the occupation in question (the would-be profession) must organize to work in a morally permissible way. Where there is no morally permissible way to carry on the occupation, there can be no profession. There can, for example, be no profession of thieves or murderers (since theft and murder are—almost always—morally impermissible). Morality limits what can be a profession. Some professions are conceptually impossible.

The moral permissibility of a profession's occupation is one way that, according to the Socratic definition, profession is conceptually connected with morality. There are two others. One concerns "moral ideals," which refer to a state of affairs all rational persons at their rational best recognize as a significant good; that is, a moral ideal is what they want realized even if the realization would mean having to help, in at least minor ways. For most professions, roughly stating the distinctive moral ideal is easy: physicians have organized to cure the sick, comfort the dying, and protect the healthy from disease; lawyers, to help people obtain justice within the law; accountants, to represent financial information in ways both useful and accurate; engineers, to improve the material condition of humanity; and so on. Health, a comfortable death, justice within the law, and the like are goods we all recognize as significant.

"Moral ideal" is not, I should add, a mere synonym for "public service." Though the ideals I just listed are all easily understood as forms of public service, some are not. For example, the natural sciences typically seek to understand "nature," with each branch of science focusing on a distinct part of nature. Although scientists seek the truth about nature without necessarily claiming to serve anyone but other scientists, they are nonetheless capable of forming a profession. The truth about nature is a moral ideal because we all like knowing about the world, even about parts of the world, such as distant galaxies, where knowing does us absolutely no good, or, at least, no good beyond satisfying our curiosity. That scientists do not seek to serve the rest of us does not mean that the ideal they serve is not a moral ideal.

Perhaps I can be a morally decent person without actively serving any moral ideal, but an occupation cannot be a profession unless it serves one. A profession serves its chosen moral ideal by setting and generally following appropriate special standards for carrying on its occupation that go beyond what law, market, morality, and public opinion would otherwise require. Without at least one such special standard, the occupation, the candidate profession, would remain nothing more than an honest way to earn a living. So, for example, the conditions that distinguish the professional soldier from the mere mercenary (however expert and honest) are the special standards of a professional soldier. To be a (good) mercenary, one need only competently carry out the terms of one's morally permissible contract of employment, but to be a (good) professional soldier, one must do more, for example, serve one's country honorably even when the contract of employment, ordinary morality, law, and public opinion do not require it.

The third way, in the Socratic definition, that professions are connected with morality is implicit rather than explicit: the special standards of a profession are *morally binding* on every member of the profession simply because of that membership. These binding standards are what constitute the profession's essential organization, not its learned societies or regulatory agencies. But how is it possible for standards that are morally permissible but not otherwise part of ordinary morality to be morally binding on members of a profession? That, I think, is the central question in the philosophy of professions. Here is my answer.

Professions must be "professed," that is, declared or claimed.[6] Physicians must declare themselves to be physicians, lawyers must claim to be lawyers, wengineers must say they are engineers, and so on. They need not advertise or otherwise *publicly* announce their profession; there is nothing conceptually impossible about a secret profession, for example, a profession of spies. But even members of a profession of spies would have to declare their profession to potential clients or employers. Professionals must declare their profession in order to earn their living by it. They cannot be hired as such-and-such—say, a professional spy—unless potential employers know that they are "spies," in the special-standards sense. They cannot, that is, be hired as a professional spy if they merely claim to know a lot about spying, to have earned a living by it for several years, and to be good at it. If their profession has a good reputation for what it does, their declaration of membership will aid them in earning a living as a spy. They will find appropriate employment (in part) by declaring their profession. If, however, their profession has a bad reputation, their declaration of membership will be a disadvantage. Compare, for example, our response to the declaration "I am an astrologer" with our response to "I am an astronomer."

Where members of a profession freely declare their membership, the profession's way of pursuing its moral ideal will be a voluntary, morally permissible cooperative practice (not so different from a football game). The members of the profession will be members because they were entitled to be (by training, experience, certification, or the like), wished to be, and spoke up accordingly. They may cease to be members simply by ceasing to claim membership.

In general, members of an occupation free to declare membership in the corresponding profession will declare it only if the declaration seems likely to benefit them, that is, to serve at least one purpose of their own at what seems a reasonable cost. If hired partly because they declared their membership, members of a profession will be in a position to enjoy the benefits of the profession. They will also be in a position to take advantage of the practice by doing less than the standards of the practice require, even though the expectation was that they would do what the standards require, because they declared the appropriate profession.[7] If cheating consists in violating the rules of a voluntary, morally permissible cooperative practice, then every member of a profession is in a position to cheat (just as contestants in a football game are). Since, all else being equal, cheating is morally wrong, every member of a profession has a moral obligation, all else being equal, to do as the special standards of the profession require. The professional standards are morally binding in much the way a promise is.

"Professionalism" is, strictly speaking, simply acting as the standards of the relevant profession require. To be a "professional" is to be a member in good standing of the profession—or, by analogy, to act as if one were, that is, to act in the way the relevant standards require. Professional standards are, of course, open to interpretation. Part of being a professional is interpreting the relevant standards in ways the profession recognizes as legitimate—for example, interpreting a certain technical standard taking into account the moral ideal it was designed to serve. Conduct is "unprofessional" if it is inconsistent with the profession's standards, properly interpreted. Since only members of a profession are subject to the profession's standards, only they can violate them. Someone not a member of the profession can be a charlatan, mountebank, or impostor but such a person cannot engage in unprofessional conduct.

Professional standards may, and generally do, vary from profession to profession. There is, for example, no reason that the professional standards of lawyers should be the same as those of physicians. A profession's standards are, at least in part, a function of opinion within the profession and therefore change from time to time as opinion changes. A profession's standards generally appear in a range of documents, including admission requirements, rules of practice, and disciplinary procedures. A profession is successfully organized insofar as its special standards are realized in the practice of its members, in what they do and how they evaluate one another.

One of the documents that states professional standards may be a "code of ethics," a formal statement of the most general rules of practice. Yet, while many definitions of profession require such a code, the Socratic definition offered here does not. That omission is both deliberate and important. While a formal code of ethics is a central feature of professions in the United States, Canada, Britain, and most other English-speaking countries, and has been since early in the twentieth century, few such codes seem to have existed outside English-speaking countries until after World War II. Yet professions seem to have existed in some of these countries without formal code or even the term "code of ethics." Both the term and a code are thus artifacts of particular cultures without being a necessary condition of the activity.

Morality, Ethics, and Law

I have so far spoken of "ethics" without defining that term. That is risky. The term has at least as many senses as "profession." What I have just said will not make much sense to someone who does not understand "ethics" as it is used here. So, I must now say what meaning I intend (beyond what appears in this volume's introduction and in ch. 1 by Deni Elliott and David Ozar).

By "ethics," I mean those special, *morally permissible standards of conduct governing members of a group simply because they are members of that group.* In this sense, Hopi ethics are for Hopi and for no one else; business ethics, for people in business and for no one else; and professional ethics, for members of the relevant profession and for no one else. Ethics—as used here—is relative even though morality is not.[8] This meaning is the one I assumed when I argued that a profession's ethics need not be embodied in a formal code. This definition makes clear why one profession's ethics may—and, indeed, should—differ from those of other professions—where the "should" implies both expectation and propriety.

Ethics in this sense is not mere *mores*. Ethics must at least be morally permissible. There can be no thieves' ethics or mafia ethics, except with ironic quotes around "ethics." Though law is also relative, changing from jurisdiction to jurisdiction, ethics is not law or even mere custom for at least two reasons. First, not all laws (or customs) are morally permissible, whereas ethical standards must, by definition, be *at least* morally permissible. Second, law applies to people whether they want it to apply or not. That is why external means of enforcement (police, courts, jails, penalties, and so on) are so central to understanding law. Ethics—or, at least, professional ethics as I have explained it— applies to people only because they voluntarily submit to it, by justifiably declaring themselves members of the profession in question and being accepted as such. Morality, an internal mode of enforcement, can therefore be—and, I think, is—the primary means of making professional ethics effective, in the same way it makes most promises effective.

Law and professional ethics are distinct in another way. An occupation's status as a profession is more or less independent of license, state-imposed monopoly, and other special legal intervention. Certified financial analysts, professors, and the like can form professions even though none of these professionals are in fact licensed. And even a country with licensed attorneys may have no legal profession (just as the United States has licensed plumbers but no profession of plumbing). Indeed, professions should maintain a certain independence from law. While some professions commit themselves to obeying the law, the commitment must be contingent. Insofar as the laws of a particular country fall below the moral minimum, any provision of a professional code purporting to bind members of the profession to obey the law would be void in that respect, just as a promise to do what morality forbids is void.[9]

Applying the Socratic Definition to Journalism

Having established the Socratic definition of "profession," I must now address how it applies to journalism. Having shown its superiority over the sociological definition of "profession," I can now quickly explain why journalism clearly is a profession.

Consider again the eight reasons with which this paper began. Though commonly offered to show that journalism is not a profession, they are, according to the Socratic definition, all irrelevant to journalism's status. Nothing in the Socratic definition requires journalists to be licensed; what is required is that someone qualified to be a journalist declare him- or herself to be one (and to be accepted as one). Nothing in the definition requires journalism to have a body of theory, only a discipline associated with the underlying occupation. The discipline may be acquired in any number of ways, not necessarily through a formal curriculum. Nothing in the definition requires a college or graduate degree. That most professions do require advanced training is a fact about the underlying occupations, not the professions as such. Nothing in the definition requires journalists to have a monopoly, that is, the power to exclude non-journalists from doing what journalists do. All that follows from the definition is that journalists can (and should) say of non-journalists that they are not journalists—or, at least, that they are not proper journalists—but *mere* bloggers, writers of the news, or the like. Journalists have a right to preserve their "trademark." Nothing in the definition requires journalists to be independent consultants, to have strict professional autonomy, independent from external regulators. Indeed, if the definition did require that, even a majority of doctors and lawyers would now lack professional status, given the rise of managed care. Journalists must, however, have autonomy of a sort, that is, the ability to act as their professional standards require. That is as possible in most large organizations as it is with most individual clients.[10] Nothing in the definition requires journalists to be members of a "professional organization," such as the Society of Professional Journalists. That is just as well. In the United States, not even law or medicine, much less many other professions, can now claim that a majority of the profession's members belong to any of its formal organizations. The only organization that journalists must belong to if journalism is to be a profession is the profession of journalism, and their membership comes with justifiably declaring membership. That membership cannot guarantee high social status or high income. All it can guarantee is that journalists who satisfy the standards of journalism, who conduct themselves as they "profess," will be "real professionals" and deserve the corresponding respect. Whether they will in fact get respect for that is, however, a contingency over which they have little or no control. They can do only as they should, and hope enough people give them the respect they deserve. Last, nothing in the definition requires a profession to have clients, only to serve a moral ideal in morally permissible ways beyond what law, market, morality, and public opinion would otherwise require.

Those eight reasons do not, then, show that journalism is not a profession. Whether it *is* one, by my Socratic definition, rests on journalists' commitment to the profession. Journalists belong to an occupation that gathers, analyzes, and reports the news, all in service to what the Society of Professional Journalists' Code of Ethics calls "providing a fair and comprehensive account of [recent] events and issues." Journalists differ from other members of the same occupation (e.g., bloggers) in that they hold themselves to this higher standard, a standard beyond that set by law, market, morality, or public opinion. Anyone can gather and disseminate information; a professional journalist, by contrast, assesses the accuracy of information from all sources, exercises care to avoid inadvertent error, diligently seeks out subjects of news stories to give them the opportunity to respond to allegations of wrongdoing, identifies sources whenever feasible, always questions sources' motives before promising anonymity, clarifies conditions attached to any promise made in exchange for information, makes certain that headlines, news teases, promotional materials, photos, video, audio, graphics, sound bites, and quotations do not misrepresent, and so on.[11] When a journalist, claims to be *a journalist* and not just a conveyor of information, it is these standards that are being professed. For the Socratic definition, the answer to the question, "Is journalism a profession?" is very much like the answer to what may seem to be a quite different question, "What is a journalist?"[12]

The Future of the Profession of Journalism

Will the profession of journalism survive commercialization of the news, the Internet's influx of amateur news bloggers, and other trends of the twenty-first century? I don't know. What seems obvious to me is that I, and everyone I know, needs journalists, that is, professionals of a certain kind, to sort through what government officials, important private persons, witnesses, and other news sources say; people who are more committed to learning the truth of significant events and to reporting them accurately. We need news gatherers upon whom we can rely. I therefore expect the profession of journalism to survive for some time. I am, however, not nearly as optimistic about the employers for whom journalists now work. The great media empires of today seem to be bound to the same wheel of destruction as General Motors, the Pennsylvania Railroad, and other former darlings of Wall Street. Journalists will need new employers—or other sources of income. Perhaps they will reverse the story of medicine and law, becoming consultants who provide journalism through their own Web sites to paid subscribers. Perhaps they will establish cooperative Web sites supported by advertising. Who knows? Nothing in the profession of journalism rules such things out—or requires them.

Notes

Early work on this chapter was carried out in part under National Science Foundation grant SES-0117471. Early versions (under various titles and focusing on various professions) were presented to a workshop, "Toward a Common Goal: Ethics across the Professions," Sierra Health Foundation, Sacramento, California, August 26, 2006; the Research Group of Ethics, Faculty of Letters, Hokkaido University, Sapporo, Japan, February 14, 2007; Second ASPCP International Conference on Philosophical Practice, Purdue University Calumet, Hammond, Indiana, May 19, 2007; Philosophy Section, Faculty of Technology, Policy, and Management, University of Technology–Delft, The Netherlands, September 24, 2007; Center for Ethics and Technology, University of Technology–Twente, The Netherlands, September 27, 2007; and the Center for the

Study of Ethics in Society, Western Michigan University, Kalamazoo, Michigan, October 4, 2007. Versions of some sections have also appeared in print (in Chinese) in "How Is a Profession of Engineering in China Possible?" *Engineering Studies* (2007), 132–41; and "Is Engineering a Profession Everywhere?" *Philosophia*, 37, no. 2 (June 2009): 211–225.

1. For more on the enormous variety of sociological definitions, see John Kultgen, *Ethics and Professionalism* (Philadelphia: University of Pennsylvania Press, 1988), esp. 60–62; or the recent exchange between David Sciulli and Rolf Torstendahl: Sciulli, "Continental Sociology of Professions Today: Conceptual Contributions," *Current Sociology* 53 (Nov. 2005), 915–42; Torstendahl, "The Need for a Definition of 'Profession,'" *Current Sociology* 53 (Nov. 2005), 947–51.

2. See, for example, the prominent place given journalism in Howard Gardner, Mihaly Csikszentmihalyi, and William Damon, *Good Work: When Excellence and Ethics Meet* (New York: Basic, 2001), a well-received recent work on the sociology of professions.

3. A recent work in this tradition is Robert Zussman's *Mechanics of the Middle Class* (Berkeley and Los Angeles: University of California Press, 1985).

4. See, for example, *Professionalism: The Third Logic* (Chicago: University of Chicago Press, 2001).

5. For a surprising example of another philosophical approach, the Cartesian, see John T. Sanders, "Honor among Thieves: Some Reflections on Codes of Professional Ethics," *Professional Ethics* 2 (Fall/Winter 1993): 83–103. For a more plausible example of the Cartesian approach, see Daryl Koehn, *The Ground of Professional Ethics* (London: Routledge, 1994). Like Kultgen, Michael Bayles, *Profesional Ethics* (Belmont, California: Wadsworth, 1981), seems to offer a sociological definition.

6. Note that most analyses of profession try to find something that is "professed." Generally, it is merely technical knowledge, skill, or expertise. In the analysis proposed here, what is professed is always something more than merely technical knowledge, skill, or expertise; it includes a morally binding commitment to a moral ideal and special standards supporting it. This brings "profession" much closer to an early meaning—publicly taking vows as part of entering a religious order.

7. Sanders, "Honor Among Thieves."

8. Morality consists of those standards every moral agent should follow. Morality is a universal minimum, our standard of moral *right* and *wrong*.

9. This point, I believe, is consistent with that made by Eugene Schlossberger in "Technology and Civil Disobedience: Why Engineers Have a Special Duty to Obey the Law," *Science and Engineering Ethics* 1 (June 1995), 163–68. While I doubt that engineers—Schlossberger's subject—have the special duty that he argues for, my point is simply that the duty's existence is independent of the claim I am making here. Engineers might both have that special duty to obey the law in general and still have good reason to violate it in certain cases (e.g., when the law is unjust). Something similar might be true of journalists, who (unlike engineers) do occasionally find themselves in jail as a result of disobeying the law.

10. For a sustained defense of this claim, see my "Professional Autonomy: A Framework for Empirical Research," *Business Ethics Quarterly* 6 (Oct. 1996), 441–60.

11. This list is derived from *The Code of Ethics of the Society of Professional Journalists*, http://www.spj.org/ethicscode.asp, accessed August 2, 2006.

12. See the article by Jay Black in chap. 7 of this volume.

7

Who Is a Journalist?

Jay Black

Who is a journalist? This is much more than a rhetorical question. It is a pragmatic one, with serious ethical, legal, and craft ramifications.

The question is disarmingly simplistic. If we're not careful, simplistic answers will emerge, but they will not satisfy. It's easy to maintain that the question is passé if we think today's 24/7, electronic, hyper information/ entertainment/persuasion world has so obliterated the lines between media functions that the death of journalism has become inevitable. On the other hand, some dogmatists find it compelling to draw hard and fast lines in the territorial sands, defining journalism in ways that include only a select few highly moral professionals while de-pressing or excommunicating everyone else. Meanwhile, it's equally problematic to broaden the definition of journalism such that everyone qualifies ("We're all journalists now").[1]

Today the majority of individuals who call themselves journalists are not full-time employees of traditional news media; they work (sometimes as freelancers, sometimes without pay) as reporters, videographers, and commentators on Weblogs (there were more than 50 million blogs by 2006, with thousands more appearing daily), cable outlets, and 'zines, locally, regionally, nationally, and internationally. One-quarter of Americans say the Internet is their main source of news. Millions rely on Comedy Central's *Daily Show* and late-night comedians, who constantly spoof mainstream media, for fresh perspectives on the "news." The Federal Communications Commission ruled in 2003 that Howard Stern's program was a bona fide news interview program. YourHub.com, founded and supported by regional newspapers concerned about the absence of youthful readers, invites people to post anything they find interesting; their motto is "Whatever story you want to share, YourHub.com is your place to do it." A goal of the public journalism movement—a movement launched in traditional media—has been citizen participation in the public sphere. That function is being served by nontraditional media, usually operating in an open rather than closed environment.[2]

Who, then, qualifies as a journalist? One can take any of several perspectives, including (but not limited to) historical, legal, ethical, technological, and performative. For instance, should journalists be defined by what they do rather than for whom they work? Do nontraditional journalists abide by the constructs that show up in traditional journalism codes—and should they? To what extent are traditional and nontraditional journalists held accountable and driven to believe in and practice what Bill Kovach and Tom Rosenstiel called journalism's central function: to produce information that enables the public to be free and self-governing?[3] Do they subscribe to the Deni Elliott–David Ozar thesis, presented in the first chapter of this volume, that journalism's central roles (over and above providing information that society needs to self-govern) are to provide information related to common social desires, be watchdogs to help people achieve autonomy, and help build community? Do traditional and nontraditional journalists agree they have an obligation to truth and a loyalty to citizens? Other individuals, crafts, and professions can share some, if not all, of these role-related tasks (teachers, politicians, social workers, and the clergy come to mind); what sets journalists apart?

My approach in this chapter is to explore the ethical and legal parameters of traditional journalism as historically understood. From this background and analysis, I conclude the best characterization of "journalist" is rooted in the performative and guided by the ethical: To be a journalist is to engage in particular activities and to perform them ethically.

Ethics and Law

When we try to define journalism and journalists and to determine who among the claimants deserves professional status (and the attendant legal privileges), we enter a foggy semantic terrain. To navigate it, we would do well to sift and sort through two domains: the domain of professional ethics and the domain of law. These domains overlap and are interdependent, but they need to be articulated for this debate to make sense.[4] In addition to considering who gets legal protection and who is subjected to legal sanctions, we should consider how various journalists and journalism wannabe's are held accountable by peers and the public. New tools and systems for gatekeeping and passing information among nontraditional reporters and active audiences are part of the equation. For instance, to what extent does online journalism, by virtue of the open environment in which it functions, hold others—and itself—accountable, and what does that mean to our notions of traditional journalism?

Ethics and law share a concern with advancing a socially shared vision of the public good, but they go about achieving that good differently. Ethics focuses on the voluntary nature of our behavior, and provides categories, principles, and exemplars by which our behavior can be judged. Ethics is "obedience to the unenforceable."[5] Law, on the other hand, deals with the arena of coerced compliance—"obedience to the enforceable"—with respect to the minimum maintenance of social stability . . . the bottom line, below which we should not fall, lest we be punished. Their respective roles are thus distinct.

The Domain of Ethics

The domain of ethics focuses on fundamental human values and moral imperatives, on principles of duty, virtue, care, and consequence—in short, on matters of character and moral autonomy, and self-imposed considerations of how we ought to treat one another in a world of voluntary relationships. As "obedience to the unenforceable," ethics entails making tough decisions—not the obvious choices between right and wrong, but the tough choices between not-quite-completely rights or even the lesser of two wrongs.

Standards of professional ethics are a sometimes confusing blend of "ideal expectations" that articulate the positive, lofty aspirations of practitioners, and "minimal standards" that spell out, usually in negative and legalistic fashion, the "thou shalt not's" of the craft, all with the goal of separating credible practitioners from hucksters and charlatans. Professional ethics applies these principles to a particular group of practitioners; hence, we see journalism ethics emphasizing freedom with responsibility, shared commitments, truth seeking, and truth telling; minimizing harm; and carefully balancing independence and accountability. The calls are often tough ones, the lines between and among conflicting moral claims often blurry. My concern here is with determining to whom the standards of professional journalism ethics should apply.

The Domain of Law

The domain of law, by contrast, demarcates the boundaries of citizens' behavior and accomplishes through coercion what ethics is often unable to achieve solely through appeals to conscience and professional censure—in short, obedience to the enforceable. This domain, as Ugland and Henderson explain, is shaped by classical liberal ideas of autonomy, reason, and self-determination.[6] Applied to journalism and public opinion, the legal domain is shaped by libertarian assumptions that society is best served by permitting only minimal interference with the media's right to gather and report information; the legal position is that "debate on public issues should be uninhibited, robust and wide open" (*Times v. Sullivan*[7]) and that the public is enriched by exposure to diverse and antagonistic sources of information. The First Amendment to the

Constitution—journalists' favorite—grants the craft of journalism a unique status among institutions, although the press's history is replete with statutory and constitutional laws, policies, administrative dictates, and informal privileges granted by government officials, all of which demonstrate that the "free press" clause is not absolute.

The domains of ethics and law, though, are also interdependent, as recognized in one of the oldest codes of journalism ethics, the Statement of Principles of the American Society of Newspaper Editors, whose preamble begins, "The First Amendment, protecting freedom of expression from abridgement by law, guarantees to the people through their press a constitutional right, and thereby places on newspaper people a particular responsibility. Thus, journalism demands of its practitioners not only industry and knowledge but also the pursuit of a standard of integrity proportionate to the journalist's singular obligation."[8]

Let's explore these two domains in more detail.

THE JOURNALISM ETHICS DOMAIN. Mechanical and craft-based skills—having a nose for news, applying good information-gathering techniques from human and stored sources, practicing good writing and presentational skills, exercising the capacity "to clearly, accurately and effectively convey the corresponding information," and maintaining an open, collaborative relationship with their audiences—are necessary but not sufficient conditions for the practice of traditional and nontraditional journalism.[9] Beyond these mechanical skills are professional and ethical considerations.

More than two decades ago, in *Committed Journalism*, Ed Lambeth put professional and ethical journalism in a historical context: "Conceived in the Renaissance, born in the Enlightenment, and nurtured to robust life in the modern West, journalism inherits the legacy of the larger society: the principles of truth, justice, freedom, humaneness, and individual responsibility."[10] Another of the classics in journalism ethics, *The Virtuous Journalist*, by Stephen Klaidman and Tom Beauchamp, challenges the press to reach for truth, avoid bias, avoid harm, serve the public, maintain trust, escape manipulation, invite criticism, and be accountable.[11]

A casual review of media ethics literature shows Lambeth, Klaidman, and Beauchamp to be on target. Academic and trade commentary on journalism describes a craft that claims to abide by the following ethical canons: truth telling, independence, courageousness, proportionality, accuracy, fairness, objectivity, impartiality, comprehensiveness, transparency, accountability, stewardship, and humaneness.

For example, Bill Kovach and Tom Rosenstiel's influential book, *The Elements of Journalism: What Newspeople Should Know and the Public Should Expect*, describes "principles that have helped both journalists and the people in self-governing systems to adjust to the demands of an ever more complex world"

(p. 5). In a statement that is quoted frequently in assessments of contemporary journalism, Kovach and Rosensteil maintain that "the purpose of journalism is to provide people with the information they need to be free and self-governing." According to them, to fulfill this task, journalism has to honor a number of commitments:

- Journalism's first obligation is to the truth.
- Its first loyalty is to citizens.
- Its practitioners must maintain an independence from those they cover.
- It must serve as an independent monitor of power.
- It must provide a forum for public criticism and compromise.
- It must strive to make the significant interesting and relevant.
- It must keep the news comprehensive and in proportion.
- Its practitioners have an obligation to exercise their personal conscience.
- Citizens, too, have rights and responsibilities when it comes to the news.[12]

Participants at a 2006 media ethics colloquium—all journalism educators—reached a similar conclusion.[13] Building on Kovach and Rosensteil's principles, they defined journalists as skilled communicators who gather and distribute information with professional commitments to:

- Truthfulness;
- Accuracy;
- Comprehensiveness/thoroughness;
- Proportionality;
- Authenticity;
- Fairness;
- Skepticism;
- Objectivity;
- Verifiable reporting;
- Articulated and appropriate loyalties;
- A watchdog function;
- Minimizing the harm that is inherent in redistributing information;
- Diversity within the ranks of journalists, and of subject matter, sources, and audiences;
- Accountability and transparency of motives and reporting practices;
- Social responsibility; and
- Independent judgment and autonomy.

The preceding list of moral values for journalists is instructive but not determinative. That is, it offers insight into what it means to be an ethical journalist but still demands autonomous moral decision making of the sort recommended in Elliott and Ozar's systematic moral analysis. I will return to these considerations at the conclusion of this chapter.

THE JOURNALISM LAW DOMAIN.   The legal argument about who is a journalist is not insignificant, for it determines who deserves special privileges. If only a select few individuals are granted special access to sources or events, or have statutory rights to protect their sources, or have constitutional protection from claims of libel or privacy invasion, then "journalist" delineates a very special class of professionals. However, if everyone is a journalist, the privileges would seem to apply universally and therefore could hardly be called "privileges."

Although it was never a no-brainer, it used to be a simpler argument. Legislatures have struggled to define, and courts have struggled to interpret, "journalist" or "reporter." *Branzburg* and other decisions suggest that all citizens are equally equipped and equally free to serve as newsgathering watchdogs—the independent pamphleteer no less than the media baron.[14] However, this "egalitarian model" contrasts with the "expert model" revealed in numerous other court cases and proposed by many legal scholars—a model holding that journalists are "uniquely qualified and clearly identified professionals who serve as agents of the public in the procurement and dissemination of news."[15] Evidence supporting the "expert model" is seen in the issuance of press passes (special seating at governmental venues), access to newsworthy events or records (prisons, crime scenes, war zones, official records, etc.), special tax and antitrust exemptions (e.g., Joint Operating Agreements and favorable postal rates)—all privileges not granted to people who don't qualify as journalists. The debate is essentially over whether the First Amendment is to be read as a "freedom of speech" document or a "freedom of the press" document, or as granting two wholly distinct freedoms. Despite the foregoing list of official and quasi-official special privileges granted to the press, courts have focused on the speech clause, emphasizing the needs of the public rather than the needs of a specific professional group. In the process, the role of "journalist" has not been well clarified.[16]

Courts and legislatures seem somewhat befuddled about some key issues: To be a reporter do you have to work for a mainstream news medium? A daily medium? (Note that *Time* magazine wasn't protected under Alabama's shield law.) Do you have to be doing investigative reporting, or could weather, travel, fashion, or food reporters qualify for protection? Do you have to "intend" to do journalism or reporting, to publish or broadcast your work product, and/ or to make money at it? Or could it be happenstance journalism? As Ugland and Henderson describe the situation,[17] Florida's shield law says a journalist is "a person regularly engaged in [newsgathering] for gain or livelihood, who obtained the information sought while working as a salaried employee"; Washington, D.C., requires the person be employed by the news media; Indiana requires the person be "an editorial or reportorial employee, who receives or has received income" for newsgathering; and Delaware requires the person be employed at least twenty hours per week before qualifying. Nebraska protects "any newspaper, magazine, other periodical, book, pamphlet, news service, wire service, news or feature syndicate, broadcast station, or network or cable television system"—a broad umbrella, yet one that doesn't shield scholars, documentarians, bloggers, and many others.

Consider the "Free Flow of Information Act" working its way through the Congress as of this writing. The act, which would establish for qualified reporters a privilege applicable in federal proceedings, passed the House of Representatives (as H.R. 2101) in the fall of 2007 by a 398–21 vote. The Senate version (S. 2035) was approved 15–4 by the Senate Judiciary Committee but has not been voted upon by the full Senate as of this writing. It would offer protection to sources and journalists alike and would apply to journalists from traditional news outlets and to some bloggers. In protecting sources, it seems to be arguing it is the needs of the public, in addition to those of elite journalists, that deserve protecting. This bill, like so many statutes and court decisions, defines journalists. In so doing, it determines that some categories of information providers are professionals and some are not. It applies to those who regularly engage in such journalistic activities as gathering and publishing news and information for dissemination to the public, and those who do so for a substantial portion of their livelihood or for substantial financial gain. Thus, it says it is not just a matter of who employs the communicators, but what the individual and institutional communicators do for a living. The key variables seem to be the nature of the work, the expectations of compensation, and the relationship between communicators and the public. According to this legislation, some communicators, including bloggers, are more deserving of the title "journalist" than are others. And, while mainstream media—including the American Society of Newspaper Editors—laud passage of a national shield Free Flow of Information law, some critics see this as a disturbing trend toward an ad hoc and perhaps arbitrary form of governmental licensing of journalists. As Gant argues, First Amendment freedoms ought to belong to all of us, because public communication is an activity rather than an institution; he says that to grant freedom to an institution means to first define and would require that you license it, which would be a violation of our basic freedoms.[18]

The New Media

So far, this introduction to the media ethics and law domains applies primarily to traditional journalists working within traditional journalism organizations— a.k.a. the "Mainstream Media," or "MSM." It is they who have laid claim to the First Amendment and other legal protections, they who claim to have historically informed the largest aggregates of society in matters of self-governance—and they who have garnered untold billions of dollars in revenue. However, we have already seen how "new media" are part of the debate.

The dramatic decline in MSM's credibility of late, and the challenges to its high status, is connected to the brave new world of alternative journalism. The exact nature of the causality chain is unclear, but there is certainly a relationship. Internet bloggers, desktop publishers, freelancers, and a host of "public communicators" who disseminate newsworthy information to others, usually in a sporadic and unregimented manner, have changed the journalism landscape.

Consider the new journalism world of Facebook, MySpace, YouTube, specialized listservs, the Daily Kos, Instapundit, Slate.com, and America's millions and millions of other cyberspace bloggers; reality (or "reality-based") television programs; the "fake news" comedians Jon Stewart and Stephen Colbert; and pundits such as Keith Olberman, Bill O'Reilly and Rush Limbaugh; along with the dozens of cable TV talking head shows and shoutfests—all examples of alternative journalism. (It's interesting to note that 65% of bloggers don't see their work as a form of journalism, but given a world with more than fifty million bloggers, that leaves millions who *do* think they're journalists. And lest we forget: When *Crossfire*'s Paul Begala and Tucker Carlson ripped into Jon Stewart for his wildly successful "fake news," Stewart ripped into *Crossfire* for harming democracy by simplifying political discourse. *Crossfire* was canceled, while *The Daily Show* is flourishing. For many of us, particularly the younger crowd, *The Daily Show* and *The Colbert Report* . . . along with tidbits from the blogosphere are primary sources of news.[19])

Mainstream media's reactions to Web-based and other new media have been fairly predictable to students of media history. At first, MSM reacted to the upstarts (technological and content innovations) as items of curiosity, then as financial and territorial threats, and only belatedly as potential partners in snagging audiences and revenue. MSM were losing their status as the United States's primary sources for information (and persuasion and entertainment), and weren't quite sure why. They soon recognized something that advertisers were already aware of: younger audiences, professional audiences, and specialized audiences were producing and retrieving media content from technology over which they had some control, rather than passively waiting for MSM to deliver whatever the media thought would sell, at MSM's convenience rather than when or where audiences wanted it. MSM's response came as no surprise to those who remembered how newspapers, magazines, film, radio, and television had responded when each had been threatened by newer delivery systems: denigrate the new media, then fear them, and ultimately integrate them into the whole media world while transforming yourself into something that makes the best use of your unique characteristics. The future of these new relationships is anybody's guess, but it's certainly noteworthy when the publishers of the *New York Times* and *Time* magazine suggest they don't care if the print versions of their newspaper and magazine continue to exist in this new media world.

Web-based media, as Gant reminds us, have had a particularly dramatic effect on MSM and journalism because they are inexpensive to access and use, they are largely unconstrained by government rules or physical scarcity, and they allow the interaction of many-to-many rather than one-to-one or one-to-many.[20] The millions of bloggers have fostered an entirely new notion of specialization, expertise, and transparency. There are, in essence, millions of fact checkers on the Web, who stand in stark contrast to the decreasing numbers of line editors or fact checkers in MSM. (Indeed, despite the fact that their own efforts at self-regulation are sporadic and inefficient, at best, bloggers seem to be doing a better job of fact checking MSM, holding established media accountable for their news and views, than MSM are doing internally.)

Citizen Journalism

Citizen journalism may be seen as one manifestation of the symbiotic relationship between MSM and new media. "Citizen journalism" describes a multifaceted environment encompassing such activities as mainstream media permitting signed or anonymous blogs on their Web sites; mainstream media recruiting non-journalists to provide expert or idiosyncratic reports and commentaries; open-source reporting—collaboration among reporters, sources, and readers; open, unedited citizen bloghouses sponsored by mainstream media; newsroom citizen "transparency" blogs, wherein citizens serve an ombudsman or public editor role; stand-alone citizen-journalism Web sites, filled with either edited or unedited stories contributed by non-journalists; and Wiki journalism, which allows anyone to write or post a news story, and for anyone to edit any story that's been posted.[21] These and other categories of citizen journalism exemplify the dramatic changes in journalism organizations' standard operating procedures and cause us to ask "who is a journalist, anyhow?"

We should also consider the ranks of public communicators, which include filmmakers, video documentarians, book authors, essayists, poets, and a wide array of public intellectuals. For all intents and purposes, many of them are "doing" journalism when they tackle significant issues of public importance, conduct research, interview sources, report data, and draw conclusions. (Some, like Michael Moore, seem to have earned the "journalism" mantle despite doing journalism "with attitude." Others, such as Oprah Winfrey's former friend James Frey, too casually blur the lines between fact and fiction, claiming their hybrid work aims to provide "greater truths."[22] To this end, Frey may fall into the same category as the *New York Times*'s Jason Blair, *USA Today*'s Jack Kelley, and the magazine journalist Stephen Glass, mainstream journalists, one and all, who egregiously violated the public trust.) Precious few public communicators have undertaken formal journalism studies, and even fewer belong to professional journalism organizations or invoke traditional journalism ethics codes or principles. Are they journalists? Do they deserve any special privileges?

New media technology, and new media practitioners, have emerged at a time when citizenship places ever more complicated demands on the population, knowledge has become more specialized, consumer behavior has become more complex, and there is increased skepticism about top-down, "voice of God" MSM authority. As Gant argues, we need more news and information than ever before, and we need it in perspective.[23] Broad-based citizen and Web-based journalism augments the knowledge base and is making a persuasive case for enjoyment of the status, rights, and protections formerly enjoyed only by elite media. Now is not the time to argue for a narrow definition of journalism.

Accountability

"Accountability" is one component of professionalism and professional ethics, and it is assuredly relevant to the notion of who deserves to be called a journalist. Clifford Christians reminds us that accountability describes how individuals and institutions can be judged with respect to their obligations. Critics can raise legitimate concerns or lay blame, and they have the right to expect reasonable answers. "An account is a reckoning properly requested and given, a statement explaining conduct to legitimately designated parties," according to Christians.[24] The question, then, is "How are journalists held accountable, and by whom?"

This is not the place to outline the history of journalism and all the ways it has or has not been held accountable. However, it is appropriate to remind ourselves (as this book does in numerous places) that to one degree or another, despite their general reluctance to be "defined" by anyone else, journalists have always been held accountable by government, by their peers and professional associations, and by the public.[25] Some aspects of accountability have been more formalized (e.g., court decisions, statutes, licensing) than have others. Some media codes of ethics have included mechanisms of accountability, if not actual enforcement. Some press councils, journalism reviews, and academic, trade, and public forums have done a better job of institutionalizing accountability and holding journalists' feet to the fire than have others. None, however, seem capable of permanently resolving the question of exactly *who* is to be held accountable for his or her journalistic performance, and precisely *how* that accountability is to be formulated and executed across time, across cases, and across individuals.

Do we want the government to license, accredit, or define who deserves protection? Given all the reasons for not entrusting the government with these rights, do we want the established media to do the licensing, accrediting, and defining? What credentialing process will legitimize journalism? What assurance do we have that the institutions of journalism would be any less biased in these judgment calls than the government would be?[26] Words such as licensing, accrediting, legitimizing, and defining are indeed troubling to traditionalists. Should any and all who "do journalism" have the right to self-define?

Accountability and New Media

Unencumbered—nay, unchecked—by mainstream media's traditional, albeit flawed, gatekeeping mechanisms—a system with layers upon layers of editors—new media practitioners are informational entrepreneurs. Some of them engage in socially significant reportage, while others subject the citizenry to half-baked ideas and unchecked prejudices. Their notions of accountability range from the nihilistic ("What do I do if I make a mistake—fire myself? Let all subjective facts and opinions flow freely.") to the pedantic ("Everybody in the blogosphere is accountable to everyone else in the blogosphere. Everything we do is transparent, while mainstream news "sausage factories" work in the dark."). Some bloggers have drafted codes of blogging ethics, attempting to garner respect and credibility and separate themselves from an Internet world peopled by "14-year-old girls imposing their bad poetry on the rest of us." Others—perhaps the majority—look with disdain upon any efforts to professionalize their enterprises and regulate (even self-regulate) their behaviors and work products.

In short, it's unwise to generalize about the new media. They appear in too many forms and have too many agendas, too many diverse practitioners, and too many differences in accountability for us to stereotype them—let alone to determine how to regulate them or to determine which among them deserve special privileges.

Conclusion

In the chapter that precedes this one, Michael Davis lays out a case for journalism being a profession and journalists being professionals. If I read him correctly, he rejects sociological definitions and opts for philosophical ones, saying that it's not just a matter of working for MSM but of having a professional attitude and accepting one's professionalism in the marketplace of ideas. The Socratic approach Davis prefers would seem to work perfectly when trying to define who is a journalist, a topic separate and distinct from the question of whether journalism is a profession. As presented in this chapter, the series of questions posed by journalists and their critics lays the Socratic groundwork that could lead to a satisfactory resolution.

The pattern of questions goes something like this:

Who does the defining? On what criteria? Awarding what privileges? Excluding whom? Benefiting whom (the individual journalist, the profession, the public, the broader system)? Should the definition be flexible, allowing entry to some who are now excluded? On what basis? Are academic and/or "professional" training and membership in "professional" organizations prerequisites? Where's the benchline? Should it be an open-source profession, defined not by where one works, but how one works? Is it a matter of an endeavor, rather than a job title, "defined by activity, not by how one makes a living, or the quality of one's work"?[27] What about accountability? Should there be seals of approval for meritorious (although not necessarily popular) performance? How does one lose professional status? What are the procedures for and consequences of being cast out of the profession? If a professional journalist represents the public in the information arena, do we deny professional status to those who violate this trust, and do we award such status to those in nontraditional media who seem to be conscientiously representing the public interest? Over and above the constitutional and pragmatic implications of licensing the "good professional," how do we deal with the troublesome implication that some journalists are in fact more ethical than others? Should the job criteria include the continued application of public service–oriented moral news values, over and above traditional craft based non-moral values?

Turning once again to Gant's text, we may agree on one of his central notions about journalism: "At its core, journalism is the way we share information and ideas with our fellow citizens. It is the lifeblood of our political system and an engine for our intellectual vitality. We cannot do without it."[28] If we accept that premise, we may also accept Gant's concluding argument:

> We must adjust our conception of journalism, and the legal
> framework built upon it, to reflect that there may be journalists
> who make it their profession, but one need not be a professional
> journalist to practice journalism. . . . [T]he First Amendment is for all
> of us. We are all given the right and the responsibility to share with
> the world our insights and inspirations.[29]

In my humble view, the issue of "who is a journalist?" and "who deserves privileges?" should not center on where one works, but on how one works. In saying this, I'm focusing on the moral or ethical domain, on issues of fundamental value and performance. The lists presented in "the journalism ethics domain" section of this chapter are highly instructive. I believe we should protect those who act as stewards of the public interest, in whatever media or for however much money they do so. If they have inculcated professional ethics while eschewing sleazeball behaviors and violations of the public trust, they should have an easier time convincing legislators and jurors that they deserve the protective mantle.

All public communicators, of course, should be given their day in court. But in the longer run, the ones who claim special privileges should pass muster in the court of public opinion as well. A fully functioning democracy—especially democracy operating at warp speed—deserves no less.

Notes

Parts of this material were included in the author's lecture, "Who's a Journalist These Days, and who deserves privileges?" presented at "Confidential Sources: What Does Branzburg Mean Now?" (conference, University of Oregon, Eugene, October 5, 2007).

1. We would be remiss to accuse Scott Gant (*We're All Journalists Now* [New York: Free Press, 2007]) of oversimplifying the issue. This essay will draw from his insightful analyses of the legal and ethical dimensions of the debate.

2. Data cited in this paragraph were drawn from Gant, *We're All Journalists Now*; Arthur S. Hayes, Jane B. Singer, and Jerry Ceppos, "Shifting Roles, Enduring Values: The Credible Journalist in a Digital Age," *Journal of Mass Media Ethics* 22 (2007), 262–79; Sandra L. Borden and Chad Tew, "The Role of the Journalist and the Performance of Journalism: Ethical Lessons from 'Fake News' (Seriously)"; *Journal of Mass Media Ethics* 22 (2007), 300–14.

3. Bill Kovach and Tom Rosensteil, *The Elements of Journalism: What Newspeople Should Know and the Public Should Expect*, 2nd ed. (New York: Three Rivers, 2007); see also the essays by Stephanie Craft (in chap. 3) and Sandra Borden (chap. 4) in this volume.

4. Eric Ugland and Jennifer Henderson, "Who Is a Journalist and Why Does It Matter? Disentangling the Legal and Ethical Arguments," *Journal of Mass Media Ethics* 22 (2007): 241–61. I rely upon their framework and that of Scott Gant (*We're All Journalists Now*) in the following paragraphs.

5. John Fletcher Moulton, "Law and Manners," *Atlantic Monthly* 134 (July 1924), 1–5, quoted in Rushworth M. Kidder, *How Good People Make Tough Choices* (Simon & Schuster, 1995), 66.

6. Ugland and Henderson, "Who Is a Journalist and Why Does It Matter?"

7. *New York Times v. Sullivan*, 376 U.S. 254 (1964).

8. American Society of Newspaper Editors, *Statement of Principles* (Reston, VA: American Society of Newspaper Editors, 1996), http://www.asne.org/index.cfm?ID=888, accessed August 15, 2008.

9. Deni Elliott and David Ozar, "An Explanation and a Method for the Ethics of Journalism," chap. 1 of this volume.

10. Edmund B. Lambeth, *Committed Journalism: An Ethic for the Profession* (Bloomington: Indiana University Press, 1986), 27.

11. Stephen Klaidman and Tom Beauchamp, *The Virtuous Journalist* (New York: Oxford University Press, 1987).

12. Kovach and Rosensteil, *Elements of Journalism*, 5–6.

13. Papers from the colloquium held at the University of St. Thomas, St. Paul, Minnesota, were published in a special issue of the *Journal of Mass Media Ethics* 22, no. 4 (2007), ed. Wendy Wyatt. The guiding principles in the Society of Professional Journalists' code of ethics further reinforce these values, if in more general terms. They call upon practitioners to (1) seek truth and report it, (2) minimize harm, (3) act independently, and (4) be accountable. Society of Professional Journalists, *Code of Ethics* (Indianapolis, IN: Society of Professional Journalists, 1996), http://www.spj.org/ethicscode.asp, accessed August 15, 2008.

14. *Branzburg v. Hayes*, 408 U.S. 665 (1972).

15. Ugland and Henderson, "Who Is a Journalist and Why Does It Matter?" 246–47.

16. Gant, *We're All Journalists Now*, 47–86.

17. Ugland and Henderson, "Who Is a Journalist and Why Does It Matter?" 248–50.

18. Gant, *We're All Journalists Now*, 81–86.

19. Borden and Tew, "The Role of Journalist and the Performance of Journalism."

20. Gant, *We're All Journalists Now*, 24–25.

21. Steve Outing, "The 11 Layers of Citizen Journalism," PoynterOnline, June 15, 2005, www.poynter.org/11layers, accessed August 21, 2008.

22. Frey's "memoir," touted by Winfrey, became a best-seller until it was revealed he had fudged many of the details of his life. Winfrey then took him to task on network television, and the debate raged about how much "truth" and how much "creative writing" were permitted in memoirs.

23. Gant, "The Transformation of Journalism and the Citizen Journalists' Battle for Equality," in *We're All Journalists Now*, 135–73.

24. Clifford Christians, "Enforcing Media Codes," *Journal of Mass Media Ethics* 1, no. 1 (Fall/Winter 1985–86): 16.

25. See, esp., Davis "Buzz" Merritt, *Public Journalism and Public Life: Why Telling the News Is Not Enough* (Hillsdale, NJ: Lawrence Erlbaum, 1995). Merritt talks about the "cultural trait of toughness" in journalism, reminding his readers that "the free press was born in a defensive crouch. Its birth certificate was a declaration—significantly, an affirmative negative—that 'Congress shall make no law . . . '" He continues:

> Of course, the amendment does not guarantee that "the press" be fair, accurate, honest, profitable, or, of course, paid attention to—only that it be free to be none or all of those things, just as can any citizen who picks up pen and paper. Although it was originally written to empower people rather than any institution, it has become, for the organized "press," a license to self-define that is unique among U.S. institutions. Neither clergy nor bar nor medicine nor academe can claim, and have validated by the courts, more latitude in action and deed. That enormous latitude is a mixed blessing. (pp. 13–14)

26. For another perspective, see Aaron Quinn's essay in chap. 18 of this book.

27. Gant, *We're All Journalists Now*, 6.

28. Gant, *We're All Journalists Now*, 200.

29. Gant, *We're All Journalists Now*, 201.

8

Norms and the Network: Journalistic Ethics in a Shared Media Space

Jane B. Singer

J ournalists, embracing the Internet with varying degrees of enthusiasm, have gradually adapted to characteristics of the medium. Many of those adaptations have involved work practices, in particular those to accommodate delivery of multimedia content—text, audio, video, and so on. Although this "convergence" involves some ethical issues, it requires adjustments mostly in skills and techniques.[1]

Other aspects of the medium lead to more explicit reconsideration of journalism ethics. The Internet delivers information instantaneously, and there were concerns, right from the start, about how the need for speed would affect accuracy. Getting a story out fast and getting it right too often seemed mutually exclusive. Today, journalists are less bothered by this issue; they still want to get it right—accuracy remains a central norm—but they and their readers seem to have accepted that the "first take" need not be the final one. There is greater tolerance for an online story evolving so that new information simply replaces what, if anything, was wrong; depending on their nature, changes may or may not be flagged for readers.

But a medium that is faster and encompasses more modalities suggests differences only in degree from a newspaper or a television news show.[2] The more fundamental difference involves the interconnected nature of a network. In their early days online, journalists adopted simple approaches to dealing with "interactivity," most of them involving the use of links to other Web pages. They turned their bylines into e-mail links, making themselves more accessible to Internet readers, and they added hyperlinks from stories to selected online documents or other source material, offering evidence to bolster an article's veracity.

Those adaptations are fine, as far as they go. But they are only baby steps toward carving out a role within a network, where both the media space and, ultimately, control over what that space contains are shared in ways quite unlike how they have been shared in newspapers. In a network, no single message is discrete; all messages connect to each other in some way. Nor are media messages either finite or fixed. Instead, the product is fluid: constantly changing, always expandable, always able to be combined with something new and different.

Message producers and message consumers also are interchangeable and inextricably linked, and roles are far less rigidly defined than in a traditional environment. You may be a producer one minute and a consumer the next—or, if you're a good multitasker, both simultaneously. And in a network, you're always connected to others who are occupying both roles.

So when it comes to ethics, the medium does matter. This it not because the Internet changes human needs or human nature—it doesn't—but because it changes how we humans interact. Ethics are all about interactions, the ways in which we deal with one another. Social life in the shared online world involves new types of relationships and connections, including some that pose challenges for media professionals.

Gatekeeper Ethics and Relationship Ethics

For various forms of twentieth-century mass media, from the newspaper through cable television, the journalist performed a privileged task: deciding what information was to be disseminated to the public. Journalistic ethics—as codified, interpreted, and voluntarily adhered to by individual practitioners, organizations, and institutions—stem from this perspective of the journalist as gatekeeper. Professional norms are a way to articulate and safeguard the role. They identify responsibilities both to the people on the other side of the gate, the audience, and to other gatekeepers, including employers and colleagues. Journalists fulfill their ethical obligations by providing information of a particular kind (accurate, credible, fair, etc.) that has been gathered in a particular way (e.g., honestly and independently).

In this perspective, the role is especially important because it is central to the broader civic good: the goal of self-government in a democracy. Journalists see themselves as fundamental to a democratic process that survives only through public access to reliable accounts of what is going on in the world. This is what Herb Gans calls the journalistic view of democracy, and what Bill Kovach and Tom Rosenstiel call the journalist's primary responsibility to provide information that citizens need to be free and self-governing.[3] Without us, the sky falls—democracy comes apart! The information is central to democracy, and the journalist is central to the information. Without the ethical journalist, in this view, information may well include disinformation or misinformation—and those are worse than no information at all.

If you see yourself as the conduit through which the information necessary to democracy must pass, it is vital to have ethical principles to guide you in that role and to serve as your pledge that you will act in a certain way. If you are a gatekeeper, the commitment to seek and report truth—the first principle in the U.S. Society of Professional Journalists' code and a universal principle in nearly all journalistic ethics codes around the democratic world—is vital because it is your responsibility not to let the misinformation and disinformation through the gate.[4] If you are the gatekeeper, it matters that you act independently in choosing, organizing, and disseminating that information because otherwise, we cannot believe what we are told, and our ability to act appropriately as citizens is diminished. In short, the underlying rationale for the ethics of the journalist in a traditional media universe both stems from and depends upon this traditional role and the traditional view of that journalist as central to the flow of information.

When journalists move to a network, the ethical principles remain essentially the same—but the rationale for them changes to one based on relationships.[5] On the Internet, where information of all kinds is ubiquitous, what people need is mainly some way to assess or judge its quality, which involves figuring out which information providers they can trust. Even relatively basic things, such as links to source material, are, in essence, a route to fostering trust. It's not so much about giving people more information, although that may be a side benefit. It's really about saying, "You can trust me because I'm providing support for what I'm telling you."

Of course, journalists ask for trust in the traditional news environment, too. But there, trust rests largely on their reputation or, more typically, the reputation of their employer as one that adheres to the norms guiding good journalism. The fact that media companies have owned the printing press for a long time suggests that they should be trusted to know what to do with it. And at the individual level, journalists simply ask readers to trust that they are being truthful, that they have been diligent and open-minded in gathering information, that they have captured the most important part of the story in the ten inches or two minutes allocated to it in today's media package. It is a lot to ask—perhaps too much, as the steadily declining reputation of news media suggests.

In ethical terms, an emphasis on relationships has all sorts of implications. Truth-telling, for instance, is as important as ever, but not because the public will not get the truth unless the journalist provides it. Rather, it is important because telling the truth is, generally, the ethical thing to do in any relationship. Truth-telling is fundamental to trust, and trust is, again, fundamental to functional social exchanges.[6] Without it—if I have no confidence you are telling me the truth as best you know it—I cannot have a viable relationship with you.

Similarly, fairness is important not just because it is the responsibility of a journalist to vet ideas in an even-handed fashion, to not deny one side the opportunity to be heard even though, as a gatekeeper, she has that power. Instead, the ethical underpinnings of fairness are based on the expectation that if I treat you fairly, you will treat me fairly in turn. It is another relationship norm, one in which the journalist is considered a participant in a more reciprocal process than that of information delivery.

The Collapse of Distance

The function of gatekeeper depends on a world in which the flow of information is linear, proceeding along a media-controlled conveyor belt with the journalist positioned between the origination point of news and its destination, audience. But a network is inherently nonlinear: information flows not only through journalists but also, continuously, around them. In this shared space, the multifaceted process of doing journalism is more collaborative. Journalists still gather and disseminate information, but they are not the only ones who do. Nor are they the only ones who verify or make sense of that information. Those processes are distributed among members of a network, particularly one in which the necessary tools are free and freely available.

If not only the roles but also the media space in which they are enacted are shared, what, if anything, makes the journalist special? Why should you, dear reader, pay any attention to what the journalist says? The time and talents that journalists bring to the tasks of gathering, verifying, and interpreting information do matter; those resources are important, and they are not universally or equally shared. But more crucial, in my view, are the ethical commitments journalists bring to those tasks—commitments to such principles as truth, fairness, independence, and importantly, accountability. Strong ethics are the hallmarks of journalism in a network.

Of course, these are hallmarks of journalism outside the network, as well. The problem is that fewer and fewer members of the audience—people who also now have the ability to gather, process, and disseminate information—seem to believe that journalists or the organizations that employ them honor these commitments. Moreover, those people have lots of alternatives. Journalists cannot afford to sit back and demand trust simply because they hold a particular occupational role or a key position in the information flow. As we have seen, the role is now shared, and the position is easily circumvented. Journalists must make their case—like everyone else—and in doing so, they must openly and explicitly demonstrate they are behaving ethically as both individuals and institutions.

This means becoming savvier about the way reputations are built and authority maintained in a constantly morphing network. Traditional media take their authority as a given, as something that comes along with the printing press or the broadcast transmitter. This stance can too readily be perceived as aloofness or even arrogance. Moreover, the notion of professional objectivity has largely blocked journalists from communicating anything about themselves, the work they do, or the rationale behind their decisions.

In a network, objectivity is inherently problematic. The concept, at least as journalists have defined and sought to enact it, involves metaphorically standing apart from the world on which the reporter reports.[7] The journalist is one who observes but is not observed, who attends—both in the sense of being physically present and in the sense of paying attention—but does not participate. Objectivity works in a world in which the end product itself reproduces the same roles: a newspaper or news broadcast that enables readers or viewers to look at the day's occurrences but not to directly engage in them.

In a digital media environment, in contrast, boundaries are difficult to sustain, whether they are among products, ideas, people, or social roles. Distances collapse online. Physical distance is erased by the immediacy with which any message can span the globe. Intellectual distance is erased by the intricate and extensive interconnections among all manner of information, and social distance by similar interconnections among all manner of people. Professional distance, such as that maintained by journalists through adherence to objectivity as a normative stance, is erased by the fact that the role of information provider is no longer limited to "professionals."

This is not at all to suggest that journalists should cease to be observers or should become participants in the events they observe. We need, and will continue to need, people willing and able to serve as trustworthy eyes and ears in places we cannot be. We need, and will continue to need, people who can convey what they saw and heard from a perspective that bears in mind the interests of the public as a whole rather than the interests of a few of its members. In fact, those needs become arguably greater than ever in an information environment to which so many can and do contribute. The primary loyalty of any journalist, in any medium, is to the public.[8]

But in a digital media environment, that public no longer occupies a distinct space or role apart from the journalist's. We are *all* citizens of the network, and we all contribute to it. Serving today's public means conveying not just the "news" but also as much as possible about who and what went into creating it. In a network, journalists do themselves a disservice when they try to hide behind the newsroom wall or the less tangible but still real wall of professional objectivity. Those walls have become barriers to the relationships necessary for effective information sharing.

Opening the Gates

The linkages I have been describing, among people and among pieces of information, not only define a network but are crucial to the creation of value within it. The more links pointing to your site, for instance, the easier it will be for a search engine to find you. The larger your social networking group, the more new people will want to join it. Standing apart from such a world is probably not feasible and certainly not desirable for the journalist. Such detachment leads to isolation, the one thing that has virtually no value in a network.

Journalists in this environment are necessarily closer to all sorts of people they have not felt close to before. The observers are also the observed, and many journalists have been startled by the scrutiny—and by the fact that most of those doing the scrutinizing reject their claims of objectivity and instead see media professionals as active and self-interested participants in the construction of news. The emergence of blogs was especially eye-opening, with their emphasis on communication not just *to* but also *with* the public, not to mention their more-than-willingness to both attack and traverse the boundaries that journalists have erected over the past 150 years.

But bloggers have a more important message to deliver than the one that comes from nipping at the heels of irritated journalists: in a network, "transparency" trumps objectivity.[9] It becomes necessary to show what goes into the process of making news—and of making decisions about news. For instance, journalists must demonstrate—not just claim—that their synthesis of information is credible. They must show that they will be accountable for what they have produced, that they will come back tomorrow to take responsibility for the information and their interpretation of it, and that they will admit and try to correct any errors.

These are not new ideas, of course; a need for accountability is formally recognized in many journalistic ethics codes. But it has been controversial. For one thing, practitioners worry about its potential conflict with autonomy: transparency can weaken the authority of members of an occupation that once held relatively unchallenged jurisdiction over information delivery.[10] Moreover, the notion that personal views or other subjective considerations should not be factors in determining what goes in the day's news product is closely connected with, yes, that old gatekeeping role. The journalist who determines, without fear or favor, what passes through the gate must be (or appear to be) impartial and uninvolved. In theory, his own beliefs are irrelevant; a news nugget is published based on its merits, not on the journalist's personal views.

Whether that was ever exactly how the process worked is debatable. But certainly, that's not how information travels around a network, and it's not how people in a network see their relationships working. As we have seen, a network demands at least some degree of mutual trust—and trust rests largely on openness. With some reluctance and not infrequent discomfort, journalists are beginning to accept this online zeitgeist and to figure out how to enact the concept of accountability in ways that fit. Two examples are through provision of greater evidentiary support for information and through increased personal disclosure.

In an online environment, with its virtually unlimited news hole, journalists have a technically enabled capability to show where their information comes from and thus to demonstrate their own standards for assessing its importance and veracity. They can and should provide background about sources, expand the depth and breadth of stories, and solicit additional input and feedback from readers. The ability to link a story to anything else in the network means that story becomes part of a multi-sourced amalgamation of information about a topic.

Personal disclosure is harder for journalists. But following the lead of independent bloggers, journalists have established thousands of their own "j-blogs," which contribute to accountability in at least two ways. First, journalists are using them to explain the rationale behind the news, particularly of controversial editorial decisions. Second, journalists are increasingly using formats such as blogs to humanize the process of making news and to describe what it is like to be a reporter: to explain how a story was obtained, why it was pursued, and, particularly if the story involves human suffering, what the journalist felt while covering it.

Journalists thus have begun to expand their interpretive role to explain not just the story but also what goes into creating it. Blogs provide a vehicle for liberating them from the strictures of traditional journalistic formats and cultural norms. Journalists have found a way to tell a companion story, one that goes beyond providing information the public needs and comes closer to what you might tell your friend about that information—including why you thought the story was worth telling and what doing so meant to you. This is another step toward establishing relationships with others in a network, not simply delivering information to a mass, anonymous civic entity called "the public." It also moves beyond saying "trust me, I'm the gatekeeper" to a more iterative approach to establishing credibility: "Here's why you should trust me. Here's why our relationship should be mutual and ongoing."

Credibility and Authority in the Network

Journalists seeking to demonstrate credibility in an interactive network also need to wrestle with changes in the nature of authority, as outlined briefly above. In a traditional media environment, ethical principles generally serve to underline and strengthen the authority of the news outlet, which typically "authorizes" its employees' practices and products as journalists. The institution essentially acts as a gatekeeper for the gatekeeper: the individual journalist vets information through the gathering and writing process, and the institution then additionally vets the work of the individual through the processes of editing and, ultimately, of publishing.

The online information associated with traditional media, such as a newspaper Web site, may or may not go through the same stages. The previously mentioned emphasis on getting information out as quickly as possible is one reason that the traditional second level of gatekeeping, the editing process, may be rushed or even bypassed, especially for breaking news.

That process also is typically bypassed for information generated by users, who are commonly asked to voluntarily adhere to a set of ethical guidelines posted on the site—an approach that, again, is based on relationships and at least some degree of trust rather than gatekeeping. Content unique to the networked environment is largely left up to the community to vet, for instance by flagging items that are inaccurate, offensive, or otherwise problematic. Journalists and their employers have taken this hands-off approach mainly for legal rather than explicitly ethical reasons: if you oversee the content, you assume some degree of legal responsibility for it, and media organizations would rather not. But there also are ethical issues here related to a shared responsibility to create a space for civic discourse, as opposed to the provision of information within a space wholly controlled by the journalist and the media organization.

Another aspect of authority relates to how information is presented. In a traditional media environment, the daily product is aggregated into a concrete and finite information package. The newspaper, the magazine, the newscast—even the Web site, though it is neither concrete nor finite—all provide bundled material from a particular organization such as the *New York Times*. Online, however, users are less and less likely to see *Times* content as part of that institutionally assembled whole. Instead, they are increasingly apt to access information as a separate unit, such as a single story or even a single blog post about a story. People find and read isolated items through search engines, news aggregators, social networking sites, and other personalizable tools rather than through the package provided by a newspaper or its Web site.

As the journalist's work is more likely to be read independently of the work of her newsroom colleagues, individual reputation becomes increasingly important. So here, too, the relationship between journalist and reader takes center stage. True, the media brand remains closely connected to, and identified with, the ethics of those who work under its banner; you may choose to click on a particular story because it has been written by a *Times* reporter. But as connections are loosened between information and its institutional "home," brands may, over time, become less important, or at least differently important, than they have been.

This shift toward greater individual authority and credibility is closely related to the notion of journalistic autonomy. U.S. journalists, in particular, have fiercely protected their freedom from external oversight as a fundamental perquisite to the credibility of a Fourth Estate able to report impartial truth. But in a network, no journalist is an island. A virtually infinite number of participants simultaneously serve as sources, audiences, and information providers—and a considerable number of those people are challenging the journalist's exclusive right to deem information credible or journalistic behavior ethical. Journalists find their autonomy challenged not so much by government—the threat they have guarded against for centuries—but by the very citizens to whom they owe their primary loyalty.

Bloggers have taken to heart the self-appointed role as watchdogs of the watchdogs. Bloggers embody the idea that democratic power is essentially distributed and that the pursuit of truth works best as a collective enterprise. They personify the marketplace of ideas with a vengeance: put it all out there, and the truth will emerge. For the first time, the capability to put it all out there actually exists.[11] That is what happens when there are no gates and no gatekeepers.

But of course, it's not just bloggers, who were merely pioneers among the digital natives coming of age along with participatory media forms and formats. The network enables—or, more accurately, demands—engagement with people of diverse beliefs and backgrounds, which in turn challenges the tendency for journalists to see only professional peers as legitimate contributors of credible news.[12] Moreover, as discussed above, no single message in this environment is discrete. No single messenger stands apart. The whole notion of autonomy becomes contested. Like objectivity, autonomy suggests at least some degree of isolation, and isolation in a network equates to irrelevance at best. Without connections, there essentially is no networked existence at all.

User-Generated Content and the *Guardian*

So far, this has all been almost wholly theoretical. How are real-life journalists negotiating this networked world? To begin to answer that question, I and a colleague, Ian Ashman, spent some time in late 2007 and early 2008 interviewing journalists at Britain's *Guardian* newspaper and its associated Web site, guardian.co.uk. As media organizations open up their Web sites to contributions from some of the people in this relationship I've been talking about, what is the effect on how journalists think about normative issues and ideals?

The *Guardian* has an atypical ownership structure in this age of corporate media: The paper is owned by the Scott Trust, and its economic framework is an explicitly ethical one. The Trust was created in 1936 with the core purpose of preserving the financial and editorial independence of the newspaper and its related media outlets, now including the Web site. Under the Trust, part of the company's mandate is to uphold a set of values articulated by the *Manchester Guardian's* former editor C. P. Scott on the paper's hundredth anniversary in 1921. "Comment is free, but facts are sacred," Scott declared. Newspapers have "a moral as well as a material existence," and "the voice of opponents no less than that of friends has a right to be heard." In other words, one of the *Guardian's* central roles is to provide a platform for a diversity of voices and viewpoints. Current editors even borrowed Scott's ringing declaration in naming the opinion and commentary section of their Web site: Comment Is Free.

Our interviews with eleven primarily print and twenty-two primarily digital journalists highlighted the themes discussed in this chapter. For instance, journalists said that while they believed they took adequate steps to ensure what they wrote was credible, they could neither assess nor affect the credibility of what users provided. They worried about how that lack of oversight might reflect on them and the *Guardian*.

Issues of authority were also important. They agreed that users posed a challenge to journalistic authority but disagreed over whether that was a good or a bad thing. Some saw enormous vitality in the online debate and saw their own role as, increasingly, to enable or facilitate that debate rather than to provide "definitive answers," as one editor said. Others weren't so sure, such as the editor who cited a need for "the expert journalist who can interrogate and understand and all those sorts of things in a way that the citizen reporter just can't."

Other challenges to journalistic authority are more direct: users are in journalists' faces all the time, with everything from personal attacks to disagreement over opinions to disputes about facts. Personal attacks are both easiest and hardest to deal with. They are easiest because the optimal response is ignoring them, but hardest because ignoring a personal attack takes a lot of self-restraint—more, some journalists confessed, than they possessed.

Differences of opinion drew mixed reaction. Most journalists said they appreciated cogent—and civilly expressed—disagreement, which several said nudged them out of complacency. But they also said that the way the disagreement was expressed mattered. As another editor put it: "When users are just saying 'I think this is crap,' what can you say to that? 'Sorry, but I don't'?"

Challenges to factual statements—to accuracy, that is—were generally valued: journalists said they were more careful about what they published because they knew if they got it wrong, they'd get slammed. In addition to being embarrassing, that of course would undermine their credibility. But there was concern, especially among a few veterans, that users were challenging what one reporter called basic assumptions—facts journalists believe speak for themselves.[13] Responding, they said, was tedious and time-consuming. In other words, users do not necessarily see the world in ways that journalists take for granted, which came as something of a shock.

Such challenges affect not only professional autonomy but also authority. *Guardian* journalists relished what they saw as considerable independence; this was especially true for online staffers, who had fewer editors to get through en route to publication. But they had misgivings about the potential effect of hit logs and comment counts and were wary about using that information to guide story judgment. More than wary, actually—many said they abhorred the very idea of what one print writer called "traffic whoring." They also saw this issue in terms of safeguarding the *Guardian* brand. Celebrity gossip and weird animals are OK for the cheesy British tabloids, but not for the *Guardian*—no matter how much usage they might generate. "You have to balance the desire for hits with what we think the paper should represent," an online editor said.

Guardian journalists saw accountability as something that differentiated them from users in important ways. For instance, they cited their willingness to publicly admit when they made a mistake, as well as to discuss and defend their ideas. They pointed out that unlike users, journalists cannot be anonymous—and anonymity harms credibility, particularly by encouraging abusive behavior. "People feel licensed to say things, in content and style, that they wouldn't own if publishing as themselves," an editor explained.

More broadly, while many *Guardian* journalists had stories of fruitful engagement with users—through formation of new community bonds, creation of a richer conversation about a topic, or enhancement of a particular story—they expressed dismay over the disturbingly confrontational nature of Comment Is Free. Several characterized it as blatantly sexist, in addition to rude to the point of being abusive, hurtful, and upsetting. "You get really, really depreciative comments," an online writer said. "Whatever kind of maxims you repeat to yourself about how anything good always has haters, it subconsciously works away."

In the meantime, a strong sense seemed to be emerging that the best approach is a carrot rather than a stick. Journalists were learning to encourage the more cogent contributions rather than trying, futilely, to discourage the hostile ones. They were going into the threads and saying "good point" when they felt that was appropriate, responding more fully to what they saw as interesting ideas—and trying, as best they could and with varying degrees of success, to grit their teeth and ignore the irredeemably obnoxious.

All these responses suggest that developing new relationships is a process that takes time, patience, a lot of trial and error, and the growth of a thicker skin than many journalists now possess. The ethical transition from professional discourse to a far more personal one is a challenge, as journalists move from a gatekeeping role to one that entails engagement with an enormously diverse range of unseen but definitely not unheard people.

Conclusion

None of these ideas about online journalism ethics is radically new. Nor do I suggest that existing commitments to core journalistic norms are not every bit as valuable, perhaps even more so, in this networked environment. On the contrary, I think they are at the heart of what journalists bring to an outrageously loud party, one with no cover charge and no one guarding the entryway. The underlying values are not just sound but crucial.

The way journalists think about and enact these values, however, needs to change to suit new and much closer relationships with the people who were once a relatively distant, distinct, and amorphous audience but who now share the communication space and control over what it contains. The task of the journalist once involved regulating the flow and content of information disseminated to the public. It no longer does. The nature of the network forces such control to be relinquished and replaced with the give-and-take of a more intimate, collaborative arrangement.

In this environment, more emphasis goes to openness and cooperation, while norms designed to erect and protect boundaries become a lot less useful, if not downright detrimental. The cliché that the Internet does not tolerate blockades is every bit as true in a social sense as in a technological one, as we have seen.

That reality is scary. It shoves journalists outside their comfort zone, and it does so rather rudely—figuratively and literally, as those at the *Guardian* are finding out. But as they are also finding out, there are ways to make the new relationships work in order to build trust, foster engagement, nurture collaboration, and create value. Ongoing interaction with users, which goes far beyond what journalists have encountered before, will continue to mean re-engagement with old ethics in new forms and new contexts.

Notes

1. Jane B. Singer, "Partnerships and Public Service: Normative Issues for Journalists in Converged Newsrooms," *Journal of Mass Media Ethics* 21, no. 1 (2006): 30–53.

2. Michael Opgenhaffen, "Redefining Multimedia: The (Dis)Integrated Use of Multiple Media and Modalities in Convergent Journalism," paper presented to the International Communication Association, Montreal, May 2008.

3. Herbert J. Gans, *Democracy and the News* (New York: Oxford University Press, 2003); Bill Kovach and Tom Rosenstiel, *The Elements of Journalism: What Newspeople Should Know and the Public Should Expect* (New York: Crown, 2001).

4. Tom Cooper, "Comparative International Media Ethics," *Journal of Mass Media Ethics* 5, no. 1 (1990): 3–14.

5. François Nel, Mike Ward, and Alan Rawlinson, "Online Journalism," in *The Future of Journalism in the Advanced Democracies*, ed. Peter J. Anderson and Geoff Ward, 121–38 (Surrey, UK: Ashgate, 2007).

6. Sissela Bok, *Lying: Moral Choice in Public and Private Life* (New York: Vintage, 1999).

7. See Stephen J. A. Ward, chap. 9 in this volume, and Carrie Figdor, chap. 10.

8. Kovach and Rosenstiel, *Elements of Journalism.* See also Stephanie Craft, chap. 3 in this volume, and Sandra Borden, chap. 4.

9. Michael B. Karlsson, "Visibility of Journalistic Processes and the Undermining of Objectivity," paper presented to the International Communication Association, Montreal, May 2008. See also Patrick Plaisance, *Media Ethics: Key Principles for Responsible Practice* (Thousand Oaks, CA: Sage, 2008), esp. chap. 3.

10. Wilson Lowrey and William Anderson, "The Journalist behind the Curtain: Participatory Functions on the Internet and Their Impact on Perceptions of the Work

of Journalism," *Journal of Computer-Mediated Communication* 10, no. 3 (2005), http://jcmc.indiana.edu/vo110/issue3/lowrey.html (accessed May 14, 2008).

11. Jane B. Singer, "The Marketplace of Ideas—With a Vengeance," *Media Ethics* 16, no. 2 (2005): 1, 14–16.

12. Mark Deuze, "What Is Journalism? Professional Identity and Ideology of Journalists Reconsidered," *Journalism: Theory, Practice and Criticism* 6, no. 4 (2005): 442–64. See also Jay Black's chap. 7 in this volume.

13. Gaye Tuchman, "Objectivity as Strategic Ritual: An Examination of Newsmen's Notions of Objectivity," *American Journal of Sociology* 77, no. 4 (1972): 660–79.

References

Much of the material in this chapter has been adapted from previously published or forthcoming works. These include:

Hayes, Arthur S., Jane B. Singer, and Jerry Ceppos, "Shifting Roles, Enduring Values: The Credible Journalist in a Digital Age," *Journal of Mass Media Ethics* 22, no. 4 (2007): 263–79.

Singer, Jane B., "Contested Autonomy: Professional and Popular Claims on Journalistic Norms," *Journalism Studies* 8, no. 1 (2007): 79–95.

———. "Digital Ethics," in *Controversies in Media Ethics*, ed. A. David Gordon and John Michael Kittross (New York: Routledge, forthcoming 2010).

———. "The Journalist in the Network: A Shifting Rationale for the Gatekeeping Role and the Objectivity Norm," *Tripodos: Llenguatge, Pensament, Comunicacio* 1, no. 23 (2008): 61–76.

———. "Objectivity in an Interconnected World," *Media Ethics* 18, no. 2 (2007): 1, 15–16.

Singer, Jane B., and Ian Ashman, "'Comment Is Free, But Facts Are Sacred': User-Generated Content and Ethical Constructs at the *Guardian*," *Journal of Mass Media Ethics* 24, no. 1 (2009): 3–21.

Singer, Jane B., and Ian Ashman, "User-Generated Content and Journalistic Values," in *Citizen Journalism: Global Perspectives*, ed. Stuart Allan and Einar Thorsen (New York: Peter Lang, 2009).

PART IV

Objectivity

Introduction

There is something very satisfying about thinking we can accurately reflect reality, much like a mirror. The associated metaphor—"the mirror on nature"—was once, in fact, the standard description of objective reporting: the reporter's task is to directly reflect the world to the reader or viewer, without any of the distortions or biases that would alter the "real" view. Many journalists still give a variant on this in their off-the-cuff comments about objectivity, and, in my experience, students are very drawn to the metaphor. We want the world to be a clear and distinct place, wholly accessible to the careful and discerning reporter, whether journalist or scientist.

Fifty years of metaphysics and epistemology have, unfortunately, put a pretty serious crimp in this "naïve empiricism."[1] The world, it seems, simply doesn't present itself in a way that makes such reflection possible. Realizing this, the academic literature and news codes now generally talk about objectivity as "fairness," as free as possible from ideological influence. For example, the *Los Angeles Times* "Ethics Guidelines" state:

> A fair-minded reader of *Times* news coverage should not be able to discern the private opinions of those who contributed to that coverage, or to infer that the newspaper is promoting any agenda. A crucial goal of our news and feature reporting—apart from editorials, columns, criticism and other content that is expressly opinionated— is to be non-ideological. This is a tall order. It requires us to recognize our own biases and stand apart from them. It also requires us to examine the ideological environment in which we work, for the

biases of our sources, our colleagues and our communities can distort our sense of objectivity.[2]

While, strikingly, the term "objectivity" does not appear anywhere in the fifty-seven-page *New York Times* "Ethical Journalism" handbook, their public editor gives it due attention, as do other respected media commentators.[3] And complaints about bias are among the most frequently expressed in letters to the editor and media blogs.

Objectivity is thus clearly a core element in the journalism ethos, even if there is no consistency in its meaning. Sometimes it's the mirror, sometimes it's fairness, sometimes a lack of bias, sometimes accuracy. Or sometimes, as with Stephen J. A. Ward and Carrie Figdor, it is, respectively, "pragmatic objectivity" or "an objectively verified report."

As a way of getting at their views, let us backtrack a bit: Why not the mirror? What's wrong with a little naïveté when it comes to reporting on reality? Isn't there a real world out there, one the careful reporter, and even more, the careful photographer, can capture and convey? Let us look at three of the more compelling problems.

Realism

Naïve empiricism assumes metaphysical realism, easily one of the more hotly debated issues in contemporary philosophy. A complex and difficult subject, realism holds that the world is, redundantly, real and, with the right methods, empirically verifiable: trees really are trees (better: sequoias, for example, are real and essentially distinct from say, magnolias), rocks really are rocks (granite is distinct from marble), dogs are dogs (Aussies are distinct from Labs), and so on. Some versions extend it to more abstract topics, such as ethics (it really is wrong to torture babies), but all take a basically scientific stance: It—reality—is out there, potentially discoverable, assuming one knows how to look correctly. The reporter's task is, additionally, to find a method for accurately conveying what's been found.

Arguments for and against realism would fill a library;[4] for our purposes it is sufficient simply to note that it turns out to be a very difficult position to defend. What we call "the world" may be a construction, driven by our concepts, needs, and desires, with some overlap with others' conceptions, but also plenty of differences. Thus it may be there is no single "real" world for the journalist to discern and communicate, and any version she conveys will necessarily reflect her particular conceptual scheme.

Ward's answer to the realism problem is to work out of the pragmatist tradition,[5] one that more or less sidesteps these metaphysical problems. Statements about the world are true if they work. It may be they work because that's what the world, in fact, allows—Ward calls those facts a "regulatory ideal"—but for most pragmatists, what the world may or may not allow is the wrong issue to address, as revealed, they suggest, by two thousand years of failed metaphysics.

But since, Ward also argues, the traditional model of objectivity assumed those very (realist) metaphysics, that model "is at a dead end; . . . [it is] a spent ethical force, doubted by journalist and academic." Yet, there are still morally powerful reasons for retaining both the term and aspects of the traditional goal: "Restraining norms are needed to ensure responsible journalism—a journalism that is accurate, fair to perspectives and not tainted by implicit or explicit bias or ideology." Such responsible journalism requires the journalist to "interpret," but within the constraints "of correct methods and tested judgments." Those methods and judgments are the right ones because, time has shown, they are the most effective at acquiring and disseminating needed information. "The task of objectivity," Ward thus concludes, "is not to eliminate active inquiry and interpretation, let alone to arrive at some perspectiveless 'absolute' description of reality, but to develop methods for testing the story's selection of alleged facts, sources, and story-angles."

Knowledge

Let us suppose, though, realism is true: the world is a real thing, and if one has the right methods, it can be empirically verified. The question remains, are persons capable of such verification? Do we have sufficient perceptual capabilities and epistemological categories? Is there any reason to think our particular set of senses provides the correct means for capturing reality? Further, when can we feel confident those perceptions haven't been skewed by our biases, fears, ideological frameworks, or moral prejudices? In short, when can we say we know something about the world, rather than just that we believe it?

As you've no doubt realized, these problems are at least as serious for science as for journalism, and epistemologists have developed an array of strategies for answering the last question. The solution, in general, has been to move away from the presumed link between knowledge and certainty, a linkage that had dominated epistemology since Plato, and instead look at whether beliefs are justified, based on the right kinds of evidence.

Objectivity, Figdor says, works on the same standard: "Objective news reports are those which can provide testimonial knowledge or justified belief about some aspect of the world to those who read or hear them. . . . For example, we ask: 'Is every sentence in the report supported by sufficient objective evidence?' A statement is objectively justified if it is rational to believe on the basis of evidence that anyone should accept." Just as we routinely make legitimate knowledge claims when we have strong empirical or analytical evidence, so also can we legitimately establish objective reports, namely, when it is rational to believe them to be true. "It follows that the inclusion of a statement in an objective news report implies it is supported by sufficient objective evidence: it's not there because the reporter made a lucky guess or wishes it were true. If s/he doesn't have that evidence, it should not be there."

Furthermore, since "value statements express what ought or should be the case, and the problem with these statements is [that] there is no consensus on how they might be objectively verified or whether they can be," objective reporting will almost never include them. Figdor thus obviously aligns with that part of the traditional standard: leave your (objectively unverified) values, preferences, and biases out of the story.

Market Forces

Even if we assume that persons are capable of empirically verifying a real world, does the business of journalism promote such reporting, or even allow it? As Ian Richards (chapter 11), Rick Edmonds (chapter 12), and Marty Steffens (chapter 13) discuss in depth, economic realities are altering how, and maybe even whether, mainstream news media practice their craft. Is it thus realistic to expect that economics-based values will not enter stories? We're not so much speaking of reporters' and editors' values, but of those of the owners of the local car dealership or major furniture store. News has, for some hundred years now, depended on advertising, and the source is running ever drier. Can the publisher afford to alienate the few remaining? When coffers were flush, it was easier for publishers to tell a complaining business owner to shove it. Can we still expect that response? Isn't it naïve to think that at least the story's slant won't reflect market-driven values?

So even if reporters are reporting, in Figdor's words, "just the facts," which facts? It's easy enough to report objectivity, to report only verified information, but to do so selectively: see FOX News. Figdor also worries about this problem and acknowledges her objectivity is very hard to achieve, given journalists' training.[6] But it is a goal worth striving for and more achievable with good editing and what she calls a more "scientific" reporting.

If the goal, then, is to save traditional objectivity, neither Ward nor Figdor comes to the rescue. Both engage in what Ward calls a "reinvention," changing the meaning and value of the principle, while also retaining core elements. For all the reasons discussed above, I am convinced they are right to give up on the traditional model. If you agree, are their models—separately or combined—sufficient alternatives? If not, can you provide one that overcomes the metaphysical and epistemological quandaries?

And even more challenging, is it possible to be objective in the face of economic pressures, particularly as these transform professional and organizational cultures. It's not that any given publisher—Rupert Murdoch notwithstanding[7]—will directly demand reporters rewrite a story to please the car dealer. Rather, over lunch with the executive editor, she'll worry out loud about revenue loss and potential layoffs. He will, in turn, express fear to the managing editor, who will pass it along to the city editor, and so forth. Such incremental change is so insidious exactly because it is so invisible. The result is, bit-by-bit, all involved believe they continue to be "fair," "unbiased," "accurate," "value free," "honest," and "transparent," when, in fact, a new, market-driven, ideology has taken root.

These are all serious problems, ones that may doom objectivity. Your task is, first, to determine whether some version of "objectivity" still makes sense; second, to define it; and, third, to develop the associated ethical norms. Or, alternatively, should we just junk it and come up with wholly distinct principles?

Whichever form of reinvention you adopt, I urge you not to take either of two popular, if also intellectually lazy, ways out. Both produce cruddy journalism and cruddy thinking. The first is to revert to the simplest version of objectivity, to use objectivity as a kind of crutch—"Hey, I'm just reporting what I see!," pretending you play no interpretative role in creating that particular narrative, that the world wrote the story and you merely passed it along.

The second is to go to the other extreme, to nihilistic relativism of the sort described by Gregory Rodriguez:

> In academia, the old-fashioned idea that there were some things that
> we could all be certain of gave way to the postmodern worldview that
> held that truth does not really exist in any objective sense, but is
> instead created by each individual through the prism of his own
> background and biases. According to this new dictum [note: it's not
> all that new and, in fact, seems to be waning within the academy],
> reality itself is fragmented and the search for commonly held truths
> is the province of fools, innocents and fundamentalists.[8]

Granting the absence of certainty need not, should not, lead to Rodriguez's cynical conclusion. Even if I can't be 100 percent certain dawn will break tomorrow morning (the sun could explode, we could be hit by a massive asteroid, etc.), I'm happy to take bets; I'll even give you quite favorable odds. As both Figdor and Ward stress, some beliefs make perfectly good sense—those that have passed evidential muster. These are beliefs the careful, thoughtful reporter will recognize as true enough, that is, beliefs backed with enough evidence that one would be a fool to be so skeptical as to feel obliged to provide contrasting opinions. And included among those highly plausible beliefs are ethical ones: one need not, for example, be fair or provide alternative perspectives on the immorality of torturing children.[9]

In other words, whatever objectivity is, it is hard work, demanding welleducated, discerning, reflective reporters not afraid to use good judgment in their interpretation of the world and in their means of communicating what they find.

Notes

1. Michael Schudson, Discovering the News: A Social History of American Newspapers (New York: Basic, 1978), 7. See also David Mindich, Just the Facts: How "Objectivity" Came to Define American Journalism (New York: New York University Press, 2000).

2. http://latimesblogs.latimes.com/readers/2007/07/los-angeles-tim.html, accessed October 10, 2008. In a July 27, 2008, editorial, however, the *Times* presents objectivity as the still-desired journalistic standard, defending opinion writing despite that it "compromises a newspaper's objectivity" (p. M2).

3. See Daniel Okrent, "It's Good to Be Objective. It's Even Better to Be Right," November 14, 2004, http://www.nytimes.com/2004/11/14/weekinreview/14bott.html, accessed October 10, 2008; Howard Kurtz, "Media Notes: Deal or No Deal?" *WashingtonPost.com*, September 26, 2008, http://www.washingtonpost.com/wp-dyn/content/blog/2008/09/26/BL2008092601063.html

4. One useful source is Stuart Brock and Edwin Mares, *Realism and Anti-Realism* (Toronto: McGill-Queens University Press, 2007).

5. Largely an American philosophical movement, pragmatism weaves through the work of Charles Pierce, William James, John Dewey, and, more recently, Hilary Putnam (in his later writings) and Richard Rorty. Ward's work is most closely informed by the latter two.

6. She examines other problems that make the practice of objectivity difficult, including reporters' egos and the methods of news gathering.

7. See the film "Outfoxed," widely available on the Internet.

8. "When all Truth Is Relative," *Los Angeles Times*, September 29, 2008, p. A-15.

9. A more telling example is reporting on climate change. See "Editor and Publisher Columnist Outing: Sack 'Objectivity' in Climate Change Reporting," Yale Forum on Climate Change & The Media, October 1, 2007, http://yaleclimatemedia-forum.org/features/0907_outing.htm, accessed October 10, 2008.

9

Inventing Objectivity: New Philosophical Foundations

Stephen J. A. Ward

The history of journalism ethics is, in large part, the evolution of models of journalism with varying ethical aims and norms. For example, there is the nineteenth-century model of the liberal press, with its emphasis on a free press for self-governing citizens; there is the twentieth-century theory of "social responsibility," discussed by Sandra Borden, in chapter 4 of this volume, which ascribes a range of duties to news media. Models of good journalism are normative responses to significant changes in society and journalism. Important engines of change include new technology, altered social habits, and fewer legal restrictions. These factors can, individually or in combination, spark experiments in journalism. If the experiments challenge existing norms of practice, proponents of journalism ethics may respond in several ways. They may invent new ethical principles to guide practice. Or they may reinterpret existing norms. They may place greater emphasis on certain values, while other values decline in importance. Why these responses are needed is no mystery. Since journalism has a far-reaching social impact, journalists are called upon to explain and justify their practices.

Today, journalists face the prospect of another ethical invention. They need a new model that responds to a revolution in media communication of global proportions. The rise of an interactive online journalism that emphasizes immediacy, interpretation, and transparency challenges an older professional model of journalism that stresses careful editorial controls and verification.[1]

The doctrine of news objectivity was one such historical invention. The time was the late nineteenth century and the early decades of the twentieth. The context was the development of a commercial press for mass society in the United States. At that time, journalists came to believe that a professional ethics disciplined by the rules of impartial news reporting was needed to respond to doubts about the existing liberal model of the press and to criticism of the mass press's aggressive information-gathering, its bold presentation of news, and its increasing commercialization. By the 1920s, the new codes of journalism ethics cited objectivity as a fundamental principle. Objectivity, as a way of reporting "just the facts" from a detached perspective, was entrenched at major newspapers in North America.

This chapter studies the invention of news objectivity, philosophically and historically. After distinguishing three senses of objectivity, the chapter outlines how news objectivity was the result of a four-hundred-year interaction between the shifting nature of journalism and shifting notions of objective knowledge and practice. The chapter then explains the doctrine of news objectivity and notes its decline, then concludes with its own attempt at ethical invention. It outlines an alternate understanding of objectivity, called "pragmatic objectivity," to replace the traditional notion of news objectivity.

Three Senses

Objectivity did not originate with journalism. When modern journalism began to appear in the seventeenth century, Western culture's pursuit of objective knowledge in the form of philosophy, mathematics, and science had been underway for about two thousand years.

Three senses of objectivity have played a major role: ontological, epistemic, and procedural. Something is objective in the ontological sense if it actually exists, independent of my mind. It is not a figment of imagination, hallucination, erroneous perception, or false belief. A belief is ontologically objective if it truly describes or corresponds to external phenomena.

Epistemic objectivity is concerned with how we know what is real and true. A belief is epistemically objective if it is well grounded on evidence and unbiased methods of inquiry. Beliefs are epistemically objective if they satisfy the best methods and standards of verification. Such methods range from the practices of everyday observation to the technical methods of scientific research.

Procedural objectivity concerns decisions and procedures in public areas of life, such as law, government, and institutional administration. The primary goal is not a theoretical understanding of some natural phenomenon, as in science, but rather to make correct decisions in social contexts, with a minimum of subjectivity, self-interest, and bias. Procedural objectivity includes objective criteria for marking academic papers, objective methods for hiring and promoting employees, and objective procedures for settling disputes.

In practice, ontological, epistemic, and procedural objectivity are closely related. One's beliefs are ontologically objective—correspond to the real—if they were formed by epistemically objective methods. Also, procedures arrive at correct decisions if they are based on facts that satisfy epistemically objective standards.

The doctrine of news objectivity, with its stress on facts, empirical methods, and impartial procedures, combines these three senses of objectivity. That is, journalists appeal to all three senses of objectivity. News reports are ontologically objective if they are accurate, factual descriptions of events, if they tell it "the way it is." Reports are epistemically objective if they are tested by good reporting methods and standards. Reports are procedurally objective if they present information in a manner that is fair to sources and impartial with respect to rival viewpoints.

Anticipating Objectivity

According to the ideal of news objectivity, a reporter (or a report) is not objective unless she has approached the story factually, impartiality, and independently. These component notions of news objectivity developed over several centuries.

The idea of impartial reporting is found at the start of modern journalism in the seventeenth century. Gutenberg's press gave birth to "printer–editors" who, in London, Amsterdam, and other European centers created a periodic press of "news sheets" and "newsbooks" for businessmen, bankers, politicians, and eventually a broad public. Despite the partisan nature of their times, these editors assured readers they printed the impartial truth based on "matters of fact" and eyewitness accounts by "reliable correspondents." Editors made these claims to persuade skeptical readers of the reliability of their news and to assure censors that their only intention was to inform.[2]

The editors portrayed journalism as one of the new discourses of fact, alongside science, travel writing, and chorography. Shapiro notes that, in England, there was a broad interest in all manner of fact during the sixteenth and seventeenth centuries,[3] including the merchant's facts of finance and the explorer's chronicle.[4] The new empirical science created societies for the impartial presentation of facts concerning the latest experiments. In English law, juries were instructed to judge the "matter of fact" in a disinterested manner. In this way, the norm of reporting impartial fact entered the lexicon of journalism from the ambient culture.

The espousal of impartial facts was often no more than rhetoric, as the line between reporting and opining was often blurred, and dubious facts were marshaled to support religious and political factions. Nevertheless, as of the 1700s many journals separated news items from opinion. For example, the new daily newspapers of London devoted much space to factual reporting on the stock market, medicines, shipwrecks, fires, and crimes. Papers began factually covering the English Parliament. Dominant London newspapers, such as the *Times*, began to send reporters to cover court cases, public demonstrations, and foreign wars. This early form of objective reporting was supported by heady notions of Enlightenment rationality, science, and the importance of public opinion. By the end of the 1700s, the press, in its reporting and opinion functions, was recognized as a Fourth Estate.[5]

The most important step toward news objectivity came in the nineteenth century with the creation of a news press for the masses, which eclipsed an opinion press for elites. The primary business of newspapers changed from providing opinion to providing news. Electricity, more powerful printing presses, trains, a national economy, and better-educated populations in growing urban centers—all combined to create large papers, with staggering increases in circulations and advertising revenue.[6] An initial "penny press" in major U.S. cities would expand into the large newspapers of press barons such as Hearst and Pulitzer.

The effect on journalism's norms was dramatic. Papers that emphasized news displayed a "veneration of the fact" and stressed the virtues of accuracy, brevity, and timeliness.[7] Technologically, the telegraph made the rapid transmission of news possible and encouraged a crisp factual style. News agencies, founded on the telegraph, showed journalists how to write objectively. In 1866, Lawrence Gobright of the Associated Press in Washington, D.C., voiced an early commitment to what would become the journalistic norm: "My business is merely to communicate facts. My instructions do not allow me to make any comments upon the facts which I communicate."[8] Meanwhile, papers for the masses began to favor less partisan reporting of public affairs so as to appeal to readers of many political views. Newspapers based on advertising and circulation reduced their dependence on political patronage. Increasing numbers of newspapers declared themselves to be "independent" in news and opinion.[9] News became a daily industrial product that required large newsrooms with many kinds of journalists. A self-conscious spirit began to grow among the swelling ranks of journalists who sought to be professional to enhance their social status and to defend their independence. Therefore, by the late 1800s, norms of news objectivity—factuality, independence, and impartial professionalism—had emerged.

Journalists in the United States and Canada began to articulate these values in codes of ethics, in editorial statements, and in journalism manuals. The expression of these norms was influenced by the prevailing popularity of positivism as an approach to inquiry and practice. Positivism, as a philosophy of science, stressed inquiry as the careful analysis of facts, as opposed to philosophical speculation. Objective knowledge of facts was separate from the subjective espousal of values and interpretations. As a matter of practice, the professional as "positivist" made judgments on an impartial consideration of facts. Objectivity came to be associated with inquiry that "stuck to the facts" and used methods to eliminate human perspective and bias. This objectivity was a naïve combination of ontological and epistemic objectivity, at the bottom of which was a common sense "realism"—the belief there is an external world that provides inquirers with independent facts. This realism is at the heart of ontological objectivity. As well, this early journalistic objectivity was also epistemic insofar as it assumed that these facts were to be known through careful observation. This attitude to objectivity was best expressed by the scientist Thomas Huxley. "Sit down before a fact as a little child," wrote Huxley. "Be prepared to give up every pre-conceived notion, follow humbly wherever and to whatever abyss nature leads, or you shall learn nothing."[10] Similarly, the reporter was to follow the facts where they led. News reporting was independent and professional if it reported "just the facts" and eliminated perspective or interpretation. The full and explicit doctrine of new objectivity was not far off.

Doctrine of News Objectivity

For clarity, we need to distinguish between traditional news objectivity and later versions. By "traditional objectivity" I mean the original notion of news objectivity espoused by print journalists in the early 1900s, first advocated by U.S. journalists, and then adopted by their Canadian colleagues. Objectivity was never widely popular in European journalism. Traditional objectivity asserts that a report is objective if and only if it is an accurate recording of an event. It reports only the facts, and eliminates comment, interpretation, and speculation by the reporter. The report is neutral between rival views on an issue.

By the turn of the twentieth century, writers and textbooks were laying down the basics of traditional objectivity. In 1894 Edwin Schuman, the *Chicago Tribune*'s literary editor, published the first comprehensive U.S. journalism textbook, *Steps into Journalism*. Echoing Gobright, he wrote, "It is the mission of the reporter to reproduce facts and the opinions of others, not to express his own." Schuman's book contained the basics of traditional objective journalism: the inverted pyramid style, non-partisanship, detachment, a reliance on observable facts and balance.[11] After World War I, "objectivity" arrived as an explicit, common term, espoused by leading editors and widely practiced in newsrooms.

Recognition of objectivity as a formal ethical principle can be traced to two major codes of ethics—the 1923 code of the American Society of News Editors and the 1926 code of the Sigma Delta Chi, forerunner of the Society of Professional Journalists. The American Society of News Editors' code, the first national U.S. code, said that anything less than an objective report was "subversive of a fundamental principle of the profession." Impartiality meant a "clear distinction between news reports and expressions of opinion."[12] The principle of objectivity was second only to the principle of truthfulness in the code of Sigma Delta Chi. "Truth is our ultimate goal," said the code. "Objectivity in reporting the news is another goal, which serves as a mark of an experienced professional. It is a standard of performance toward which we strive." Objectivity reached its zenith in the 1940s and 1950s when, for example, Herbert Brucker saluted objective reporting as one of the "outstanding achievements" of U.S. newspapers.[13]

Traditional objectivity was more than a definition or an abstract ideal, it was a doctrine, a web of norms, standards, and rules that governed practice. The doctrine elaborated on journalism's commonsense empiricism, disciplining it with six standards:

1. Standard of factuality: reports are based on verified facts;
2. Standard of balance and fairness: reports balance and fairly represent the main viewpoints on an issue;
3. Standard of non-bias: the reporter's prejudices and interests do not distort reports;
4. Standard of independence: journalists are free to report without fear or favor;
5. Standard of non-interpretation: reporters do not put their interpretations into reports; and
6. Standard of neutrality: reporters do not take sides in disputes.

By the 1950s these standards were operationalized in newsrooms by rules on newsgathering and story construction: all opinion must be clearly attributed to the source, accompanied by direct quotation and careful paraphrasing; reporters must verify facts by reference to documents, scientific studies, government reports, and numerical analysis; and reports must be written from the detached tone of the third person. Phrases that indicate a bias or that are an unjustified inference from the facts are eliminated, or translated into neutral language. As these standards reveal, traditional objectivity was nineteenth-century ontological and epistemic objectivity adapted to journalism—a procedure with strict norms, required attitudes, and a detailed set of rules. Objective reporters were to be completely detached, to eliminate all of their opinion, and to report just the facts.

Why Objectivity?

Why did so many journalists and newspapers adopt objectivity, this language of restraint and exclusion? Some of the reasons have been noted: the development of a news press, a demand for unvarnished news, a readership of varied political views, and new technology. But these factors explain only why reporters focused on factual reporting, not why they adopted the restraints of traditional objectivity. What happened between the late 1800s and the early 1900s to prompt journalists to turn their casual empiricism into a stern method that limited their freedom? Why did they think this ideal was appropriate for the hurly-burly of daily journalism?

The answer resides in a deepening doubt about, and disillusionment with, journalism as a source of truthful information and as an agent of democracy. The doubt arose from two sources. First, there was a loss of confidence in the existing liberal model of the press. Second, there was skepticism about journalism's capacity to report truthfully and factually about a more complex modern world. Both kinds of doubt seemed to justify the tough ethic of objectivity.

The liberal model of the press in the nineteenth century held out the hope that a free, unregulated press would be an independent, responsible educator of citizens on matters of public interest. That hope flagged as the commercial press was accused of being sensational, "yellow,"[14] directed by press barons and influenced by advertisers and other interests.[15] A powerful corporate press, driven by commercial imperatives, seemed to be no better for journalism or democracy than a partisan press, dependent on political patronage.

Meanwhile, there was a growing awareness that reporters' chronicles of events were being distorted not only by their own subjectivity but also by agents in a manipulative public sphere. The rise of the press agent and the success of propaganda during World War I called for a journalism that tested alleged facts.[16] In sum, trends in journalism and in society threatened the naïve idea that reporters could easily obtain the truth through mere observation. What was fact and what was fiction in such a public sphere? An impulse to chronicle the world was not enough for truthful, independent journalism.

The answer, it seemed, was traditional objectivity. Reporters should stick to, and verify carefully, the facts, separating them from opinion. This would eliminate the reporter's own bias, in addition to the interpretations (and manipulations) of others. Also, journalists were to remain impartial among the many conflicting interests of society. If the press reported the facts, the public could make their own judgments on what was true or false. As Walter Lippmann said, journalism served democracy if it provided objective information about the world, not "stereotypes."[17] According to this view, what was needed was a professional, independent news press that was disciplined each day by the rules of objectivity.

Therefore, the development of traditional objectivity, as a doctrine distinct from journalistic empiricism, was due to an ethical response to these challenges within and without journalism in the early twentieth century. It was a doctrine that sought to repair, by enhancing the existing liberal model.

Challenge and Decline

The heyday of traditional objectivity was from the 1920s to the 1950s in the mainstream broadsheet newspapers of North America. The doctrine was so pervasive that, in 1956, the press theorist Theodore Peterson called it "a fetish."[18] However, the second half of the century is a story of challenge and decline that resulted from new forms of journalism, new technology, new social conditions and, hence, new models.

Despite being widely adopted, objectivity always had its critics. For example, Henry Luce, who founded *Time* magazine in the 1920s, dismissed it outright. "Show me a man who thinks he's objective and I'll show you a liar," Luce declared.[19] He argued that events in a complex world needed to be explained and interpreted. The "muckrakers" of the early 1900s rejected neutrality in reporting, and the emergence of television and radio created more personal forms of media where a strict objective style struggled. In the 1960s, an "adversarial culture" that criticized institutions and fought for civil rights was skeptical of objective experts and detached journalism. Other journalists practiced a subjective personal journalism that looked to literature for its inspiration.

In academia, philosophers, social scientists, activists, and others challenged the authority of objective science. Thomas Kuhn's influential writings were interpreted as showing that scientific change was a non-rational "conversion" to a new set of beliefs,[20] while others declared all knowledge is "socially constructed."[21] Postmodernists such as Jean-François Lyotard and Jean Baudrillard questioned the ideas of detached truth and philosophical "meta-narratives"—large historical narratives that make sense of human experience.[22] Media scholars treated objectivity as the tainted dogma of a dominant corporate media, arguing objective routines did little more than protect journalists from criticism.[23]

In the final decades of the twentieth century, online journalism gave further support to interpretive or opinion journalism. New media technology allowed almost anyone with a computer to publish their commentary or photos online, or to claim that they were a citizen journalist or blogger. This "new media" values immediacy, interactivity, sharing, and networking, limited editorial checks, and the expression of bias or opinion in an "edgy" manner. As Jane Singer argues below, the trend in media values on the Internet has been to move away from, and to be skeptical of, the ideas of professionalism and objectivity.

Today, the questioning continues. In an influential article, the journalist Martin Bell urged replacing objectivity with a journalism of "attachment,"[24] and the Annenberg Public Policy Center published a "manifesto for change," noting that objectivity is "less secure in the role of ethical touchstone," while norms such as accountability are increasing in importance.[25]

In retrospect, we can see journalism ethics in the twentieth century as representing both the rise and the decline of objectivity, the latter represented in the new forms of interpretive and personal journalism with increasing global reach. Amid these changes, there have been four criticisms of objectivity: First, the naïve realism on which it rests—the idea of an objective, discoverable world—has been widely challenged. Second, it is too demanding an ideal, and its rules are routinely broken by profit-seeking news organizations. Hence, objectivity, in practice, is a "myth." Third, objectivity, even if possible, is undesirable because it forces writers to use restricted formats, encouraging a superficial reporting of official facts, thereby failing to provide readers with needed analysis and interpretation. Further, objectivity ignores other vital press functions, such as commenting, campaigning, and acting as public watchdog. Finally, a democracy is better served by a diverse, opinionated press. In particular, a nonobjective model of journalism is best for an interactive media world.

Pragmatic Objectivity

A century after the doctrine of news objectivity was adopted, we arrive at a dead end. Traditional objectivity is a spent ethical force, doubted by journalist and academic.

In practice, fewer journalists embrace the ideal; objectivity gradually disappears from codes of journalism ethics, while newsrooms adopt a reporting style that includes perspective and interpretation.[26] Three options loom: abandon objectivity and replace it with other principles, "return" to traditional objectivity in newsrooms, or redefine objectivity.

Simply abandoning objectivity is not a viable option, since without it journalists lose an important restraint; they need clear principles to guide their activity. Unfortunately, much criticism of objectivity "deconstructs" the ideal without constructing an alternative. The decline of objectivity has left a vacuum in ethics just as journalism undergoes rapid, disorienting change. If journalists do not need to be objective, what other restraining norms are needed to ensure responsible journalism—a journalism that is accurate, fair to perspectives, and not tainted by implicit or explicit bias or ideology? Without objectivity as a principle and set of methods, without some basis for distinguishing the objective from the subjective, how do we distinguish between ranting and informed opinion, propaganda and well-evidenced interpretations, factual reports and fiction? Objectivity is not the only principle that can help journalists seek truth for the public, but historically it has operated as one such principle.

The best option is to reform the conception of objectivity in journalism through philosophical examination.[27] A new conception of objectivity starts with a diagnosis of where traditional objectivity comes up short. My diagnosis is that, as we've seen, in the late 1800s, when journalists sought a doctrine to discipline the rush for news, they adopted a popular but deeply flawed version of objectivity—a stringent positivism that reduced objectivity to "just the facts." Traditional objectivity was built on an indefensible epistemology and a questionable metaphysics, both of which falsely characterized reporting as passively empirical. Traditional objectivity was rooted in a misleading metaphor of the journalist as a recording instrument who passively observes and transmits facts. When positivism and its passive model collapsed, so did traditional objectivity.

In the long run, the traditional conception of objectivity would engender futile debate, preventing the construction of a more defensible ideal. As criticism of objectivity arose in academia and in journalism, defenders of objectivity lacked the concepts to adequately defend their view. Debate became focused on the wrong issues; for example, whether journalists could be perfectly objective. Both the defenders and critics of objectivity tended to assume that traditional objectivity was the only one on offer. It had to be defended, despite its flaws, because the option was flimsy, irresponsible reporting. All of this was occurring as other disciplines were developing richer notions of objectivity that acknowledged knowledge as an interpretive achievement.[28] This turmoil ignored an obvious question: Why is traditional objectivity the only notion under discussion? In what follows, I outline what I believe to be a better notion: pragmatic objectivity.[29]

Idea of Pragmatic Objectivity

Like traditional objectivity, pragmatic objectivity adopts the epistemic and ontological sense of objectivity. It agrees with traditional objectivity that there is an external world that our inquiries attempt to know and that serves as a check on what we would like to believe. The idea of an external world is a sort of regulatory ideal—it sets up as a cognitive norm the pursuit of better and better knowledge of the world. This is "minimalist" realism: what is true or false is what is or what is not the case. There is not much more we can say about the nature of truth than the idea that our beliefs strive to describe what is the case. All of the really interesting and difficult questions about objectivity belong to epistemology: How do we know what is presumably the case? How do we inquire objectively and carefully into the nature of the world? Moreover, pragmatic objectivity regards most of what we believe to be true about the world to be a matter of interpretation, hypothesis, and theory. It views knowledge as an interpretive accomplishment. Therefore, the heart of pragmatic objectivity is not ontological objectivity but the ways and means of epistemic objectivity, especially within journalism. Pragmatic objectivity is a matter of correct methods and tested judgments from within some conceptual scheme.

My view also agrees with traditional objectivity that objectivity disciplines the process of journalism, via established tests for appropriate reporting. But pragmatic objectivity takes a different view of how that testing proceeds and what its goals should be. Whereas traditional objectivity rejects the idea of the interpreting journalist, pragmatic objectivity starts from the idea that journalism is an active, interpretive, cultural activity. All works of journalism are regarded as interpretations in that there is an element of interpretation in even the most basic reports. The basis of this view is the fundamental epistemic thesis that we do not have direct and immediate contact with reality but rather that humans know the world through the use of various, interlocking conceptual schemes. The task of objectivity, then, is not to eliminate active inquiry and interpretation, let alone to arrive at some perspectiveless "absolute" description of reality but to develop methods for testing the story's selection of alleged facts, sources, and story angles. The goal of the objective newsroom is to produce well-grounded interpretations, tested through criteria appropriate to the evaluation of journalistic inquiry, that is, criteria that detect bias, challenge alleged facts and viewpoints, ask for evidence, and prevent reckless, uncritical reporting. The central question thus is not, "How can I report only the facts and avoid values and interpretation?" but "How well does my report, as an interpretation, satisfy objective criteria of evaluation?"

How does this method work? We implement pragmatic objectivity in the newsroom by constructing stories according to a certain attitude and by testing statements within the story, according to criteria and procedures, which, together, combine epistemic and procedural senses of objectivity and define rational, objective inquiry in journalism.

The attitude in question is what I call the objective stance. It consists in a number of intellectual virtues such as a willingness to place a critical distance between oneself and the story, to be open to evidence and counterarguments, to fairly represent other perspectives, and to be committed to the disinterested pursuit of truth for the public as a whole. One is "disinterested" in not allowing one's interests to prejudge or distort a story. The objective stance requires the integrity to admit error and to recognize blind spots in one's thinking.

However, it is not enough to have an objective attitude. One has to apply this attitude to the construction and evaluation of stories by employing criteria of three general kinds: First, criteria that test the stories for correspondence with carefully obtained and collaborated evidence. Second, criteria that test the coherence of claims in the story with existing knowledge and expertise. Third, criteria that test the story for how well it has framed the issues, and whether it has consulted a diversity of perspectives.

The practical task is to translate the objective stance and these broad criteria into more specific standards and procedures useful to working journalists and varied forms of journalism. This presumes that the general ideal of objectivity is interpreted and practiced in different ways in different domains. For example, in health research, objectivity entails procedures such as triple-blind drug tests. In criminal trials, jurors are asked to adopt the objective stance when the judge instructs them to follow the rules of evidence and the coherence of testimony. In journalism, reporters apply the three general criteria when they adopt specific procedures, such as collaborating stories across independent sources, cross-verifying the claims of a whistleblower, or using computer-assisted reporting to find patterns in the data. Journalists respect these criteria when they compare the clinical trial of a drug with existing studies or seek an appropriate diversity of perspectives. By putting these attitudes and criteria into practice, journalists display a desire to be objective as far as the conditions of journalism allow. They honor norms at the center of journalism ethics.

The approach of pragmatic objectivity to the testing of reports and stories is different from traditional objectivity in several important ways. First, as noted above, the goal is different. The latter seeks stories of fact; the former seeks well-supported interpretations. Second, traditional objectivity has one narrow test of stories—whether what is said is a fact, usually interpreted as a fact of observation or some form of empirical data. Pragmatic objectivity tests stories by holistically employing a set of tests that go beyond observable fact, including ones for coherence and consistency. It also tests for the diversity and quality of perspectives, as part of the objective approach.

Ultimately, the appropriateness of pragmatic objectivity is a pragmatic matter. It depends on whether the reformed notion serves the purposes for which we invoked objectivity in the first place—the search for norms to encourage reliable, tested journalism for the public good amid a media revolution where new forms of journalism question traditional notions of news objectivity. Only attempts to employ the norms of pragmatic objectivity over time will allow us to determine whether the new definition is helpful.

Implications

What are the implications of this approach to objectivity? First, good journalism is regarded as standard-guided interpretation, the importance of which is revealed in the coverage of complex topics, such as developments in science. A good science story has at least four layers. On one level, there is the article's factual accuracy and completeness. On the second level, there is the correct interpretation of statistical information and the identification of uncertainty in a study, such as a drug trial. There is a third level of clearly covering the positive and negative implications of a new discovery, and why the public should care about these issues. And, finally, there is a fourth level, where journalists are aware of the metaphors and language they employ, the way they frame the story, and possible conflicts of interest. Each of these represents a move to a richer and more sophisticated notion of objectivity, one beyond the traditional "just the facts" approach.

Second, pragmatic objectivity avoids a hard distinction between news and opinion—a forced choice between objective fact and subjective opinion. Instead, it posits a continuum that ranges from straight news at one end to ranting on the other. Between these opposites, the continuum includes the more complex forms of interpretive news reporting, informed analysis, and well-evidenced commentary. Stories differ not by an absence or presence of interpretation, but by their degree of interpretation and theorizing. This implies that the objective stance is not limited to what we call straight reporting. For example, news analysis can be evaluated according to the standards of empirical fact and coherence, and so can commentary. Similarly, there is no reason that bloggers cannot adopt elements of the objective stance. In fact, it is possible to use the interactive nature of new media to question stories through a continuing dialogue among many online voices—a communal, intersubjective testing.

These examples reveal objectivity need not be applied to the same degree everywhere; it depends on the form of communication. For instance, objective standards of accuracy, factuality, and fairness should be applied firmly to reporting on criminal trials because of the seriousness of the event and the effect of reporting on the justice system, while such standards are inappropriate for satirical journalism.

Third, pragmatic objectivity does not require neutrality but rather an open-minded attitude to a story as one begins to inquire into it. Objectivity is the disposition not to prejudge the story and to be willing to change one's mind as facts run against the initial hypothesis. This allows the reporter to draw conclusions, especially as these relate to a commitment to truth and the public interest, so long as such conclusions are well evidenced. Rather than avoid judgment, journalists should strengthen how they research and test their claims. Rather than fudge the fact that journalists select sources, facts, and angles, journalists should justify their selections.

Fourth and finally, to adopt pragmatic objectivity is to put to rest the misunderstanding that objectivity is perfect knowledge of reality. The judgment that something is objective is about well-grounded belief and fallible methods, not absolute knowledge. Objectivity, pragmatic or otherwise, is no miracle worker; it doesn't guarantee truth but instead wears a human face. It is about what imperfect journalists can accomplish in testing their data, under deadlines, just as that which is achieved every day by judges, referees, educators, conflict-resolution experts, and peacekeepers. Nor does objectivity require an uncaring Olympian detachment. The choice is not between an aloof objective reporting and a caring, attached journalism. Passion and attachment are about motivation; objectivity is about testing that motivation. Passion and objectivity are different aspects of the journalistic process, and the best journalism judiciously blends both to produce engaging and objectively tested reporting. Journalism based only on passion is reckless; journalism based only on objectivity is accurate but lacks depth.

The best feature of objectivity is that it encourages journalists to subject their work to critical reflection and standards. An honest desire to confirm and cohere is the essence of good journalism and is vital to its public role. The

objective stance restrains journalists, but it also prods them to do better-re-
searched stories. Adopting the objective stance helps counterbalance a public
sphere redolent with instant analysis, instant rumor, and manipulative sources.
In this expanding universe of media, we still need, at the heart of our media
system, a solid core of journalists, across all media platforms, committed to
objective public journalism, properly understood.

Notes

Some of the ideas in this article are taken from my *The Invention of Journalism
Ethics*.

1. See Friend and Singer, *On-Line Journalism Ethics*, and Jane Singer in chap. 8
of this volume.
2. Ward, *Invention of Journalism Ethics*, chap. 3.
3. See Shapiro, *A Culture of Fact*.
4. Mary Poovey argues that the modern fact began in the double-entry bookkeep-
ing of sixteenth century merchants. Poovey, *A History of the Modern Fact*, 29–91.
5. This history is examined in *The Invention of Journalism Ethics*, chaps. 3 and 4.
6. See Baldasty, *The Commercialization of the News*.
7. Stephens, *A History of News*, 244.
8. Mindich, *Just the Facts*, 109.
9. By the 1890s, one-third of U.S. newspapers listed in newspaper directories
identified themselves as independent. By 1940, that number had risen to 50 percent.
"Newsroom independence" had various meanings. In the beginning, it meant no
more than the freedom to take positions that differed from those of the newspaper's
political party. Hence, newspapers sometimes called themselves "Republican independent." Eventually, "independence" would develop into the idea of a complete
independence from all external influences. This ideal was described as a "wall"
between the editorial and non-editorial divisions of the newspaper.
10. Quoted in Stephens, *A History of News*, 221.
11. Shuman, *Steps into Journalism*.
12. Pratte, *Gods within the Machine*, 205–7.
13. Brucker, *Freedom of Information*, 21.
14. The term "yellow journalism" was put into circulation in 1897 in an editorial
written by Ervin Wardman, editor of the *New York Press*. Wardman used the term as a
dismissive epithet for the sensational journalism of Hearst's *Journal* and Pulitzer's
World. Wardman chose the word "yellow" apparently because, at the time, Hearst and
Pulitzer were in competition for the services of R. F. Outcault, who drew the popular
yellow-colored cartoon, the "Yellow Kid." The cartoon depicted the antics of an
irreverent, jug-eared child from the tenements of New York. See Campbell, *Yellow
Journalism*, and Spencer, *The Yellow Press*.
15. Skepticism about journalism goes back to the beginning of the modern news
press. However, in the late 1800s, a trickle of criticisms and worried analysis of the
role of the press in society turned into a stream of articles and books. More than a

hundred magazine articles on the press, many of them expressing concern about trends in journalism, appeared in the United States during the 1890s. The criticism continued into the twentieth century. Part of the criticism was that the press was "yellow" (i.e., sensational). See Ward, *Invention of Journalism Ethics*, 211–13.

16. Schudson, *Discovering of News*, 142.

17. Lippmann, *Public Opinion*, chapter 1.

18. Peterson, "The Social Responsibility Theory of the Press," 88.

19. Baughman, *Henry R. Luce and the Rise of the American News Media*, 29.

20. See Kuhn, *The Structure of Scientific Revolutions*. Kuhn later denied that his model of scientific revolution implied a non-rational conversion.

21. See Barnes and Bloor, "Relativism, Rationalism and the Sociology of Knowledge," and Hacking, *The Social Construction of What?*

22. For an introduction to postmodern thought, see Connor, *Postmodernist Culture*, and Butler, *Postmodernism*.

23. Hackett and Zhao, *Sustaining Democracy?*; Tuchman, *Making the News*.

24. Bell, "The Truth Is Our Currency."

25. Overholser, *On Behalf of Journalism*, 10–11.

26. The first code of ethics for the Canadian Association of Journalists, created in 2002, does not contain the word "objectivity," let alone make it a fundamental principle. Revisions to the code of the Society of Professional Journalists in the United States have removed objectivity as a major principle. See the codes at www.caj.ca and www.spj.org.

27. For an elaboration of the following, see chap. 7 of *The Invention of Journalism Ethics*.

28. Theorists have advanced notions such as "interpretive sufficiency" and "positional objectivity." On interpretive sufficiency, see Christians, "Preface." On positional objectivity, see Sen, "Positional Objectivity."

29. I provide a detailed explanation of pragmatic objectivity in chap. 7 of *Invention of Journalism Ethics*.

References

Barnes, Barry, and David Bloor. "Relativism, Rationalism and the Sociology of Knowledge." In Rationality and Relativism, ed. Martin Hollis and Steven Luke, 21–47. Oxford, UK: Blackwell, 1982.

Baldasty, Gerald. *The Commercialization of the News in the Nineteenth Century*. Madison: University of Wisconsin, 1992.

Baughman, James L. *Henry R. Luce and the Rise of the American News Media*. Boston: Twayne, 1987.

Bell, Martin, "The Truth is Our Currency." *Harvard International Journal of Press/ Politics* 3, no. 1 (1998): 102–9.

Brucker, Herbert. *Freedom of Information*. New York: Macmillan, 1949.

Butler, Christopher. *Postmodernism: A Very Short Introduction*. Oxford: Oxford University Press, 2002.

Campbell, W. Joseph. *Yellow Journalism: Puncturing the Myths, Defining the Legacies*. Westport, CT: Praeger, 2001.

Christians, Clifford G. "Preface." In *Communication Ethics Today*, ed. Richard Keeble. Leicester, UK: Troubadour, 2005.

Connor, Steven. *Postmodernist Culture*. Oxford, UK: Blackwell, 1989.

Cunningham, Brent. "Rethinking Objectivity." *Columbia Journalism Review* 4 (2003): 24–32.

Friend, Cecilia, and Jane B. Singer. *On-Line Journalism Ethics: Traditions and Transitions*. Armonk, NY: M.E. Sharpe, 2007.

Hackett, Robert A., and Yuechi Zhao. *Sustaining Democracy? Journalism and the Politics of Objectivity*. Toronto: Garamond, 1998.

Hacking, Ian. *The Social Construction of What?* Cambridge, MA: Harvard University Press, 1999.

Kuhn, Thomas S. *The Structure of Scientific Revolutions*. Chicago: University of Chicago Press, 1962.

Lippmann, Walter. *Public Opinion*. New York: Macmillan, 1922.

Mindich, David T.Z. *Just the Facts: How "Objectivity" Came to Define American Journalism*. New York: New York University Press, 1998.

Overholser, Geneva. *On Behalf of Journalism: A Manifesto for Change*. Annenberg Public Policy Center. Philadelphia: University of Pennsylvania, 2006.

Peterson, Théodore. "The Social Responsibility Theory of the Press." In *Four Theories of the Press*, ed. Fred Siebert, Theodore Peterson, and Wilbur Schramm. Urbana: University of Illinois Press, 1956.

Poovey, Mary. A *History of the Modern Fact*. Chicago: University of Chicago Press, 1998.

Pratte, Paul Alfred. *Gods within the Machine: A History of the American Society of Newspaper Editors, 1923–1993*. Westport, CT: Praeger, 1995.

Ross, Charles G. *The Writing of News: A Handbook*. New York: Henry Holt, 1911.

Schudson, Michael. *Discovering of News: A Social History of American Newspapers*. New York: Basic, 1978.

Shapiro, Barbara. A *Culture of Fact*. Ithaca, NY: Cornell University Press, 2000.

Shuman, Edwin. *Steps into Journalism: Helps and Hints for Young Writers*. Evanston, IL: Correspondence School of Journalism, 1894.

Spencer, David R. *The Yellow Press: The Press and America's Emergence as a World Power*. Evanston, IL: Northwestern University Press, 2007.

Stephens, Mitchell. A *History of News: From the Drum to the Satellite*. New York: Viking, 1997.

Tuchman, Gaye. *Making the News: A Study in the Construction of Reality*. New York: Free Press, 1978.

Ward, Stephen J.A. *The Invention of Journalism Ethics: The Path to Objectivity and Beyond*. Montreal: McGill-Queen's University Press, 2004

10

Is Objective News Possible?

Carrie Figdor

Never bury the lead; of course, objective news is possible. Unfortunately, I will also conclude, it is not earnestly pursued.

The structure of this chapter is as follows. I briefly explain the nature of objective news and of the debate regarding its possibility. I then assess the main arguments for the unattainability of objective news. A close examination of these arguments shows that, contrary to widespread belief, journalists who try to provide objective news are not striving in vain. I close by discussing the effect of competing journalistic aims and other limitations on our efforts to generate objective news. I suggest that the unwarranted skepticism regarding the possibility of objective news is an artifact of the changing priorities of journalists and inadequate journalistic methods, and that the only real issue is how we can better train those journalists who want to generate objective news.

The Nature and Problem of Objective News

Objective news is essentially an epistemic kind. What is sometimes now called the "journalism of verification" is merely what yields objective news: verification (or justification) is an epistemic notion.[1] The editorial adage "When it doubt, leave it out" also expresses its epistemic nature. More specifically, objective news reports are those that can provide testimonial knowledge or justified belief about some aspect of the world to those who read or hear them. To satisfy this requirement we apply epistemic standards of evaluation. For example, we ask, "Is every sentence in the report supported by sufficient objective evidence?" A statement is objectively justified if it is rational to believe on the basis of evidence that anyone should accept. For example, observing ten inert bodies in the road after a roadside bomb explodes is evidence on the basis of which it is rational to believe the statement that at least ten people died in the explosion.[2]

The ultimate aim of an objective news report is, of course, truth, but many statements in objective news reports may turn out to be false, despite our best efforts to verify. This is why it is not necessary for an objective news report to consist entirely of *true* statements. What is necessary is that it consist entirely of *objectively verified* statements. Thus, if a fact is a statement that expresses what is the case (what's true) or what reliably or logically follows from what is the case, to report "just the facts" is to include only objectively verified statements in a news report. (This is only a necessary condition for objective news; editing, discussed later, also plays a role.) It follows that the inclusion of a statement in an objective news report implies it is supported by sufficient objective evidence: it's not there because the reporter made a lucky guess or wishes it were true.[3] If he or she doesn't have that evidence, it should not be there.

Although the presence of *any* unverified statement in a news report detracts from its objectivity, the debate over objective news focuses on that subset of sentences that expresses or immediately implies the reporter's values, preferences, biases, or personal opinions (values, for short), which may or may not be shared by his or her social peers.[4] Value statements express what ought or should be the case, and the problem with these statements is there is no consensus on how they might be objectively verified or whether they can be. However, it is sufficient reason to leave them out of objective news reports if we're not sure whether they *are* verified, whether or not one thinks they *can't* be. Value statements may automatically appear to many readers or listeners as claims for which the reporter does not have sufficient objective evidence, based on their belief that such claims *can't* be verified. This appearance is sufficient reason to leave them out, even if (contrary to their belief) there *are* facts of the matter when it comes to values and even if value statements *can* be objectively verified.[5]

Journalists try to purge their news reports of objectively unverified statements, including but not limited to value statements, by following a bundle of professional practices. Mindich provides a standard description of the traditional features of objective news reports.[6] These include (1) detachment (use of neutral language), (2) nonpartisanship (inclusion of all relevant sides of a story; fairness), (3) the inverted pyramid style of writing (presentation of facts in order of importance), (4) naïve empiricism (factual accuracy), and (5) balance (lack of distortion, such as by omission of relevant facts).

This list is best seen as a complex description of a traditional objective news report, not a set of rules to follow for producing reports that satisfy the description, nor a set of necessary and sufficient conditions for any objective news report. For example, there is no essential connection between a report's being objective and its being written in the inverted pyramid style. And at least some of the practices traditionally used to generate news reports that satisfy Mindich's description may be poorly conceived (never mind poorly executed).

For example, the practice of getting an official statement and an opposition statement (what Cunningham has called "he said, she said" journalism) is one method for trying to generate a nonpartisan report, but not the only or best one.[7] As Kovach and Rosenstiel emphasize, journalism does not have a profession-wide set of rules for generating objective news reports, although individual news outlets, editors, or reporters generally do, from which a set of standard practices might be developed.[8]

Arguments against the possibility of objective news try to show that human cognitive limitations prevent us from leaving all values out of our news reports. One type of argument blames these limitations for the inevitable inclusion of sentences or descriptions expressing values; the other blames these limitations for editorial choices that shape news reports in ways that inevitably reflect values.[9] This reference to human cognitive limitations is crucial but liable to be misunderstood. The question is whether objective news is possible *for journalists*, not whether it is logically possible, since logical possibility refers only to the absence of contradiction. Of course, it is logically possible. The worry here is whether it is possible, given human cognitive capacities and the laws of nature.

The misunderstanding involves the goal of the professional practices that may result in objective news. The goal is not to cleanse reporters' minds of values. It is to cleanse their news reports of statements for which they lack sufficient objective evidence.[10] Methods for achieving balance involve making sure verified relevant facts are not omitted; loaded descriptions are omitted because they imply values; and so on. If adopting a particular psychological attitude (sometimes called "objective" in a non-epistemic sense of the word) makes it easier for journalists to follow the practices, that's an interesting psychological fact. It says nothing about the objectivity of the report, which lies in its sentences' being backed by sufficient objective evidence, whether that evidence is gathered by a human, a robot, or a robotic human.[11]

The problem of objective news, then, is not whether journalists can purge themselves of their values by following the practices, but whether they can generate news reports purged of unverified facts by following the practices. In other words, the premise that human beings inevitably have subjective points of view, which is uncontroversially true, does not entail the conclusion that news reports are inevitably subjective, for the validity of making such an inference is precisely the issue. Einstein inevitably had a subjective point of view, too, but it doesn't follow that $E = MC^2$ is inevitably subjective.

The Argument from Value-Laden Observation (VLO)

The impossibility of objective news doesn't follow from the fact that reporters are fallible. Fallibility means only that we need to be careful to "get the facts"; it doesn't make it impossible to do so. As we've also seen, concluding that "human beings inevitably have subjective points of view; therefore, news reports are inevitably subjective" also fails because we can't infer anything about the epistemic status of news reports from a fact about human psychology without additional premises. Can critics of the possibility of objective news do better than this?

If we change the language of the above statement slightly, we can see why it is a popular argument that at least *seems* plausible: We can only observe the world from our own subjective perspectives; therefore, objective news is not possible.[12] Stated this way, the statement summarizes another argument inspired by complicated debates in the philosophy of science that challenge what Mindich calls the "naïve empiricism" of many journalists.[13] The central claim in that debate is that, contrary to what most of us believe, values are embedded in perceptual observation. If observation is value-laden, no statement in a news report that is verified by observation can be accepted as objectively verified. For example, seeing and smelling ten dead people after a bomb blast may appear to objectively verify the statement that at least ten people died in the blast, but since values are suspect, any statement supported by value-laden observation is suspect as well.

The full argument can be stated as follows:

1. We can only observe the world via our own perceptual observations.
2. These observations are essentially value-laden.
3. Therefore, they cannot provide objective verification.
4. Consequently, objective news is not possible.

Note that the value-ladenness of observation is not the claim that we make observations and then interpret them in ways that reflect our values. Value-ladenness claims that two observers in exactly the same perceptual conditions who are identical biologically and psychologically except that they have different values will literally observe different things. The claim also is not that we can perceive only that for which we have concepts: If person A has the concept "cancer" and person B does not, then only A literally can see cancerous tissue when looking at an X-ray; B literally cannot see cancer, only (maybe) black dots. The claim here is that perception is constrained by the values we hold, not merely by the concepts we possess. If, for example, a reporter for the *Jerusalem Post* believes that Jews ought to have a homeland in Israel and a reporter for Al-Jazeera believes that Jews ought not to have a homeland in Israel, this difference in their *values*—not their *concepts*, which these two beliefs share—constrains their sensory capacities such that they literally cannot observe the same things. Looking at what we intuitively might consider the same object doing the same thing, the *Post* reporter literally cannot see an armed oppressor entering Gaza, even if she has the concepts "armed oppressor," "entering," and "Gaza," while the Al-Jazeera reporter literally cannot see an Israeli soldier entering Gaza even if he has the concepts "Israeli soldier," "entering," and "Gaza."

Value-ladenness of observation also is utterly different from standard problems of eyewitness testimony, in which people are very unreliable and often offer pure conjecture with a feeling of utter certainty.[14] Two eyewitnesses may be 100 percent reliable regarding their respective value-laden observations.

Of course, when value-ladenness is properly understood, many of those who think the initial inference is a good argument will find VLO implausible. There is more to be debated here, but it doesn't matter. For even if we accepted premise 2 as true, VLO is invalid: the conclusion doesn't follow. This is because even if observation is value-laden, all that follows is that to see what someone else sees I must share that person's values. This is obviously possible. So, to get to the conclusion, we will need another premise:

1. We can observe the world only via our own observations.
2. These observations are essentially value-laden.
3. Values cannot be objectively verified.
4. Therefore, our observations cannot provide objective verification.
5. Consequently, objective news is not possible.

In short, value-laden observation cannot provide objective verification, not because we have different values (so what, if values can be shared?), but because values themselves cannot be objectively verified.

The problem here is that premise 3 may not be true; it trades on the popularity in some circles of value relativism (if there is no fact of the matter regarding values, then there's nothing to verify) and epistemic relativism (there are no objective methods of verification). But both positions are controversial. There may well be values that anyone should hold and evidence on the basis of which a belief is rational for anyone to hold. It's true that objective news is possible only if objective verification is possible. But VLO doesn't argue that this necessary condition can't be satisfied in the case of values; it just *asserts* it can't. We were looking for a reason to doubt the possibility of objective news, but VLO doesn't give us one.

In sum, the argument from value-laden observation claims that a reporter can't generate objective news because observation can't provide objective verification. (The problem *isn't* that we can't share values or "worldviews"—which include values—or come to know what others are thinking.) It's not obvious that observation is value-laden. But even if it were, value-laden observations can provide objective verification if values can be objectively verified. Since the argument gives us no reason to think they can't be, it fails to show that objective news is not possible.

The Argument from Value-Laden Editing (VLE)

A second line of argument claims that the editorial filter itself is value-laden. Not every activity counts as an event, not every event counts as news, not every feature of a newsworthy event is considered newsworthy, and not all the statements that describe the newsworthy features of newsworthy events are given equal weight. These selection processes—collectively, I'll call them editing—involve value judgments along two dimensions: in or out, high or low (e.g., the lead is in and high). The argument from value-laden editing claims that editing choices inevitably reflect the values of those doing the choosing and that whatever passes through a value-laden filter is itself value-laden. We can state this argument as follows:

1. Generating news reports (individually or through a whole edition) necessarily involves editing.
2. Editing is essentially value-laden.
3. The product of a value-laden editing process is itself value-laden.
4. Therefore, objective news reports are not possible.

Of course, objective news reports are not data dumps or lists of unrelated statements. At a minimum, news reports (objective or otherwise) are linguistic narratives offered for public consumption by a news outlet. This weak criterion is not a sufficient condition (e.g., a newspaper might contain a short piece of fiction), but it enables us to distinguish news reports from non–news reports without begging any questions raised by value-laden editing.

The strength of VLE lies in its simplicity and specificity. Unlike VLO, it does not rest on complex philosophical positions or on premises that threaten the justification of any belief based on perception. It argues that objective news reports must not just get the story right; they must get the story. But getting the story involves a framework of editorial choices, which rely on judgments of importance. Since these judgments will inevitably be affected by one's values, the argument goes, the reports cannot be objective in the sense that any competent editor or reporter should make the same judgments in the same circumstances.

Before addressing VLE, some preliminary issues can be set aside. First, the possibility of objective editorial choices also does not require infallibility. Editors and reporters omit important facts, bury the lead, and miss stories all the time. Reporters are constrained by what they know when they look for what they don't. But omniscience is not a condition of objective news, and ignorance is not bias. Second, even if values or biases inevitably taint editing in general, it doesn't follow that every story inevitably is tainted by bias. As Mindich argues, it took an outsider, Ida B. Wells, to break the story of the segregation and terrorizing of African Americans in the South before the civil rights era.[15] Mainstream reporters missed it. But if leaving a story out is a form of value-laden editing, then Wells's story was not value-laden; she got the story (as did later reporters). The push to hire minorities in newsrooms is predicated on the idea that editing biases of this sort can be overcome in news reports. Whether individuals must overcome their biases is not the issue.

Third, not all editorial choices detract from the possibility of objective news. Many judgments of importance are not problematic. For example, the fact that an ant crawled across a reporter's sleeve will not be included in his or her report on a street demonstration. At least some editorial choices reflect differences in the facts that each reporter has discovered or the quality of the evidence he or she has obtained by deadline. Fourth, the editing filter is typically not one person. Unlike columns or blog entries, objective news reports are generated by news staffs, even if one person gets the byline. Therefore, most editorial filters are multiperspectival. If the second premise is right, multiperspectival editing processes will still be value-laden, however.

So why think premise 2 of VLE is true? Value-laden editing is correct to emphasize that editorial choice involves judgments of importance and that these judgments are as important for objective news reports as is verifying the statements in them. The question is whether these judgments can be based just on objective reasons; if not, they are value-laden. An editorial judgment is objectively justified if it is rational to make that judgment on the basis of reasons that anyone should accept, just as it is rational for a person to obtain eggs and break them if he or she wants to eat an omelet. If at least some stories are the result of choices that satisfy this condition, then the second premise is false.

Consider the following: if no editorial choice is objectively justifiable, then such choices may as well be made by a rookie reporter. Conversely, if some editorial choices can be objectively justified, that would explain why seasoned journalists are put in editorial positions. They are there because they have acquired the ability to base their editorial choices on reasons that any skilled editor would accept as constraints on their judgments—facts about audience interests and values, background knowledge of related issues, competing stories, the size of the day's news hole, the quality of a reporter's evidence by deadline, and so on. We can satisfy ourselves of the objectivity of these choices by putting other skilled editors in those circumstances and seeing if they make the same choices. We don't, in fact, do this in journalism, but we could; the replication of experiments in science by independent research teams is the same sort of test.

There can, of course, be more than one way to report objectively on the same event (by the same or different news outlets), for each editorial filter will be objectively determined by different constraints, particularly audience values and background knowledge. The fact that Al-Jazeera, the BBC, and CNN cover events in the Mideast differently does not mean that their editorial choices are value-laden in the sense that they cannot be fully constrained by these facts about audience interests and so on. Differences in these constraints can be sufficient to explain the editorial differences. It remains true that editorial staff values may play a role in some or even many editorial choices. But the second premise claims that editorial choices are inevitably value-laden—that is, not fully constrained by objective reasons. We have no reason to think that this stronger claim is true. It was not an accident that news outlets everywhere reported the September 11 attacks on the World Trade Center towers, even if distinct audience values or other constraints also dictated different ways of reporting the story. The test of objective editing remains: replicate all the constraints to replicate the choices.

There is, however, one particular value that does affect all editorial choices: the value of satisfying the audience's (or publisher's) interests. Journalists, like anyone else, need not value the interests of others; bloggers, in particular, may make a point of not doing so. But acknowledging and responding to the fact of other people's interests may itself be a reason for editorial choice that anyone should accept, particularly if doing so is instrumentally valuable for its role in making knowledge possible. Bloggers who ignore others' interests and yet want to generate objective news may be acting irrationally in something like the way someone who wants an omelet but refuses to get eggs would be. If objective news is a form of testimonial knowledge, it makes little sense to try to generate it if one pretends there is no one else who might care. I might have reason to seek evidence for my beliefs all for myself, but that is not sufficient reason to publish it.

I conclude that while VLE raises an important and problematic aspect of objective news, it does not succeed in showing that it is impossible for editorial choices to be dictated by the constraints in which journalists operate. I do concede that it is open for journalists to refuse to accept those constraints, in particular by refusing to value other people's interests. So editorial choices will be value-laden in this respect. But this value may itself be one that anyone ought to hold.

The Real Problem of Objective News

I have defended the possibility of objective news from claims that our values inevitably infiltrate either the statements in news reports or the editing filter through which these statements pass. The argument from value-laden observation does not give us a reason to think that observation is not a source of objective verification. Arguments from value-laden editing do not acknowledge the role of knowledge in constraining editorial choice. Although bias in news reports is inevitable in general, it does not follow that every news report is inevitably biased.

However, it is undeniable that many actual news reports are not objective— they do not contain just objectively verified facts chosen just on the basis of objective constraints. If it is possible, and if the conditions for its possibility have nothing to do with journalists' attitudes, why is this so? I'll discuss two reasons.

The first is that actual news reports reflect competing goals, each of which leaves its stamp on the published product. The epistemic goal of objectivity is one constraint. Economic, aesthetic, and egoistic goals are the foremost non-epistemic constraints. The effect of these three non-epistemic goals on the objectivity of a news report can be roughly gauged by comparing news reports with scientific research papers published in peer-reviewed scientific journals, which strive for the same epistemic goal but not the other goals (or not nearly to the same extent). *Scientists* may well be as ego-driven as journalists, but their *papers* are not about themselves or their opinions.

Economically, we value accuracy highly and are willing to pay a lot to get it. Science is hugely expensive largely because sophisticated instruments for making accurate observations are costly. Generating news reports to an analogous degree of accuracy is also expensive. But you get what you pay for, and the objectivity of a news report will reflect this economic constraint.

Aesthetically, news stories must be interesting enough to catch and keep the audience's attention. That means color—which may mean using descriptions that are loaded with positive or negative connotations or provoke emotional responses. For example, we often describe the characters of public figures even if we don't really have sufficient evidence for our descriptions. It also can mean a judgmental style—not analysis, which can be based objectively on valid deductive or strong inductive arguments, but colorfully expressed opinion that may not be supported by any valid argument at all (e.g., vivid ad hominem attacks). It also can mean using anecdotes to illustrate or make vivid, even though truly representative cases are rare and non-representative cases often distort or distract (hence the temptation to form a composite person from various sources or make one up from scratch). Being objective and being interesting are compatible goals but can be difficult to combine successfully. No wonder objective news is often described in highly unappealing terms.[16]

Egoistically, journalists—like many people—are often motivated by the goal of social status.[17] Objective journalism is intrinsically self-effacing: it's not about you. And who, in this day and age, wants that? The article that does not have the reporter's identity stamped all over it does not garner the public recognition for its author that a blog entry, an opinion piece, a television appearance, or any of the other media in which journalists assert themselves in the public sphere can. Few non-journalists read bylines, and the work that goes into discovering and verifying facts, rewriting, and editing is invisible to the public. Extensive wire service reporting may garner only a mention of the service's having contributed to a news report that runs with a local reporter's byline. No wonder Ivy League graduates often fill the newsrooms of the most prestigious news outlets and that opinion journalism has again become so popular.

The second reason that objective news is difficult has to do with the practices that have traditionally been associated with its pursuit. It is debatable whether these practices do lead to objective news (even when properly followed). Much of the discontent with objective news may simply be belated recognition that the traditional practices are not adequate. I have emphasized that objective news is an epistemic category. But compare the professional training journalists get with that of students of the sciences. The latter spend a great deal of time learning epistemological techniques—how to design an experiment that will yield a useful result, how to derive a prediction from a theory, how to generate and critically assess alternative hypotheses. These critical and analytical skills are not had just by having normal cognitive abilities.[18] Moreover, it took time to develop these techniques: courses in experimental design and data analysis did not just appear with Galileo and Newton. Analogous training in journalism schools would be what Kovach and Rosenstiel have called a "science of reporting," which emphasizes methods of verification. They suggest the following as the "intellectual principles of a science of reporting":

1. Never add anything that was not there.
2. Never deceive the audience.
3. Be as transparent as possible about your methods and motives.
4. Rely on your own original reporting.
5. Exercise humility.

The Rule of Transparency (#3) is explained as follows:

It is the same principle as governs scientific method: explain how you learned something and why you believe it—so the audience can do the same. In science, the reliability of an experiment, or its objectivity, is defined by whether someone else could replicate the experiment. In journalism, only by explaining how we know what we know can we approximate this idea of people being able, if they were of a mind to, to replicate the reporting. This is what is meant by objectivity of method in science, or in journalism.[19]

These cognitive skills, possessed by seasoned journalists, can be made explicit and taught. Arguably, the core of what in journalism is called an "objective attitude" or even "skepticism" is just critical and analytical thinking.

Ultimately, the problem of objective news is not that it is an unattainable ideal, but that, relatively speaking, it can be boring, costly, and dissatisfying to the ego. We want it, but not enough to outweigh our other goals. In the meantime, we have a hodgepodge of traditional practices that may not be adequate to this epistemic goal; only now are we beginning to focus on the epistemic nature of objectivity.[20] I conclude that while objective news is attainable, we have barely begun to pursue it in earnest.

Notes

1. See, e.g., Bill Kovach and Tom Rosenstiel, *The Elements of Journalism* (New York: Three Rivers Press, 2001).

2. See Paul Boghossian, *Fear of Knowledge* (Oxford: Oxford University Press, 2006), 63–69. We need not be infallible for evidence to be objective; what matters is that beliefs based on such evidence can be considered rational.

3. This is why when we aren't sure (i.e., when we don't have sufficient objective evidence) we do not claim that we are. Instead, we write a sentence for which we do have sufficient objective evidence (e.g., that official estimates on Tuesday put the number of dead at *N*).

4. Often, the disputed values are those familiar from the culture wars; even Bernard Goldberg's critique of the mainstream media (*Bias: A CBS Insider Exposes How the Media Distort the News* (Washington, D.C.: Regnery, 2002) does not target news reports in general but stories on gay rights, abortion, affirmative action, and the like.

5. Michael Schudson, *Discovering the News: A Social History of American Newspapers* (New York: Basic Books, 1978), urges journalists to seek objective news via an allegiance to the fact/value distinction. This is imprecise, for even partisan journalists can be professionally committed to that distinction. More precisely, it is an allegiance to the objectively verified/unverified distinction, which need not coincide with the fact/value distinction at all. If values can be objectively verified, they can be included in objective news reports; and if a fact is not objectively verified, it should be left out.

6. David T. Z. Mindich, *Just the Facts: How "Objectivity" Came to Define American Journalism* (New York: New York University Press, 1998).

7. Brent Cunningham, "Re-thinking Objectivity," *Columbia Journalism Review* 3, no. 4 (July/August 2003), p. 3, and online at http://www.cjr.org.issues/2003/4/objective-cunningham,asp?printerfriendly=yes.

8. Kovach and Rosenstiel, *Elements of Journalism*.

9. E.g., some suggest replacing the norm of objectivity with a norm of accuracy (Michael Kinsley, "The Twilight of Objectivity," *Washington Post*, March 31, 2006, p. A19) or of reliable information (Victor Navasky, *A Matter of Opinion* [New York: Farrar, Straus & Giroux, 2005]). Presumably, this means just getting the facts right, whether or not values are also excluded.

10. Jack Newfield, "Journalism: Old, New and Corporate," in *The Reporter as Artist: A Look at the New Journalism Controversy*, ed. Ronald Weber (New York: Hastings House, 1974), 54–65, and Kinsley, "Twilight of Objectivity," are among the many who make this mistake. After listing a set of values commonly held by U.S. reporters ("belief in welfare capitalism, God, the West, Puritanism, the Law, the family, property, the two-party system, and perhaps most crucially, in the notion that violence is only defensible when employed by the State"), Kinsey writes: "I can't think of any White House correspondent, or network television analyst, who doesn't share these values. And at the same time, who doesn't insist he is totally objective" (p. A 19).Whether or not the correspondents and analysts are correct in describing *themselves* as objective (whatever they mean by that), *nothing* immediately follows about the objectivity of their news reports.

11. Schudson (*Discovering the News*, 8) discusses the "objective attitude." See also Stephen J. A. Ward's essay in chap. 9 of this book.

12. Molly Ivins seems to offer an argument of this type. As Victor Navasky writes:

As far as I'm concerned, when in 1993 Molly Ivins achieved the ripe middle age of forty-nine, she disposed of the objectivity question for all time: "The fact is that I am a forty-nine-year-old white, female, college-educated Texan. All of that affects the way I see the world. There's no way in hell that I'm going to see anything the same way that a fifteen-year-old black high-school dropout does. We all see the world from where we stand. Anybody who's ever interviewed five eyewitnesses to an automobile accident knows there's no such thing as objectivity." (*A Matter of Opinion*, 409)

13. See Mindich, *Just the Facts*, 8. For one of the original arguments in philosophy of science, see N. R. Hanson, *Patterns of Discovery* (Cambridge: Cambridge University Press, 1961).

14. Elizabeth F. Loftus, *Eyewitness Testimony* (Cambridge, MA: Harvard University Press, 1979); Gary L. Wells and Elizabeth F. Loftus, eds., *Eyewitness Testimony: Psychological Perspectives* (New York: Cambridge University Press, 1984).

15. See Mindich, *Just the Facts*, 113–137.

16. Mindich (*Just the Facts*, 109) notes the "bland gruel, without the spice and piquancy of partisan criticism and local dialect" of early Associated Press reports, while Schudson (*Discovering the News*, 77–87) describes the "dull discipline" of objective news editing imposed on reporters who sought to launch literary careers.

17. For example, Richard Perez-Peña ("Top Editor to Step Down at the *Washington Post*," *New York Times*, June 24, 2008, p. C3) describes Leonard Downie Jr. as "a calm, unassuming leader in an often frenetic business known for outsize egos."

18. Anthony Serafini, "Applying Philosophy to Journalism," *International Journal of Applied Philosophy* 3, no. 4 (Fall 1987): 45–49. Reprinted in *Philosophical Issues in Journalism*, ed. Elliot D. Cohen (New York: Oxford University Press, 1992), 256–63.

19. Kovach and Rosenstiel, *Elements of Journalism*, 79.

20. For example, Columbia University's Graduate School of Journalism introduced a course in evidence and inference in the 2006–7 academic year. See also the critical analyses of media recommended by Brent H. Baker (*How to Identify, Expose and Correct Liberal Media Bias* (Alexandria, VA: Media Research Center), even though his goal is exposing liberal biases in particular.

The Practice of Journalism

PART V

The Business of Journalism

Introduction

> Only a great white shark on speed is more frighteningly, mindlessly ruthless than a profit-challenged corporate executive in search of a new idea. It is, in fact, virtually suicidal to place yourself between the average media company CEO and a dollar.

So wrote Pulitzer Prize–winning *Los Angeles Times* columnist Tim Rutten in 2005, as he contemplated the fate of television news, given the steady decline in viewership. He finished the column with a cynical, yet oddly hopeful admonition: "It's commonplace nowadays to hear the three network news divisions compared to dinosaurs. But if they follow the giant reptiles into extinction, it won't be because their brains were too small. It will be because they were too cheap to buy bigger ones."[1] I say "hopeful" because Rutten implies news executives can save mainstream news sources if they have realistic profit expectations and are smart enough to sustain a high-quality product, rather than succumbing to the latest corporate fad.

Rutten wrote that column just as the *Times* was starting a series of job cuts subsequent to the paper's sale to the Tribune Company. Since then, the paper has lost hundreds of news positions, while also carving through a series of editors and publishers, most of whom quit or were fired over disputes regarding layoffs.

And, of course, the *Times* is hardly unusual. Newspapers around the world, and particularly in the United States, are experiencing sharp circulation declines, layoffs, and even closures. Some celebrate these numbers. Here's a sample blog from the Huffington Post, written in response to James Boyce's posting about newspapers' decline:

That newspapers are going the way of the dinosaurs (and our oil) is . . . a good thing. A great thing, in fact. And I celebrate their death, as I believe all sane people do. There are a few of us sane souls who refuse to read the daily swill, who refuse to buy the endless propaganda, who refuse to be told what the news is, what the truth is, by people who have no idea what either are. Instead of an alarmist article, shouldn't you be looking at this as a good thing, Mr. Boyce? The pendulum is swinging back—toward reality, toward the truth.[2]

As I argue in various places in this book, despite online journalism's considerable potential, the loss of newspapers would be a devastating blow to society and to democracy. Not just because there is something deeply gratifying, at least to us dinosaurs, about holding a newspaper, being able to take it everywhere, not having to worry about maintaining an Internet connection or about one's battery dying, but also because core journalistic values are embedded in the history and culture of newspapers.

Those values are certainly not always wholly consistent with broader ethical values—see, for example, chapter 20 of this volume—and those that are, too often are also corrupted by news organizations' prudential needs. Nonetheless, the foundational moral justifications for news media—protecting rights, enhancing community, promoting democratic engagement, challenging power—are historically best reflected in the practice of newspaper journalism. If I were confident that new media could sustain those foundations, then tactile or convenience motivations would hardly suffice. I'm not so confident, though, in part because much of new media's appeal lies exactly in its rejection of the perceived elitism and anachronism of mainstream media.

But . . . there are, as two of the following authors argue, increasing grounds to think mainstream media has yielded to exactly what worried Rutten: they've given up on the reasons for journalism so as to make money off it. This raises a whole host of questions, including: If it's all about the money, how can the once sacrosanct wall between the editorial and the business sides be sustained? Can news that speaks only, or at least most forcefully, to a moneyed elite—those whom advertisers want to reach—still truly be called *news*? And, most importantly, what of legal protections? The Framers of the U.S. Constitution assuredly did not provide First Amendment protection so the Tribune Company's stockholders could insist on an 18 percent return.[3]

The reality, Ian Richards tells us, is news "has become a commercial commodity even though it does not fit easily into standard economic theory." It does not because questions of scarcity don't readily apply to news and because of difficulties in determining the basic unit for sale: "Depending on the context, it could be a news story, an article, a program, a bulletin, or a combination of these." These problems, in fact, contribute to news organizations' financial troubles. When they were the only, or at least the best, game in town for advertisers, questions of scarcity loosely applied; while news itself was not scarce, newsprint or airtime was; or, better, access to advertisers' potential customers was. As media have proliferated, however, so have the options for reaching customers. So what's left to sell? Will people really pay for news, pay enough to keep papers in business?

Richards thinks so, while also arguing standard business models will not, should not, apply: "News continues to be an important commodity, being bought and sold and distributed in various forms and by various means among a range of news platforms and consumers. The commodification of news would not matter if it was a product such as detergent or floor polish, but, obviously, news is rather more than this."

The alternative, he argues, is to move away from a standard profit model and place ownership of news organizations within "social responsibility theory," reinforced by a code of ethics—not for the reporters, but for the business executives and employees. Key to such a code, Richards stresses, is a reinforcement of the purpose of journalism: "to find and report truth," as this is understood in light of Hilary Putnam's notion of "rational acceptability."

All that may be well and good, Edmonds argues, but newspapers still have to make enough money to hire reporters, buy paper and ink, run the presses, and deliver the product. Such profitability is assuredly tenuous. Edmonds paints a pretty bleak picture: even before the 2008 recession, newspapers were hit with the loss of substantial classified ad revenue and declining circulation. In all but a few cases, these led to significant job cuts and even the closing of newspapers. Given current trends, Edmonds suggests, the future will likely mean a few regional and national papers (he gives, for example, high marks to the national *Wall Street Journal*), with much smaller local papers, some of which will be print–online hybrids.

Marty Steffens takes these organizational and professional-level discussions and brings them home, giving a firsthand, on-the-street account of what it is like to be a journalist, a business journalist no less, reporting on the very conditions that may produce an upcoming pink slip. She raises all the right concerns and gives some recommendations, but the general conclusion one draws from her essay is, *times are tough.* One can only hope they are also survivable. I deeply fear the consequences otherwise.

Notes

1. Tim Rutten, "News' Fate in Today's Corporate Culture," Regarding Media, *Los Angeles Times*, January 22, 2005, p. F1.

2. James Boyce, "Is This the Last Newspaper Stand?" Huffington Post, April 28, 2008; http://www.huffingtonpost.com/james-boyce/is-this-the-last-newspape_b_99085.html, accessed October 25, 2008.

3.   This is the reported figure that investment managers were insisting, in the first decade of the twenty-first century, that various Tribune holdings had to produce. In 2007 Sam Zell bought the Tribune Company (including the *Chicago Tribune* and *Los Angeles Times*) and now, like many owners and investors, is just struggling to make *any* profit. In fact, the company declared Chapter 11 bankruptcy in early December 2008.

II

Journalism's Tangled Web: Business, Ethics, and Professional Practice

Ian Richards

For the pain, suffering and hurt of these stolen generations, their descendants and for their families left behind, we say, "sorry." To the mothers and the fathers, the brothers and the sisters, for the breaking up of families and communities, we say, "sorry." And for the indignity and degradation thus inflicted on a proud people and a proud culture, we say, "sorry."

> —Australian Prime Minister Kevin Rudd,
> address to the Australian Parliament,
> February 13, 2008.[1]

With these words, Australia's newly elected Labor prime minister Kevin Rudd apologized on behalf of the nation for the past treatment of Australia's indigenous population. This was a moving and dramatic moment in the country's history, rendered even more so by the twelve-year refusal of the previous Liberal government to take such action. It was reported as the lead story in television and radio news bulletins, on Internet news sites, and on the front pages of the nation's newspapers. With one exception. In the Northern Territory, where a large proportion of Australia's indigenous population resides, coverage of the apology was absent from the front page of the *Northern Territory News*, the main newspaper in the territory's capital, Darwin.[2] Instead, the page carried reports about a car crash involving the son of a local senator and a minister's resignation from the territory's government. There was just a small pointer letting readers know that, inside the newspaper, they could read about the prime ministerial apology.

This was a remarkable omission, by any standards. While assessments of news events are often variable, the national and international response to this event left no doubt that it was the major Australian news development that day. How, then, to explain its treatment by the *Northern Territory News*? Although no public explanation has been offered, the uninspired positioning of the story appears to indicate that those responsible for putting out the paper that day decided that fewer readers would be interested in the topic than in the alternatives. Given that the newspaper's circulation area includes some of what are widely considered to be the more racist elements in Australian society, it seems likely that this was the case, and that a decision was taken not to risk offending them.

In other words, the presentation of a major news event appears to have been significantly influenced by its perceived audience reception. If so, this would hardly be surprising. In common with newspapers around the world, the *Northern Territory News* is having trouble maintaining its readership, and the last thing the paper needed was to risk antagonizing a significant number of readers by giving prominence to material to which they might object.

News as Commodity

The forces that appear to have been at work in this case are common throughout news media. While they operate to varying degrees and in many different ways, such considerations are a fact of life for most media organizations around the world. Historically, most newspapers—and, later, most television and radio services—needed to make money in order to survive, and many of the earliest publications were primarily vehicles for providing merchants with information relating to trade.[3] Most sections of contemporary news media still need to make money, although the greatest returns are no longer on income from subscribers but, rather, income from mass advertising.

> The shift to an advertising rather than subscriber business model, where advertisers "bought" consumers, brought the market into the centre of the frame and [brought] heavy pressure to bear on content. Content became the "bait" to catch readers and viewers for advertisers[,] and audience figures the key to evaluating success.[4]

A key part of this content is news, which has become a commercial commodity even though it does not fit easily into standard economic theory. Reading, watching, or listening to news doesn't diminish someone else's ability to enjoy it, which means news defies "the very premise on which the laws of economics are based—scarcity."[5] Indeed, it is difficult to define what constitutes a basic unit of news—depending on the context, it could be a news story, an article, a program, a bulletin, or a combination of these.

Media organizations today operate in an intensely competitive commercial environment in which market forces exert "an almost irresistible pressure on every activity to justify itself in the only terms it recognizes: to become a business proposition, to pay its own way, to show black ink on the bottom line."[6]

Market forces themselves are neither ethical nor unethical; they make no moral judgments about the commodities to which they apply, operating in the same way with regard to trade in sugar or oranges as for trade in heroin or child pornography.[7] But while they make no moral judgment on news, market forces have ethical implications because they can influence both what is selected as news and the way that news is shaped. The "bottom line" generally demands maximizing ratings and circulation and, through this, revenue from advertising, which means that the information needs of citizens who do not fit the categories desired by advertisers are generally met poorly or not at all. For some media organizations, audience maximization means trying to obtain the largest possible circulation and ratings, while for others it means maximizing the number of readers, listeners, and viewers who possess the income, education, occupation, age, and spending habits considered most desirable by advertisers. The imperative is to retain and consolidate the "right" readers, listeners, and viewers, which means shunning "boring" stories and avoiding alienating audience members, lest they look elsewhere and never return. This helps explain why, in most media, coverage of celebrities and gossip generally outweighs reportage of issues of substance, and why many events capture media attention for a brief period and then, if unresolved or not dramatically changed, drop from media view.

Although such pressures have always existed, the expansion of corporations into most sections of news media has exacerbated the situation. As Stuart Adam explains, "Journalism has always been circumscribed by interests which have reasons for wanting to rein journalists in. The difference now is that the constraining systems are larger and more powerful, and the outcomes potentially more threatening."[8]

Convergence and globalization have strengthened trends towards concentrated media and cross-media ownership. While corporations can bring some positives,[9] the negative consequences of corporate takeovers of news media have been well documented (see, e.g., Bagdikian 1997; McChesney 1999).[10] Such takeovers often include retrenchment of journalists; declining support for more expensive approaches to newsgathering, such as investigative reporting; greater use of material from "sister" outlets; the proliferation of lighter stories about lifestyle, entertainment, and celebrities; and a greater preparedness to use material provided through public and corporate relations.

Corporate expansion across news media has occurred at the same time as rapid technological change. Some idea of the increased pace of this change can be gained from the fact that it took forty years for radio in the United States to gain an audience of fifty million, and fifteen years for the personal computer to reach that number, but a mere four years for the Internet to be regularly used by fifty million Americans.[11] The ethical implications of new media are discussed in more detail in chapter 8, but it is important to understand that the rise of these media has also had implications for the economic context in which journalism is practiced. At one level, the rise of blogging and "citizen journalism" has challenged the very definition of what constitutes a "journalist"; at another, it has challenged the domination by conventional media organizations of the gathering, selection, and presentation of news and information. In some organizations these changes have induced what one commentator has described as "blog terror" because "people are getting their understanding of the world from random lunatics riffing in their underwear, rather than professional journalists with standards and passports."[12] This appears to be something of an exaggeration because media corporations have fought back strongly, responding to the threat posed by new media with everything from online news and journalists' blogs to discussion groups and chat rooms. Indeed, a recent U.S. study by the Scripps Survey Research Center found that newspapers, radio news, local television news, and network television news are used by five or six times as many people as those who use blogs, and that "furthermore, those who use blogs use the mainline media more than the people who do not use blogs."[13] The fact remains, however, that newspaper circulations and television news audiences are largely static or in decline around the world. As Matthew Taylor has observed, "Newspaper sales are falling [and] TV viewing figures are falling because there's a multiplicity of channels and more and more people are developing their own media through the Internet."[14]

Newspapers are the section of news media most threatened by the new technologies, primarily because the conventional newspaper business model has been seriously undermined by the movement of advertising revenue to the Internet, and the preference of an increasing number of readers for accessing their news via the Internet.[15] The consequences are so serious that the prominent British academic, media commentator, and former newspaper editor Roy Greenslade has claimed that "newspapers are dying in the United States and the death knell is also sounding for newsprint in Britain and across the rest of Europe."[16] Having worked in newspapers for four decades, Greenslade has concluded, "We are in the process of moving from one news platform to another. The stagecoach is giving way to the train. The great change does not spell the end of journalism itself."[17]

The key point in relation to this discussion is that news continues to be an important commodity, being bought, sold, and distributed in various forms and by various means among a range of news platforms and consumers. The commodification of news would not matter if it were a product such as detergent or floor polish, but, obviously, news is rather more than this. (For fuller discussion of journalism's purpose and goals, see the essays by Stephanie Craft, in chapter 3, and Sandra Borden, in chapter 4, of this volume.) Society needs news media, Matthew Kieran argues, "to know what is happening and so that we can judge whether our representatives are doing their job, whether the right policies are being pursued, whether we should make representations to government against some policy, and whether true justice is being carried out."[18]

Many non-media corporations have recently relied on the notion of corporate social responsibility as a guide to ethical decision-making, although, because of the special social role of news organizations, a model which specifically acknowledges that role such as social responsibility theory (SRT) appears to be more appropriate.[19] However, while compelling, this model also has problems:

> If the people have a right to know about government business, why
> are the media rather than the government responsible for exercising
> this right? Why should the media watch the governors any more than
> the governed? From what should the media be "free" and what
> should they be "free" to do? Whose duty is it to ensure that the media
> carry out any responsibilities they might have? And to whom are
> individual journalists responsible—their publics, their news sources,
> their editors, their proprietors or, perhaps, themselves?[20]

The answers to these questions are generally grounded in the wider responsibilities of the news media as outlined in SRT. These obligations include servicing the political system by providing information, discussion, and debate on public affairs; enlightening the public so as to make it capable of self-government; and safeguarding the rights of the individual by serving as a watchdog on government.[21] Despite its problems, and recognizing that no model is perfect, a modified SRT provides a useful means of assessing the consequences of the corporatization of news media.

Business and Ethics

Ethical behavior in journalism is the outcome of a complex amalgam of social and other forces. Increasingly, these include factors identified in the field of business ethics, such as competitive pressures, individual values conflicting with organizational goals, personal gain, greed, and managers' values and attitudes. The single most influential factor in setting the ethical agenda in an organization, however, is the behavior of the chief executive and senior management, meaning what they actually do when confronted with ethical dilemmas, rather than what they might say or write about ethics.[22]

The extension of non-journalistic values across much of news media generally has been motivated by the increasing tendency of media corporations to appoint as senior managers individuals who have been trained in management rather than in the professional practice of journalism. This means that they bring different understandings to their role, and these understandings seldom include a deep appreciation of the place of the press in democratic society. The values, ideas, experience, and training that such individuals contribute might be useful for increasing corporate profits, but these qualities are not necessarily conducive to the ethical practice of journalism. This is not to suggest that corporate managers are intentionally unethical or "anti-journalism" but, rather, that traditional journalistic values often suffer a form of collateral damage from the drive to run an efficient business. Some idea of just how removed some business attitudes are from the traditional values underlying journalism can be gained from the observation of the former Australian media executive Cameron O'Reilly:

> In terms of content, there is no doubt that the consumer is more
> promiscuous than ever before, and that the only way to ensure that
> your relationship with him or her is more than a one night stand is to
> make the experience compelling. If all we do is report the news fairly
> and accurately, we haven't got a chance.[23]

Part of the explanation for this situation appears to lie with the view of the world as shaped by management theory. This field has for some years been influenced by stakeholder theory, which focuses on individuals or groups of individuals affected by or able to affect the achievement of an organization's objectives.[24] Stakeholders commonly identified include shareholders, management, employees, customers, suppliers, communities, and the environment. The notion of stakeholders provides an alternative model to the stockholder view of business, meaning the view that investment returns to shareholders have absolute priority over all other considerations. But while the notion of stakeholders is useful for identifying and organizing the multitude of obligations that corporations have to various groups,[25] it has come under mounting criticism in recent years. Damien Grace and Stephen Cohen assert that the notion of stakeholder "can lead you to believe that you have moral responsibilities to any number of 'interested' parties, when in fact there is no particular duty to them simply because they have taken an interest in your activities. An interest is not necessarily a stake."[26]

Among other things, stakeholder theory has been labeled "an ideology which induces managers to bargain directly with particular interests in society in terms which satisfy the managers and the particular stakeholders irrespective of the ethical and cultural basis of the social milieu in which they are situated."[27] Such criticisms raise many questions, some of which are directly relevant to journalism. If a media organization and the journalists who work for it function as "stakeholders" in a given situation, then they risk being compromised when reporting that situation. As Mackey points out, treating journalists as stakeholders can lock them into a special relationship with a particular organization or section of society, thereby eroding their ability to perform a watchdog role in relation to that organization or group, and undermining their responsibility to represent the broader interests of society.

Partly through the influence of theories such as this, many managers have misconceptions about the role of the news media. At the same time, many of them also have misconceptions about ethics, often acquired from the way in which the subject was—or was not—presented to them in management programs or training courses. While such programs and courses generally include some treatment of business ethics, there is considerable variation in course content, the way it is taught and the suitability of those who teach it. There is also an ongoing debate among those who teach business ethics as to whether ethical values and behavior can actually be taught in the first place (see, e.g., Kohlberg and Hersh 1977; Trevino and Brown 2004).[28]

In the wake of the wave of dramatic corporate scandals in the United States late in the last century, debates about business ethics became more intense than ever, and some observers blamed "where careers begin—with management education."[29] Although a number of studies have concluded that education alone cannot address widespread unethical corporate acts,[30] the content of management courses appears to have *some* lasting effect, as argued in a recent paper by the late Sumantra Ghoshal.[31] Ghoshal was professor of strategic and international management at the London Business School, a member of the committee of overseers at the Harvard Business School, and coauthor of a book nominated by the *Financial Times* (UK) as one of the fifty most influential management books.[32] In the paper, he presents a devastating critique of what is taught in business schools, arguing that many of the worst excesses of management have their roots in a set of ideas that emerged from business school academics over the previous thirty years.[33] Ghoshal makes a plea to business academics to think more broadly and inclusively as to what constitutes valuable scholarship, invoking Ernest Boyer's well-known typology of scholarship—the scholarship of discovery (research), the scholarship of integration (synthesis), the scholarship of practice (application), and the scholarship of teaching (pedagogy).[34] In Ghoshal's view, business schools have been dominated by those who excel at the scholarship of discovery (researchers) to the detriment of those who excel at the other forms of scholarship.

He argues that the dominance of research has given impetus to attempts to make business studies a science, and that a direct consequence of these attempts has been the explicit denial of any role for moral or ethical considerations in the practice of management.[35] Instead, most of the disciplines in which management theories are rooted have been penetrated by an ideology that is grounded in a set of pessimistic assumptions about individuals and institutions.

> While the philosophy [of radical individualism] has influenced the
> work of many scholars in many different institutions, its influence on
> management research has been largely mediated by the University
> of Chicago. It is in and through this institution that "liberalism," as
> Friedman called it, has penetrated economics, law, sociology, social
> psychology, and most other core disciplines, yielding theories such as
> agency theory, transaction cost economics, game theory, social

network analysis, theories of social dilemmas, and so on, that we now routinely draw on both radical individualism and Friedman's liberalism to frame our research and guide our teaching.[36]

Ethics does not fit easily into this liberal frame, being viewed largely as an individual concern that should be excluded from social theory. If Ghoshal and his supporters are correct, there may well be consequences for journalism's ethical standards. If ethics is given inadequate treatment in management education, and if those so trained become managers of news organizations, then many journalists are eventually answerable to managers with a limited or nonexistent understanding of ethics. The consequences of such a situation are obvious.

Ways of Responding

The most common device used to bolster journalists' standards around the world is the code of ethics. There has been extended debate as to the real purpose of codes, which have been criticized because they "leave a lot to be desired in terms of implementation and efficiency."[37] However, codes constitute "the bedrock for a shared moral worldview," and it seems obvious that "even a flawed code is preferable to moral chaos."[38] More to the point, perhaps, codes can be a useful device for resisting corporate pressures to behave unethically:

> Such codes have been constructed from an understanding of the best journalistic practices and have evolved not only to guide journalists in the performance of their duties, but to strengthen the ability of journalists and editors to manage relations with business offices and departments of advertising within media companies.[39]

While it is clear that codes have a place in journalism, it is also clear they alone cannot provide the solution to pressures from management. Apart from the problem of enforcement, most codes place the onus for ethical behavior squarely on the shoulders of individual journalists, which reverses the usual direction of corporate authority.[40] In the corporate world, the real power to withstand pressures to behave unethically lies with chief executives and other senior management, not with individual practitioners. Yet journalism's ethics codes seldom, if ever, apply to those in such high positions.

On a more positive note, there are signs that the study of business ethics is becoming more central to the education of aspiring managers. Although the role of journalism in democratic society is generally not part of this education, it is not unduly optimistic to expect that the extension of business ethics will eventually produce some media managers with a greater understanding of the ethical issues faced by journalists. Paradoxically, some hope also lies with the very commercial pressures that have done so much to erode journalism standards in the first place. If journalism is to survive in anything like its current form, it will need to remain in demand by vast numbers of ordinary people, which means it will need to retain credibility with readers, listeners, and viewers. Those who employ journalists will need to support the retention of this credibility or risk further declines in audiences and profits. Thus, even if they would prefer not do so, they may find they have no choice but to back off and allow their journalists to report accurately and ethically.

Any society should support what is best for its citizens overall—and there seems little doubt that what is best for a democratic society is a free press. As stated by the prominent U.S. journalist Davis Merritt, a free society cannot determine its course without three things: "shared relevant information; an agora (that is, a place or mechanism where the implications of that information can be discussed); and shared values (at a minimum, a belief in personal liberty)."[41] At its best, a free news media can provide each of these. To do so, however, does not require unconditional freedom; rather, boundaries are necessary to encourage accurate and ethical reporting because, as Onora O'Neill has stated, "A press that serves rather than damages democracy needs to aim for accuracy in its reporting: its claims should be truthful, even if they cannot be guaranteed to be true."[42]

Finding and reporting the truth has, of course, long been one of the main goals of journalism, and truth telling continues to be the primary justification for journalism. This goal has been challenged by contemporary critiques of traditional theories of truth, especially those grounded in naïve empiricism. At a minimum, though, journalists should strive for what Hillary Putnam calls "rational acceptability," that is, an appeal to coherence rather than correspondence epistemology.[43]

This standard allows one to distinguish true from false characterizations of events and, for journalists, can be summarized as the qualities of accuracy, completeness, fairness, and objectivity (for a fuller discussion, see Richards 2005)[44]. Considering the battering to which the notion of objectivity has been subjected in recent years, it is perhaps necessary to add that "objectivity" in journalism has at least four interpretations. It can mean:

> being non-partisan, in the sense of not advocating a position on controversial issues; maintaining balanced partisanship, as when a newspaper provides a fair representation of opposing partisan viewpoints, either in general or regarding particular issues; maintaining value neutrality, in the sense of stating facts without making value judgments; or not distorting facts and understanding.[45]

The type of press required by democratic society is one that is free to exercise the criteria of rational acceptability. However, to encourage and strengthen them requires appropriate structures, such as O'Neill's suggestion that reporters, editors, and owners be required to declare and disclose conflicts of interest. As she says, "Why should those who work in the media be exempt from the disciplines faced by others working in other powerful organizations?"[46]

Conclusion

In a world of global corporations and the globalization of the practice of journalism, journalism ethics has little choice but to become global.[47] This is not straightforward for many reasons, not least because journalism is a culturally established practice that has developed in the particular historical circumstances of each country where it is practiced.[48] However, ethics can be both universal and rooted in particular contexts, and it is possible to accommodate considerable differences. Some ethical values expressed in different and distinctive ways—such as honesty, trust, integrity, sincerity, loyalty—transcend particular cultures, while others—such as marriage customs, social stratification, and kinship obligations—do not.[49] Accordingly, Grace and Cohen suggest that values that transcend cultures be regarded as primary values, while those that relate to the expression of primary values be regarded as secondary values. Truth telling, understood as rational acceptability, is surely a primary value in journalism.

For going global to be effective, it will be necessary for the awareness and appreciation of journalism's primary values to extend beyond journalism practitioners. As Clifford Christians has argued, we need to increase moral literacy because "moral literacy understands moral behavior in interactive terms, with reporters, advertising executives, script writers and producers and public relations practitioners operating in the same areas as citizens themselves."[50] To this list should be added those who manage media organizations. In the paper discussed earlier, Ghoshal concludes that, to enable students to contribute to building a positive future, it is necessary to reinstate ethical concerns in management practice and in mainstream theory.[51] Precisely what these concerns should be requires negotiation, but the reinstatement of a range of primary values in the field of management seems likely to produce newsroom managers who understand why journalists need to report accurately and ethically. The British wartime leader Winston Churchill once observed that democracy is the worst form of government there is—except for all the others. In a similar vein, journalism is the worst form of communication there is—except for all the others. Despite the corporate context in which much journalism is conducted today, there is cause for cautious optimism that this will continue to be the case for a long time to come.

Notes

1. Kevin Rudd, "Address to the Australian Parliament," ABC News Online, February 12, 2008, http://www.abc.net.au/news/events/apology/text.htm (accessed February 20, 2008).

2. Richard Farmer, "Richard Farmer's political bite-sized meaty chunks," Crikey. com.au, February 13, 2008. Accessed February 14, 2008.

3. Karen Sanders, *Ethics and Journalism* (London: Sage, 2003), 129–131.

4. Sanders, *Ethics and Journalism*, 129.

5. Gillian Doyle, *Understanding Media Economics* (Cheltenham, UK: Edward Elgar, 2006), 10.

6. Christopher Lasch, *The Revolt of the Elites and the Betrayal of Democracy* (New York: Norton, 1995), 97–98.

7. David Croteau and William Hoynes, *The Business of Media: Corporate Media and the Public Interest* (Thousand Oaks, CA: Pine Forge, 2006), 17–26.

8. G. Stuart Adam, "A Preface to the Ethics of Journalism," *Journal of Mass Media Ethics* 19 nos. 3 & 4 (2004): 247–57.

9. For example, after it began publication in 1964, Australia's first national daily newspaper, *The Australian*, was subsidized for almost two decades by other operations within Rupert Murdoch's News Corporation Ltd.

10. See, e.g., Ben Bagdikian, *The Media Monopoly*, 5th ed. (Boston: Beacon, 1997), and Robert McChesney, *Rich Media, Poor Democracy* (Urbana, University of Illinois Press, 1999).

11. Anthony Giddens, "Globalisation," Lecture One, BBC Reith Lectures 1999, BBC Online Network, April 7, 1999. http://news.bbc.co.uk/hi/english/static/events/reith_99/week1/lecture1.htm (accessed May 5, 2008).

12. Michael Kinsley, "Do Newspapers Have a Future?" Time-CNN, September 25, 2006, http://www.time.com/time/magazine/article/0,9171,1538652,00.html (accessed March 22, 2008).

13. Thomas Hargrove and Guido Stempel, "Use of Blogs as a Source of News Presents Little Threat to Mainline News Media," *Newspaper Research Journal* 28, no. 1 (2007): 99–102.

14. Matthew Taylor, "The Perception Gap," *Counterpoint*, ABC Radio, March 3, 2008, http://www.abc.net.au/rn/counterpoint/stories/2008/2176710.htm (accessed March 3, 2008).

15. Roy Greenslade, "Move Over: Journalists Will Have to Share Their Space," Sydney Morning Herald Online, May 1, 2008, http://www.smh.com.au/news/opinion/journalists-to-share-their-space/2008/04/30/1209234954732.html (accessed May 6, 2008).

16. Greenslade, "Move Over."

17. Greenslade, "Move Over."

18. Matthew Kieran, *Media Ethics: A Philosophical Approach* (New York: Praeger, 1997).

19. For a fuller discussion of social responsibility theory, see, e.g., Clifford Christians, Ted Glasser, Denis McQuail, Kaarle Nordenstreng, and Robert White, *Normative Theories of the Media: Journalism in Democratic Societies* (Urbana: University of Illinois Press, 2009); Clifford Christians and Kaarle Nordenstreng "Social Responsibility Worldwide" *Journal of Mass Media Ethics* 19, no. 1 (2004): 3–28; J. Herbert Altschull, *Agents of Power*, 2nd ed. (New York: Longman, 1995); John Nerone, ed. *Last Rights: Revisiting Four Theories of the Press* (Urbana: University of Illinois Press, 1995).

20. Ian Richards, *Quagmires and Quandaries: Exploring Journalism Ethics* (Sydney, University of NSW Press, 2005), 9.

21. Fred Siebert, Thomas Petersen, and Wilbur Schramm, *Four Theories of the Press*(Urbana: University of Illinois Press, 1956).

22. Peter Brokensha, *Corporate Ethics: A Guide for Australian Managers* (Adelaide, Australia: Social Science Press, 1993), 14.

23. Cameron O'Reilly, *The Media Report*, ABC Radio National, September 3, 1998.

24. John Boatright, *Ethics and the Conduct of Business* (New Jersey: Prentice Hall, 2000), 355.

25. Boatright, *Ethics and the Conduct of Business*, 356.

26. Damien Grace and Stephen Cohen, *Business Ethics* (Melbourne, Australia: Oxford University Press, 2000), 59.

27. Steve Mackey. "Misuse of the Term "Stakeholder" in Public Relations," *PRism* 4, no. 1 (2006): 7 http://praxis.massey.ac.nz/fileadmin/Praxis/Files/Journal_Files/2006_general/Mackey.pdf (accessed March 22, 2008).

28. See, e.g., Lawrence Kohlberg and Richard Hersh, "Moral Development: A Review of the Theory," *Theory into Practice* 16, no 2 (1977): 53–59, and Linda Trevino and Michael Brown, "Managing to Be Ethical: De-bunking Five Business Ethics Myths," *Academy of Management Executive* 18, no. 2 (2004): 69–81.

29. Jennifer Merritt, "What's an MBA Really Worth?" *Business Week Online* 22 September 22, 2003, pp. 90–102.

30. See, e.g., Jeri Beggs and Kathy Dean, "Legislated Ethics or Ethics Education? Faculty Views in the Post-Enron Era," *Journal of Business Ethics* 71 (2007): 15–37.

31. Predictably, Ghoshal's paper produced an intense debate, but, significantly, many of those working in the field came out in support of his assessment (see, e.g., the series of articles in *Academy of Management Learning & Education* 4, no. 1 (2005).

32. Sumantra Ghoshal, "Bad Management Theories Are Destroying Good Management Practices," *Academy of Management Learning & Education* 4, no. 1 (2005): 75–91.

33. Ghoshal, "Bad Management Theories," 75.

34. Ernest Boyer, Scholarship reconsidered: priorities of the professoriate. Princeton NJ: The Carnegie Foundation for the Advancement of Teaching, 1990).

35. Ghoshal, "Bad Management Theories," 79.

36. Ghoshal, "Bad Management Theories," 84.

37. Kaarle Nordenstreng, ed., *Report on Media Ethics in Europe* (Tampere, Finland: University of Tampere, 1995), 12.

38. Mike Martin, *Meaningful Work: Rethinking Professional Ethics* (New York: Oxford University Press, 2000), 33.

39. Adam, "Preface to the Ethics of Journalism," 256.

40. John McManus, "Who's Responsible for Journalism?" *Journal of Mass Media Ethics* 12, no. 1 (1997): 5–17.

41. Davis Merritt, *Knightfall: Knight-Ridder and How the Erosion of Newspaper Journalism Is Putting Democracy at Risk* (New York: Amacom, 2005), 17.

42. Onora O'Neill, "Freedom of Speech," *BBC News International Viewpoints*, BBC World Service, December 9, 2007. http://news.bbc.co.uk/2/hi/in_depth/7127423.stm#middle (accessed February 20, 2008).

43. Hilary Putnam, "Fact and Value," in *Pragmatism: A Reader*, ed. Louis Menand (New York: Vintage, 1997), 338–62.

44. For a fuller discussion, see Richards, *Quagmires and Quandaries*, 27–47.

45. M. W. Martin, *Journalistic Objectivity*, in Journalism Ethics: A Reference Handbook, ed. E. Cohen and D. Elliott (Denver: ABC-CLIO, 1997), 54–58. See also the essays by Stephen Ward (ch. 9) and Carrie Figdor (ch. 10) in this volume.

46. Onora O'Neill, "Freedom of Speech."

47. See the essay by Herman Wasserman in chap. 5 of this volume.

48. Martin Conboy, *Journalism: A Critical History* (London: Sage, 2004), 37.

49. Grace and Cohen, *Business Ethics*, 182.

50. Clifford Christians, "The Media and Moral Literacy," *Ethical Space: International Journal of Communication Ethics* 1, no. 1 (2003): 13–19.

51. Ghoshal, "Bad Management Theories," 87.

12

The Decline of the
News Business

Rick Edmonds

A t the December 2001 media week conference for investors, sponsored by
Credit Suisse and staged in the grand ballroom of the Plaza Hotel, Arthur
Sulzberger Jr. led the New York Times presentation team. Business was only
fair after eight months of recession, but Chairman Sulzberger bantered lightly with then CEO Russ Lewis. Putting on his publisher's hat, an exuberant
Sulzberger turned to editorial matters. He bobbed on the balls of his feet at
the podium as he talked about his flagship paper's coverage of the September
11 tragedy and its aftermath, still unwinding in hundreds of "Portraits of Grief"
profiles. "We absolutely own that story," he crowed.

A lot has changed in the years since. The venerable Plaza quit the hotel business and mostly converted to condos. Credit Suisse was one of many investment
houses to drop its newspaper analyst position, and ceded hosting the December
conference to its competitor UBS. Sulzberger doesn't come to these meetings
anymore. His designee, CEO Janet Robinson, is a stern, all-business presenter.
If she speaks of the *New York Times* content at all to investors, it usually is to tout
growth of the luxury-advertiser-driven "T" magazine supplements.

With dismal 2008 results and 2009 expected to be worse still, there is
no bounce left in the industry's step. Clearly, newspapers have entered a
race against time to trim costs as quickly as print advertising revenues arc
tumbling— more than 15 percent year-to-year as the current deep recession
plays out. At the same time, newspaper execs—not exactly guys who cook up
brilliant inventions in their garages—are pressed to experiment to find new,
sustaining revenue streams. Success is by no means assured. Serious discussion
has begun to turn to which prominent metro paper will fail first. Print, some
new media critics say, could be largely a relic by early next decade.

What went so wrong, so fast? The leading edge of the leading problem surfaced at that same 2001 meeting. Jeff Taylor, the founder of Monster.com, had been invited to give a provocative luncheon talk, and obliged, claiming his fast-growing electronic service would bury traditional print job listings. The first afternoon speaker, then Tribune CEO John Madigan, departed from his text and heatedly countered that the industry was just starting to fight back—as it indeed did quite successfully with the copycat CareerBuilder service. Later the Newspaper Association of America (NAA) commissioned a McKinsey Company study to determine how much of the huge help-wanted decline over a decade was recession related and how much was being lost to electronic competitors. When the consultant concluded in April 2005 that much of the business was gone for good and rates were being driven down for what remained, former NAA chairman Tony Ridder denounced the report as a "very shallow and superficial effort."

That lese-majesty denial persisted for several years more in the face of powerful evidence to the contrary. Craigslist blossomed, offering free electronic classified listings for general merchandise, apartment rentals, and autos. Like Monster.com customers, users found they had a wide range of quick and well-targeted choices. Sellers could tout their goods at length and could even include a couple of color photos. Less conspicuously, Realtor.com developed sites that could sort by location and price, plus provide a virtual tour of the property. The print *Auto Trader* had been making inroads in used car listings even before the Internet had cranked up an electronic counterpart. Car manufacturers found success with their own sites that allowed prospective buyers to decide options and ship a new car if they chose. All the while, Google recorded quarter after quarter of explosive growth with search advertising, another drain on dollars that used to go to newspapers and other traditional media.

Classifieds had been nearly the biggest category of advertising for newspapers and by far the most profitable—selling it mainly consisted of taking orders and cashing checks. By the end of 2008 (adjusting for inflation), it had been sliced in half and appeared in freefall. Nearly any transaction for which newspaper classifieds used to be an essential can now be done more cheaply, and often more effectively, with an online competitor.

Still, through 2006 and early 2007, the prevailing view seemed to be, as Ridder put it, that the industry was "under pressure" commercially but that there was no cause for alarm. Industry leaders seemed to think the business would rock along with slow rates of growth but high profitability, making up much of the lost print revenues with online advertising growth or other new ventures. And they put money behind the sunny rhetoric. McClatchy bought Ridder's Knight-Ridder for $6.5 billion in stock and debt in March 2006. The real estate mogul Sam Zell borrowed $13.5 billion to take Tribune Company private in April 2007 and assume its debt. Smaller companies made similar acquisitions at business-as-usual rates.

In the spring of 2007, as the economy gradually moved into recession, negative trends suddenly accelerated and the industry went into something pretty close to a crash. Print ads declined sharply, again mostly in the classifieds, as online growth slowed. Total ad revenue was down 7 percent in 2007 and in the first quarter of 2008. Bad, but it got much worse. The rate of losses doubled to 15 percent or more for the remainder of 2008, as a broad recession slashed ad budgets and put some retail advertisers out of business. Newsprint prices picked a bad time to jump 20 to 30 percent from the previous year. Even with frantic cost-cutting in newsroom head counts and paper use, companies saw profit margins narrow and earnings plummet. And that was average—some metro papers had much higher rates of advertising decline and locked-in union agreements that slowed the cost-cutting. Papers in states such as California and Florida, which had experienced the faux real estate boom mid-decade, tumbled to an especially precipitous thud. Companies that had made big acquisitions between 2004 and 2007 at the prevailing optimistic prices suddenly were pressed to make interest payments and honor other aspects of their debt covenants.

At the outset of 2009, some small-town papers or those in growth communities continue to operate at reduced but comfortable profit margins. For many, though, the wolf is at the door. A number of papers are up for sale with no evident buyer interest. Wall Street has clobbered the publicly traded companies to a small fraction of their value in better times.

What about the Audience?

Since 2004 newspaper circulation has declined. First the losses were in the 0.5 to 1.5 percent range year-to-year. By the end of 2008, the average had risen to 4 to 5 percent. Results at some big metro papers were considerably worse. So isn't the heart of the problem that print newspapers are losing readers, especially young ones, to Internet alternatives? Not exactly.

Audiences at newspaper Web sites cannot be measured in strictly comparable terms to print circulation or readership. But by any measure it has grown steadily. Newspapers can fairly argue that as many people are reading their journalism, in one format or the other, as ever.

Circulation at U.S. papers accounts for only 15 to 20 percent of revenue (at European and Asian papers, the split is typically 50–50). Small declines in circulation revenue are not a big deal financially, especially since there can be savings on paper and delivery expenses. Many papers also eased up on soliciting new subscribers, an expensive proposition, especially after the federal do-not-call rule took effect. Also, print advertising rates do not tightly correlate with circulation gains or losses. Papers may not be able to raise rates as aggressively as they did in the good old days of monopoly pricing power, but they can at least hold the line or add a little for inflation.

Print remains a popular medium for many advertisers, especially if sales prices are relevant, and thus commands a premium rate. Sunday papers, especially, are fat with inserts and coupons, which many readers use to plan their shopping. To a point, this is good news for newspaper organizations. Retail and national advertising are soft but not the same sort of disaster zone as classified.

But the residual strength of print display and insert advertising masks some surprising weaknesses that developed in online advertising at newspaper Web sites. Most people consume online news very differently from how they read a traditional newspaper. Often it is in short sessions, many of which occur at work. So there is not the equivalent of a leisurely spin through the print paper, glancing at ads as you turn the pages.

Conversely, when an Internet user is in a shopping mood, she may go directly to a shopping site like eBay or Amazon, or one more narrowly targeted. News content is redundant to the "man on a mission" seeking shopping information or looking to buy. In fact, it would be viewed as an intrusion and distraction. The reverse is also true—online news consumers may simply be annoyed by the likes of pop-ups, welcome screens, and dancing mortgage ads. This does not mean online adverting is a dud for newspaper organizations—there is a substantial and growing volume, though the growth slowed significantly in 2007 and 2008.

But the ads and news that were so lucratively packaged in the traditional newspaper print business model are, to a large extent, "unbundled" online. Add to that the proliferation of blogs and social media sites, and there is so much generic inventory online that rates, low already, are falling.

For historical and business reasons, news content on the Web, except for specialized financial and professional information, is free. Charging for content drastically reduces traffic, driving advertising rates further down. It also blocks links from Google and other search engines—a side door that brings in more visitors than the front door to a typical newspaper site's home page.

So even as Web traffic builds, the Internet is proving a disappointment for newspapers. As readers migrate to the Web, the company is trading paying customers for free riders in a setting that generates less value for advertisers. For now, online revenues are not building at anywhere near the volume needed to replace the print revenue falling away.

Other News Businesses

Television has not been hit as hard as newspapers because the medium has seen nothing comparable to the classifieds bloodbath. However, local stations and the networks (including their entertainment shows) are losing audiences and advertising to digital alternatives. Automotive is an especially important category for local stations, so they are hurt as dealerships close and domestic automakers flounder.

By 2008, local television news operations were beginning to ape some of the cost-cutting that has become common in newspapers. Not only were staffs reduced, but a number of longtime, highly paid local anchors were let go. Groups of commonly owned stations began pooling graphics and other production functions at a single site. WUSA-TV in Washington, D.C., announced in late 2008 that it would no longer send two-person reporter–camera crews out on stories. Instead, reporters would do their work one-man-band style, setting up the camera then jumping in front of it to do the story.

Looking forward, those in the TV news business share print's apprehension. Advertisers want to move more of their budgets in the years ahead to digital formats. To an extent, some are sticking with traditional media only until they develop more confidence in what works in the new media.

Collateral Damage

Predictably, the newspaper industry's response to plunging revenues has been to scale back costs. Since revenue losses in 2007 and 2008 totaled 20 to 25 percent on average—more at the hardest-hit papers—a little nip and tuck does not do it. Instead, major reductions are occurring throughout the newspaper operation, including outsourcing such major functions as printing and delivery.

What faces outward to the reader, however, is a conspicuous reduction in the space allocated to news (to save on paper) and cuts in news staff, through buyouts and layoffs. Typically, these are targeted at the most senior and expensive reporters and editors. These two forms of cutting are reinforcing. With fewer staff, you don't need as much space to display their work; with less news space, you don't need as many reporters and editors.

There is a reasonably good count of how many news professionals have lost their jobs, but the figures used for comparison are not concurrent. The American Society of Newspaper Editors (ASNE) conducts a yearly employment census. Started decades ago to measure progress in adding more minorities to news operations, the census also yields a total job count. A majority of U.S. newspapers, especially larger ones, choose to participate; totals for the remainder are projected.

According to ASNE's 2007 count, 2,400 fulltime professional news jobs were lost, leaving about 52,600. So the one-year loss was close to 5 percent, and the reduction for the first years of the decade about 10 percent. Although figures for 2008 and the early part of 2009 are not yet available, it is clear the pace and depth of cuts have increased. So it is fair to assume that 20 percent of the industry's news force is gone. Hard-hit papers in San Jose, Philadelphia, Dallas, and Minneapolis, among others, are operating with about half the news staff they once had.

What coverage is being lost? At least four areas have clearly been hit:

Metros have typically cut to the bone any effort to cover more distant suburbs or outlying cities. Papers can still afford to cover their home city council but not one ten miles beyond the city limits. So, for people who live in these places—and there are millions of them—rudimentary government coverage, formerly provided by at least a few professional reporters for the metro, is now hit or miss. A suburban daily or strong weekly might plug the gap, but, just as likely, public business now goes on with no one watching.

Specialty beats have been trimmed way back or shut down. For example, not so many years ago many metro papers had weekly science sections and at least a half dozen knowledgeable reporters. Health and environmental issues still get coverage, but nearly all the rest is gone, except at national papers. In 2008, with stock tables dropped and many freestanding business sections folded into the local report, papers are finding they do not need so many business reporters. Arts criticism—especially the local movie critic—may be ditched as nonessential.

Depleted bureaus in both the statehouse and Washington have become the norm. A reasonably ambitious metro paper used to have a cadre of senior reporters keeping an eye on their congressional delegation and agency news of local interest out of Washington. The statehouse was often the epicenter of high-end, tough-minded watchdog journalism. Bigger papers such as the *Los Angeles Times* and *Chicago Tribune* had big Washington bureaus. All that is more ambition than most can afford these days, especially given a trend to focus on local news as a strategic advantage. A person or two, at best, is all that the typical metro can afford anymore. They trust to the wire services to do the rest.

Most national papers continue to operate foreign bureaus, though most have cut the number of reporters. Regional papers, including such one-time players as the *Boston Globe, Baltimore Sun,* and *Philadelphia Inquirer,* have shut theirs down altogether. What was once a source of vital and varied reporting from abroad is now, at best, the occasional reporting trip to pursue a story of local interest.

The *New York Times, Wall Street Journal,* and *Washington Post* are honorable exceptions to these trends. All have had some cuts in staff and space but still manage intelligent and aggressive reporting on a full range of topics. The *Journal* increased its space and staff for international news after Rupert Murdoch's News Corporation took over. The *Post* produced a model exposé, leading to broad reforms, in its 2007 stories on the shabby treatment that wounded veterans of the Iraq War were receiving at Walter Reed Hospital.

Some observers—such as the respected retired *Los Angeles Times* editor John Carroll—think the numbers tell only part of the story of the ongoing damage.[1] There is also a deep demoralization in the ranks as reporters view the departure of valued colleagues, wonder whether they will be next, and get confusing signals from the top guns in the corner offices.

Looking for good news about news requires some searching, but here are three modestly hopeful trends:

Small and midsized papers, while beginning to take nicks from online competitors and the 2008 recession, are holding readers and advertisers better than the big metros. Often they are the only vehicle for local news and local retail advertising. So their prospects are comparatively bright.

In the Internet age, most staffs are now geared to post stories quickly to the Web. Newspaper Web sites are also enhanced with blogs, reader discussions, audio, and video—all of that an upgrade to what the traditional paper can do. If online advertising perks up, an attractive news report is already in place in many cities.

There have been promising, freestanding online news start-ups in Minneapolis, San Diego, and other cities. They are supported by philanthropy and a member-support model like that of public radio, but so far they lack a mature business model for sustainability. Already, though, they are generating a volume of serious journalism at a fraction of the traditional costs.

On balance, however, the prospect of some major cities losing their only newspaper no longer seems remote. More to the point, what newspapers do to invigorate democracy and informed civil life is melting away, month by month, like the polar ice cap.

So What Will Happen?

A long-range forecast for an industry under intense short-term pressure is perilous.

However, late 2008 and 2009 yield some pretty good models of what will get worse before—*if*—anything gets better.

There will be more cutbacks of space and staff. How much and how many depends on how severe and protracted the recession proves. Newspaper executives were reluctant to make the last round of cuts and are aware of the danger of going too far—that is, leaving the print newspaper, still responsible for bringing home most of the revenue, a shell of itself with little appeal to serious and loyal readers.

So there will be experiments. For example, the *Detroit Free Press, Detroit News*, and some smaller papers are trying to suspend home delivery or eliminate print altogether on certain days. The remaining print editions will be on Sunday or near the end of the week where advertising already is concentrated. They will have some of the bulk and depth readers expect of a print paper. Other days of the week, readers and advertisers will be asked to make do with the online report or with a condensed print version sold on a single-copy basis. The move will yield major savings on paper use and delivery costs. It also constitutes a real-time test of what alternatives readers and advertisers will accept, perhaps reluctantly, as their choices become limited.

Some newspaper companies will seek bankruptcy protection, most likely to reorganize, but in some cases to be sold entirely. The Tribune Company blazed that trail in late 2008 crushed by $13.5 billion in debt that its owner Sam Zell had agreed to pay eighteen months earlier when earnings prospects were better. Generally, companies carrying a lot of debt from recent acquisitions have had trouble making the interest payments and complying with other loan covenants, even if most or all of their individual newspapers are profitable. Most of the newspapers will continue to operate and work toward a more gradual transition to digital news and new revenue streams.

Some papers, though, are flat-out losing money. With little prospect of turnaround anytime soon and a depleted pool of potential buyers, they will close. Untested is whether substantial online alternatives will spring up in those cities once the void in coverage is real and obvious.

For newspaper organizations that do get through, prospects brighten. The recession won't last forever, and some hard-hit advertising categories will bounce back. Already, by late 2008, the cost pressure of high paper and fuel costs had softened.

A potentially important boost could come with partnerships (notably one with Yahoo) to display online ads more widely and target them better. By harvesting information about the interests readers show on site, ads can be directed to likely buyers. Rates increase and newspapers can effectively sell the same display space several times over. The new alliances go directly to fixing what has been most disappointing about newspapers' online advertising to date—comparatively low volume combined with very low generic rates.

There also appear to be opportunities—serving news and advertising to mobile devices, for one, and special editions for download to electronic devices like Kindle—that could yield substantial new revenue streams. Users would pay for content in these formats, and advertisers would pay to reach them— much the way it worked in the allegedly dead traditional newspaper business model.

These are prospects, however, not certainties. The unpalatable alternative is that both news consumers and advertisers will accelerate their movement to digital options. That would leave professional journalists with more limited and untested venues in which to do their work and get paid. It would also leave much of the United States scrambling to replicate the vanished benefits of a once-vibrant press.

Notes

1. Personal communication, February 2008.

13

Covering a World That's Falling Apart, When Yours Is Too

Martha Steffens

B etween falling media revenues and the global financial crisis, the world in autumn 2008 had become topsy-turvy for journalists. The Dow Jones Index had lost $1 trillion in just one week, and the newspaper industry was in such disarray that fifty media CEOs huddled in a closed-door "crisis summit" to attempt to resuscitate the industry and stem the tide of declining ad revenues and resulting journalist layoffs.

Television ratings and news readership soared as panicked Americans turned to journalists for any scrap of information. Should they take what's left of their money out of the stock market? Renegotiate a mortgage that's more than their house is worth? How can they protect their jobs in a time of massive layoffs by U.S. companies?

Journalists had a front-row seat for the crisis, interviewing weeping home-foreclosure families and fumbling to find new ways to describe another staggering day on Wall Street, all while worrying about their own investments and employment future.

Business journalists were in a tightening vise. Their expertise was in high demand, but their numbers were dwindling, as reporters and editors were laid off or took buyouts. Business sections at papers like the *Allentown (Pa.) Call* and *Honolulu Advertiser* disappeared altogether because banks and investment houses weren't buying ads.

In those disheartening times, it became usual for the board of directors of the Society of American Business Editors and Writers (SABEW) to have a "gut-check" at the beginning of each meeting.

The SABEW board members spanned the range of those who report on financial and economic matters for newspapers, wire services, broadcast, magazines, and Web sites. Each took a turn, at the twice-annual meetings of the board, to describe the newsroom mood and pending changes.

The reports from the newspapers staffers were, at first, merely sad, but as the months wore on, horrific. First, stock-listing pages vanished. Then, whole special sections and, with them, groups of reporters. And then the business section itself became mere pages behind the sports section, and once-prized columnists and top editors were shown the door.

It became so bad that personal finance columnist Gail MarksJarvis of the *Chicago Tribune* penned a special advisory guide for members on how to evaluate a buyout, or what to do if laid off.[1]

The weekly business journals and wire services fared better. They were the glimmering exceptions picking up readership (and staff) as local papers pared down business coverage. But then the great Wall Street tsunami of 2008 even had those media running for high ground. With financial services in the dumper, Bloomberg News and Dow Jones Newswires weren't selling as many services, and the hiring climate became downright chilly. Covering the meltdown itself was exhausting.

One FOXBusiness reporter wrote on his Facebook site that after covering the freefall of the markets in late September 2008, he went back to his apartment and cried. A Bloomberg reporter dusted off her résumé. Though her job was secure, she just couldn't face spending another day riding, and reporting on, the market roller coaster.

The decline in market value was just another nail in the coffin of publicly held media companies. They'd already been buffeted by higher delivery costs; advertisers were shredding contracts, and consumers decided that if they weren't buying a latte at Starbucks, then they weren't buying a newspaper either.

In November 2008, SABEW posted dire news on its BizBuzz job column about recent mass layoffs at the *Kansas City Star*:

> Gene Meyer, the longtime personal finance writer at the *Kansas City Star* who left the paper last month amid its downsizing, plans a Web site to continue reporting personal finance news and trends. Also leaving the business desk during the downsizing was Jennifer Mann, an advertising writer who joined the paper in 1983, and Bob Cole, another reporter.[2]

Admittedly, the anxiety level became so high that you could just hear Scotty from *Star Trek* shouting from the engine room in his trademark brogue: "Captain, we cannae take anymore . . . she's gonnae blow!"

In these overheated newsrooms-cum-boilerrooms, we revisit the ethical questions: Do financial pressures lead to ethical lapses? Does workload pushed onto shrinking staffs lead to cutting corners? Do job-loss anxiety or low salaries tempt journalists to court jobs from the very companies they cover?

Just two months before, a group of business editors and reporters chatted in roundtable format with Steve Buttry, a trainer for the American Press Institute. Buttry, now also executive editor for the *Cedar Rapids Gazette*, was conducting a training session in Kansas City on ethics and technology. One midlevel newsroom editor admitted the quest for newspaper revenue—any revenue—led her to seek out Web or print projects that could garner advertising dollars. "Two years ago, I'd never have done that," she said. Clearly, the thought of losing more staff, versus finding the dollars to keep them, has won out. Her comments resonated with colleagues, who nodded in silent agreement.[3]

Of course, when pressed, most of us think we would still be in firm grasp of our ethics even if we were exhausted from chasing down the revenue bus. When money is a consideration, doesn't it always compromise our independent judgment? Or is that merely a virulent subterfuge since commercial interests have always influenced content in the history of ad-supported media? Food sections, chock full of recipes, were created by newspaper publishers to wrap the midweek food ads. Luxury advertisers needed more sports content, so hours of golf tournaments now air to meager but affluent audiences.

During journalism's golden age of the late 1970s through the early 1990s, newsroom budgets swelled as plentiful retail ads served the burgeoning consumer culture. It was easier for business staffs to shun freebies sent by eager PR people and for editors to shrug at the occasional ad boycotts from angry car dealers. Aggressive codes of ethics became the norm, with the biggest and best news organizations such as the *New York Times* even suggesting that what your spouse did for a living could color your judgment. Most business journalists refused to take even a cup of coffee from a source, much less a ride on the corporate jet to visit the new factory in Mexico. Journalists were content with flying the ethical flag and seemed to willingly forgo the forbidden active involvement in buying and trading individual stocks, trusting that their retirement investments were safe in 401K mutual funds. But that changed in the financial crisis of October 2008, when on-air news presenters and print reporters palpably grieved over their lost nest eggs.

Freelancers have always been the canary in the ethical coalmine. Living from paycheck to paycheck, they had to mix higher-paying industry work with journalism. One Midwestern freelancer, who specialized in covering the insurance industry, knew she was flirting with disaster by continuing to earn money on both sides of the fence. "I'd love to be able to stop [working for the insurance companies], so I could really write about them," she said.

And with tighter budgets and smaller staffs, all media are using more freelance work, making it even tougher to maintain a consistent approach to ethical standards. For those journalists who still populate desks in emptying newsrooms, doing "more with less" has turned into doing "less with less"—cutting time spent on stories, and forgoing costly editing. Tighter budgets, too, often mean the hiring of younger (cheaper) and less experienced journalists. And what about the anxiety effect? When reporters feel the breeze of a swinging ax coming toward them, doesn't it provoke a survival instinct? Or will reporters take the high road, and choose to leave before they choose to rationalize unethical behavior, or even worse, to engage in self-censorship? After all, you could be applying to your sources for a job when you lose yours.

When SABEW members rewrote their ethics code in 2007, members attending a conference in Anaheim responded to several ethical dilemmas. One was this:

> For the last four years you've covered tourism. There's a high-paying PR job open. A mutual friend tells you that he hears the job is yours if you apply. Do you:
>
> a. ignore the comment and keep on doing your job,
> b. tell your editor about the rumor, even though you might get pulled from the beat, or
> c. ask how much the job pays before deciding what to do?

An overwhelming number—62 percent—chose the last one, a clear sign that self-interest was paramount.

We already know that in areas where the salaries of business journalists are low, such as Africa, Eastern Europe, Russia, and China, the practice of paying journalists for stories is thriving. In Russia, the tradition of *zakazukha*, or paying for publicity, runs the spectrum of companies paying for coverage to reporters extorting businesses by threatening to write negative stories if not paid. In China, as in other parts of Asia, the "red envelope" phenomenon—where reporters are "compensated" for their expenses just for attending press conferences—continues without much comment. For the former *Shanghai Daily* reporter Martin Guo, walking an ethical tightrope meant showing up late for press conferences. He thereby avoided the handout line for the red envelopes without insulting his generous hosts.[4]

Outside of the Great Depression, there's never been a worse time in U.S. journalism. The chaos in the newsrooms, and on Wall Street, prompts us to hope that journalists won't adopt an "end of the world" mindset. As we're packing bags to change careers, let's hope that we don't jettison all our ethics while running for the door.

Notes

[Editor's Note: Some interview subjects have not been identified so as to protect confidentiality.]

1. Marks Jarvis, Gail, "So You've Been Laid Off or Taken the Buyout? Here's What You Do Next," July 1, 2008, http://www.sabew.org/news/2008/92-planningahead.htm.Accessed November 2, 2008.

2. Chris Roush, managing editor, SABEW.org, http://www.sabew.org/news/2008/114-BizBuzzNovember2008.htm. Accessed November 10, 2008.

3. Personal communication, September 2008.

4. Personal communication, November 2008.

PART VI

Privacy

Introduction

Shortly after I took my current job, there was a horrific accident in which a teenage driver was trapped in her burning Volkswagen Beetle. Lois Henry, a young reporter recently hired by the *Bakersfield Californian*, happened upon the scene within moments of the crash. She, along with other motorists, helplessly watched the poor girl's agonizing death.

Unlike the others, though, and being a well-trained reporter, Henry broke out her pad, took careful notes, began interviewing witnesses and emergency personnel, and called for a photographer. Her powerfully written front-page story the next day, with photo, described in graphic detail the girl's final moments. The story also incited a high number of complaints, most of which voiced displeasure at being confronted with something so graphic over their morning Cheerios. Others worried about the harm caused to the girl's loved ones.

Henry, now an assistant managing editor for the *Californian*, was coincidentally scheduled to talk to my media ethics course a few weeks later. No surprise, much of the conversation centered on the accident story. She was quite proud of her reporting, of her ability to set aside her own emotional response to accurately convey the scene's horror.

Most of the students focused on the "yuck" factor, on how distasteful the coverage was, along with fears of added harm to the family. Henry was appreciative of both concerns but gave the two standard journalistic answers: the deontological, "we have the right to cover and the public has a right to know," and the consequentialist, "if this story motivated even one driver to be more careful, then those harms are well-justified."[1]

Henry was, however, pretty flabbergasted at my main concern, that the story invaded the girl's privacy. "How could it?" she asked. "It occurred on a public street, in full view of dozens of people." She then accurately quoted California law, which says if the information in question is visible from a public area without technological enhancement (e.g., telephoto lens), one does not invade privacy by viewing, photographing, or disseminating it.

Henry is now a terrific reporter and columnist—smart, reflective, insightful, curious, and a great writer—all the qualities one could hope for in a journalist. She also embodies the traditional journalistic ethos—"Get the story!"—as reflected in her comments, then and now, on the accident story: moral directives on privacy, as opposed to legal ones, are too subjective, and journalistic activities are both too time-constrained and too important to spend time in the street pondering moral or definitional niceties. The law, as representative of well-established public sentiment, provides perfectly good guidance.

All good answers, and all also a moral copout. In Cliff Christian's words, "Legal prescriptions are an inadequate foundation for the news business. Privacy is not a legal right only, but a moral good. For all of the sophistication of case law and tort law in protecting privacy, legal definitions do not match today's challenges."

There is, in fact, widespread agreement in the philosophical and ethics literature on the correct definition of privacy, and it differs considerably from the legal. In Candace Gauthier's language, privacy entails "control over access to oneself and to certain kinds of information about oneself." Christians agrees, quoting two well-known but philosophically divergent scholars (Sissela Bok and Alan Westin): "Privacy is the condition of being protected from unwarranted access by others—either physical access, personal information, or attention" and "the claim of individuals, groups, or institutions to determine . . . when, how, and to what extent information about them is communicated to others." In all three definitions, control—over one's body and legitimate property and over information about oneself—is the essential characteristic. Unlike the legal approach, while location may sometimes be incidentally relevant, it is anything but a central feature. Should I autonomously choose to dance the chicken dance in the local shopping mall, I can hardly complain when that information is later shared by and with others. Should one, however, be forced at gunpoint to do so, that is, when we are thrust, beyond our control into a personally revelatory circumstance, we should not be further victimized by a privacy invasion.

What happened to that poor girl would thus surely qualify as a private moment, and it should have been her, or her surviving surrogates,' right to determine who should have access to information about her agonized final moments.[2] While they cannot practically preclude immediate witnesses, they should have a prima facie right to veto wider dissemination.

The "prima facie" qualifier is, though, key to this conclusion. In my experience, too many reporters conflate the *definitional* question with the *justificatory* one. Determining whether an event qualifies as private is only the beginning of the analysis. Since, like all rights, privacy is not absolute, it can be, often should be, overridden by other moral concerns. Take an obvious example: Parents have a strong right of privacy in their child-rearing practices, but that right should be overridden upon evidence of abuse. Their right to privacy is outweighed by the child's right to safety. Similarly, access to an elected official's private financial activities is generally justified by her constituents' right to know how her governmental decisions might be correspondingly affected.

Determining whether a given case represents such justified privacy invasion is the hard work of ethics, hard work that first necessitates a thorough explication of privacy's moral importance: Why do humans value it so; what role does it play in the fulfillment of a rich human life?

Gauthier and Christians address these questions in a nicely complementary way. Gauthier's approach more closely aligns with the traditional liberal view: "Privacy is essential for our sense of ourselves as persons and as self-determining moral agents." It is a key means by which humans develop and maintain the autonomous ability to establish life goals and projects, to order values, and to form intimate relationships.

Christians's communitarian position begins with such relationships: "Human identity is constituted through the social realm . . . we know ourselves primarily as whole beings in relation." Since such relations are largely defined by their degree of intimacy, privacy control is essential. Think about how uncomfortable you feel when someone you barely know reveals a close intimacy or, by contrast, when you learn through a mutual, but mere, acquaintance that a dear friend has made a life-altering decision. In the former case, there's a strong sense of, "oh, bleh, too much information," while in the latter it may elicit a feeling of betrayal: "Didn't you trust me enough to tell me?"

These, again complementary, perspectives reveal privacy to be a profound value, vital to confirming our status as autonomous, social beings. They also thereby reveal the tough task of ethically weighing values—privacy versus the other rights or goods attached to a story. Put another way, they reveal why a facile appeal to pat answers—"the law allows it" or "the public has a right to know" or "privacy trumps all"—will too often result in real moral harm.

Gauthier and Christians provide, thus, a method for helping reporters resolve real cases. Gauthier uses a utilitarian-tinged version of Elliott and Ozar's SMA (Systematic Moral Analysis), while Christians provides a practical application of communitarian norms and ideals.

Their arguments also give the lie to another facile and all-too-common journalistic belief—that public figures enjoy no privacy right. The short version of both authors' view: being a public figure does not negate one's personhood. Celebrities often choose to forfeit control over some personal information for career gain, and public good often justifies the revelation of activities or information public officials might like to keep to themselves. But neither reason creates a free-for-all; one must still determine whether any particular revelation of information is ethically justified—either due to the person's choice (thereby nullifying its status as private) or to a more compelling moral good.

A final important point: The sorts of information over which each of us wishes to have control vary widely. One way of getting at those differences is by working through an exercise such as the one below. That you and your classmates will undoubtedly rank some of these differently is part of the point; respect for privacy dictates *you* get to determine what counts. Others must respect those choices or have a compelling moral justification to intrude.

Privacy Exercise

On a scale of 1 to 5 indicate how upset you would be if the following information were revealed about you (1 = couldn't care less; 5 = royally ticked off).

1. How you did on your last quiz.
2. What score you received on your last major research paper.
3. What you had for lunch today.
4. Details of your first sexual experience.
5. How much money you made last year.
6. How you've decorated your home.
7. Images of you partially clothed.
8. Details of your religious beliefs.
9. Your sexual orientation.
10. Images of the mess in your car.
11. Your bank account number.
12. Details of your most recent sexual experience.
13. Images of you having sex.
14. Details about conflicts with your family.
15. Images of you in the bathroom.
16. Details about your most embarrassing childhood moment.
17. Images of you nude as a baby.
18. Images of you, in a public setting, breaking down in profound grief.
19. Images of you, in a public setting, expressing great joy.
20. Details of the most negative work (or academic) review you've ever received.
21. How you ranked this survey.

Notes

1. The *Californian* is best known in ethics circles for its decision, in 1986, to print the now infamous "drowning photo," showing a young boy in a half-zipped body bag lying at the feet of his anguished family. The photo was on the front page of the

Sunday paper, in column three, half above the fold. The paper received a record number of phone calls, including a building-clearing bomb threat. Bob Bentley, then executive editor, acknowledged his own poor judgment for putting it on the front page but also defended the decision on consequentialist grounds: "If it motivated one family to more closely watch their children. . . ." (Gauthier discusses this case, in chap. 15 of this volume; for a full commentary from two of this volume's authors, see http:// commfaculty.fullerton.edu/lester/writings/what_is_news.html [accessed October 21, 2008]).

2.   I use "right" language here for stylistic ease, with such usage intended to incorporate both its traditional, liberal meaning and more contemporary, virtue-based "moral good" characterizations.

14

The Ethics of Privacy

Clifford G. Christians

In nearly every survey of public opinion and the media, privacy is a premiere issue if the press wishes to main its credibility. The laws safeguarding privacy are impressive, but legal prescriptions are an inadequate foundation for the news business. Privacy is not a legal right only but a moral good. For all of the sophistication of case law and tort law in protecting privacy, legal definitions do not match today's challenges. Merely following the letter of the law presumes the law can be determined accurately. There are several reasons that establishing an ethics of privacy that goes beyond the law is important in the gathering and distribution of news.

First, the law that conscientiously seeks to protect individual privacy excludes public officials. While the body of law developed to date condemns intrusion on personal matters, it also allows the exposure of all secrets bearing on public concern. In general, the courts have upheld that political personalities cease to be purely private persons, in addition to ruling that First Amendment values take precedence over privacy considerations. Court decisions have given the media extraordinary latitude in reporting on public persons.[1] Even falsehoods relating to official conduct have been protected, unless made with actual malice or reckless disregard of the facts. Though uncertainties exist, the Supreme Court typically chooses not to curtail the press's freedom to provide indispensable service to democratic life. The press has thus been granted the legal freedom to treat elected officials unethically. Though the law does not explicitly rule out falsehood, innuendo, and exaggeration—or invasions of privacy—human decency and basic fairness do.

Second, the press has been given great latitude in defining newsworthiness. People who are exposed to the public eye by events, even unwittingly, are generally classified with elected officials under privacy law. The courts have ruled that material is newsworthy because a newspaper or station carries the story.[2] But the meaning of newsworthiness is susceptible to trendy shifts in news values and often is adjusted when competition for markets is fierce. Additional determinants are needed to distinguish gossip and voyeurism from information necessary to the democratic decision-making process.

Third, legal work on privacy begs many questions about the relationship between the self and society. For democratic political theory, the relation between the individual and the collective is typically understood as too complex for legal analysis; the relationship must thus be reduced and narrowed for legal conclusions to be drawn. Professor Thomas Emerson's classic summary is commonly accepted:

> The right to privacy attempts to draw a line between the individual
> and the collective. It seeks to assure the individual a zone in which to
> be an individual, not a member of the community. In that zone he
> can think his own thoughts, have his own secrets, live his own life,
> reveal only what he wants to the outside world. The right of privacy,
> in short, establishes an area excluded from the collective life, not
> governed by the rules of collective living.[3]

Shortcuts and easy answers arise from boxing off these two dimensions. Glib appeals to "the public's right to know" are a common way to cheapen the richness of the private–public relationship. Therefore, sensitive journalists who struggle with these issues in terms of real people, put more demands on themselves than only considering what is technically legal. They realize that ethically sound conclusions cannot emerge unless various privacy situations are faced in all their complexities.

From a communications perspective, this argument for an ethics of privacy beyond the law entails a specific definition of private life. According to Sissela Bok, "Privacy is the condition of being protected from unwarranted access by others—either physical access, personal information, or attention."[4] In Alan Westin's terms, privacy is "the claim of individuals, groups, or institutions to determine for themselves when, how, and to what extent information about them is communicated to others."[5] Privacy is not merely a legal right but a human condition or status in which humans, by virtue of their humanness, control the time, place, and circumstances of communications about themselves. A private domain gives people their own identity and unique self-consciousness within the human species; such a domain is a precondition for developing a healthy sense of personhood.

Democracies as a system of rule by the people (*demos*) distinguish themselves in these terms. Democracy is inconceivable without the presumption that human self-identity as one's own possession is foundational. Legally, it means that citizens have freedom from government control over what they themselves control. As Louis Hodges notes, "Historically, it is clear that totalitarian societies use high visibility—the near absence of privacy—as a major ingredient to produce a homogenous and servile populace. . . . One who has no privacy, who is completely open, is readily coerced."[6]

Because privacy is embedded in our humanness, it is fundamentally moral in character. Its health or violation harms or injures the human species as a species. Privacy as a moral good is nonnegotiable because controlling our life's core is essential to our personhood. However, while unalterable, privacy cannot be an absolute since we are cultural beings with responsibility in the social and political arena: We are persons; therefore we need privacy. We are social beings; therefore we need public information about each other. Since we are individuals, eliminating privacy would eliminate human existence as we know it; since we are social, elevating privacy to absolute status would likewise render human existence impossible.

For work in communication ethics, the definition of privacy as control over communication about oneself is of particular importance. This definition also sharpens our understanding of the ethics of privacy in this revolutionary era when the technologies of public communication are being transformed. In the digital age of networking, search engines, computer bases, cyberspace, mobile phones, MySpace and iPod, establishing a credible ethics of privacy is especially urgent. The issues have been articulated to date primarily in terms of print and broadcasting. But massive storage capacities, global transmission online, code composites, and electronic intervention make privacy protection increasingly fragile and unenforceable. Because digital intrusion has been made a wide-ranging public issue, the ethical framework ought to be commensurate in scope. A credible ethics of privacy thus needs to be rooted in the common good rather than in individual rights. And with this communitarian turn, privacy concerns in society open up beyond those centered on journalism, as I will discuss at the end of this chapter.

The Common Good

The common good has a long pedigree in political philosophy. For example, Aristotle's "common interest" is the basis for distinguishing defensible constitutions in the people's interest from illegitimate ones on the rulers' behalf.[7] For Locke, "the good of the people," along with peace and safety, are the ends of political society.[8] Rousseau understood "the common good" as the object of the general will and the end of the state, in contrast to "particular wills."[9] In Habermas, discourse in the public sphere must be oriented "toward mutual understanding" while allowing participants "the communicative freedom to take positions on validity claims."[10] Despite differences on the precise content of the common good and how to promote it, there is a core meaning that the welfare of all citizens, rather than that of factions or special interests, should be served impartially. Moreover, it is a normative principle, not just the majority results of an opinion poll or voting as argued by positivistic social science. The common good cannot be understood statistically, but as Bernard Diggs concludes, it is a "fundamental concept of social morality."[11] And in terms of the privacy under discussion here, asking journalists or government officials or data companies to respect it is little more than moralistic pleading, unless such demands are grounded in a defensible notion of the common good.

In mainstream legal terms, privacy is an individual right. While not included per se in the U.S. Constitution, since *Griswold v. Connecticut* the Court has considered it necessary to guarantee other rights. The Warren and Brandeis law review article in 1890 that launched the legal understanding of privacy ever since is appropriately titled, "The Right of Privacy."[12] The liberal democracy that this legal perspective presumes entails a commitment to individual autonomy as the first principle. "Each person," says John Rawls, has an "equal right to the most extensive system of basic liberties" compatible with similar liberty for all.[13] From the classical liberalism of Locke and Mill to the typical thinking on the Supreme Court today, individual liberties have priority. We are constituted as selves antecedently, that is, in advance of our engagement with others. As Stephen Mulhall and Adam Swift remind us, a sense of communal commonness describes a possible aim of individuated selves but is "not an ingredient of their identity."[14] A liberal politics of rights presumes that people are distinct from their ends; that is, persons are separate from their conceptions of the good. Individual identities, in other words, are established in isolation from history and culture. Ignoring the importance of goods held in common, the political community is merely "a system of cooperation between mutually disinterested individuals."[15]

Rights, as understood from this perspective, provide no conceptual apparatus for coping with the intolerance that flourishes when settled traditions turn cold. When faced with the need for broadly shared values as societies fragment and break down, rights language is mute. Appealing to asocial and ahistorical rights tends to justify selfishness and buys the freedom to be ourselves at too dear a price. In contrast, the Canadian philosopher, Charles Taylor, emphasizes the possibility and importance of a constitutive bonding to goods. The human preoccupation with life's worth and meaning is best understood as situating ourselves in relation to moral goods in common rather than to political formations. Our sense of the good is woven into our lives as we relate to others.[16]

In contemporary forms of social democracy—either its participatory or deliberative forms—the community is understood to be logically prior to persons. Human identity is constituted through the social realm. In this communitarian perspective, our selfhood is not fashioned out of thin air. We are born into a sociocultural universe where values, moral commitments, and existential meanings are either presumed or negotiated. Social systems precede their occupants and endure after them. Therefore, morally appropriate action intends community. Unless our freedom is used to help others flourish, our own well-being is negated. Contrary to the Lockean dualism between individuals and society, we know ourselves primarily as whole beings in relation. Rather than paying lip service to the social nature of the self while presuming a dualism of two orders, human freedom is interlocked with communal well-being. Some forms of association are authoritarian, hierarchical, exclusionary, or gender-biased. Instead of insisting on my individual autonomy within them, we ought to call ourselves to active participation in articulating a common good and mutuality in implementing it. As Craig Calhoun insists, "We should build the conditions of public life so that publics, always in the process of making themselves, might also make themselves good."[17]

There is another way to describe a legitimate common good that can serve as the ground of ethics of privacy. The common good entails obligations to one another. Liberal theory claims that this obligation results from a recognition of the rights of others and a voluntary contract to respect them. The assumption is that political obligation is self-assumed, a commitment into which we enter freely. In the liberal heritage of contract theory, communal obligation is unproblematic. Through the voting process, individuals decide for themselves how to order their obligations and offer their consent. In Locke's version of tacit consent, an individual's acceptance of community benefits gives rise to obligations. Using schools or highways, for example, obligates citizens to the government that builds and maintains them.

Despite hints at the importance of community in Locke and other classical liberals, their emphasis was clearly on the individual. The communitarian approach represents a reversal of that emphasis and is thereby a kind of starting over intellectually.[18] We assume obligations to others because we consider them to be distinctive as our own species. In acknowledging their human dignity, we carry an obligation to treat them accordingly. Consenting humans freely create their own relationships on the grounds that the dignity of the other warrants them. Thus, obligations are not directed primarily to the state, but to one another. Duties are constituted by the presumption of dignity, and therefore are owed to fellow members of institutions and participants in social practices. The primal notion of human dignity is the basis of moral agency. All meaningful action is for the sake of community building. Unless I use my freedom to help others flourish, I deny my own well-being. John Macmurray argues that since the relationship among beings with dignity "constitutes their existence as persons," it follows that a "morally right action is [one] which intends community."[19] In other words, the common good is accessible to us only in personal form; it has its ground and inspiration in human being itself, rather than in contract. The reciprocity it considers essential for community existence is itself built on the assumption of a human dignity in which we regard others as basically like ourselves.

General Morality

An ethics of privacy inscribed in the common good does not merely add a moral dimension to the mainstream view centered on legal rights. It builds its ethics in distinctive terms from the ground up and the inside out. Specifically, this means that the ethics of privacy is constructed within the general morality rather than within professional ethics per se. Instead of appealing to the apparatus of professional codes and practitioner conventions, the ethics of privacy ought to arise from and be accountable to the general morality. How the ethics of privacy works itself out within communal values ought to be the focus, not first of all what practitioner norms dictate. The ultimate standard for media professionals in the case of privacy is not role-specific prescriptions but the general morality.

Certainly, professional roles require some special norms. Physicians have role-specific obligations to patients, and lawyers to clients, and reporters to sources. Special duties exist when their recognition has better moral consequences than would be true in refusing to recognize them. But what is penultimate ought not be made one's final and all-inclusive appeal. Mass media organizations are institutions of power whose decisions and policies can be self-serving. Practitioners often turn defensive when criticized. Competition and careerism typically cloud the application of professional codes or ethical guidelines. Sometimes following canons of professional practice allows self-defined exceptions for the professional as expert.[20] Rather than refining professional codes of ethics, the challenge for journalists, as for all professionals, is the moral life as a whole—no harm to innocents, truth telling, keeping promises, beneficence, gratitude, reparations for wrong actions. With this focus, reporters operate in the same arena as their readers and viewers, rather than being seen as distant and preoccupied with the self.

Giving priority to the general morality and making professional ethics derivative from it turns the issue of privacy on its head. Instead of a bevy of rules and constraints that journalists use to determine whether they are violating privacy or not, the issue is whether the victims consider journalists' behavior invasive. Instead of thinking in professional terms, reporters shape their perspective in terms of the people's perceptions. The ethics of privacy is fundamentally a citizens' ethics, understood and implemented by professionals as human beings first of all, not as practitioners. On an elementary level, journalists will need to distinguish gossip, pandering, innuendo, exaggeration, and falsehood from news. These are minimalist tasks involved in all newsgathering and dissemination; that is, determining newsworthiness by separating what the public wants to know from what it needs to know. But the overall ethics of privacy, its formulation and implementation, has the general morality as its axis. The common good is the alpha and omega, rather than professional considerations the beginning and end. Public journalism is an analogue—journalists living with the public and interacting with their ideas will understand privacy and act on it, rather than be narrowly preoccupied with internal prescriptions from the newsroom.

Hence the formal criterion for the ethics of privacy: since human dignity entails control of private life space, information is communicated about human beings to others if and only if a reasonable public considers it permissible in terms of the common good.[21] By way of contrast, Hodges summarizes the formal criterion of the mainstream view rooted in journalistic interests: "It is just for a journalist to violate the privacy of an individual if and only if information about that individual is of overriding public importance and if the public need cannot be met by other means."[22] The common-good version eliminates entirely the claim to "overriding public importance" as determined by journalists. Certainly "overriding importance" prevents journalists from feeding the public's curiosity and prurient interests. But the prerogatives here belong to the journalist instead of with the public. Journalism's self-interested definition of newsworthiness, rather than the common good, becomes the standard. Similarly, journalists may have an understanding with their sources that all information will be treated confidentially, but then change their minds when they come under pressure and conclude that the public has a right to know this privileged material after all.[23] Whereas we agree with the general morality that we ought to keep our promises, canons of professional practice, in this case, allow an exception for the journalist as expert. While the decision to disclose may yield a beneficial result in the short term, insisting on exceptions undermines the press's ability in the long term to serve as the agent of democratic flourishing. In terms of democracy's very definition, the credibility of its institutions, such as the press, depends on their adhering to the same standards as the public they are said to serve.

Application

Privacy is a complicated domain, and the gains made to date in the law and in ethics have evolved over more than a century. Starting over intellectually cannot produce an immediate set of policies and practices. Here are five areas in which an ethics of privacy based on the common good stimulates our thinking and action.

(1) Innocent victims of tragedy. We should report zero about them unless for their own reasons they give permission to publish. This category is singled out for illustration since it is often regarding innocent victims of tragedy that the "public significance" criterion creates too many exceptions. In a common-good ethics, there are no exceptions for any human beings in tragic circumstances as human beings. The "overriding consideration of public interest" as

determined by the journalist does not exist. Whether or not the persons in grief or distress are elected officials or public persons, celebrities or temporary heroes, or ordinary citizens, they exclusively control their life space. Families of firemen killed on duty should not be covered unless at their request. Reporters at a burning home leave the sufferers alone; they tell the story without interviewing or filming the victims. The fact that readers and viewers are attracted to the intimate details of human misery has no salience. As the classic story of the Good Samaritan makes clear, flesh-and-blood humans have preference over abstract categories. Real people have first priority over such abstractions as the public, audience, readers, and viewers. Innocent victims totally and categorically make the decision whether their grief is shared outside their own communities of intimacy.

Obviously "innocence" is open to dispute. Criminals violate the common good and threaten communities rather than find their identity within them. Their actions and thinking as criminals therefore do not warrant the exceptionless protection of the innocent. But criminals do not deny their humanity altogether and as raw meat have no life space to control. The common good still sees delinquents as members of the species and interacts with them constructively, as in the classic film, "Dead Man Walking." "Rejecting the sin but not the sinner," "think the best of people," and "innocent until proven guilty" have become clichés, unfortunately, but in their own way represent the common-good perspective.

(2) National security and surveillance. In the United States, the goal of the Department of Justice after September 11, 2001, was no longer prosecuting terrorists but preventing terrorism. Data gathering became the key ingredient in stopping terrorist activity before it begins. In the name of homeland security, the FBI has access to records maintained by businesses if government agents can claim they are working on international terrorism—including medical records, library records, records of credit card purchase, and financial records. The USA PATRIOT Act (Uniting and Strengthening America by Providing Appropriate Tools Required to Intercept and Obstruct Terrorism) permits unannounced "sneak and peek" searches that the target is notified of only at a later date. It requires that the records of international students must be kept up-to-date and made available because such students are considered a potential source of espionage and terrorism. Through public outrage and revision, some safeguards have been added, though the basic provisions continue.

In terms of common-good privacy, there is one domain that is inviolable. The common good protects human dignity. Should government surveillance demand personal records outside of the owner's control, human dignity requires absolute protection. Security measures that intrude upon personal information without notification have, in the process of securing a nation–state, denied its democratic character as a civil society. If governments use common-good language to justify intrusion, they have eviscerated the common-good idea of its inscription in human dignity.

(3) Commercial databanks. The business of private investigators is boom-
ing as the availability of digital data grows. It is already a $10 billion-a-year
industry. Before computer storage, the average person could often escape scrutiny. Cumbersome recordkeeping was a shield from marketers, employers, and
the suspicious. With remote mainframes, information was difficult to access,
even for the technically sophisticated. The move to desktop PCs and local serv-
ers in the 1990s established the privacy problem we now face. Today the information boom has left virtually nothing private. Computers hold half a billion
bank accounts, half a billion credit card accounts, hundreds of millions
of mortgages and retirement funds, and medical claims and more. The
e-commerce businesses link them together. Kroll Associates is the largest for-
profit investigative agency in the world, with agents in every state and on every
continent except Antarctica. They search courthouse records, confidential banking information, personal data (through Auto Track and IQ Data), credit reports
from Equifax, news facts about anyone in the news, online databases that sell
data to subscribers, and so forth. Equifax, for example, keeps records on 200
million Americans and shares them with 114,000 clients. Docusearch promotes itself as the premiere provider of "online investigative solutions" and
sells information about anyone to those with a Visa card—their staff made up
of private investigators, former FBI and CIA agents, and surveillance experts
with years of inside experience (http://www.docusearch.com). Its clients include lawyers, insurers, detectives, the Los Angeles Pension Union, and Citi-
bank's legal recovery department.

Congress continues to work on legislation that outlaws the gaining of
financial information from banks by deceptive means. It has initiated reforms
that require the data owner's consent before others may profit from the data.
Such legal activity may be beneficial, but the most productive approach for citizens, politicians, and those in the investigation business and the press is the
ethics of the common good. In common-good terms, dealing with for-profit
data companies does not occur primarily through institutional policies (laws
from the government and safeguards agreed to by the business community).
Responsibility here belongs to the civil society, and includes the careful entry of
personal data only when absolutely necessary. Nongovernmental organizations
(NGOs) with special expertise in surveilling e-commerce are encouraged and
supported. The press includes commercial data companies on its beat. The
press does not cover such companies only when they break the law but
becomes the mouthpiece for those NGOs, who serve as watchdogs.

(4) Journalism, privacy and the common good. With an ethics of privacy
grounded in the common good, the common good's vitality becomes the press's
preoccupation, as compared with liberalism's focus on each individual. While
each case of privacy violation is troubling, a communitarian approach considers those violations within the larger context of their effect on the common
good. This approach is parallel to public journalism, which sees the mission of

the press in community terms—not just transmitting facts from expert sources but helping public life go well. This is an analogue of the press and privacy in the common-good model. The stress is not first of all reporters covering private matters, but their commitment to a healthy public. To the extent that the common good is known and appreciated, the details of privacy in law and professional practice will be interpreted correctly.

(5) Technology's impact. In a highly technological age, our authentic humanness tends to suffer. Technological metaphors and the vocabulary of machines have more resonance than does the mystery of personhood. Technological values are radically at odds with a world of human wholeness and moral imperatives. The instrumentalism driving the technological age subverts our ability to make moral judgments. We concentrate on the efficiency of instruments, on means, and neglect ends. A calculus of averages and probabilities replaces ends, the common good, and sacred human dignity—the technological order constituting the moral order in terms of technique. The crises we face are not technologies per se, but a technological understanding of being. The values underlying the technological enterprise present the challenge, and only when instrumental values are revolutionized will humans be able to recognize and live by the morality of human dignity. Nourishing the moral realm in which human civilization is situated, and in which privacy makes sense, is the news media's overall purpose in the digital age—similar to stressing physical fitness, diet, and preventative medicine rather than concentrating resources on surgery and emergency medicine. In fulfilling this mission, the media strengthen secondary schools and higher education where the issues of society and technology can be worked on in depth.

Conclusion

A sophisticated ethics of privacy is a sine qua non for news media, with the common good being the primary principle. For communications, the best definition of privacy is the protection of one's innermost self by determining who or what enters our personal life space. In the digital era of networking and cyberspace, establishing an ethics of privacy is especially urgent. Because intrusion is a wide-ranging public issue using digital technology, the ethical framework ought to be commensurate in scope. A liberal ethics of human dignity for print or broadcast media, even one that appears able to stand on its own, needs to be expanded into an ethics of the common good. Thus, privacy must be understood primarily in terms of the general morality, not in terms of professional standards. The ethics of privacy is not focused on decisions that journalists make but is centered on the victims' need to control information about themselves. A reasonable public determines whether, when, and how information

THE ETHICS OF PRIVACY 213

about them is communicated to others. From the common-good perspective, important social concerns regarding privacy are made transparent and inescapable.

Notes

1. In its 1964 ruling (*New York Times v. Sullivan*), the U.S. Supreme Court supported the press's role as crucial to democracy. In 1971 the Court applied its 1964 opinion to an individual caught up in a public issue—a Mr. Rosenbloom, who was arrested for distributing obscene books. Subsequent opinions have created some ambiguities though continually reaffirming broad media protection.

2. In its rulings involving newsworthiness, the courts have favored the media's definitions by broadly construing the "public-interest exemption to privacy" developed by Samuel Warren and Louis D. Brandeis ("The Right of Privacy," *Harvard Law Review* 4 [December 15, 1890]: 193–220).

3. Thomas I. Emerson, *The System of Freedom of Expression* (New York: Random House, 1970), 545.

4. Sissela Bok, *Secrets: On the Ethics of Concealment and Revelation* (New York: Pantheon, 1983), 10–11.

5. Alan H. Westin, *Privacy and Freedom* (New York: Atheneum, 1967), 7.

6. Louis W. Hodges, "The Journalist and Privacy," *Social Responsibility: Journalism, Law, Medicine* 9 (1983): 12.

7. Aristotle, *Politics: A Treatise on Government*, trans. W. Ellis (London: George Routledge, 1888), Bk. III, chs. 6–7, pp. 90–93.

8. John Locke, *Second Treatise of Government*, ed. T. Pearson (New York: Liberal Press, 1954), ch. 9, p. 73, para. 131; ch. 13, p. 91, para. 158.

9. Jean-Jacques Rousseau, *The Social Contract and Other Political Writings*, ed. V. Gourevitch (Cambridge: Cambridge University Press, 1997), Bk. II, ch. 1, p. 57.

10. Jürgen Habermas, *Justification and Application: Remarks on Discourse Ethics*, trans. C. Cronin (Cambridge, MA: MIT Press, 1993), 66. See also Habermas, *Moral Consciousness and Communicative Action*, trans. C. Lenhart and S. W. Nicholson (Cambridge, MA: MIT Press, 1990).

11. Bernard J. Diggs, "The Common Good as Reason for Political Action," *Ethics* 83, no. 4 (1973): 284.

12. Samuel D. Warren and Louis D. Brandeis, "The Right of Privacy," *Harvard Law Review*.

13. John Rawls, *A Theory of Justice* (Cambridge, MA: Harvard University Press, 1971), 302.

14. Stephen Mulhall and Adam Swift, *Liberals and Communitarians*, 2nd ed. (Oxford, UK: Blackwell, 1996), 49, 52. Cf. Michael Sandel, *Liberalism and the Limits of Justice* (Cambridge: Cambridge University Press, 1982), 59–65.

15. Mulhall and Swift, *Liberals and Communitarians*, 56; cf. pp. 54–55.

16. Charles Taylor, *Sources of the Self: The Making of the Modern Identity* (Cambridge, MA: Harvard University Press, 1989), 89.

17. Craig Calhoun, "The Public Good as a Social and Cultural Product," keynote address to Lilly Foundation Conference, Indianapolis, Indiana, November 1993, p. 6.

18. See Carole Pateman, *The Disorder of Women: Democracy, Feminism and Political Theory* (Stanford, CA: Stanford University Press, 1989), 26–29.

19. John Macmurray, *The Form of the Personal: The Self as Agent,* vol. 1 (London: Faber & Faber, 1961), 38.

20. See Alan Goldman, *The Moral Foundations of Professional Ethics* (Totowa, NJ: Rowman & Littlefield, 1980).

21. Following Sissela Bok (*Lying,* New York: Vintage, 1978), concrete moral choices must be tested against Rawls's concept of publicity, "as directed to reasonable persons" (p. 97). "We now have little public discourse about moral choice. It is needed in classes, in professional organizations, in government. It should be open, not closed to special interest groups . . . giving a chance for all views to be heard" (p. 103). Bias creeps into any evaluation and every decision, and "an inflamed and threatened public can be unreasonable in the extreme" (p. 108). Even with adequate information, just how reasonable a public actually is in its practices and conclusions, is debatable. But Bok argues that, alongside the flesh-and-blood public, an imagined reasonable public is possible—one that distinguishes argument from force and includes a variety of viewpoints rather than a dictator's mandate. Despite the limitations of both the concept and application of reasonable persons, the test of publicity "can nevertheless reduce the discrepancy of perspectives, shed light on moral reasoning, and facilitate moral choices" (p. 108).

22. Hodges, "Journalist and Privacy," 12.

23. See Aaron Quinn's chap. 18 in this volume.

15

Understanding and Respecting Privacy

Candace Cummins Gauthier

This essay will address the practical conflicts for journalists, their employers, the owners of news organizations, and the public regarding issues of privacy in reporting the news. Privacy will be understood, here, as control over access to oneself and to certain kinds of information about oneself. First, the relevant interests of the public, journalists, and news organizations will be discussed. Then, building on Deni Elliott and David Ozar (chap. 1 in this volume), ethical principles will be recommended for considering, discussing, and resolving issues of privacy in journalism. Finally, these principles will be applied to news stories and images that invade the privacy of public officials, celebrities, and ordinary citizens.

Relevant Interests to Be Balanced

There are several interests to be balanced in the consideration of privacy and the practice of journalism. The first three are interests held by all individuals in (1) maintaining their privacy, (2) respecting the privacy of others, and (3) obtaining information about the world. The remaining four are interests specific to journalists and the organizations for which they work: (1) producing appealing stories, (2) meeting their professional moral standards, (3) maintaining the trust of the public, and (4) sustaining a profitable business.

The Interests of Individuals in Relation to Privacy

Maintaining our privacy is a matter of control over access to us and to certain kinds of information about us. Others could gain access to us through seeing or touching us and through photographs or audiovisual recordings. Our control over access to ourselves through touch is legally protected, with laws against battery. We control access to ourselves through sight, photography, and audiovisual recording by choosing to be in places where there is a reasonable expectation of privacy, or choosing to appear and speak in public.

When we are in public, photographs, audiotapes, or videotapes made of us do not normally invade our privacy, since these are recordings of public behavior. On the other hand, if photographs or tapes are made in situations where there is a reasonable expectation of privacy, our privacy has been invaded. For example, there is a reasonable expectation of privacy in a doctor's office or a drug treatment center, but not en route to or from these places. A photograph of someone being examined in the doctor's office would be a private image, while a photograph of someone entering a doctor's office would not. One example of a borderline case would be a photograph of Brittany Spears being carried by stretcher from her home to a waiting ambulance. Although she is in public, she certainly did not choose to collapse at home and have to be taken to the hospital.

A similar distinction can be made in the case of information about us. Some information about each of us is publicly available. For example, our date of birth, arrest records, degrees earned, and, at some public universities, annual salary, are matters of public record. Clearly, we cannot control this kind of information, since anyone may search public records to obtain it. Publishing this kind of information does not invade privacy, since the information is publicly available.

On the other hand, most information about us is not a matter of public record. This will be considered "private information," in this chapter, just as most images that are not of public behavior will be considered "private images." Some of our private information is legally protected, such as our medical records, credit card and bank statements, and tax returns. Whether private information is legally protected or not, publishing or airing it will invade our privacy, unless, that is, we have provided this information ourselves or have given permission for it to be published. These are the two ways in which we exercise control over who has access to this kind of information.

Human beings have both a social need and a natural desire for control over access to themselves and to private information about themselves. Privacy is essential for our sense of ourselves as persons and as self-determining moral agents for, as Jeffrey Reiman puts it, privacy is necessary for the development and confirmation of moral personhood. He writes, "Privacy is a social ritual by means of which an individual's moral title to his existence is conferred."[1] Privacy, he says, "conveys to the developing child" that she has "exclusive moral rights" over her own body, in addition to her thoughts.[2] These rights include the right to decide what to do with one's body and thoughts and the right to control who has access to them.[3]

Recognizing these rights in ourselves and having them respected by others is essential for the development of personhood.[4] I would also add that this is the way in which individuals become self-determining moral agents. Respect for privacy also "confirms, and demonstrates respect for, the personhood of already developed persons."[5] As Reiman summarizes his argument, "The right to privacy . . . protects the individual's interest in becoming, being, and remaining a person."[6]

Privacy is also necessary for the development and maintenance of meaningful human relationships through our ability to control the kinds and amounts of information we share with others.[7] According to Julie Innes, the value of privacy is based on respect for persons as "emotional choosers."[8] Privacy protects individual self-determination with regard to our emotional choices and actions by protecting the ways in which we experience and express our emotional attachments to significant persons in our lives.[9]

In addition to the social need for privacy, we also have a personal desire for some level of privacy. Even those who seek public attention often set limits on media access to themselves and their families. While they are willing to give up some privacy in order to have successful careers, they often also attempt to reserve some areas of privacy, particularly regarding their emotional attachments and personal relationships.

It follows, then, that respecting the privacy of others is one of the ways in which we respect persons as self-determining, emotionally engaged, and relationship-oriented moral agents. In this way we recognize their legitimate need and desire to maintain control over access to themselves and to certain information about themselves.

In tension with the moral demand of privacy is the vital interest in obtaining information about the world around us, information that allows us to become connected to our world and other people in it. In some cases, we need this information to make important decisions, such as which candidates to support in an election. In other cases, we simply enjoy having information about other people and their activities, through entertainment and sports news.

Our interest in obtaining information about our world and, particularly, other people, leads to an important distinction between information that we need and information that we simply would like to have. Commentators have described this distinction in terms of "need to know" and "want to know" or a "right to know" and an "interest in knowing." [10] This distinction is also found in Deni Elliott and David Ozar's ethics theory piece. The authors first discuss information "people of any society *need* in order to function effectively as a society and to effectively pursue any of their collective or individual goals." This category of "needed information" includes information about "governments and other institutions and centers of power in the society," health and safety, and "new forms of social and organizational power" within the society. Second, they consider information that "enables the people of the society to respond to their *desires*," insofar as these are common to most members of the society.

The authors argue that providing "information related to *needs* outranks information related to *desires*." However, both "are central values of journalism." These two categories are contrasted, then, with a third category of information, based on "individualized pursuits" or "preferences." Because this information is neither needed by citizens nor concerned with the widely shared interests and desires that bind the society together, providing this last kind of information is "not a central value of journalism."

As will be developed later in this essay, if the information is actually needed by citizens—for example, because it involves their government and government officials—invading privacy to provide that information may very well be morally justified. On the other hand, it will be very hard to justify invading privacy to provide information that is based merely on the individual preferences of some members of the society.

Interests of Journalists and News Organizations in Relation to Privacy

Journalists have interests in getting stories that appeal to their audiences and that meet the demands of their employers. Again, the public wants information—some needed, some only desired—about their world and the people in it. Publishers, editors, and news directors want stories that provide such appealing and vital information so that their news outlets will succeed in the competition for readers, listeners, and viewers.

Journalists who can meet the informational needs, social desires, and even the individual preferences of their target audience are likely to have good success with their news organizations and reap corresponding benefits in terms of salary, promotion, and awards. Unfortunately, the release of private information and images often accomplishes the goals of journalists, editors, and news directors alike. In short, respecting news subjects' privacy often conflicts with choices that may enhance one's career.

But journalists also have interests in living up to the standards of their profession. For example the Society of Professional Journalists *Code of Ethics* includes the following guideline: "Recognize that private people have a greater right to control information about themselves than do public officials and others who seek power, influence or attention. Only an overriding public need can justify intrusion into anyone's privacy."[11] Another guideline admonishes journalists: "Show good taste. Avoid pandering to lurid curiosity."[12]

Such tensions also exist within profit-seeking news organizations. With the growing ownership of news outlets by large publicly traded corporations comes an increasing demand for adequate returns. As long as the release of private information about and images of those in power or those whose careers put them in the public eye continue to appeal to the public, these interests will lean toward invasions of privacy.

However, news organizations must also be mindful of the dual reactions of the public. Citizens need a certain amount of private information about those in power and those who seek power through election or appointment. A large segment of the public also wants private information about and images of entertainment and sports stars. Yet, the public is also quick to criticize news outlets that cross boundaries in terms of invading privacy.

In summary, all of these interests compete: journalists and their organizations strive to provide information sought by the public, information that often pushes the boundaries of respect for privacy. Hence, the challenge: how to provide appealing and important information in a way that also serves journalists' professional interests, advances corporate financial interests, and meets professional ethical standards?

Ethical Principles Relevant to Privacy Issues in Journalism

The first ethical principle that is relevant to privacy issues in journalism is the Principle of Respect for Persons. This principle requires that persons be treated with respect for their self-determination, their relationships and emotions, their reasonable goals, and their privacy. This principle is based on Immanuel Kant's "practical imperative": "Act so that you treat humanity, whether in your own person or in that of another, always as an end and never as a means only."[13] Abiding by this principle requires providing, where feasible, information necessary for persons to be capable of genuine self-determination. In addition to respect for self-determination (from Kant), the Principle of Respect for Persons includes respect for the relationships, emotions, reasonable goals, and privacy of persons.

The requirements of the Principle of Respect for Persons are clearly relevant to the practice of journalism and issues of privacy invasion. Self-determination includes the ability of persons to control access to themselves and to private information about themselves. Those who provide private information or give permission for this kind of information about themselves to be published or aired are being treated as an end, with respect and dignity. For the most part, this will also be true of those who are photographed or filmed in public. Their privacy is not being invaded because they have exercised control over access to their private information and images.

When private information is published or aired without permission and when images that were recorded in places where there is a reasonable expectation of privacy are released, privacy is invaded. Moreover, these persons are treated as a mere means to the goals and ends of journalists and their news organizations, including career advancement, selling papers and gaining audiences, and ultimately increasing profits.

Respect for relationships and emotions places limits on the access journalists should have to the families and friends of those under public scrutiny, including candidates for office, public officials, and celebrities. Respect for these persons includes recognition of their emotional connection to the important people in their lives and their desire to protect their loved ones from public view.

Those who seek public office or have attained these positions, in addition to entertainment and sports stars, may desire to have their names and images in the public eye, for example, to win financial support and votes or to attract audiences for their films, music, or sports events. That they wish such publicity, however, does not give journalists total access. Many of these people also have the understandable goal of placing limits on media access. These limits will often be based on the desire to protect those with whom they have important relationships and emotional attachments.

Because of the fundamental importance of all of its elements for personhood (self-determination, relationships and emotions, setting goals for oneself, and privacy) the Principle of Respect for Persons provides a prima facie barrier against invasions of privacy. This means that it should be the starting point for any discussion about news stories that clearly invade privacy and, moreover, it establishes a presumption in favor of respecting the privacy of the subjects of those stories. Thus, the burden of proof falls on those who wish to violate others' privacy.

The second ethical principle that is relevant to issues of privacy in journalism is the Utilitarian Principle. Elliott and Ozar's chapter pointed out that the most important obligation of the journalist was "the obligation to avoid causing unjustified harm." We also saw, in that chapter, the comparison of the "overall good" and "overall harm" of an action as one of the ways used to determine if the harm that will be caused by an action is justified. This is the point of the Utilitarian Principle.

The Utilitarian Principle requires that benefits be maximized and harms minimized. This principle is concerned with promoting more good than harm in the world. It is based on the ethical theory of John Stuart Mill. According to Mill, "Actions are right in proportion as they tend to promote happiness; wrong as they tend to produce the reverse of happiness."[14] By "happiness," Mill means "pleasure and the absence of pain;" by "the reverse of happiness," he means "pain and the privation of pleasure."[15] Mill makes it very clear that the happiness to be promoted by the Utilitarian ethical theory "is not the agent's own happiness but that of all concerned" and that between our own happiness and that of others, we must be "strictly impartial."[16]

Applying the Utilitarian Principle begins with an identification of the potential harms (in terms of unhappiness, pain, and the loss of pleasure) and expected benefits (in terms of happiness, pleasure, and the absence of pain) of a particular action, for all those concerned. The next step is an impartial comparison of those harms and benefits. If the harms, impartially considered, are greater, the action will be morally wrong. If the benefits, impartially considered, are greater, the action may be morally right. This is true even though the action does have the potential to cause harm. In this case, the potential harms will be justified by the expected benefits of the action, as long as the benefits cannot be gained in any less harmful way.

Consider the release of private information or images in the news media. According to the Utilitarian Principle, the publication of private information or images will not be morally justified unless the expected benefits outweigh the potential harms and there is no other, less harmful, way to promote these benefits. However, an important part of this principle is the fact that the harms and benefits to be compared must include those that will be experienced by everyone affected by the action. In this case, they would include the person whose privacy is being invaded, those with whom she has close relationships, and the public, in addition to journalists and their news organizations.

Because journalism ultimately serves "the public," as noted in the Elliott and Ozar chapter, the benefits to the public of the release of private information or images must be of primary importance. Thus, the value of this principle is that it asks not only journalists, editors, and news directors, but also the owners of news organizations, to take into serious consideration the potential harms to the person whose privacy is being invaded and those to whom this person has significant emotional attachments, in addition to the expected benefits to the public, rather than focusing exclusively on the benefits to themselves and their own organizations.

Combining these two ethical principles provides an initial framework for addressing ethical issues concerning privacy invasion by the news media. Based on the Principle of Respect for Persons, we begin with a presumption in favor of respecting privacy. Invading someone's privacy, then, can be justified only if the expected benefits outweigh the potential harms and the benefits cannot be produced without risking those harms, based on the Utilitarian Principle.

Invading privacy has the potential harms of threatening a person's conception of herself as a self-determining moral agent, damaging her self-respect and emotional well-being, and destroying reputations, relationships, and lives. This will always need to be justified by expected benefits for the public and not simply for the journalist and the news organization. This method of resolving ethical issues for privacy thus requires journalists and their news organizations to justify invasions of privacy; because such invasions are initially prohibited under the Principle of Respect for Persons, that justification must involve some overwhelming benefit to the public.

Illustrating the Application of These Principles to Cases of Privacy Invasion

In the remaining sections, the release of private information and images by the news media will be considered for three particular groups of individuals: (1) public officials and candidates for public office; (2) celebrities, such as entertainment and sports stars; and (3) so-called private citizens, those with no interest in public attention.

When the release of news reports or images would invade an individual's privacy, the journalists involved, and their editors and news directors, should begin with a presumption in favor of respecting privacy by not releasing this information or image. This is based on the Principle of Respect for Persons, which requires respect for an individual's self-determination, emotions, relationships, reasonable goals, and privacy. Since invading privacy has a great potential to harm people's sense of themselves as self-determining moral agents, in addition to their emotions, relationships, and goals, this harm must be outweighed by the expected benefits for the journalists and their news organizations, and most importantly, for the public. Moreover, the prospective benefits must not be possible without causing this kind of harm. This is based on the Utilitarian Principle.

Certainly there may be benefits to the journalists and their news organizations in terms of professional recognition, career advancement, and increased profits. However, the primary benefits to be considered are those to the public, and these must be determined to be more important than the harm done to the person whose privacy is invaded, with no less harmful way to produce them, in order for the release of private information or images to be morally justified.

Privacy for Public Officials and Candidates for Public Office

Given the presumption against invading the privacy of public officials and candidates for public office, based on the Principle of Respect for Persons, it will be essential to justify the release of private information or images using the Utilitarian Principle. Journalists, editors, and news directors will need to convince themselves that the expected benefits to the public, primarily, and then to themselves and their news organizations, are more important than the potential harms to the person whose privacy is being invaded and that there is no way to promote those benefits without the risk of harm.

Potential harms to those whose privacy is invaded, and their families, include loss of self-determination and self-respect, loss of reputation and political office, emotional damage, and the destruction of important relationships. Benefits to the journalists and their news organizations include things such as financial success, promotions, awards, and increased market share and profits. The major benefit for the public in these cases would be providing the citizens of a democracy with information they need in order to participate in the democratic process, for example by voting for certain candidates or calling for the censure, resignation, or removal of those already in office.

The word "need" reminds us of the category, noted in the Elliott and Ozar piece, of information "that the people of any society *need* in order to function effectively as a society and to effectively pursue any of their collective or individual goals." That category includes "a lot of information about governments and other institutions and centers of power in the society, and about the persons who hold offices or in other ways wield such power." However, this description does not specify the *kinds* of information that would be needed about persons who hold offices, or seek or wield such power.

Of the wide variety of information potentially available, that which would justify privacy violations must be *relevant*, that is, there must be a significant connection between the private information being released or conveyed by an image and something about the individual in her role as a public official or candidate for public office. For example, the connection might be to an individual's ability to execute the duties of her office. The connection might also be to the individual's character and the question of whether or not she deserves the trust of the citizens for whom she is or will be making important public policy decisions. The connection might also be to positions on public policy questions the individual has expressed.

When private information is connected to the job performance of a current or potential public official, this information is certainly relevant and needed. For example, while medical information is considered to be highly private in our society, based on medical confidentiality, a diagnosis of early Alzheimer's disease in a candidate or an elected official is relevant to her ability to perform the duties of a political leader.

Information about traditionally private concerns, such as sexual conduct or the use of drugs, may become issues of character for those who are seeking or already holding public office. This will be true, particularly, when they have lied about these activities or when the activities are illegal, for example in the case of using controlled substances.

This is a controversial area because some may argue that lying was justified by the private nature of the information, while others will argue that lying or using illegal substances indicates a character flaw about which citizens need to know, as an issue of trust. In regard to drug use, whether alcohol or illegal drugs, many will argue that the time when the drug use occurred also matters, so that a candidate's alcohol addiction, or marijuana or even cocaine use thirty years ago should not be exposed thirty years later. I think this latter argument makes sense. As our pool of candidates for public office increasingly includes those who came of age in the 1960s and 1970s, we will naturally see an increase in youthful alcohol and drug use that was left behind as these individuals matured and took on the responsibilities of their adult lives.

Finally, private information may be connected to the stated values or public positions of the official or candidate, in the sense that it would shed light on the sincerity of those values and positions. For example, when Eliot Spitzer served as the attorney general of New York, he aggressively pursued corruption and prosecuted prostitution organizations as part of this effort. As governor of New York, he even signed a bill that most severely penalized those who patronize prostitutes, rather than penalizing the prostitutes themselves. When his long-term involvement with an international prostitution organization came to light, Spitzer was forced to resign. It was, in this case, the hypocrisy of his public stand on prostitution that made the release of private information about him relevant to his tenure as governor.[17] His hiring prostitutes, as a married man with daughters of his own, also speaks to his character and makes his exposure more relevant.

If the private information or images under consideration are connected to the ability of a public official or candidate for public office to perform the duties of that office, the official or candidate's character, or the sincerity of the candidate or elected official's stated positions on public policy issues, this information is relevant and needed by the public. In these cases, the presumption against privacy invasion provided by the Principle of Respect for Persons may be overridden because the potential harms of invading privacy would be outweighed by the public's need for this information, and, in particular, for their informed participation in the democratic process, and there is no other, less harmful way, for them to gain it.

Privacy for Entertainment and Sports Figures

It is often argued that celebrities, such as entertainment and sports stars, give up their privacy as they seek notoriety in their fields. However, no one can be expected to give up all of their privacy, regardless of their chosen career. Everyone deserves the respect that is owed to all persons, so that violations of privacy will always need to be justified by some overwhelming benefit, primarily to the public, and not just to those in the news business. This is as true of celebrities as it is of those who hold or seek public office.

As we saw in the last section, invading the privacy of public officials and candidates must be justified by the expected benefits to the public of having information they need as citizens of a democratic society. In those cases we used the concept of relevance to determine when the information in question was actually needed by the public and, thus, when private information and images could be justifiably released.

In the case of entertainment and sports stars, as well, we begin with a presumption in favor of privacy, based on the Principle of Respect for Persons. Privacy invasions must be justified by showing, first, that the expected benefits outweigh the potential harms of releasing private information and images of celebrities. The harm to celebrities from invasions of their privacy may include loss of self-determination and self-respect; loss of reputation, status, and revenue; emotional damage; and damage to meaningful relationships. Celebrities' families may be similarly harmed.

The benefits to journalists and their news organizations may include promotions, better salaries and awards, and increased market share and profits from offering the audience sensationalized news stories. The main benefit for the public is entertainment and the satisfaction of their natural curiosity about the lives of famous people. Because the public wants to know all about these people, they may be entertained by the release of private information about their favorite celebrities and private images of them. Yet, there are certainly many other ways in which the public could be entertained that don't invade people's privacy.

Where celebrities are concerned, the concept of relevance is not going to be helpful in justifying invasions of their privacy. This is because the public really has no need for private information or images when they pertain to entertainment and sports figures. This kind of information also does not fall under Elliott and Ozar's category of "common social desires," in the sense of desires that bond the members of society together. It seems, instead, to belong under the category of "preferences," since this is information about "things we humans are interested in and seek information about that do not have a significant impact on the strength of the society."

Since this kind of information is not needed by the public and does not even satisfy widely shared common desires, the potential harms caused by releasing it are greater than the expected benefits, particularly the rather weak benefit of mere entertainment, which may be provided in other ways. In addition, not only are the celebrities and their families harmed by invasions of privacy, but news organizations are, too, as they come to be perceived more as purveyors of gossip than as providers of real news. This kind of focus tends to destroy the public's trust in a news outlet. Reputable news organizations would do well to focus attention on the successes and failures of celebrities in their professional fields, rather than delve into their private lives.

Consider the case of the retired tennis legend, Arthur Ashe. In 1992, a *USA Today* reporter called Ashe to confirm a rumor that he had AIDS, one day before the story of his illness was to be released in the paper. Even though Ashe asked for the story to be held for thirty-six hours, the sports editor refused. Ashe was forced to call a press conference for the next day. Ashe later said that *USA Today* had put him in the "position of having to lie if he wanted to protect his family's privacy."[18]

In this case there was no need for the public to have this private medical information about a former sports star. No one's health or safety was threatened. There was certainly no benefit to the public, only the satisfaction of idle curiosity. The harm that was done to Arthur Ashe, to his reputation, his emotional well-being, and his family relationships (at a time when AIDS created even greater fear and stigmatization than it does now) is clearly more important than the benefits for the public, the individual journalist who wrote the story, and *USA Today*. In fact, the newspaper came under heavy criticism for its actions.

Some journalists argued that the release of this information benefited society by showing that AIDS was not just a gay disease. I would respond that the benefit to society was not great enough to justify invading Ashe's privacy and destroying his reputation and his personal life. In addition, this benefit could have been, and, in fact, was, provided by other less invasive means, for example, when a middle-school student, Ryan White (1984), and basketball star Magic Johnson (1991) came forward voluntarily to discuss their HIV status. Finally, the journalists' argument illustrates perfectly how *not* to treat persons. According to the journalists' argument, it is acceptable to treat Ashe as a mere means to educate society about AIDS, rather than as an end, with choices about how his private medical information will be used. Kant would disagree, citing the practical imperative.

Contrast the Arthur Ashe case with that of another celebrity, the well-known model Naomi Campbell. In 2001, Campbell's efforts to overcome drug addiction were reported by the *Daily Mirror* of London and documented with a photo of her entering a Narcotics Anonymous meeting. The story also included details about what went on in the meeting.[19] While the photograph of Campbell going into the Narcotics Anonymous meeting does not invade her privacy, since it was public behavior, I would argue that publishing reports about the meeting does. There is a reasonable expectation of privacy in these support groups. It may not be as high as that for a private treatment clinic, but it does and should exist for those who seek support during recovery in these widely respected community treatment programs.

Certainly those who seek fame and fortune through sports and entertainment have the reasonable goal of capturing the attention of journalists in order to enhance their popularity. Many celebrities want to be seen and heard as much as possible. When they choose to appear in public, their public behavior may be reported with no invasion of privacy. This is because it is under their control when and where they appear, with some exceptions, such as being taken by ambulance to the hospital. Similarly, when they provide information to reporters or give their permission for private information to be published or aired, they have exercised control over the release of this information and are respected as persons, so there is no violation of their privacy.

Because there is really no need for the public to have access to private information or private images and there is unlikely to be any overwhelming benefit to the public that cannot be produced in less harmful ways, celebrities must be allowed to set the limits on what private information about them and what private images of them are published or aired. This is the essence of respecting privacy, in the end: allowing people to control who has access to them and to private information about them.

Privacy for Those with No Interest in Public Attention

Violating the privacy of what are aptly called "private citizens," those who are simply living their lives and not seeking office or public attention, is the most difficult to justify. Journalists and their news organizations should begin, once again, with a presumption that favors respecting the privacy of private citizens. Then they will need to justify these invasions of privacy by citing the expected benefits for the public (and themselves) that cannot be produced in any other way and that outweigh the potential harms to the individuals involved, to their families, and to the news organizationst.

Consider those who are accidentally thrust into the public eye, simply by being the victims of crimes, accidents, or natural disasters, or gain notice by their own heroic actions. For example, the *Bakersfield Californian* published a photograph of a five-year-old drowning victim, at the edge of a lake, surrounded by his grieving family. Readers and media critics charged the paper with invading the privacy of the family and showing a "callous disrespect of the victim."[20] The managing editor originally thought publishing the photograph was justified by its potential to warn families and prevent similar drowning accidents in the future. He later came to believe the photograph should not have been published, based on the public outcry against it.[21]

The first question to be asked is: was this a photograph of public behavior? While the family was in public, it could be argued that they did not choose to place themselves in the situation of loss and grief that was captured on film and that there is a reasonable expectation of privacy when faced with such a situation, wherever it occurs. This case also illustrates a comparison of the harm caused to the family by lack of respect and invading their privacy, with the possible benefit for the public in being warned of the dangers of children drowning. The newspaper's reputation was also probably damaged in this case, as many readers were offended by the photograph of a dead child and his grieving family.

Journalists and editors will certainly disagree over whether or not the harm to the family and the newspaper was outweighed by the potential public benefit. My own view is that a story describing the incident and the reaction of the family, without the photograph, could have provided a similar benefit, without causing this kind of harm to the family and the reputation of the newspaper.

Another example illustrates the problem with the label "public figure." In 1975 Oliver Sipple was brought to the attention of the public when he saved the life of President Gerald Ford in San Francisco. A few days later, a number of newspapers revealed Sipple's involvement in the gay community, although he refused to comment and clearly wanted to keep his sexual orientation private. This invasion of Sipple's privacy resulted in serious emotional damage and caused his family to abandon him.[22]

Journalists may argue that once crimes, accidents, natural disasters, and heroic acts are reported, the individuals involved are considered "public figures," so that further privacy-invading coverage of their lives is justified. This sounds suspiciously self-serving, in the sense that if journalists take it upon themselves to bring someone to the public's attention, even without that individual's intent and permission, they are then fair game for further investigation and media coverage.

Throughout this essay, I have avoided the term "public figure" for just this reason. It is too broad a term and too easily applied to those who do not see themselves, and have no interest in being described, in this way. No one is a "public figure" simply because journalists give them this label. Individuals become "public figures" when they choose to define themselves as such because they seek or have attained public office or desire public attention for some other personal or professional reason and the media agrees that they deserve public attention. For example, the editor of the local paper or a professor who gives controversial speeches and writes op-ed pieces may or may not want to be considered a "public figure." Either way, privacy invasions by the news media will not be justified, without some overwhelming benefit to the public that cannot be produced in any less harmful way.

In the case of publishing private information about accidental "public figures," journalists and their news organizations may appear to benefit with promotions, financial success, and awards, in addition to increased market share and profits. The public may also be said to benefit if private information or images warn them of dangerous situations. However, a written description of an accident, using information available through public records and follow-up interviews with those who agree to speak to reporters and be photographed, could produce a similar benefit, without invading anyone's privacy. News organizations also need to remember that the public tends to lose trust in news outlets that invade privacy for no discernible reason except to sensationalize their news coverage.

When someone is labeled a "public figure" and privacy invasions seem to be justified on that basis, journalists and their news organizations should look back to how that individual became a so-called public figure. Is this person running for public office or does she already hold public office? Is she putting herself into the public eye to publicize her team, her films, her music, her university, or her newspaper, for example? Or has this person been thrust into the media spotlight for no other reason than random circumstances: being in the wrong place at the wrong time?

As with entertainment and sports celebrities, it will be difficult to justify releasing private information and images of ordinary people on the basis of some overwhelming benefit to the public that would not be possible without invading privacy. Private citizens may offer private information for publication or give permission for private information or images to be published. If they do, they are afforded respect since they have retained control over their private information and images.

Thus, the same rule for privacy issues in the news applies to these two groups of individuals. Normally, public behavior may be reported and recorded in photos and on audiovisual tape, with some exceptions, such as when people are placed in situations over which they have no control. Information that is publicly available may be reported. But the release of private information and images should be based on permission to publish or air them.

Conclusion

As we have seen, the invasion of privacy often yields benefits for the public, journalists, and news organizations. It also has the potential to cause great harm to candidates and public officials, entertainment and sports stars, and private individuals, and to the reputations of the news organizations involved. Journalists and their editors and news directors should begin with a presumption against invading privacy, based on the Principle of Respect for Persons. If privacy invasions are considered, they should be justified, using the Utilitarian Principle, by some overwhelming benefit to the public and to journalists that cannot be produced otherwise. The potential harm for those whose privacy is invaded and those with whom they have important relationships should never be discounted.

With public officials and candidates for public office, their privacy may justifiably be invaded for important benefits to the public. As we have seen, this will often be the case when private information is relevant to their ability to perform the duties of their office, their character, or the sincerity of their stated positions on public policy issues. In general, celebrities and private citizens, even if they consider themselves to be "public figures," should retain control over information that is not publicly available and over images of themselves that are recorded when they have a reasonable expectation of privacy. For these last two groups of individuals, invasions of privacy need to be justified by serious benefits to the public that are not possible without invading their privacy, and this is going to be very difficult to do.

In the end, journalists and their editors and news directors need to discuss and be able to defend invasions of privacy in their news reports. They should ask themselves and each other why they are invading an individual's privacy. They need to be able to articulate their reasons as though they were explaining this to the individuals involved, their families, and the public. Finally, the reasons need to be based on some overwhelming benefit to the public, benefit that clearly outweighs the harm done and cannot be produced in any less harmful way.

Notes

1. Jeffrey Reiman, "Privacy, Intimacy, and Personhood," *Philosophy and Public Affairs* 6 (1976): 39.

2. Reiman, "Privacy, Intimacy, and Personhood," 39, 43.

3. Reiman, "Privacy, Intimacy, and Personhood," 42–43.

4. Reiman, "Privacy, Intimacy, and Personhood," 39.

5. Reiman, "Privacy, Intimacy, and Personhood," 39.

6. Reiman, "Privacy, Intimacy, and Personhood," 44.

7. James Rachels, "Why Privacy Is Important," *Philosophy and Public Affairs* 4 (1975): 323–33.

8. Julie Innes, *Privacy, Intimacy, and Isolation* (New York: Oxford University Press, 1992), 106–7. See also Charles Fried, *An Anatomy of Values* (Cambridge, MA: Harvard University Press, 1970), 137–52.

9. Innes, *Privacy, Intimacy, and Isolation*, 105–12.

10. Regarding need/want, see Philip Patterson and Lee Wilkins, *Media Ethics: Issues & Cases*, 6th ed. (Boston: McGraw Hill, 2008), 155–57; regarding right/interest, see Christopher Meyers, "Justifying Journalistic Harms: Right to Know vs. Interest in Knowing," *Journal of Mass Media Ethics* 8 (1993): 133–46.

11. Society of Professional Journalists, *Code of Ethics* (Indianapolis, IN: Society of Professional Journalists, 1996), online at http://www.spj.org/ethicscode.asp. Accessed May 28, 2008.

12. Society of Professional Journalists, *Code of Ethics*.

13. Immanuel Kant, *Foundations of the Metaphysics of Morals*, trans. Lewis White Beck (1785; Indianapolis, IN: Bobbs-Merrill, 1959), 47.

14. John Stuart Mill, *Utilitarianism*, ed. George Sher (1861; Indianapolis, IN: Hackett, 1979), 7.

15. Mill, *Utilitarianism*, 7.

16. Mill, *Utilitarianism*, 16.

17. Hendrik Hertzberg, "Falling," *New Yorker*, March 24, 2008, pp. 25–26.

18. Philip Patterson and Lee Wilkins, *Media Ethics: Issues & Cases*, 5th ed. (Boston: McGraw Hill, 2005), 155–56.

19. Patterson and Wilkins, *Media Ethics*, 6th ed., 333–34.

20. Patterson and Wilkins, *Media Ethics: Issues & Cases*, 3rd ed. (Boston: McGraw Hill, 1998), 37–39.

21. Patterson and Wilkins, *Media Ethics*, 3rd ed., 37–39.

22. H. Eugene Goodwin, Groping for Ethics in Journalism (Ames: Iowa State University Press, 1983), 220–23.

PART VII

Approaching the News: Reporters and Consumers

Introduction

This part is, in many ways, the heart of the book, especially from a practitioner's perspective. The chapters directly address what it means to be an ethical producer or consumer of news, considering this via specific issues, like torn loyalties, conflict of interest, and source protection.

As I noted in the main introduction and as should be clear from the book's structure, I don't think one can effectively address practical ethics problems until one has first developed an informed and sophisticated theoretical and conceptual foundation. Without these, ethics analyses are typically case-driven and ad hoc; hence the predominantly theoretical and conceptual focus on Section One's four parts.

Such abstractions, though, have to eventually find a home; otherwise, ethics remains at a theoretical level only. That home, for journalists, is rich with ethical choices. Among the myriad choices faced on any given day are whether to treat subjects and sources as a mere means to a story; whether one can live with an editing process that tends to reduce complex problems to simple ones, so as to fit a shrinking news hole; whether acquiring or disseminating a piece of information invades others' privacy and, if so, whether doing so is nonetheless justified; whether scoop competition produces better or just faster stories; whether one may accept a lunch offer from a future potential news source; whether the nature of contemporary market forces allows for sophisticated and critical reporting; and what counts as proper attribution. Furthermore, as Wendy Wyatt argues, consumers also have choices to make, in particular of whether to be literate enough and engaged enough to demand real journalism from news organizations.

How should budding practitioners prepare for such choices? Jay Black provided, in chapter 3, a set of guiding principles; there are also the various societies' codes of ethics. But, even if Michael Davis is right about journalism being a profession, the nature of the journalistic enterprise precludes it from fitting neatly within the traditional professional model; for example, it has no accreditation standards nor even manifests universal agreement on what counts as excellent—or for that matter, as ethical—journalism. There are certainly traditional models (see, for example, the lede's pyramid structure), but if we've learned anything from online journalism, it is that there are many different ways of effectively conveying information. Similarly, there is certainly a journalistic ethos, at least within MSM—see chapter 20. Again, though, that ethos is being explicitly challenged by non-MSM journalists—as it should be, since it is largely driven by prudential rather than ethical imperatives (as it is, I would note, with all professions).

In these respects, journalism is much closer to mental health practice than it is to, say, engineering. Mental health ethics literature is striking in how much it stresses the relationship between good ethical choices and *competency*. In other fields, like engineering, medicine, and law, competency is assumed and ethics is more about the dilemmas that emerge from conflicting principles. Like journalism, though, mental health practice does not have a single accepted method; theories and treatment techniques are almost as varied as the number of providers, and thus many ethical concerns emerge from marginally competent (or worse) care and its effect on clients.

In my experience, mental health professionals try to compensate for the amorphous nature of their practice by setting down hard and fast, absolutist rules, for example, a strict adherence to the American Psychological Association's code of ethics. Such rules, though, make it tough to manage the cases that don't fit the box. Rather, as Aristotle argued, the virtuous person should instead rely upon *phronesis*—practical wisdom—to discern when rules should be followed and when bent or broken. Take truth telling—a fundamental ethical principle among all professions. The virtuous, practically wise person wholeheartedly commits to being honest but also recognizes that sometimes truth telling is simply cruel, obeyed because the rule says to tell the truth, not because it is the morally right choice.

Thus what it means to be a good mental health professional, and, I'd suggest, a good journalist, is to have the right character, built upon intellectual virtues, technical skills, and practical wisdom, including the wisdom to know when to abide by and when to bend professionally situated ethical principles. Practical wisdom within journalism would entail that one must be knowledgeable about the world, be good at acquiring and communicating information, know the core moral principles and their place in journalism practice, and have enough experience to know how to apply those principles.

The last, "how to," criterion can be enhanced, I think, via four steps: First, one must understand what the issues are. This volume provides an overview, made more specific by individual chapters, as exemplified by the four in this part. Second, one must acquire an understanding of such key terms and concepts as "objectivity" and "privacy." Third, one must become comfortable with an ethics decision-making process, like Elliott and Ozar's SMA. Fourth, and maybe most importantly, one must learn from role models.

The importance of role models is one of the reasons this is such a valuable part. Three of the chapters are by scholars who started their careers as successful journalists, including a Pulitzer Prize winner (Jacqui Banaszynski), a former newspaper editor and publisher who still writes a biweekly column for the *Miami Herald* and the *Palm Beach Post* (Edward Wasserman), and a former managing editor of a weekly (Aaron Quinn). All now have academic positions, including two in endowed chairs (Banaszynski and Wasserman). In other words, you have in these authors impressive role models, people who were and are successful in the practice and in the evaluation and teaching of that practice.

Banaszynski's chapter, for example, extends the *phronesis* point to the daily practice of reporting, particularly with respect to the tension between the ethos-driven adherence to personal detachment from story sources and "personal values and instincts." Her goal is to break down this perceived dichotomy: "Walking onto the job doesn't mean walking away from ourselves. Presuming to do so is, at best, dishonest. At worst, dangerous." Rather, a journalist's humanity is what allows her to get closer to the truth of a situation, thereby serving journalism's highest purpose.

Banaszynski thus reinforces the book's "this is hard stuff" mantra; ethical journalists cannot just engage in knee-jerk adherence to standard principles, such as detachment, but must carefully think through the values underlying those principles and determine whether they should be followed in specific cases.

Wasserman picks up on one of the "must avoid" ethical principles: conflict of interest, concluding it is a far more complex and widespread problem than generally acknowledged in, for example, codes of ethics. Wasserman has written one of the more important articles in the book, both because of its insight and powerful reasoning and because of its far-reaching implications. If he's right, and I think he is, the practice of journalism faces a structural and endemic conflict of interest, one that cannot be cured but only better managed. It is a challenging chapter, in both senses of the word: it demands a careful read, for the argument proceeds through a number of steps, each building upon the previous, and it provides a critical take on the business, forcing one to think hard about probably inevitable ethical pitfalls and their best management.

After a conceptual analysis of the nature of conflict of interest and of its ethical impact on practice, its endemic presence in journalism—both mainstream and emerging—Wasserman provides a series of recommendations for better managing conflicts. All are compelling, even if some appear, to my eye, too idealistic. As you talk through the chapter, and assuming you find his "endemic" arguments convincing, can you come up with other management techniques?

Aaron Quinn also takes on a difficult issue: Are promises to sources absolute? His conclusion: "Contrary to the journalistic convention that once a confidential agreement is made, it cannot be broken . . . journalists are at least permitted, even, at times, obligated to break confidential agreements." This conclusion falls exactly within the Aristotelian model discussed above: after a rich defense of the use of confidential sourcing and a strong prima facie commitment to confidentiality agreements, Quinn makes the *phronesis* move—these cases demand respect for other moral considerations (particularly for "justice") and thus require a wise balancing.

He does not make this move lightly, nor should he. Keeping promises is among the highest of moral duties, justly violated only in rare circumstances. The temptation, though, is to treat promises as conversation-enders, or worse, *thought-enders:* "I made a promise, so case closed. I don't care about, and don't want to have to think about, the moral ramifications." Unfortunately, life doesn't always fit this neat approach. One should, for example, of course break a promise to meet a friend for coffee so as to provide aid to an accident victim, or, when, as in one of Quinn's reporting illustrations, "the public's interest is in conflict; for example, harboring the identity of a source who is a danger to innocents."[1]

Quinn's argument sits within the specific public policy question of whether to provide a Federal Shield Law. He argues in favor but in doing so notes this brings more explicit duties than are currently associated with journalism's professional status. That is, he argues for "something akin to professional licensure, suggesting a change in journalism education and self-regulation." While other chapters in the book include arguments that might imply a regulatory move, Quinn is the only one who sticks his neck out on this highly controversial point. Your gut reaction, if you have been at all inculcated in the journalism ethos, is undoubtedly negative; how can a vibrant free press be consistent with regulation? Quinn nicely challenges that instinct; if he's wrong, it is not for obvious reasons.

Wyatt, as noted above, reminds us that these issues rub both ways. Yes, reporters have a duty to provide high-quality and ethical journalism, but the public also has a duty to demand it and, thus, to be discerning enough to tell the difference. Her argument begins where Craft's and Borden's leave off: if journalism is necessary to a vibrant, participatory democracy, even the very best of it will fail in this task if it lands in a vacuum. Participation requires, Wyatt stresses, recipients of information, persons who will critically engage it and, where appropriate, act accordingly. She notes, "And in societies as vast and complex as most modern-day democracies, participation relies on a means of conversing that stretches across the vastness and through the complexities. We cannot rely only on direct interpersonal communication to make our democracy work; we require a mediated form of public discourse, and . . . journalism's central purpose in a democracy is facilitating this discourse."

Wyatt's argument develops via a melding of Walter Lippmann's "pessimism" and John Dewey's "idealism" regarding the likelihood of an informed, engaged citizenry. As per Lippmann, modern democracy is fraught with impediments to civic engagement, but, per Dewey, "any hope of maintaining what has been accomplished and building on those accomplishments relies on our own internal motivation to embrace obligations beyond simply obeying the law . . . [and such motivation] must emanate from our conscience, our sense of moral seriousness, our integrity, and our realization of what it means to be a full member of a community." Wyatt translates this into six obligations each of us should embrace and through which a journalism-enhanced, truly participatory democracy can emerge.

I received the first draft of Wyatt's chapter in May 2008. At that time it was hard not to be a Lippmannish curmudgeon, skeptical about whether genuine democracy, built upon an informed and engage electorate, was even possible. The public, especially those under thirty, was apathetic, even cynical, about civic engagement. Since then, however, Barack Obama was elected in a record-turnout election, a victory built on a campaign greatly enhanced by a grassroots Internet-based activism, largely driven by eighteen- to twenty-five-year-olds, 70 percent of whom supported Obama.

Maybe we've turned the corner; maybe the Internet can live up to its hype and provide the means for participatory democracy. If so, good journalism will be all the more vital, given the unfiltered nature of Internet information. The concerns and challenges presented by this part's authors thus have, to paraphrase Wasserman, a robust past, present, and future.

Notes

1. Although I'm obviously rejecting Kant's absolutism on promise keeping, his emphasis does remind us to take promises quite seriously. This includes, in addition to the insistence on having justified grounds for their violation, the admonition to be circumspect in their use. Thus, to stick with the example, one should probably never *promise* to meet someone at a certain time or place, since so many factors beyond our control could get in the way. A lesser verbal assurance will surely suffice, if our companions know and trust our character.

16

Conflicting Loyalties and Personal Choices

Jacqui Banaszynski

A reporter and a photographer covering AIDS in Africa are asked to buy rubber gloves and bleach for a woman who is caring for her dying daughter; without those simple protections, the woman could become infected. A reporter learns that public school officials look the other way as children steal food from the cafeteria to take home to empty cupboards. If she reports it, the school could be forced to crack down—and kids could go hungry. A reporter covering Hurricane Katrina in New Orleans finds a woman and her grandson stranded on a freeway. Their story is as compelling as it is desperate: the woman wrote her grandson's name and date of birth on his arm so he can be identified when he is found—alive or dead. They have no water or transportation and beg the reporter to take them to a shelter.

Every day, journalists confront situations that ask us to weigh our journalistic principles and practices against our personal values and instincts. Many seem minor: Do you indulge in the buffet table at a political meeting when there's nothing else to eat? Do you let your spouse donate money to an environmental group? Others cut deeper: Can you cover an abortion-rights bill if abortion is against your religious beliefs? Can you protest the closing of your child's school if you sometimes fill in on the education beat?

Most can be addressed by newsroom policies or resolved by consulting a good editor or respected colleague. Almost all require some level of disclosure or transparency—either within the news organization or directly to the public. But many situations journalists wrestle with are not neatly managed by boilerplate policies. They cut to the bone and seem to pit our values as "objective" journalists against our values as compassionate, caring human beings. We are to report the news fully, "without fear or favor;" yet our reporting could expose vulnerable subjects—undocumented immigrants, crime victims, the home-less, or the mentally ill—to embarrassment or risk. We are to divorce ourselves from personal involvement or bias; yet we wade into worlds where injustices are rampant, and where our sense of outrage screams for action. We pledge to remain independent of special interests and agendas; yet we are members of a society that, if it is to work, needs its citizens to donate, volunteer, and vote.

Popular mythology about—and, sadly, sometimes within—news media indicates that these value systems are in conflict: the profession is bound by conventions that set us apart from society. We clutch our notebooks like talis-mans against emotion, and hide behind the safe shield of conflict-of-interest policies and ethics codes. We observe but don't engage. We record but don't react. We chronicle a situation but don't care about the outcome. The pres-umption is that we must put down our personal values—perhaps even our humanity—when we pick up our notebooks or cameras. What a mispercep-tion. And what a shame. Because the best journalism is driven by passion—passion for the truth, and passion for society's right to that truth. And passion is a decidedly human trait, one that comes from a deeply personal place.

Throughout history the best journalism has revealed the either/or con-struct of professional versus personal to be false. It is essential for journalists to remain independent of special interests, to rise above harmful bias, to verify the accuracy of stories, and to be transparent about the sources of information. None of that demands that we unplug our humanity.

Jacob Riis roamed the streets of New York City at the end of the nineteenth century to expose the plight of immigrant families huddled in tenements and immigrant children pressed into hard labor. An immigrant himself, who often slept in police-run poorhouses, Riis was shocked by the myth of the promised land. He was compelled to tell that story out of his personal experience and values.[1]

Ernie Pyle marched shoulder to shoulder with soldiers in World War II and experienced firsthand how courage and fear walk hand in hand. He was an unapologetic champion of the little guy, who he humanized through his walk-in-their-boots reporting. Pyle died on the battlefield, but his stories helped define a genre of journalism that, by its very name—human interest reporting—defies a separation between the two.[2]

Edward R. Murrow delivered searing portraits of migrant farm workers in his acclaimed television series *Harvest of Shame*, all but daring America to take action. He turned the same professional outrage on the powerful and vindictive Sen. Joseph McCarthy, and helped end an ugly episode in American govern-ance.[3] Murrow understood the symbiotic relationship between good journal-ism and humanity. In a 1958 speech, he noted the potential of the then new media of broadcast television: "This instrument can teach, it can illuminate; yes, it can even inspire, but it can do so only to the extent that humans are determined to use it to those ends. Otherwise it is merely wires and lights in a box."[4] All human beings are shaped by the circumstances of our lives—our childhood, our education, our culture, our religion, our friends and family and experiences. Journalists can no more shed that shaping than can lawyers or doctors or teachers or priests. Walking onto the job doesn't mean walking away from ourselves. Presuming to do so is, at best, dishonest. At worst, dangerous.

Journalists make more mistakes—act more unethically—by *not* acknowledging their emotions and humanity, argues Butch Ward, the former managing editor of the *Philadelphia Inquirer* and now a distinguished fellow at the Poynter Institute.[5]

"The best work that's been done throughout history has been done by human beings, not by machines," Ward says. "Our unwillingness to admit we're human beings has gotten us into a lot of trouble."

That doesn't mean journalists should abandon independence for advocacy or activism. We serve society through our detachment from most causes or agendas. We stand in for the public—and apart from power—at civic meetings so we can ask probing questions, sort out truth from spin, and help society function with full, and fully vetted, information.

But babysitting civic life is a small part of what journalists do. We also investigate, uncover, challenge, entertain, and, yes, engage. When we're at our best, we expose the bad guys, explain consequences, and help citizens take action.

We also tell stories—stories that remind us of our connections as human beings.

We can't engage others unless we, ourselves, are engaged. How can a reporter relay the emotional truth of a situation—the anguish of a mother whose son is killed in war, the panic of a working father who loses his job, the dual hopes and fears of an immigrant family seeking a toehold for the future—if he doesn't bring his own emotional intelligence to that reporting?

"It's naïve to think that you can capture the emotion of a situation without your heart being involved in your work," says Ward. "It comes down to the lens through which you see situations. Is it going to be a purely intellectual lens? Or are you going to bring all your senses to bear?"

"AIDS in the Heartland"

On a cold March evening in 1988, I stood in the waiting room of a hospital in Ortonville, Minnesota, notebook in hand, pen poised, leaning against a pillar, listening.

In front of me, a family stood in a circle holding hands. They had just been told that Bert Henningson Jr.—they called him "Randy," and knew him as son, brother, uncle—was losing his battle with HIV/AIDS. He had lapsed into a semiconscious state and was being kept stable on a respirator. Unplug the machine, the family was told, and he'll likely die. Leave him on the respirator, and he could go on—alive in body but not mind—for weeks, maybe months.

So the family circled, and held hands. A passage in my story, "AIDS in the Heartland," described it this way:

> One by one, nudged by matriarch Ailys Henningson, they spoke their piece. It was family tradition, to vote on matters of import. One such family vote, years earlier, involved the color of the kitchen. With a little urging from mischievous Berton Henningson Sr., the four children chose flamingo.
>
> On this night, the vote was unanimous. They would let Henningson die.[6]

What the story didn't say is that when it came time for Ailys, Bert Jr.'s mother, to cast the last vote, she instead turned to me. "Jacqui, how do you vote?"

No matter how we justify our involvement in stories—we affect things by our presence no matter how hard we try to do otherwise—this was way outside the bounds. Yet it was hard to shake off: I was allowed to witness something profoundly important and profoundly private; how, then, could I deny a direct and simple request?

My decision was made harder by the back story: I had gotten to know Bert Henningson intimately during the year photographer Jean Pieri and I immersed ourselves in his relationship with his partner, Dick Hanson, and their march together towards death from AIDS. I grew especially close to Bert, who became the storyteller as Dick grew sicker and sicker and finally, eight months earlier, died. Now it was Bert's turn, and I was given the chance to write about someone who had already had a dress rehearsal for his own death.

But for most of that time, Bert's family had declined to talk to me. Their position was made clear by Ailys, who, at seventy, was as formidable as she had been as an elementary school principal. They supported their son, she said, but wanted nothing to do with "you or your kind."

Now, at this crucible moment, she was asking me to join the family vote. I offered to put down my notebook. No good. I offered to leave the room with the understanding I would reconstruct the scene later. No, Ailys said, I need to know how you would vote. That's when, out of desperation, my journalistic instincts kicked in. I asked another question: "Why?"

Her answer: She wanted to know how I would vote because she wanted to know how her son would vote. She figured I knew because she figured I had asked him.

It would have been easier not to know. It would have been a lot easier not to care. Not to care about the smart, honest, witty man dying in the bed down the hall. Not to care about these people in front of me who had sacrificed their privacy for a story their son/brother/uncle wanted to tell. But I did know. And I did care. So what did I do?

Minefields and Challenges

Before I answer, let's consider the challenges. I have admitted getting "especially close" to a story subject. I have admitted having information that, if shared, could affect an outcome. I have admitted caring about the people I was covering.

That's quite a professional minefield to negotiate. The only way I know to get through it is to take it step by careful step, sometimes forward, sometimes sideways, sometimes back, always with journalistic intent, always with the public good in mind, and always with others around to guide us as we make our way. What I don't know how to do is avoid the minefield—unless we think it's our job to stand always on the sidelines, safe notebooks in hand, as stenographers.

There's a story told in a newsroom I worked in about a veteran reporter who was as sweet as he was dogged. One afternoon, after an especially difficult interview, he slammed down the phone and said, "I do things as a reporter that I would never do as a human!" Any journalist worth his byline knows the feeling. Our jobs often take us outside the conventions of polite company. Who among us has been raised to invade privacy? To challenge someone's truthfulness in public? To knock on the door of a grieving family at the height of their sorrow? But because those actions seem abnormal doesn't mean they aren't ethical, human, and, sometimes, noble. It probably never feels entirely normal for a cop to interrogate a suspect, or for an EMT to blast someone's heart with shock paddles. They do those things in the pursuit of a greater societal good. In other words, they do them with a clear and ethical purpose in mind. It's when purpose gets lost, or when our personal values don't jive with our professional purpose, that we need to reconsider our fit for the job or, more likely, how we do the job.

I once saw a television reporter stop the burial of a child at a refugee camp in Sudan because she was so broken up she couldn't get through her stand-up. She asked that the funeral be paused while she composed herself. I also once watched a newspaper photographer and TV cameraman brawl in a snow bank outside the estate where former vice-president Hubert H. Humphrey lay dying. They were fighting over camera position.

In both cases, the journalists lost sight of the real purpose of their work, and let their values—professional *and* personal—slip. In the case of the fist-fighting photographers, that's clear. But even the TV reporter, as "human" as her anguish was, let that get in the way of a greater act of humanity, which would have been to toughen up and let the funeral continue uninterrupted.

Commitments, Choices, and Solutions

So what happened in that hospital waiting room back in 1988?

I didn't join the family vote, of course. Instead, I kept a commitment I had made to everyone involved in the story: I outlined what was in my notebook that I planned to write. I told them that Bert, a PhD economist, had told me that his greatest fear was losing mental acuity and becoming a burden on his family. He had told me he had considered suicide but rejected it out of respect for his parents. I would have reviewed that information with the Henningsons as part of my fact-checking process anyway. My situational response was to do that in the moment rather than waiting for a more standard prepublication fact-check.

"AIDS in the Heartland" was as intimate as it was controversial. From the outset, Pieri and I tried to follow a process that would neither exploit nor romanticize. That started when we got the assignment—take readers inside the life of a gay AIDS patient at the pitch of the epidemic, when society's terror of the disease often attached to its revulsion of homosexuality. We promised everyone we interviewed that we would review relevant information before publication. With Dick and Bert, the primary subjects, we outlined the likely consequences of their participation, positive and negative. We stipulated that nothing was "off the record." But there were times we would talk more casually, not recording them verbatim, but returning later for a formal interview. We agreed to few conditions, and only when our reporting supported that decision. For example, Bert had been married and didn't want his ex-wife and stepdaughter included in the story. I determined they had nothing to do with Bert's daily life, his relationship with Dick, or his illness. The fact of his marriage was mentioned in the story, but the names of the ex-wife and her daughter were not. Exposing them would not have added to the story substantively and could have caused them undue harm.

Those agreements helped us gain the trust of the story subjects, including, eventually, Bert's mother Ailys. It also allowed us to write candidly about Dick's lifestyle, which likely brought AIDS into the relationship. To do less would have been to whitewash reality and lose faith with readers. It would have been dishonest.

Throughout our reporting, our editors at the *St. Paul Pioneer Press* asked the toughest of questions. They helped us weigh our responsibility to readers and to the story subjects. We brainstormed alternatives that kept us off the shoals of either/or decision-making. We kept our purpose in mind.

One last thing. I mentioned caring and closeness. I don't think it's possible to spend months with people facing death without coming to care about them. But Jean and I regularly reminded Dick and Bert that ours was a professional relationship; telling their story was our primary goal. That clarity of purpose became crucial when Dick railed against the first story in the series—he felt it was too negative—and when I had to describe Bert's deteriorating mental condition in the final installment. It broke my heart to write things that hurt them, but it was the ethical thing to do.

Foundational Principles

In practicing and teaching journalism, I've found the most useful guide to ethics in the work done by Bob Steele and others at the Poynter Institute. These living guidelines adapt to changing times and technology, recognize that there is no one-size-fits-all answer, but keep three foundational principles in mind:[7]

- Seek truth and report it as fully as possible
- Act independently
- Minimize harm

Those principles are demanding: they expect journalists to work with both courage *and* compassion. We must be purposeful and independent in gathering information and interpreting it for the public good. We also have to be aware of the consequences of our work.

The best journalists may use different words but believe in the same practice. Bruce de Silva, a writing coach for the Associated Press, puts it this way: "Write only what you know to be true, don't misrepresent yourself, avoid all conflicts of interest, always be fair and avoid hurting anyone who doesn't deserve it. The rest is situational."[8]

Notice that De Silva doesn't say, "Avoid hurting anyone." Journalists live with the knowledge that the spotlight they shine can often burn. That means we have to report deeply enough to get to the truth, and to believe some greater public good will come of publishing it.

De Silva's second provocative reference—*The rest is situational*—would seem to leave the journalist without a sure rudder, out there as a rogue operator, not bound by any bottom-line rules or ethics. It hints at cavalier behavior, in which a journalist can rationalize whatever action he or she finds useful in the moment.

Not so. Each situation a journalist encounters demands that she adhere to professional standards and think about how those standards apply in various scenarios and to various stakeholders. The impact of a decision—especially a decision to publish—can be vastly different on a source than it is on a story subject than it is on the readers. And it demands that the journalist, rather than ignore his personal frame of reference, be aware of what he brings to the situation and figure out how to manage that as part of his journalism.

Drawing Lines

In 2002 reporter Paula Bock and photographer Betty Udesen traveled to Zimbabwe for the *Seattle Times* to write about the cultural, political, economic, and emotional ravages of HIV/AIDS. The prompt for the trip was local: a Seattle-based nonprofit, PATH, with funding from the Seattle-based Gates Foundation, was developing woman-controlled contraceptives, then working with agencies in Zimbabwe to put education and prevention in the hands of women there. Bock and Udesen learned that women and children are the primary victims of HIV/AIDS in parts of the world where prostitution is an economic imperative and where men control the sexual dynamic. Most men disdain the use of condoms within marriage. Whether street workers or wives, coming of age sexually puts women at high risk for AIDS.

Bock and Udesen wanted to tell the story through that prism. They found the ideal family: three generations of women—Amai Caty, fifty-eight, a wife and mother of twelve children; her daughter, Ruth, twenty-four, who was widowed by AIDS and now dying of it herself; and Ruth's daughter, Martha, five, who represented the generation of African children next in line to inherit AIDS unless something dramatic happens to intervene.

Bock and Udesen visited the family at its home outside Harare. Ruth was very ill and Amai Caty was caring for her. Bock asked Amai Caty if she was taking precautions against becoming infected herself. A passage from the story:

> Amai Caty knew her daughter was infected with the same virus that killed her son-in-law, but she'd hoped Ruth wouldn't get sick. Then Ruth's cough turned to vomiting and diarrhea. For days now, she's been too weak to walk. She soils her blankets.
>
> Each time, Amai Caty cleans up. She wipes her daughter's bottom with warm rags. She scrubs the bedding with hot water and rocks.
>
> At church, Ruth's mother says, she learned about home-based care for "this disease that has come among us." Use bleach and detergent and gloves, they told her.
>
> She can't afford these things.
>
> She repeats: I don't have any gloves.
>
> This, in a few understated words, is her plea for help.

That plea posed a dilemma for Bock and Udesen. For a few cents, they could buy bleach and gloves. A small thing—perhaps the only humane thing. Bock addressed it in her story: "What if you can help, but don't? What if Ruth soils the sheets tonight? What if Amai Caty has cuts on her hands?" But they didn't find it an easy decision at all. Buying supplies would make them direct actors in the story they were there to cover. And while something so small would not seem to blur the boundary between them and their subjects, their reporting told them otherwise.

Faced with a global epidemic, what do you do?
   Faced with a plea for one pair of rubber gloves, what do you do?
   In impoverished Africa, people want and need to be paid for whatever they do, including sharing their time and their lives. But if we pay for information, a source might exaggerate or lie. Neighbors or relatives might grow jealous. If we buy gloves for one mother, why not bleach for another, drugs for a third? Where do you start? Where does it end?
   Instead we tell a story, because that's what we do.
   In journalism, that's ethics.
   In the heart, it rings hollow.

Rather than remain paralyzed by an either/or—either they buy bleach and gloves or don't—Bock and Udesen sought options that would honor their humanity and their journalism. The solution they hit on: they would make a donation to a local group that supported AIDS families, ensuring that many people—not just Amai Caty's household—received help. Amai Caty would get her bleach and gloves but not know where they came from.
   But before Bock and Udesen could make their donation, Ruth died. When they asked Amai Caty about it later, they gained one of the most powerful moments in their story, one that helped readers understand the demands that HIV/AIDS places on love:

So when the end came for Ruth, Amai Caty showed her love with her hands. "I would wash everything that came out of Ruth," she says. "I never used any gloves. If I was to take plastic bags, like from the sugar and mealy-meal, Ruth would see me wearing the plastic on my hands and she would have stress. 'Oh my mother is seeing me like I am a toilet. My mother does not love me.' So I was touching everything with my hands. I wanted Ruth to know that I loved her and would touch her. It was up to God as to whether I would be infected or not."

Bock and Udesen had to respect the culture they were in, despite their own leanings. But their tensions didn't end there. Back in Seattle, Bock felt she couldn't tell the story of Ruth's family honestly without being honest about her own involvement. She weighed her ethical obligations to the family but also to the readers of the *Seattle Times* and to her own sense of to professionalism.
   In the end, she saw that the helplessness she and Udesen felt in Zimbabwe sat near the heart of the story. It mirrored the helplessness we all feel in the face

of such a vast tragedy—one that can mire entire governments in indecision. Bock used her personal conflict to serve as a metaphor for society's inability to combat HIV/AIDS. Her solution wasn't to turn her back on the emotional intensity she felt—but to share it with readers.

What's one pair of rubber gloves? Nothing. Everything.

Bock and Udesen's story, "In Her Mother's Shoes" (for which I was the editor), was published December 1, 2002, in the *Seattle Times*. It won several national and international awards, including the Ernie Pyle Award for Human Interest Writing and the Global Health Council's Excellence in Media Award. The story circulated around the globe and was cited by President George W. Bush when he signed a $15 billion AIDS package. It also became the centerpiece of a traveling exhibit designed to educate the public about efforts to prevent HIV in developing countries.

Honoring the Profession

Bock found different solutions for her story on AIDS than I did for mine, but we honored a similar process. We sought options that retained our professional independence while responding to an emotional situation. Our actions were informed by our journalistic purpose, and ultimately made our journalism better.

This approach to ethical journalism is as liberating as it is challenging. Liberating because it doesn't lock you in to rigid responses. Challenging because there are so many variables to consider. For example, a college journalist is sent to profile a star high school athlete who just joined a powerhouse team in the local school district. The athlete tells the reporter "off the record" that his family hasn't moved into the district yet—putting him in violation of league rules. If the journalist reports that, the athlete could be kicked off the team, and the team suspended from the season's play.

The reporter doesn't want to jeopardize the athlete's future, so files a nice profile without exploring the residency issue. That approach, while understandable, doesn't take others into account. What if school officials knew the family wasn't living in the district but recruited the athlete anyway? What about teams from other schools who might be put an unfair advantage? What about other athletes who will be competing for similar college scholarships but won't get the same attention?

That doesn't mean the reporter should rush to publish a "gotcha" piece. But he and his editors should consider the broader implications of their actions. Bottom line: they should do more reporting. The only way to make ethical decisions is with as much consideration and information as possible.

Central to the Poynter Institute's ethical guidelines are questions. Not rules but questions, which are the core of all good journalism. Among them:

- What do I know? What do I *need* to know?
- What is my journalistic purpose?
- Who are the stakeholders—those affected by my decision?
- What are the possible short- and long-term consequences of my actions?
- What are my alternatives to maximize truth telling and minimize harm?

This is tricky terrain, especially when a journalist walks a line between personal values and professional obligations. If that line is fuzzier than we'd like—if the boundary between us and our sources and subjects, and between us as individuals and us as professionals, isn't wide, firm, and bright, how do we know where to stand?

Ward says it comes back to values: "I don't have one set of values as a human being and another as a journalist," he says. "I have the same values as both. I believe in fairness as a human being and as a journalist. I believe in service to others as a human being and as a journalist." The key is how those values inform our actions. It is a journalist's actions—not private opinions or personal beliefs—that are ethical or not.

Ethics in journalism is not a convenient checklist, but a process of critical thinking and action that actually takes us closer to a story—not farther away. It engages rather than distances. It defines independence as a protection against improper influence rather than as a disconnect from the world or those we write about. And it requires us to be better journalists—to ask more, know more, and care more about what we do, why we do it, and who we do it for.

Notes

1. For more on Riis, see his *How the Other Half Lives* (Mineola, NY: Dover, 1971), or Tom and Annette BukSwienty's new biography, *The Other Half* (New York: W. W. Norton, 2008).

2. To learn more about Pyle, see Indiana University's collection at journalism. indiana.edu/news/erniepyle.

3. Murrow's conflict with McCarthy was featured in the 2005 Oscar-nominated film "Good Night, and Good Luck," directed and cowritten by George Clooney.

4. Speech to Radio-Television News Directors Association conference, October 15, 1958, Chicago, Ill., available on the Web at http://www.turnoffyourtv.com/commentary/hiddenagenda/murrow.html.

5. These and subsequent Ward quotations are from a December 2008 phone interview with the author.

6. Jacqui Banaszynski, "AIDS in the Heartland," *St. Paul Pioneer Press*, Special Section, April 3, 1988.

7. Robert Steele, "Guiding Principles for the Journalist," available at http://www. poynter.org/column.asp?id=36&aid=4349, accessed December 2, 2008.

8. Personal communication, December 3, 2008.

17

A Robust Future for Conflict of Interest

Edward Wasserman

Conflict of interest has become a signature element in the claim by Internet-based commentators to moral superiority over their legacy news media counterparts. The insistence of so-called mainstream journalists that they are free not just of private material entanglements but of personal sympathies that might tilt their reporting and commentary is brandished as a prime exhibit in the indictment of the media establishment as hypocritical, secretly biased, and unworthy of public trust.[1]

Much of the criticism comes under the banner of transparency and accountability and centers on narrow matters such as alleged partisan leanings among reporters. That trivializes the matter. The exuberant rise of New Media and the steady collapse of established media business models are raising issues related to independence and conflict of interest in much more profound ways than allegations over mere campaign giving would imply.

As I will suggest, innovations such as online advertising tied to specific editorial content, highly targeted Web sites intended to nurture demographically attractive micro-publics, nonprofit funding of editorial initiatives, and an increase in amateur or non-full-time journalists are all potentially problematic in ways that pre-Internet formulations of conflict of interest do not fully anticipate.

So, conflict of interest has a bright future. It also has an illustrious past. Indeed, it is virtually a cultural archetype of journalistic corruption: the business writer who covers a company in which she owns shares, the politics reporter who accepts a weekend junket from a wealthy office-seeker, the publisher who kills an embarrassing story about an advertiser arrested in an anti-prostitution sweep, the media company that diverts resources to promotional coverage of the products of a corporate affiliate.

Nature of Conflict of Interest

At its broadest, conflict of interest comprises a variety of situations where undeclared obligations or loyalties exist that might plausibly stand between journalists or journalism organizations and the public they principally serve. Those obligations engender a set of rival objectives, usually unknown to the audience, that the journalist would reasonably be expected to be mindful of and be inclined to help fulfill, and which could, accordingly, influence her reporting or its presentation.[2] Although the traditional notion of "interests" suggests a material stake rather than a personal bond, the conception here is not so narrow; any affiliation that the person values may suffice to produce a conflict.

Conflict of interest has recently come to be applied still more broadly to a wide array of mental predispositions and sentiments that might conceivably have a discernible effect on the journalist's output.[3] A key question is when such loyalties, affections, sympathies—an inescapable consequence of living in society—do indeed create conflicts that are ethically problematic for journalists.

Plainly, not all do. For that matter, material holdings may not either. It is easily imaginable that even a journalist who has what certainly seems to be a financial stake in the subject of a story might attach so little importance to the apparent entanglement that the reporting would be unaffected.

Role of Judgment

So, how then does a potential influence become ethically problematic? How is it expressed? Here, it seems appropriate to posit a mediating agency that gives the influence practical consequence, which Meyers and Davis[4] do by assigning a pivotal role to judgment. Accordingly, conflict of interest does its harm less by giving the journalist another constituency to serve than by affecting the way she thinks, by impairing her judgment. Because of the conflict, the reporter looks for different matters to report, selects different facts, presents them differently, pursues angles she might not otherwise care about—in sum, performs a range of professional operations differently and creates content that is different from what a journalist free of the conflict would produce.

The strength of this formulation is that it frames the consequences of a conflict of interest in a way that seems intuitively true: After all, a conflict need not turn the reporter into a straight-line agent of the problematic influence.[5] It works both more subtly and more comprehensively, by re-sensitizing the reporter, recalibrating cognition, redirecting attention, promoting an off-stage constituency not so much to serve as to be mindful of and to care about.

Such is the value of recognizing the role of judgment and recasting the harm done by conflict of interest as consisting of impaired judgment—and of content that, consequently, is transformed.

But a danger with this construct is that if not handled properly it changes the subject. It shifts critical attention away from the corrupting force of the outside influence and the propriety of the reporter's engagement with it, and onto the journalist's internal capacity to cope with that influence and safeguard his work from its effects. Ethics yields to psychology. Instead of an inquiry into values and loyalties, we have interrogation on motives and susceptibilities. Plus, the construct invites evasion and denial, since the reporter is the main authority on whether his judgment is altered. Perfectly outrageous influences could be defended as ethically permissible in light of the individual's purported integrity and strength of character.

Plausibility

So how should judgment fit into the conflict-of-interest model without tipping into that psychologistic trap? Here, the notion of plausibility—combining both reasonableness and likelihood—seems helpful. Accordingly, conflict of interest exists when it is plausible that the influence would impair the journalist's professional judgment to the detriment of her public service obligations.[6] It therefore requires two conclusions: that it is reasonable to expect the outside interest to have an influence, and that the influence would be deleterious. This formulation explicitly acknowledges that the finding that a conflict exists requires an outside determination of plausibility; disharmony cannot be inferred automatically from the existence of overlap between professional duty and other interests.

A final point on the moral harm done by conflicts. Because conflict of interest impugns not just the communicator's performance but her motives, the damage it does goes beyond the possible distortions or inaccuracies a given conflict might engender in a single story. The notion has power as an exemplar of cultural villainy because it implicates the fundamental trustworthiness of communication. Trusting somebody, as Annette Baier reminds us, is quite different from relying on that person for a particular service. It is an expression of confidence not just in the technical competence but in the goodwill of the other, especially when the power, knowledge, and capacities of the two parties are widely unequal and when the trusted party necessarily operates within a wide grant of autonomy and self-direction.[7] Little strikes quite so devastatingly at the basics of communicative trust than the suspicion that messages are motivated and shaped by a self-serving agenda that the other person is deliberately concealing.

"Apparent" Conflicts

How does this discussion illuminate the perplexing status of "perceived" or "apparent" conflicts of interest? Contemporary codes interpret conflicts expansively to embrace activities whose effects on journalism are hard to discern and that may not constitute ethical breaches at all.[8] Among them are actions that might expose employers to public reproach, dilute their brands, deny them credit or payment for outside work their employees do, and otherwise put them at a commercial disadvantage—without, however, necessarily influencing the information and commentary delivered to the public, which constitutes the journalist's main duty and ground for ethical criticism.

So this usage is widespread, and its popularity is troubling. Perceptions, after all, are not usually considered valid reasons for moral action unless they are accurate. Moral philosophers from Plato on have insisted on the fallibility of perception and the need to subject it to rigorous verification and thought. The alternative is to say, in effect, "There's nothing wrong with the action except that others might view it as objectionable." Such a statement privileges the opinion of outsiders as ethically authoritative, rather than as a view that needs to be tested and, if ill founded, disputed or disregarded. Sometimes "the public" is wrong, sometimes "the public" may not even be audible above the clamor of denunciations whose real purpose is to disable a news organization.

In our formulation, if it is not plausible that the activities or relationships that seem problematic would have a discernible effect on the quality of journalism delivered to the public, there is no conflict of interest, real or potential. The problem is a misperception and, as Michael Davis argues, the solution is to show that it is a misperception so that a reasonable outsider will agree. In his discussion of "apparent" conflict of interest, which he defines as a situation where no conflict exists but an outsider might justifiably suspect one, resolution requires "making available enough information to show that there is no actual or potential conflict."[9]

Scope of Conflicts

Powerful—perhaps the most powerful—conflicts arise not from outsiders bearing threats or blandishments, but from within normal journalistic practice.[10] The logic of conflict of interest implicates routine features of the organizational sociology of contemporary journalism. The beat system, whose operating rationality entails nurturing a stable network of productive source relationships, creates strong incentives to use or withhold information to sustain those relations.[11] The White House correspondent who learns the aging president catnaps during Cabinet meetings understands reporting that fact may cost him his access, and consequently, his highly esteemed beat. The desire for personal, professional advancement itself constitutes an interest that may well come into conflict with the duty to report publicly significant facts. Consider the ambitious columnist who vets potential topics with an eye to those that will get him on TV talk shows and thence onto the lucrative speaker circuit.[12] Or the city editor who hungers for a big prize and devotes an outsized proportion of her staff to a glamorous project at the expense of coverage of matters of continuing, but less prize-worthy, importance.

If we look beneath the level of professional practice to the institutional political economy that enfolds the newsroom,[13] what makes conflict of interest even more insidious is that its logic incriminates the economic essentials of news as a business. A commercial news operation, especially if chiefly dependent on advertising rather than on circulation revenue, is under unrelenting pressure to assess coverage options by their appeal to demographically desirable markets, not by their value in nurturing an informed and sovereign citizenry. Redeploying newsroom resources away from foreign bureaus to lucrative home-furnishing sections, or taking precious time within a half-hour evening program away from news and selling it to advertisers, may have reasonable economic justification, but these are nonetheless responses to conflicts of interest.

Those vexing elements related to the organizational sociology and political economy of journalism are captured in the formulation offered by Black, Steele, and Barney: "Conflicts of interest occur when individuals face competing loyalties to a source or to their own self-interest, or to their organization's economic needs as opposed to the information needs of the public."[14] That formulation correctly describes realities inextricably woven into the contemporary practice of journalism, where journalists routinely confront competing loyalties to sources and their organization's economic needs and face pressure to privilege those relationships over their primarily public duty.

In that respect, the problem of conflicts derives from the reality that the people who produce journalism are embedded in the organizations that employ them and the communities they serve. They practice journalism within partly overlapping layers of obligation and loyalty—personal, professional, and institutional. Journalists, in everything they produce, must balance the demands of multiple constituencies: sources, colleagues, bosses, competitors, family, posterity, and—above all, one hopes—the general public. All, it is important to remember, may have legitimate claims on the journalist's loyalty.[15] The interests of each sometimes overlap and sometimes clash, and those areas of agreement and discord are etched onto the journalism that results. Journalists suffer or benefit from the coverage they offer in ways that may not be apparent, and their anticipation of those consequences cannot help but color their professional output.

Journalism need not be corrupt. But as a truth-telling practice it is inevitably a negotiated approximation, and the notion that it can be practiced within a zone of undiluted dedication to the public good is impossible to support. Instead, it seems fair to say that conflicts of interest are an unavoidable feature of the terrain that journalists navigate, which cannot be eliminated but must be managed, more or less successfully, more or less honestly and ethically.

Historical Background

Identifying conflict of interest as a distinct concern first required articulating broader principles of communicative ethics, such as independence and fair-mindedness. Until those emerged as values, the notion of a conflict could have no normative edge; a hidden loyalty cannot constitute a conflict unless there is some principal obligation it conflicts with. Moreover, on the level of political culture, only after the idea was advanced that the journalist had some public duty did it make sense to deplore private influences that might subvert it.

Although the term itself dates only from the mid-twentieth century,[16] early expressions of the doctrine of journalistic objectivity suggest a sensitivity to what we now call conflicts of interest. In his history of journalism ethics, Stephen Ward identifies, starting in seventeenth-century England, two sources of objectivity as a professional norm.[17] First was the rise of periodic publishing, an economic model based on building return business. The publisher's wish not just to reach today's readers but to ensure that readers come back for the next issue spawned standards of reliability and trustworthiness that, although not explicitly couched in conflict-of-interest language, are functionally equivalent to a claim to be approaching the public with clean hands.

In the following century, Ward argues, that marketplace incentive was joined to a second source, an emerging conception of the informed public as a political force, allied to and nourished by a press whose leanings were subject to open speculation and critique.[18] The press, admittedly, was riven by contending allegiances, but the notion that it had a principal obligation to the public was born in this period, and a fuller conception of conflict of interest became possible. In his 1800 work, Tunis Wortman explicitly connected impartiality with resistance to contending pressures: "Neither fear on the one side, nor hope of reward on the other, should intimidate or influence its enquiries. . . . The moment that corrupt or foreign considerations are suffered to bias, or stain their pages, they become injurious to the genuine interests of the society."[19] In the United States the idea that journalists have a primary loyalty to the public good took modern form in the late nineteenth and early twentieth centuries, apace with the appearance of news media as profit-seeking industrial enterprises, the rise of the mass-circulation advertising-support model, and the

movement of journalism toward self-identification as both a professional practice and an instrument of popular sovereignty.[20]

It has been argued that concern about "institutional conflicts of interest"—
powerfully corrupting pressures on journalists that originate within their own
businesses—arose only a century later, with the late-twentieth-century emergence of media conglomerates whose wide-ranging manufacturing and sales
operations regarded their affiliated news divisions as a potential source of
"synergies"—or PR support.[21] While the potential for improper influence undoubtedly grew with the industrial diversification of news owners, fear of the
corrupting influence of undisclosed private loyalties arising from the owning
institutions themselves was voiced much earlier.

The first industry-wide ethics code, that of the American Society of Newspaper Editors,' in 1923, warned: "Promotion of any private interest contrary to
the general welfare, for whatever reason, is not compatible with honest journalism."[22] A decade later, the American Newspaper Guild's ethics code identified
several areas related to conflicts of interest, such as taking money for publicity
work and covering matters that clash with the policy of newspaper owners.[23]
The Journal of Mass Media Ethics, launched in 1984, reported in its first issue
that most ethics codes assigned central importance to conflicts of interest, especially such matters as extracurricular political involvements and outside income.[24]

A Typology

The way in which conflict of interest has metastasized into a catchall charge
leveled against a great number of activities—from putting bumper stickers on
one's car to moonlighting—suggests more systematic analysis could be useful.
Accordingly, I suggest analyzing journalistic conflicts along two dimensions:
the degree to which they are endemic to the practice of journalism or the business in which it is embedded, and the degree to which they are directly consequential, meaning they are likely to have discernible effects on what the journalist does.

Dimension 1: From Endemic to Extraneous

Conflicts are endemic to the degree that they arise from the nexus of institutional, professional, and personal relationships in which the journalist works.
They are extraneous to the degree that they originate outside those relationships.[25]

As discussed earlier, reporters' reliance on sources may oblige them to ignore newsworthy stories that, if published, would damage valuable relationships that enhance the reporters' effectiveness and enable them to advance

professionally.[26] That is a conflict inherent in the terrain on which journalism is practiced and is hence endemic. Similarly, the TV station manager who kills a story because it would imperil a valuable advertising contract is responding to a reality internal to the reality of ad dependency: Advertisers may withhold support from media outlets whose coverage they view as harmful. That does not mean the station manager's decision is ethically sound, which it almost certainly is not. My point is that it is a response to a conflict endemic to commercial news.[27]

By contrast, consider a reporter's decision to campaign on her own time for a political candidate she favors. That is not a response to challenges or opportunities inherent in her work as a journalist. Likewise, if a reporter buys property whose value might be influenced by things she writes, the purchase is not one of those tough decisions that she must weigh as part of her job. The conflict arises from goals external to her journalism, and, in the terms proposed here, is extraneous: nothing in the practice of journalism itself engenders it.

Dimension 2: From Conflicts with Clear Impact to Those without

Some conflicts seem more laden with consequences than others. But while it is easy to offer examples of loyalties or obligations that seem certain to affect reporting, the opposite case is harder to imagine. Is a non-consequential conflict ethically problematic? Is it a conflict at all?

The question is a reasonable one, yet, as we have seen, news organizations routinely promulgate rules that forbid ties of dubious consequence. A sports writer is disciplined under a conflict-of-interest prohibition for attending a political fundraising concert even though she will never write about that or any other campaign event (or even about the music.) A politics reporter faces limits on her financial portfolio not because investments might predispose her to write one thing rather than another, but because her employer craves a reputation for integrity. Are such restrictions justified as responses to conflicts of interest?

While it is important to be skeptical about the appropriation of ethics language for the purpose of workplace supervision and brand management, there may still be a principled reason to forbid some entanglements that have no direct, immediate, or substantive effect on the journalist's output: they may still clash with the reporter's duties in real ways.

Consider outside commitments that may induce a reporter to privilege certain obligations that ought to be subordinated to a primary duty to inform the public—celebrity journalism, for instance, where journalists are rewarded with lavish fees on the national speaker circuit once they establish themselves by appearing on high-profile news talk shows. They have a huge careerist incentive to anticipate, in their day jobs, the kind of topics and treatments that will make them talking heads on TV. That unacknowledged agenda might plausibly guide their journalism toward covering some things and not others.

Similarly, book publishing and blogging, in which the journalist is seeking to turn her reporting into a vehicle for other business ventures or professional avenues, are vulnerable to criticism on conflict-of-interest grounds. In those instances, as with the classic conflict, the journalist allows a set of interceding loyalties to stand between content and audience, burdening her professional activities with undisclosed purpose and entitling her to rewards unrelated to her obligation to serve her public ably and independently.[28]

Such conflicts have no clearly discernible impact on a particular area of coverage and represent no specific, undisclosed loyalty or obligation that the reporter might be advancing through textual framings, omissions, or distortions. Yet they frame larger alignments that, it is reasonable to presume, affect the journalist's judgment when it comes to the way she carries out her professional duties. So the argument that they may still be conflicts of interest seems sound.

Hence, we have two dimensions of conflicts: the degree to which they arise from the ways in which journalism is practiced and institutionalized, and the degree to which they have discernible, direct consequence on information and commentary delivered to the public.

Handling Conflicts

This typology offers clues as to how to handle conflicts of interest and mitigate the harm they cause. In general, conflicts can be eliminated, disclosed, or managed. How effective—and how available—those remedies are depends on the specifics of the conflict, and whether it is endemic or extraneous, consequential or non-consequential.

Elimination

Clearly, this is the most effective response to a genuine conflict of interest. It could mean severing the outside relationships or commitments that are problematic, or reassigning or modifying the specific duties that produce the conflict.

By their nature, non-endemic conflicts are easiest to eliminate without harming important processes or relationships. The real estate reporter need not buy the property in the neighborhood she covers. The publishing company can still publish if it does not buy naming rights to the new stadium that will be financed by a bond issue that its newspaper is urging voters to approve.

That is not to suggest that such conflicts can be eliminated without cost, which may well involve abridging customary freedoms. Even if getting rid of non-endemic conflicts may not threaten business as usual, doing so still comes at a cost, which may not be trivial. That makes it necessary to consider whether the conflicts are sufficiently vexing or consequential to bother.

Endemic conflicts are far more intractable. How can anyone eliminate the editor's desire to pursue prize-winning coverage, the publisher's incentive to deploy staff on new sections that draw fresh advertising, the news director's hunger for sensational items for sweeps week, the corporate manager's insistence on cutting statehouse bureaus to raise the news division's contribution to the consolidated bottom line? Endemic conflicts, by and large, cannot easily be eliminated.

Disclosure

What Louis Day calls the "moral minimum,"[29] disclosure amounts to alerting the public to otherwise hidden loyalties or obligations that might influence what they see or hear.

It is rarely a satisfactory response for several reasons. First, disclosure typically cannot be specific as to how the outside entanglement might shape the journalism. If readers are supposed to be forewarned to possible bias by knowing that the writer used to work for the subject of the story, they may still not have a clue as to what direction that bias may lean. (Indeed, the writer herself may not be sure.) Second, even if the disclosure did suggest a broad direction of improper influence, it does nothing to rid the report of it or to indicate the extent of its reach.[30] Third, as noted, rival loyalties may manifest themselves not so much in discernible bias but in impaired judgment. Disclosure does not enable readers to compensate fully for that impairment.[31] Fourth, some powerfully consequential conflicts may be impossible ethically to disclose. Take the negotiation with a source that obligates the reporter to withhold a good story now in hopes of a better story later. The reporter must keep that negotiation secret, yet the agreement compromises her duty to report publicly significant information.[32]

How does disclosure relate to the typology of conflicts? Disclosure is most practicable with conflicts that are non-endemic—that is, those that do not arise from fundamental journalistic processes—and most illuminating with conflicts that are plainly consequential, where the link between conflict and content is clearest. It does little to mitigate endemic conflicts, in part because they are likely to be both difficult to convey and so sensitive that few organizations would disclose them. If used as a response to conflicts that are not clearly consequential—meaning they affect predisposition and context, not the substance of available work—disclosure is liable to be either unintelligible or impracticable, or both.

Managing Conflicts

Earlier, I suggested that conflicts of interest are an inescapable feature of the terrain on which journalism is practiced, and derive, in part, from the reality that journalists work within a nexus of interwoven and overlapping obligations, most of them perfectly legitimate. The conventional responses to conflicts—elimination and disclosure—work best with conflicts that are the least vexing: those that are non-endemic, meaning they do not arise from the nature of the work, the character of its commercial setting, or the boundaries of its institutional structure; and are plainly consequential, in that they clearly relate to content the journalist produces.

Endemic conflicts work a subtler, longer term, and ultimately more corrupting influence on the independence of journalism, and typically have consequences toward the less discernible side of the scale. Accordingly, other responses may be appropriate, as described below.

FOSTER IN-HOUSE DISCOURSE. Internal discussion of conflicts may produce benefits quite different from those of public disclosure. (Perhaps the public should know and take part in this discussion, but the key point here is to encourage self-awareness and self-criticism among journalists themselves.) The problem of conflicts of interest is one that journalists experience directly and personally. They should be encouraged to address such questions as "What are the best stories you know about but cannot write? Why not?"

PROVIDE INTERNAL OVERSIGHT. Does anybody watch for sacred cows? Are they not persistent threats to journalistic independence? If the organization has a news ombudsman or public editor, is that person a customer-service supervisor and a public complaints department—or is she empowered to look for ways in which, say, institutional or commercial inducements are allowed to shape coverage? Endemic conflicts of interest require vigilance and a determination to guard against their corrupting coverage to the detriment of the public need for significant information.

SEGREGATE FUNCTIONS. A typical professional conflict of interest arises when the same individual is expected to fulfill more than one role in regard to the same client.[33] News organizations, in the name of calibrating editorial operations to business goals, have in recent years given senior editors financial incentives linked not to journalistic success but to cost containment or even revenue enhancement.[34] Managing endemic conflicts honestly requires making them manifest and addressing them forthrightly. As unfashionable as this conclusion might be, this argues for reasserting the traditional church–state distinction and re-segregating news from commerce.

SUPERINTEND DUTIES. Creating fixed areas of editorial responsibility—for example, beats, specialist editors, section chiefs—encourages staff to develop enduring loyalties to particular outside constituencies, and in some cases even to view their own prospects as dependent on the success of those constituencies. A reporter assigned to a presidential campaign might well view her future and her candidate's future as intertwined; both, after all, might land in the White House. Staff should be rotated regularly; fixed beats should be understood as a potential boon to expertise but a constant threat to reportorial independence and an incubator for endemic conflicts.

WIDEN OMBUDSMANSHIP. The test I suggested using to determine whether a conflict exists is whether it is plausible to conclude that the relationships would have a discernible impact on the journalism the public sees. But determining plausibility requires the existence of both standards of reasonableness and people to apply them. Plus, since the undertaking is intended to keep journalists' behavior consistent with public expectations of probity and independence, it might be valuable to create permanent in-house panels composed of journalists and outsiders to fill the ombudsman's role to examine conflicts, evaluate cases, and, when appropriate, issue findings. Those findings could be made public or, if the conflict at issue is one that cannot ethically be disclosed, kept private.[35]

Conflicts in the Emerging Media Regime

While resisting conflicts of interest remains a cornerstone of the ethic that is normally thought constitutive of journalistic professionalism, that view is not universally shared among the rapidly growing corps of New Media practitioners whose work—reporting and commenting on matters of public significance—is essentially journalism. Some see the conflict rules of legacy media as a fig leaf that conceals—poorly—an arrogant refusal by journalists to own up to the inherent biases they are prone to and help propagate. (Others argue that bias is inherent in all cognition and expression, and the solution is disclosure and transparency.) But the changing economic model of Internet-borne journalism lacks the clarity of conventional news operations and the cultural safeguards that have arisen to provide journalists with, for instance, some insulation from commercial pressure. Undisclosed payment in exchange for influence appears to be en route to becoming not just incidental, but common to some successful blogs.[36]

New varieties of endemic conflict are arising with the emergence of Internet-based news media and the migration of legacy media online. That migration involves not so much a straightforward transference to an electronic distribution platform as a cascade of transformations affecting almost everything news media do, from fact gathering to revenue generation to editorial imagination. What follows are some notable new areas where conflicts of interest seem unavoidable.

CALIBRATED ADVERTISING. Online tracking technologies enable news managers to determine with unparalleled precision who is clicking through to which coverage. Through so-called third-party cookies, they, or their revenue-side colleagues, can also learn a great deal about the online—and offline—behavior of those same readers, and can thereby assemble a profile of demographic and psychographic desirability for purposes of selling advertisers adjacency to coverage likely to draw a suitable crowd.[37]

Hence, the revenue potential of particular elements of coverage is knowable as never before. The promise is tantamount to the Holy Grail of commercial news—the ability to monetize coverage in a tightly focused, granular fashion, to know that an article or video report on, say, the latest home-fitness machines will draw so much ad revenue, and to make editorial-coverage decisions accordingly.

Such behavioral surveillance is difficult to square with a practice that professes to respect privacy, but our concern here is with the sharp conflict between rival resource-allocation choices; that is, a conflict between coverage with or without clear revenue payback. When the editorial options that are left orphaned include matters of civic importance, the conflict is between business prudence and public service.

USER-GENERATED CONTENT. The push to integrate audience segments into the process of producing journalism—also known as crowd-sourcing—creates incentives to enfranchise people who have the requisite skills, motivations and technical capabilities at the expense of others, and privilege coverage areas that are likely to appeal to population groups that are easier to mobilize and draw reporting and analytical support from. The 2006 Fort Myers, Florida, case, in which the local paper orchestrated an impressive outpouring of citizen zeal, is illustrative. The stories concerned the excessive impact fees charged residents of a local town in connection with their power company's expansion. The ensuing investigation was fueled by—and largely conducted by—a flood of amateur help in gathering and analyzing evidence of municipal irregularities, and led to a rollback of assessments.[38]

This seems to exemplify the kind of coverage most ripe for crowd-sourcing: an issue where the main challenges are empirical and narrowly analytical, rather than conceptual and political, and where the motivation of the amateur labor base—saving money, in this instance—is strong. The danger is that assigning priority to projects susceptible to crowd-sourcing could mean giving short shrift to highly worthwhile inquiries whose constituencies are less easily mobilized, less mainstream, and less richly skilled.

Integrating outside amateurs can also mean introducing new sources of conflicts of interest: individuals who have conflicts of their own, or whose collaboration might derive from loyalties or obligations among existing staff. Such was the problem in an ill-starred 2007 project at the Los Angeles Times in which illustrious outsiders were solicited to serve as guest editors of a new Sunday section. The first amateur editor, it turned out, was a movie producer who had had a professional relationship with the girlfriend of the *Times* editor who led the project, who resigned in the aftermath. The entire project was scrapped.[39]

VERTICALITY. Mass-circulation media are seeking to splinter their broad audiences into market slivers that correspond to categories that are meaningful and useful to advertisers. Those categories may be geographic in nature—neighborhood-based, for instance—or may relate to specific interests, age groups, ethnicities, and the like. The consequences are apparent in Dallas, where the monopoly metro newspaper has 50 microsites, and Cincinnati, whose newspaper has spawned 129 microsites. Is this problematic? It might be. It involves harnessing journalism to the purpose of identifying and targeting subpopulations because a constituency of potential advertisers wants to reach them without paying for audience overlap.[40] It also involves developing tightly targeted information based on particularities that distinguish one population subset from another. Conflict arises, as with the problem of calibrated advertising, between the broad conception of public service and the highly particularized iteration of journalism as an informational wedge that pries open access to people of determinate value to marketers.

WORKPLACE TRENDS. Several such trends—the increasing role of unpaid commentators, reductions in full-time newsroom staffs, a greater use of part-time contributors and consulting analysts, use of outside materials (e.g. video news releases)[41]—suggest a common theme: the predominant reliance by news media on paid staffs of full-time journalists and the materials they produce is changing. News organizations are growing more porous, and the traditional clarity of anti-moonlighting rules[42] is being eclipsed by an era in which many journalists will construct careers around serial moonlighting.

NONPROFIT FINANCING. The growing weaknesses of the advertising-support model have prompted a search for nontraditional funding sources, notably from philanthropies and foundations. The 2007 creation of ProPublica was a significant moment, in which an entirely new organization conceived around a specific kind of journalism—investigative reporting—came into being through a single, bold act of private largesse.[43] The more typical pattern is for foundations to bankroll reporting on a given subject, influencing not what journalists report, but what they report about.[44]

It is inconceivable any funder would be wholly indifferent to the journalism its money makes possible, and it is unlikely that deeply committed foundations will not have some idea of the sort of findings they want to pay to help produce. Paradoxically, the very fact that nonprofits do not intend to use programming as a lure for commercial messages, but explicitly seek to make certain programming possible, may make the potential for improper influence greater than with commercial advertisers.

The continuing problem is to safeguard a professional space for independently gathering and sharing publicly significant information and comment. Conflict of interest is a concept that captures some of the most potent threats to that space. Finding ways to avert, brand, and neutralize the harm of such conflicts remains one of the most difficult challenges facing U.S. journalism at the dawn of the new millennium.

Notes

1. See, e.g., "Journalists as People," *On the Media*, National Public Radio, September 10, 2004, transcript, http://www.onthemedia.org/transcripts/2004/09/10/06 (accessed June 18, 2008). "Jeff Jarvis on Transparency versus Objectivity," *Big Think*, May 8, 2008, www.bigthink.com/media-the-press/10367 (accessed June 18, 2008). Jeff Jarvis, "The Objectivity Myth," Guardian.co.uk, February 19, 2008, http://www.guardian.co.uk/commentisfree/2008/feb/19/theobjectivitymyth (accessed June 18, 2008).

2. This interpretation, which emphasizes attitude and predisposition, not material interest, is similar to that advanced by Christopher Meyers, who writes "that the effect upon judgment is more important than is the type of gain received," in "Clinical Ethics Consulting and Conflict of Interest: Structurally Intertwined," *Hastings Center Report* 37, no. 2 (2007). Meyers pointed me to the work of Michael Davis, esp. his "Introduction," in *Conflict of Interest in the Professions*, ed. M. Davis and A. Stark, 8–21 (New York: Oxford University Press, 2001). The classic conflict, for Davis, is one where someone is in a professional relationship that requires her to exercise judgment on behalf of another person yet at the same time has a special interest that is likely to interfere with "the proper exercise of judgment" (8).

A possible problem here, however, is that the analysis presumes it is possible to tell good judgment from bad judgment. Similarly, in introductory notes to Kenneth Kipnis, "Conflict of Obligation and Conflict of Interest," in *Ethics and the Legal Profession*, ed. M. Davis and F. A. Elliston (Buffalo, NY: Prometheus, 1986), 283–99, the editors write that conflicts occur "when someone cannot satisfy one obligation without failing to satisfy another" (280). Here again, the line between satisfying one obligation and failing to satisfy the other is thought to be clear, and the relation between the two to be "zero-sum." Similarly, Andrew Stark argues that the influence of conflicting interests is readily detectable in the work of judges and reporters because "there is an empirical reality, a fact of the matter, against which their reporting or judging can be measured to see if it moved off course" (Stark, "Comparing Conflict of Interest across the Professions," in *Conflict of Interest in the Professions*, 345).

Our conception of conflicts does not require such clarity because, as a practical matter, the influence of the conflict on a journalist's performance may not be unambiguous and, indeed, may not be sufficiently harmful to constitute failure to serve the primary interest. But it would still be a conflict, I will argue, if it is plausible to conclude that its influence is detrimental to the primary duty. To what degree that detriment amounts to "failure" to deliver the expected service varies. The detriment may not take the form of impaired service; consider the reputational harm to a journalist whose friendships with sources yield privileged access and exclusive coverage. (See note 6 below.)

3. The persistent controversy over "media bias" represents a further iteration of the customary notion of the conflict of interest. See, e.g., Bernard Goldberg, *Bias: A CBS Insider Exposes How the Media Distort the News* (New York: Regnery, 2001), and Eric Alterman, *What Liberal Media? The Truth about Bias and the News* (New York: Basic Books, 2003.) Here, ideological predisposition or political sympathy is elevated in importance to be roughly equivalent to material interests in its potential to corrupt. Our position is that preferences and opinions are not equivalent to interests as considered here, unless they are embraced as sufficiently obligatory that it would be plausible to expect them to influence professional performance.

4. Davis, "Introduction."

5. For a narrower conception, which defines interests by their direct link to action, see Sandra L. Borden and Michael S. Pritchard, "Conflict of Interest in Journalism," in *Conflict of Interest in the Professions*: "An interest is something we pursue, act in behalf of, or act for the sake of" (80).

6. Note that the formulation includes detriment: It requires that a conflict of interest be harmful to journalism's primary duty, which is public service. The notion that for something to be ethically problematic it must require a harm seems axiomatic. But the injunction, for example, to "act independently" (Society of Professional Journalists, "Code of Ethics," http://www.spj.org/ethicscode.asp [accessed June 28, 2008]) makes no mention of tainted coverage or any specific detriment. Can there be conditions that do no discernible harm and yet are still properly characterized as conflicts? Suppose a journalist's personal relationship with a source wins her unusual access; the public benefits from disclosures it would not otherwise get. Does that friendship therefore not constitute a conflict of interest? I say it does. Our argument is that it would still be problematic. True, evidence of public benefit would be a partial defense. But, in a larger sense, the relationship would remain a detriment: the reporting itself is likely to suffer from favoritism; if the relationship were kept secret it would be a frontal assault on the obligation to reveal circumstances pertinent to important coverage, and if disclosed it would set unpalatable precedents about the proper relationship between personal ties and coverage and undermine the confidence of potential sources in the impartiality of the journalist.

7. Those are the elements of trust relationships as described by Annette Baier, "Trust and Antitrust," in *Moral Prejudices: Essays on Ethics* (Cambridge, MA: Harvard University Press, 1994), 95–129, which treats trust as a moral fundamental. Davis, too, notes that a trustee, unlike an agent, is not under the direct control of a principal and has a considerable range of autonomy ("Introduction," 8.) The inequality between journalist and public—what Baier calls "asymmetry"—is an important aspect noted by Borden and Pritchard ("Conflict of Interest in Journalism," 76).

8. The Society of Professional Journalists' code admonishes: "Avoid conflicts of interest, real or perceived," (in *Doing Ethics in Journalism: A Handbook with Case Studies*, 3rd ed., ed. Jay Black, Bob Steele, and Ralph Barney (Boston: Allyn & Bacon, 1999), 149. (A useful selection from the codes is found on pp. 145–60.) Similarly,

Wilkins and Brennen reflect this dual thrust in current codes: "Conflict of interest is one of few areas of professional ethics where perception of 'reality' has equal standing in a moral sense with the actual reality. The goal here is twofold: first, to circumscribe the sorts of influences that can erode professional judgment, and second, to maintain the bond of trust and authority between professionals and the larger society" (in Lee Wilkins and Bonnie Brennen, "Conflicted Interests, Contested Terrain: Journalism Ethics Codes Then and Now," Media Ethics Division, AEJMC 2003 Annual Conference, Kansas City, MO, http://eric.ed.gov/ERICDocs/data/ericdocs2sql/content_storage_01/0000019b/80/23/44/39.pdf, pp. 183–216 (accessed June 28, 2008). Also published in *Journalism Studies* 5 no. 3 (2004): 297–309.

For a more recent compendium of codes, see Dale Jacquette, *Journalistic Ethics: Moral Responsibility in the Media* (Upper Saddle River, NJ: Pearson Prentice Hall, 2007), 82–291. The *New York Times* code offers an especially expansive reading of conflict of interests. See *Ethical Journalism: A Handbook of Values and Practices for the News and Editorial Departments*, http://www.nytco.com/pdf/NYT_Ethical_Journalism_0904.pdf.

9. Davis, "Introduction," 18. However, even if outside activities do not constitute a conflict of interest, they may still be objectionable on reasonable professional grounds. If they keep the journalist from doing her job effectively and if she is unwilling to curtail them, she might have to be reassigned or dismissed. Suppose the activities are so prominent and controversial that some potential sources are deterred from talking to the reporter and some potential readers distrust or disregard what she writes. The writer with the education beat who is a high-profile abortion rights activist might find that her ability to report and to reach her readers is impaired. (See the Vero Beach, Florida, case, described by Deni Elliott, "Freedom of Political Expression: Do Journalists Forfeit Their Right?" *Journalism Ethics Cases Online*, Indiana University School of Journalism, http://journalism.indiana.edu/resources/ethics/covering-politics/freedom-of-political-expression; accessed June 15, 2008.) The reporter's outside commitments may have nothing substantive to do with the matters she covers. But if a reporter's notoriety shuts down incoming channels of information and prompts listeners to close their ears, her journalism will be harmed. Journalists are communicators, and they must have people willing to talk to them and to listen to them. Still, that is a judgment on workplace practicalities, not a verdict on ethical wrongdoing, and if management is bowing to bigotry or ignorance in the name of eliminating a conflict of interest, it may be committing an injustice and compounding it with a high-sounding misrepresentation.

10. Some formulations downplay or ignore conflicts engendered by the practice of journalism itself: "Conflicts of interest in journalism arise in circumstances in which there is reason to be concerned that the judgment and performance of journalists might be unduly influenced by interests they have that lie outside their responsibilities as journalists" (Borden and Pritchard, "Conflict of Interest in Journalism," 74, emphasis mine.)

11. Edward Wasserman, "The Insidious Corruption of Beats," January 8, 2007, http://journalism.wlu.edu/knight/2007/01-08-2007.htm (accessed June 27, 2008).

12. See James Fallows, *Breaking the News: How the Media Undermine American Democracy* (New York: Vintage, 1992), 83–126.

13. Michael Schudson offers the useful analytical distinction in media studies between the levels of organizational sociology, which examines how work is performed and authority applied within media institutions, and of political economy, which concerns the larger boundaries and inducements associated with broad lines of institutionalization and principles of economic operation. See his "Sociology of News Production Revisited (Again)," in *Mass Media and Society*, 3rd ed., ed. James Curran and Michael Gurevitch (New York: Oxford University Press, 2000), 177.

14. Black, Steele, and Barney, *Doing Ethics*, 15.

15. As Borden and Pritchard note, the secondary interests that conflict with the journalist's primary public service obligation are in themselves legitimate ones and would be perfectly allowable if not for the conflict ("Conflict of Interest in Journalism," 80).

16. Davis finds that the term itself dates to a 1949 New York federal court case, and says the Index of Legal Periodicals had no heading for the term until 1967 (Davis, "Introduction," 17).

17. Stephen J. A. Ward, *The Invention of Journalism Ethics: The Path to Objectivity and Beyond* (Ithaca, NY: McGill–Queen's University Press, 2004), chap. 3. These historical arguments are summarized in Ward's essay in this book.

18. Ward, *The Invention of Journalism Ethics*, chap. 4.

19. Cited in Jacquette, *Journalistic Ethics*, 12. Original available at http://books. google.com/books?id=UuoRAAAAIAAJ&printsec=frontcover&dq=%22Tunis+Wortman %22+Political+Enquiry (accessed June 12, 2008).

20. For accounts, see Ward, *Invention*, chap. 5; Michael Schudson, *The Sociology of News* (New York: W.W. Norton, 2003), chap. 4; and Jeremy Iggers, *Good News, Bad News* (Boulder:Westview Press 1999), chap. 3.

21. Charles Davis and Stephanie Craft, "New Media Synergy: Emergence of Institutional Conflicts of Interest," *Journal of Mass Media Ethics* 15 no. 4 (2000), 219–31.

22. American Society of Newspaper Editors, "Code of Ethics or Canons of Journalism," http://ethics.iit.edu/codes/coe/amer.soc.newspaper.editors.1923.html.

23. In Lee Wilkins and Bonnie Brennen, "Conflicted Interests, Contested Terrain: Journalism Ethics Codes Then and Now." *Journalism Studies* 5 (no. 3, 2004), 297–309.

24. Wilkins and Brennen, "Conflicted Interests."

25. Andrew Stark captures part of the distinction I propose between endemic and extraneous in his discussion of in-role ("professional") and out-of-role ("person-al") conflicts. ("Comparing Conflict of Interest across the Professions," in *Conflict of Interest in the Professions*, 335–51.) He offers the example of a government bureaucrat who supports a new program because she believes that support will advance her career. That careerist ambition, which arises from within her role as a civil servant, compromises her professional judgment. What I am calling endemic conflicts include those in-role conflicts but are also composed of institutional conflicts arising from the organizational and political–economic levels of news—say, a decision to shift editorial resources onto coverage likely to lure new classes of advertising—which are matters outside the discretion of the individual journalist and distinct from her professional role.

Endemic conflicts include those created when a professional plays more than one role with respect to the same principal, as with the legislator who is expected to be both a special interest advocate and public interest arbiter (Stark, "Comparing Conflict of Interest," 336–37.) Similarly, in the case of the TV station that kills a story to appease an advertiser, the sole principal, arguably, is the public, but the station faces conflicting public roles: as a news purveyor, and as a business entity obligated to act responsibly toward its employees (e.g., by avoiding decisions that drive down revenues and cost jobs), stockholders, and advertisers.

26. See note 11.

27. Is endemic/extraneous also a distinction between avoidable and unavoidable conflicts? There is a surface similarity. But "avoidable" is a judgment I would rather not apply here. True, endemic conflicts are harder to avoid. Can anybody report sensitive information without engaging in horse-trading with a source? Can a station manager avoid recognizing that financial harm might come from embarrassing a big advertiser? Avoiding either endemic conflict is costly in narrow terms of operational efficiency. But avoiding non-endemic conflicts carries costs, too, although who bears the costs may differ. Take the reporter's outside electoral advocacy: If the reporter were solely a journalist, such activity would be easily avoided. But the reporter is also a citizen, and restricting her carries the cost of curtailing a right to political expression we normally cherish. To be sure, the conflict is avoidable—but only when the cost of curtailment is regarded as acceptable. Avoidability thus rests on an ethical priority that we assign to the duties associated with her role as a professional journalist. We need not make that judgment in order to determine that those conflicts are extraneous to the journalist's duties.

28. Such a conflict may well be institutional, not individual. In a disquieting 2006 instance, Pakistan's President Pervez Musharraf included in his memoir the allegation that immediately after the attacks of September 11, 2001, a senior U.S. official told a Pakistani defense official that the United States would bomb Pakistan if U.S. forces were denied access to suspected al Qaeda staging areas. The anecdote was highlighted in a CBS News press release issued on a Thursday, which triggered a question the next day at the Washington, D.C., joint press conference of Presidents Musharraf and Bush. There, Musharraf said he would not discuss the matter until his appearance Sunday on *CBS 60 Minutes*. That interview was timed to help the Monday morning launch of book sales by CBS's sister company, the publisher Simon & Schuster (See Edward Wasserman, "Holding News until the Time Is Right," October 2, 2006, http://journalism.wlu.edu/Knight/2006/10-02-2006.htm [accessed June 28, 2008]). A situation that raised similar questions arose in regard to Bob Woodward's 2006 third book on the Bush administration's conduct of the Iraq War, *State of Denial: Bush at War, Part III* (New York: Simon & Schuster, 2006). The book contained sensational material that had been in the possession of Woodward and, by extension, his employer the *Washington Post*, for some considerable period before it was made public. The question is whether Woodward and the *Post* had an obligation to go public with such disclosures when they were confirmed and otherwise publishable instead of holding them back to maximize sales of Woodward's book. In this regard, assuming that the *Post* management was kept informed as to his findings—as both parties agreed—the *Post*'s institutional behavior was even more problematic than was Woodward's. At a minimum, the newspaper acquiesced in an arrangement that denied

its readers the timely disclosure of publicly significant information in the hands of one of its star employees, whose reporting was a benefit that *Post* readers could reasonably trust the paper to provide. See "Coverage of Bob Woodward's New Book," *CNN Reliable Sources*, October 1, 2006, transcript, http://transcripts.cnn.com/TRANSCRIPTS/0610/08/rs.01.html (accessed June 27, 2008).

29. Louis A. Day, *Ethics in Media Communications*, 2nd ed. (New York: Wadsworth, 1997), 195.

30. This was a point made by Wilkins and Brennen in "Conflicted Interests," p. 303. Also, consider the case of Maria Bartiromo, the CNBC anchor who interviewed the chairman of Citigroup on-air, after telling her audience that she was a shareholder in his company. See Martha Graybow, "CNBC Tightens Rules on Stock Ownership," *USA Today*, January 13, 2004, http://www.usatoday.com/money/media/2004-01-13-cnbc-invest_x.htm (accessed June 28, 2008). Did Bartiromo's disclosure neutralize the potential for harmful partiality that having holdings in the company implies? Admittedly, her admission would prompt her audience to assume that any "puffball" questioning of Citicorp's boss Sanford Weill were a result of her protecting her financial interests, and it might prompt some to suspect that her investment had sharpened her desire to get Weill on-camera to begin with. But it does not indicate which other companies or individuals Bartiromo might steer coverage toward or away from, or which areas of business activity she might be sensitive to—in short, to the whole range of market-related happenings she might well view differently because of her investments, current and prospective. Would she remind viewers of her Citicorp holdings before reporting on any of hundreds of entities that compete with one of its subsidiaries?

31. "The question which any conflict-of-interest situation raises, of course, is whether a professional's judgment has been impaired or compromised" (Stark, "Comparing Conflict of Interest," 344). Similarly, Davis argues, even though disclosure eliminates the problem of deception, "Conflict of interest can remain a technical problem after it has ceased to be a moral problem" (Davis, "Introduction," 12).

32. That said, even when disclosure is not feasible, the willingness to come clean may still be a valuable moral exercise. Such willingness may be an illuminating test to self-administer before entering an arrangement that might constitute a conflict of interest. The authors of *Doing Ethics* suggest that a reporter ask himself, "Am I willing to publicly disclose any potential conflicts?" (Black, Steele, and Barney, *Doing Ethics*, 119). The question recalls Annette Baier's "expressibility" test, which holds that people in a trust relationship should be able to disclose to each other the bases of that trust. They may choose not to so disclose, but if they believe doing so they would not undermine the relationship, the trust, arguably, is morally sound (Baier, "Trust and Antitrust").

33. For the problem of professions that fuse judging with advocacy, and the desirability of segregating the two, see Stark, "Comparing Conflict of Interest," 337. It is notable that news organizations that are scrupulous about keeping reporters from writing commentary may require editorial chiefs to take part in sales or marketing decisions with the explicit purpose of tilting coverage toward areas likely to lure the right shoppers. That bias is rarely seen as problematic.

34. See, e.g., Leonard Downie and Robert Kaiser, *The News about the News: American Journalism in Peril* (New York: Vintage, 2003), 93.

35. That ombudsmen should be outsiders rather than journalists is argued by Christopher Meyers in "Creating an Effective Newspaper Ombudsman Program," *Journal of Mass Media Ethics* 15, no. 4 (2000), pp. 248–56. The idea is that otherwise they would be "deeply enmeshed in the profession's ethos," unable to critique it appropriately. The variation I'm suggesting sees advantages to internalizing a process of negotiation over standards between professional and public. As to sanctioning authority, I agree with Meyers that ombudsmen should have it, but I see no likelihood that editors or senior producers would ever let them. Creating ombudsmen panels, as suggested here, even if they had only deliberative and advisory powers, could still be a major step toward creating the "ethical climate" Meyers advocates.

36. Josh Friedman, "Blogging for Dollars Raises Questions of Online Ethics," *Los Angeles Times*, March 9, 2007, http://www.latimes.com/business/printedition/la-fi-bloggers9mar09,1,2985214,full.story. Also, see the comments of the federal elections commissioner Bradley Smith in "Newsmaker: The Coming Crackdown on Bloggers," by Declan McCullagh, CNet News.com, March 3, 2005, http://news.com.com/The+coming+crackdown+on+blogging/2008-1028_3-5597079.html, and the self-regulation proposal of Robert Cox, president of the Media Bloggers Association, "Credentials and Access Program," posted December 14, 2006, http://www.mediabloggers.org/rcox/credentials-and-access-program. See also Edward Wasserman, "Selling the Blogosphere," October 17, 2005, http://journalism.wlu.edu/knight/2005/10-17-05.html, and "Can the Internet Be Saved?" December 25, 2006, http://journalism.wlu.edu/knight/2006/12-25-2006.htm. (All of the above links were accessed on June 28, 2008).

37. For efforts to integrate conventional sources of personal data, see Kevin J. Delaney and Emily Steel, "Firm Mines Offline Data to Target Online Ads," *Wall Street Journal*, October 17, 2007, p. B1.

38. For background on the Fort Myers project, see Jeff Howe, "The New (Investigative Journalism," posted November 6, 2006, on *Crowdsourcing: Tracking the Rise of the Amateur*, http://64.233.167.104/search?q=cache:TbNcXlu8DUsJ:crowdsourcing.typepad.com/cs/2006/11/the_new_investi.html+Fort+Myers+News-Press+%22user-generated+content%22&hl=en&ct=clnk&cd=2&gl=us (accessed June 17, 2008). See, more generally, Jeff Howe, "The Rise of Crowdsourcing," *Wired Magazine* 14 (June 2006), http://www.wired.com/wired/archive/14.06/crowds.html (accessed June 17, 2008).

39. James Rainey, "Times Opinion Chief Quits," *Los Angeles Times*, March 23, 2007, http://www.latimes.com/news/printedition/front/la-fi-grazer23mar23,1,211948,full.story?coll=la-headlines-frontpage (accessed March 24, 2007).

40. Sue Clark-Johnson, "2007 Knight-Batten Symposium Keynote Speech," Institute for Interactive Journalism, September 17, 2007, Washington, D.C. http://www.j-lab.org/ba07clarkjohnsonspeech.shtml (accessed June 17, 2008). See also Edward Wasserman, "Narrowing the Vision," *Miami Herald*, April 14, 2008, p. 19A.

41. Diane Farsetta and Daniel Price, "Still Not the News: Stations Overwhelmingly Fail to Disclose VNRs," Center for Media and Democracy, November 14, 2006, http://www.prwatch.org/fakenews2/execsummary (accessed June 18, 2008). For use of "analysts" and independent commentators, see David Barstow, "Message Machine:

Behind TV Analysts, Pentagon's Hidden Hand," *New York Times,* April 20, 2008, p. A1, and Edward Wasserman, "Get Rid of Unchallenged Consultants," *Miami Herald,* April 28, 2008, p. 19A.

42. See Yehiel Limor and Itai Himelboim, "Journalism and Moonlighting: An International Comparison of 242 Codes of Ethics," *Journal of Mass Media Ethics* 21, no. 4 (January 2006): 265–85. Their survey found that roughly half the codes address moonlighting; of those, three-quarters ban all government work—perceived as the most sensitive source of conflict—and 21 percent prohibit any employment that might engender conflicts of interest.

43. Richard Perez-Peña, "Group Plans to Provide Investigative Journalism," *New York Times,* October 15, 2007, http://www.nytimes.com/2007/10/15/business/media/15publica.html?_r=1&ref=media&oref=slogin (accessed June 18, 2008).

44. See Carol Guensburg, "Nonprofit News," *American Journalism Review,* February/March 2008, http://www.ajr.org/article.asp?id=4458 (accessed June 23, 2008). See also "Commercial Public Radio?," "Local Radio Stations," and "How Strong the Firewall?," a three-part series on public radio underwriting, *Marketplace,* Public Radio International, May 24, May 31, and June 7, 2004, http://marketplace.publicradio.org/features/underwriting (accessed June 28, 2008).

18

Respecting Sources' Confidentiality: Critical but Not Absolute

Aaron Quinn

Confidential sourcing has proven to be an effective tool for investigative journalism, particularly when highly secretive or high-public-impact information is at stake and there are too few transparent sources to adequately inform a news story. Nonetheless, many journalists choose to use confidential sources sparingly or not at all because the potential harms in using confidential sources, in their view, outweigh their potential benefits. This chapter will explore three key facets of confidential sourcing in an effort to provide a practical model of ethical deliberation for the use of confidential sources.

First, I will argue that there are justifications for the use of confidential sources in journalism. Second, I will discuss what conditions are necessary for the use of confidential sources, what procedures should be in place to use them best, and why in these cases confidential sourcing is at least morally permissible, if not morally obligatory. Finally, contrary to the journalistic convention that once a confidential agreement is made, it cannot be broken, I will argue for why journalists are at least permitted—even, at times, obligated—to break confidential agreements. Each of these arguments underlies a larger question that has been debated for several decades: Should journalists have a federal shield law protecting their confidential agreements?

Confidentiality as a Professional Tool

Confidential agreements are not only crucial for journalists but are a hallmark of established professions such as medicine and law. In each occupation, confidentiality is invoked to increase the flow of information available to at least one party. In journalism, confidential sourcing is crucial for maintaining a free flow of information to the public. This moral good, though, weighs against at least two significant moral costs: First, in gaining information from a confidential source, the audience loses information regarding the identity of the source and, thus, knowledge of the source's credibility or trustworthiness; and, second, confidential sources or journalists sometimes use confidentiality as a means to achieve personal gain by corrupting the legitimate purposes of confidentiality agreements. Recently, high-profile journalists, such as Bob Woodward of the *Washington Post*, have come under fire for making confidential agreements with high-powered sources upon which they regularly rely, perhaps only for the purpose of maintaining good relationships with them.[1]

As a consequence of indiscriminate uses of confidential sourcing, journalists have failed to inspire the requisite trust among the public, the judiciary, or legislators to warrant support for creating federal laws protecting confidential agreements—protection that would ensure journalists' ability to maintain legitimate confidential sources in the face of legal challenges, say, from law enforcement, or, more commonly, from judicial inquiry. As one media critic said in regard to the increasing number of subpoenas to journalists in recent years, "Public esteem for the media is low, and neither Congress nor the courts seem inclined to grant special protection to journalists."[2]

One possible reason for this lack of support is that many journalists aren't making morally defensible decisions on when and how to make confidential agreements, nor are they *breaking* confidential agreements in the rare but critical circumstances in which it is appropriate to do so. As I will argue below, journalists have a clear prima facie moral duty—fidelity—to keep confidences. Overriding that duty, thus, can be justified only by another more stringent duty, such as justice.

Journalism and Justice

Journalism has at least a two-pronged relationship with the philosophical concept of justice, broadly conceived, and both aspects of the relationship play an integral role in guiding the use of confidential sources. *Particular justice* guides journalists in their determination of whether individual actions are fairly conceived and acted upon. *Social justice* regards the fairness of institutional norms and the rules or laws that affect society broadly conceived.

Particular justice is relevant to confidential sourcing insofar as it guides one in determining whether a confidential agreement is worth making or breaking in a given instance. Confidential sourcing is also linked with social justice in regard to its sustained effect on society as an institutional practice. Journalism's institutional norms, including its use of confidential sourcing, must be aligned with reasonable moral standards so that they best serve the public, as public well-being is the goal of social justice and, given journalism's social role, also a basic goal of journalism. The often-used journalistic term "public interest" is intimately linked, therefore, with social justice, such that when one claims that one is acting in the public interest, one is simultaneously claiming to be acting justly.

To extend this argument, as Stephanie Craft and Sandra Borden argue in this book, journalism is part of a justice system necessary for a democratic state. That is, journalism is a crucial component of a check-and-balance system; this Fourth Estate role is vital to ensuring that no single branch of government, nor any other social institution (including big business), attains illegitimate power.

Moreover, journalism's role as a check on government is only a small part of a larger justice-based symbiosis among multiple public institutions; for example, government also places checks on journalism insofar as it is responsible for constraining media ownership, libel, slander, and so on. Also, journalists and the judiciary rely on information that law enforcement provides about criminal arrests, while watching that police power does not get too strong or too weak to achieve its ends. Both government and journalists check the activities of big business, in part through legislation and government agencies and in part through investigative journalism. Finally, police investigators, prosecuting attorneys, and investigative journalists are similar in several core teleological foundations: their purpose is to impartially gather physical and anecdotal evidence about wrongdoing and present it to their relevant audiences for judgment. In the case of police, the audience is a prosecutor; in the case of a prosecutor, the audience is a judge or a jury; in the case of a journalist, the audience consists of readers, listeners, or viewers of news. There is thus a codependence in the justice-affirming check-and-balance system that involves journalism as a major component.

In light of these complementary roles, journalism, by virtue of its role as public investigator, is clearly a component of the justice system within a democracy. As key players in this system, shouldn't confidentiality be central to journalism in much the same way it is to other such other social institutions as medicine, the law, and the clergy?

My answer is that, for the above-noted reasons, confidentiality is a prima facie right and duty of journalists. As *prima facie*, though, it can be overridden by other moral considerations. First, journalists—probably more than lawyers or judges—are often mediocre investigators because they are insufficiently trained in investigation and research. Audiences are thus sometimes left with poor or even misleading information with which to render a judgment. Furthermore, journalistic audiences are often less competent than other justice based audiences because they are presumably less informed about determining what is relevant about the information they are offered—for example, they are not necessarily coached to consider evidence or testimony in the careful way in which a U.S. jury would be instructed.

Though the audience-judgment problem is unavoidable, the journalistic-competence problem may be correctable. Professional education and training, along with regulatory penalties for professional negligence, would raise the level of journalistic investigation and presentation by minimizing incompetence and motivating compliant behavior. Other professions, such as medicine, have education and training that is suited to achieving the goals they pursue. If, as Michael Davis argues in chapter 8, journalism were a profession, with standards and regulation comparable to other professions, then it should be granted confidentiality as a professional right and duty. It might thus be time to require a standardized education, with corresponding professional enforcement.

By way of comparison, if a doctor were poorly educated and trained but managed to be licensed and as a result harmed her patients, she could face, in addition to possible civil or criminal penalties, severe regulatory consequences from within the profession, including loss of licensure. In journalism, however, there are no professional or regulatory repercussions for sub-par investigations that sometimes lead to disastrous consequences for innocents—unjust public judgments that, for example, sometimes ruin businesses and/or reputations.[3]

Moreover, there are few effective avenues of legal recourse for people wrongly accused by journalists, particularly if they are public figures. In the United States, public officials must by law endure intense public scrutiny, so long as there is no "actual malice," a historically very tough burden for litigants to prove.[4] Last, there is neither mandatory accreditation for journalists nor a central professional organization widely recognized as central; thus, there is no highly recognized method of self-regulation apart from implicit newsroom values or journalists' personal moral values.

Summarizing the argument to this point:

- Journalists play a vital role in promoting public interest, in part through their watchdog role over other powerful social institutions;
- That role makes journalists key players in the democratic system of social justice;
- Like other such players, journalists can effectively fulfill their function only if they have the prima facie right and duty of confidentiality;
- The duty brings with it something akin to professional licensure, suggesting a change in journalism education and self-regulation.
- Establishing the right and duty, though, is just the first step. We need also consider the circumstances in which journalists are justified in making, and also in *breaking*, confidentiality agreements. I turn now to that set of guidelines.

Making and Breaking Confidential Agreements

Traditional confidential agreements consist of a journalist and a source who agree that the journalist will receive information from the source under the condition that the journalist will not disclose the source's identity.[5] Typically, the biggest moral risk in such cases of confidential sourcing is public trust. Thus the virtue of trustworthiness is paramount in determining how a good journalist ought to act in the circumstances. The first matter in establishing public trust is thus to determine what conditions are necessary to justify *making* a confidential agreement.

Most newsroom guidelines say journalists should enter into confidential agreements only when the public importance of the information sought warrants the secrecy of the source's identity and when no viable transparent source is available. Given that journalism should inform the public as transparently as possible, journalists ought to withhold sources' identities only when there is no reasonable alternative; indiscriminate use of confidential sources has a tendency to erode public trust and runs contrary to long-established journalistic principles regarding attribution. Sources, though, especially within government, have come to expect confidentiality, often for good reason. A general unwillingness by reporters to grant or uphold confidentiality agreements would, hence, erode sources' trust in journalists, making balance in this area critical.

For example, although it would have been preferable that Bob Woodward and Carl Bernstein's famous confidential source, Deep Throat, were named (for the sake of transparency and public evaluation), given what we now know of his—Mark Felt's—position in the FBI, he could have continued providing information only in secret. It was therefore justifiable for Woodward and Bernstein to establish that confidentiality. Indeed, it was probably obligatory, given what was at stake: the information was vital to the public interest—namely, deposing a corrupt president—and the agreement prevented potential harm to the source—he might have become a target of those against whom he made accusations. Therefore, in the interests of justice, Woodward and Bernstein, lacking an alternative transparent source of information, used a confidential source.

This case serves as an exemplar and thus reveals the two broad conditions that must be present when making a confidential agreement, the first being the normative condition and the second the epistemic condition. I provide more detailed description of the application of these conditions in my final section.

- Public-interest Value (the normative condition): Confidential agreements must be made only when the public-interest value of a source's information is significantly greater than the loss of transparency. In these cases, journalists ought to be guided by the virtue of justice in order to determine what cases are severe enough cases of injustice to warrant use of this special tool.
- Source Quality (the epistemological condition): When invoking confidential agreements, journalists must carefully consider the quality of a source's testimony to ensure that the testimony—because it is unattributed—is reliable, since readers will not be able to assess a

source's legitimacy for themselves. Adding a generic title like "high-ranking administration official," for example, may bolster source credibility in the eyes of the public—so long as it is not overused—since it involves some description of a source's legitimacy. Even then, though, journalists must carefully evaluate a source's accuracy, or his likelihood to have correct information, and his honesty, particularly whether he is likely to act in good faith.

However, despite the occasional necessity of anonymous sources in serving the public interest, the corruption of confidential sourcing often occurs when sources manipulate journalists to meet their personal ends. Recently, for example, in the Valerie Plame-Wilson affair, it seems likely that I. Lewis Libby and other Bush administration officials manipulated the journalists Matthew Cooper, Judith Miller, and Robert Novak, among others, to threaten a political enemy.[6] Plame-Wilson, an undercover CIA agent, apparently had her cover blown by Bush administration officials in retaliation for the *New York Times* op-ed piece of her husband (former U.S. ambassador Joseph Wilson IV), which disputed the Bush administration's rationale for the war in Iraq. Wilson, who had been commissioned by the CIA to investigate, found no evidence to show that any materials changed hands between Niger and Iraq, as President Bush had claimed in his 2003 State of the Union address. Shortly after the *Times* op-ed piece, administration officials confidentially spoke to journalists, trying to undercut Wilson's credibility, but in the process they outed Plame-Wilson as a CIA operative. Following an independent prosecutor's investigation, Libby was eventually convicted of perjury and obstruction of justice and was sentenced to thirty months in federal prison. President Bush, however, commuted Libby's sentence before he served any time.[7]

Journalists also sometimes use confidential sources to send specific political or social messages, or even to bolster their own fame or fortune; for example, many journalists and media critics claim that Bob Woodward withheld the identity of a clearly malicious confidential source involved in the Plame-Wilson affair—even in the face of inquiry from a special prosecutor—because he needed to maintain a strong relationship with that source for future journalistic work. Woodward's colleagues, such as the longtime *Washington Post* columnist and national correspondent David Broder and the *Post* associate editor Eugene Robinson, were critical of Woodward on NBC's *Meet the Press*.[8] Broder said Woodward caused "consternation" at the *Post* because he had withheld the information about Plame-Wilson from his colleagues for more than two years. He said Woodward left his editor "blindsided for two years, and . . . went out and talked disparagingly about the significance of the investigation without disclosing his role in it." Broder added, "Those are hard things to reconcile."[9] Robinson implied that Woodward might have had self-serving motives for withholding leak information: "You know, I think that's a very interesting question in this whole incident about confidential sources, about access, about the trade-offs that we all make for access in granting anonymity to sources. And, you know, I think that's going to continue. I think people are looking at us skeptically."[10]

These are both cases, I maintain, in which the duty of justice would ethically demand revelation of a source's identity. The first, as I explain in greater detail below, demands identifying the source because there were, it became apparent, national security and criminal justice considerations; the second demands identifying the source because Woodward, it seems, maintained the confidence for his personal advantage rather than for the public good.

There is also the problem of source deception. If a source intentionally or negligently deceives a journalist, does the prima facie duty of fidelity persist? Traditionally, journalists have maintained a near-absolute standard that all confidential agreements must be maintained, regardless of the circumstances. A look at two highly influential U.S. journalism ethics codes reveals several absolutist commandments that *all* confidential sources be maintained in all circumstances.[11] As evidence of their commitment to this unwavering standard, journalists have been convicted, fined, and even jailed because of their perceived duty to protect confidential sources, even when those sources have been deceitful.

By contrast, Gannett, the parent company of many U.S. newspapers, made a commonsense policy that all of its journalists make confidential agreements conditional on the source acting in good faith—any lies or deception may nullify an agreement.[12] Gannett rightly adopted this policy because absolutist rules cannot appropriately account for the nuances of confidential sourcing, including the occasional deceptions sources commit against journalists, some of which surface only after a confidential agreement is made. Thus, even if journalists carefully evaluate a source and find there are no obvious ulterior motives and that the source is in a good position to know, it may still be the case that the confidence should be broken, if the source's information is later proved fraudulent. This violation of a prima facie duty is justified when another moral consideration demands, for example, that revealing those sources could contribute to justice either against the source or toward some other person or entity about whom the source holds crucial information.

Justifiably Breaking Confidences

The reason that journalists strictly maintain confidential sources can largely be reduced to trust. Journalists need sources to trust that confidential agreements will be maintained. Nonetheless, there are both practical and theoretical flaws with the way journalists often emphasize trust over broader and more complex matters, including their justice-based commitment to the public. For what is ignored in the race to win the trust of key sources is the fact that journalists may lose the trust of the public for compromising their overarching goal—to serve the public interest.

Journalists risk using strict rule-based reasoning to determine right action in a given circumstance because the most emphasized source of moral authority is a company or industry-wide code of ethics. Thus, if there is a code-based rule that dominates journalistic protocol in a given domain, journalists run the risk of following that rule without considering its potential circumstantial weakness. They do this because following protocols such as codes of ethics is an easy, if often problematic, mode of self-governance;[13] it is simply the perceived authoritative power of the rule that matters, without consideration of the harm following such a rule may cause. As noted above, the American Society of Newspaper Editors' and the Society of Professional Journalists' codes of ethics both demand that journalists maintain confidentiality absolutely.[14] Journalists who unwaveringly abide by this rule thus operate under the notion "I shall never break my promise." While all human beings, including journalists, ought to value promise keeping, there are, of course, instances in which keeping a promise conflicts with other valuable moral considerations. I wish, thus, to recommend an alternative to often simplistic rule-based moralities. Instead, one must consider an alternative form of guidance such as the systematic moral analysis (SMA) that Elliott and Ozar offer in chapter 1 of this volume. The SMA, through its demand for moral depth and consistency, guides journalists to act justly and thus, as I argue above, in the public interest, which is the ultimate aim of confidentiality agreements.

Journalists most often establish confidentiality agreements with every intent to keep them. In the vast majority of cases, it is appropriate to keep these agreements because they allow journalists to serve the public interest insofar as they keep the public informed about crucial social issues. However, one can imagine instances in which the public's interest is in conflict; for example, concealing the identity of a source who is a danger to innocents, deceiving the journalist, or simply promoting evil each constitute a reason for breaking confidence.

For, as much as a healthy society should value promise keeping, it should also put a high premium on treating people justly; that is, treating people according to what they deserve. Although someone to whom a promise is made has a prima facie expectation of that agreement being respected, there are several potentially mitigating factors. For example, the journalist is just one party to the confidential agreement and is not the only member with moral obligations; thus, such agreements ought explicitly include that the source must offer truthful information, or, at least, give what she believes to be accurate information in good faith. Therefore, sources who deceive journalists knowingly or negligently do not deserve to have their confidentiality upheld, since they have violated the agreement.

Judith Miller and the Valerie Plame-Wilson Affair

To illustrate agreements like the one described above, consider again the Miller and Plame-Wilson affair. In this case, Miller likely would have been morally justified if she had broken her confidentiality agreement with her source, Libby, prior to being officially released of liability by him (which effectively ended her eighty-five-day stint in federal prison on charges of contempt of a grand jury). Though Miller made a formal and legally binding confidentiality agreement with Libby, he at least tacitly violated that agreement when he revealed Plame-Wilson's identity simply for the sake of political advantage and revenge. The violation would consist of Libby's malicious intent toward innocents (Plame-Wilson) and his calculated deception of Miller.

Furthermore, I contend that Miller was not only justified in breaking the agreement but in fact had a moral obligation to expose Libby to the grand jury if the consequences of his anonymity would likely be so egregious that his protection would run contrary to the public interest. For example, if Libby and other administration officials were likely to continue acting vengefully toward political opponents, and in cases such as that of Plame-Wilson, putting the lives of innocents in danger, Miller would be morally obliged to prioritize the protection of others over promise keeping.

In determining which action best serves the public interest, we must consider the competing moral considerations. On the one hand, one ought to be compelled to keep the agreement because of the initial contractual promise and because keeping these agreements perpetuates trust among journalists and sources, thereby serving the long-term public interest. On the other hand, if journalists keep agreements with sources who deceive them and/or who do unjustified harm to others by gaining anonymous impunity, then the public interest is not well served and the agreement should be broken. When such a decision is made, however, the news organization also has a duty to provide a public, transparent, explanation of their reasons.

Joe Budd and the Courier-Journal

The vast majority of confidential cases do, however, demand that journalists maintain their sources, even in the face of significant value conflict. For example, in Australia in March 1992, the Brisbane *Courier-Journal* reporter Joe Budd was jailed when he refused to disclose his sources for a story that uncovered numerous "riotous" acts by Queensland police officers. Several Queensland police officers on retreat in Toowoomba were charged on a variety of counts relating to raucous behavior in several pubs and business establishments in the town. However, charges against all nine officers were dropped, with the allegation that a deal was struck between the police and local prosecutors, which involved witness intimidation. Budd claimed he had a source who had evidence to support those claims, though he refused to identify him to a court hearing arguments over journalistic defamation.[15]

Budd's article contained verbiage—from accounts of witnesses and damning information from a confidential source—that was critical of the police and the prosecutor. The prosecutor later sued the *Courier-Journal* for defamation and won more than AUS $50,000 in damages. Meanwhile, Budd was charged with contempt of court and served half of a two-week sentence for refusing to reveal his source.[16] In determining whether Budd should have maintained his agreement, the crux of the moral argument here relates to the value of the information sought by the court and withheld by the journalist.

On the one hand, it is in the interest of the court (and the *Courier-Journal*) to have testimony from the confidential source; the court would have used the testimony to make a more informed judgment, and, for the newspaper, the source could provide a defense from the defamation charge insofar as the source might legally validate the allegations in Budd's articles. However, there are several more compelling reasons that the source *not* be revealed.

- In the broader scheme of public interest, the agreement was necessary to secure the source, who in turn was necessary to give credence to the claim that the Queensland police and the prosecution had acted corruptly. Without this source, it is not certain anyone would have made the police rioting public, which is the seminal matter of public interest. However, this entails that the journalist carefully evaluate the source for informational legitimacy and good faith.
- Bringing corrupt police and prosecutors to justice clearly outweighs the good that the confidential source could contribute to bolster a defamation claim. Given their social power and ability to cause great harm, police and prosecutorial corruption is more important than the defamation of a prosecutor, which, though regrettable, is something a public official should expect as part of his role.[17]
- Finally, because the confidential source seems to have acted in accord with the confidential agreement, it would require a morally mitigating circumstance to override the agreement; a confidential source should be revealed (assuming he or she has abided by the agreement) only if such revelation is necessary to avoid a monumental injustice; for example, if doing so could prevent the loss of life, limb, or property.

Although the consequences against Budd and the *Courier-Journal* were morally unjust—Budd spent time in jail and the paper paid a hefty award in the defamation case—they did, even against great adversity, deliver what was most in the public's interest: the apparent truth about corruption between police and a state prosecutor. In fact, Budd's news report seemed to have delivered both truth (about the matter) and justice (exposing the guilty), all of which delivered what was most in the public interest.

Conclusion

It is clear that journalists require the ability to effectively attract and protect confidential sources so as to enhance the free flow of information that benefits the public. I hope it is also clear that public interest ought to guide journalists' behavior in making appropriate decisions regarding confidential sources. As we have seen, confidential sourcing, when successful, is a boost to the public interest; however, we have also seen how it can be manipulated by self-interested sources and journalists. Thus, it is not surprising that the powers that be—public opinion, legislators, and the judiciary—have been loath to give a wide-ranging legal privilege to journalists.

Because journalists do not currently hold the standards and self-regulating procedures of other professions, they have not earned a strict legal confidentiality privilege; should that change, such a privilege should be granted accordingly. In the meantime, the following general guide should be followed when making confidentiality agreements:

- Public-interest value: Confidentiality agreements must be made only when the public-interest value of a source's information is significantly greater than the loss of her transparency. In these cases, journalists ought to be guided by the public interest in order to determine what cases are sufficiently unjust as to warrant use of this special tool.
- Source quality: When invoking confidential agreements, journalists must carefully consider the quality of a source's testimony to ensure that the testimony—because it is unattributed—is reliable, since readers will not be able to assess a source's legitimacy for themselves. And in all cases, journalists must carefully evaluate whether a source is accurate, whether he is in a position to have correct information, whether he has been honest, and, particularly, whether he is likely to act in good faith.

Furthermore, journalists must, in order to perform their job well, be willing to break confidentiality agreements when justice—and thus the public interest—is best served by doing so. In the cases provided, we have seen the error in the journalistic tradition that demands that all confidential agreements must be upheld. However, in cases like Joe Budd's, journalists often must be prepared to endure consequences for making good decisions.

Notes

1. NBC, *Meet the Press with Tim Russert*, November, 27, 2005. Nicholas Lehman, "Telling Secrets," November 7, 2005 (rev. January 3, 2008), http://www.newyorker.com/fact/content/articles/051107fa_fact.Accessed December 1, 2005.

2. Jeffery Toobin, "Name That Source," January 16, 2006 (rev. January 3, 2008), http://www.newyorker.com/fact/content/articles/060116fa_fact. Accessed June 15, 2007.

3. *Cohen v. Cowles Media Co.*, 501 U.S. 663 (1991).

4. In the 1964 landmark lawsuit *New York Times v. Sullivan*, it was decided that it is the burden of public officials to establish "actual malice" to recover compensation for libel. Actual malice occurs when the accused has "knowledge that the information was false" or that it was published "with reckless disregard of whether it was false or not" (376 U.S. 254 [1964]).

5. Variations of this traditional model exist. The Gannett news company, for example, lists the following confidential-agreement variations:

(a) The newspaper will not name them in the article.

(b) The newspaper will not name them unless a court compels the newspaper to do so.

(c) The newspaper will not name them under any circumstances.

Gannett, "Principles of Ethical Conduct for Newsrooms," rev. January 5, 2003, http://www.asne.org/ideas/codes/gannettcompany.htm (accessed July 9, 1999).

6. Elisabeth Bumiller, "Debating a Leak: The Director; C.I.A. Chief Is Caught in Middle by Leak Inquiry," *New York Times*, October 5, 2003, p. 1A.

7. CBS, *The Exposure of Valerie Plame*, October 28, 2008 (rev. April 21, 2008), http://www.cbsnews.com/stories/2005/10/28/60minutes/main994753.shtml (accessed October 30, 2005).

8. NBC, *Meet the Press*, November 27, 2005.

9. NBC, *Meet the Press*, November 27, 2005.

10. NBC, *Meet the Press*, November 27, 2005.

11. See American Society of Newspaper Editors, *Code of Ethics*, 1975, and Society of Professional Journalists, *Code of Ethics*, 1996.

12. Gannett, "Principles of Ethical Conduct for Newsrooms."

13. See Renita Coleman, "Moral Development and Journalism," chap. 2, in this volume.

14. The Society of Professional Journalists' *Code of Ethics* uses the following language to guide confidentiality agreements: "Always question sources' motives before promising anonymity. Clarify conditions attached to any promise made in exchange for information. Keep promises." The American Society of Newspaper Editors uses this: "Pledges of confidentiality to news sources must be honored at all costs, and therefore should not be given lightly."

15. Caslon Analytics, "Media Privilege," rev. February 2006, www.caslon.com.au/censorshipguide22.htm. Accessed July 15, 2007.

16. Queensland Parliament, transcript of the Proceedings of the Review of Section 3.1 of the Criminal Justice Act 1989, Brisbane, Australia, 1993.

17. The claim that public officials should expect a higher degree of public criticism in their capacity as public servants is consistent with American defamation laws, which, mentioned earlier, require proof of "actual malice," which means that one makes a claim with knowledge that it is untrue or recklessly disregards the truth.

19

The Ethical Obligations
of News Consumers

Wendy N. Wyatt

M uch of the literature on journalism ethics considers journalists' duties in light of their responsibilities to multiple stakeholders, including, importantly, citizens. James W. Carey took seriously this connection between the press and the public. In one of his more eloquent and memorable passages, Carey described the bond this way:

> The god term of journalism—the be-all and end-all, the term without
> which the entire enterprise fails to make sense—is the public.
> Insofar as journalism is grounded, it is grounded in the public.
> Insofar as journalism has a client, the client is the public. The press
> justifies itself in the name of the public: It exists—or so it is regularly
> said—to inform the public, to serve as the extended eyes and ears of
> the public, to protect the public's right to know, to serve the public.
> The canons of journalism originate in and flow from the relationship
> of the press to the public. The public is totem and talisman, and an
> object of ritual homage.[1]

The press clearly has obligations to the public. But is this relationship between journalism and the citizenry one-sided? Does the public make sense without the press? And if it doesn't, what must the public do to ensure the perpetuity of journalism that exists to serve it?

In this book's ethics theory chapter (ch. 1), Deni Elliott and David Ozar claim that journalism and the public should have a collaborative relationship: "The ideal relationship of journalist and audience is to see them as partners in the project of judging what information is needed, what information responds to common social desires, what enhances autonomy, and what builds community." Elliott and Ozar's chapter—and most of this book—focuses on the journalist's role in the collaborative relationship. This chapter fleshes out the citizen's side of the partnership—the obligations that audiences have to journalism.

The Citizen Democracy Needs

First, what obligates citizens to the press? Journalists enter the news profession because they want to help tell the stories of the day. But how do you or I get implicated in this collaborative relationship just by virtue of being citizens? After all, consuming news takes time; journalism can be dull and sometimes even complicated; and it's easier to just plug into my iPod, log on to my Facebook account, or tune in to my favorite reality TV show.

It's true, we cannot be compelled to actively engage in a relationship with journalism. In fact, as political theorists have pointed out time and again, democratic societies *require* very little of us beyond obeying the law. But the very notion of a democracy—the god term, if you will—is participation, and in societies as vast and complex as most modern-day democracies, participation relies on a means of conversing that stretches across the vastness and through the complexities. We cannot rely only on direct interpersonal communication to make our democracy work; we require a mediated form of public discourse, and as previous chapters in this book have argued, journalism's central purpose in a democracy is facilitating this discourse.

But journalism can serve its purpose only when audiences participate, when they join the conversation. If audiences choose not to, we must ask: Why even bother with democracy? A benevolent dictator may ask less of us and serve us just as well.

The difference between a citizenry that opts in and one that doesn't can be illustrated by the historic debate between the journalist Walter Lippmann and the philosopher John Dewey. In three books penned during the 1920s, Lippmann systematically took on the notion of participatory democracy and the rational public that is supposed to comprise it. Eric Alterman explained Lippmann's revelation in a 2008 *New Yorker* magazine article:

> Lippmann identified a fundamental gap between what we naturally
> expect from democracy and what we know to be true about people.
> Democratic theory demands that citizens be knowledgeable about
> issues and familiar with the individuals put forward to lead them.
> And, while these assumptions may have been reasonable for the
> white, male, property-owning classes of . . . Colonial Boston, contemporary capitalist society had, in Lippmann's view, grown too big and
> complex for crucial events to be mastered by the average citizen.[2]

Lippmann assumed that average citizens live in a world they cannot fully see, do not fully understand, and are unable to direct. The public is "slow to be aroused and quickly diverted . . . and is interested only when events have been melodramatized as a conflict."[3] In other words, Lippmann saw a public that— even if it could master the issues of the day—simply couldn't be bothered by them. To solve this disconnect between theory and practice, Lippmann was ready to recommend doing away with democracy altogether and eventually with journalism as well. Replacing journalism would be "intelligence bureaus" made up of an elite class of social scientists who would access needed informa- tion, assess the government's actions, and then develop expert opinion on the relevant issues of the day. The average citizen need do no more than look to the experts. Voilà! Through his intelligence bureaus, Lippmann had found a way to create "public opinion" without all the messiness of the public.

John Dewey followed Lippmann's work with keen interest and even called Lippmann's analysis "perhaps the most effective indictment of democracy as currently conceived ever penned."[4] But while Dewey may have agreed with Lippmann's diagnosis, he didn't concur with the prognosis. For Dewey, it wasn't that democracy had failed; rather, it had yet to be tried. Yes, the public was in eclipse, but the concept of an active, engaged public was not an impos- sibility. The United States had become what Dewey called a Great Society, char- acterized not only by complexity but by isolationism and individualism. Dewey was concerned that human thought would begin to emulate the overly mecha- nized and technological social processes of the time. Social scientists and a governing elite were not the answer; they would not help a Great Society be- come a Great Community. Dewey believed that human beings had the capacity for intelligent judgment and action if proper conditions were furnished. These conditions included democratic schools, voluntary associations, and, impor- tantly, newspapers, which would offer "a subtle, delicate, vivid and responsive art of communication."[5] In this kind of environment, the public could redis- cover itself and achieve its fullest potential.

Today, we can recognize the validity of both the pessimistic journalist Lipp- mann, who dismissed any notion of citizen obligations, and the idealistic phi- losopher Dewey, who had high expectations of citizens. Therefore, rather than siding exclusively with one of them, perhaps the best way to approach the pros- pects for a truly democratic citizenry is to recognize both views. John Durham Peters does just this when he calls for an accounting of democracy's troubles that, in turn, allows for more productively coping with its possibilities.

> Rather than fighting the losing battle of keeping one's democratic
> heart pure and one's wit intact, it is better to take democracy as
> tragically flawed and yet still worthy of admiration. In fact, the flaws
> are what make democracy admirable; they are not things to be
> transcended. Democracy, I argue, is a form of government and a way
> of life whose peculiar strength lies in its ability to cope with the
> inevitable failure of our best-laid plans.[6]

Of course, democracy was born when Athenians could gather in the amphitheater and was reborn when colonists could meet in the town hall, but that's clearly not the case today. Modernity may have created conditions that challenge the democratic project, but the enterprise is not altogether lost. Any hope of maintaining what has been accomplished and building on those accomplishments relies on our own internal motivation to embrace obligations beyond simply obeying the law. No theory—democratic, philosophical, sociological, or otherwise—can guarantee that motivation. As the political scientist Bhikhu Parekh has argued, it must emanate from our conscience, our sense of moral seriousness, our integrity, and our realization of what it means to be a full member of a community.[7] According to Parekh, people who have a sense of belonging to a cohesive community tend also to have the intrinsic and rational motivation to nurture and improve the quality of collective life. They feel morally obligated to participate in public affairs, to speak up against injustices, and to protect the integrity of the public realm where public discourse occurs.[8] Today, this means discourse facilitated almost exclusively through media.

Put simply, if we want democracy to flourish—even if it is destined for imperfection—we must voluntarily commit to meeting certain citizen responsibilities. One of the more important of these is joining in a collaborative relationship with journalism, one that depends on mutual participation. Journalism, as democracy's primary tool of public communication, is what binds us together as citizens. In the democratic project, the press and the public are interdependent; the entire endeavor rises or falls on the health of this collaboration.

Six Citizen Obligations

It is all well and good to assert that citizens have obligations to journalism in a democratic society, but the claim is ineffective without offering ideas on the specific responsibilities citizens ought to assume. Below, I offer a list of six obligations that help give form to the citizen side of the journalism–citizen relationship.[9]

OBLIGATION #1: DEVELOP MEDIA-LITERACY SKILLS. Media literacy is best described as a set of skills that empower audiences to be critical analysts rather than passive consumers of media messages. A media-literate citizen is imbued with a healthy skepticism and approaches media content with cautious eyes. In refusing to be easily taken in by a message, the media-literate reader, viewer, or listener asks questions not only of content but also of the sources from which it derives, realizing that those sources shape the reality being portrayed. What's more, someone who has developed media-literacy skills recognizes that meanings are negotiated, that different audiences make different sense of media messages.

Media literacy is not media bashing but rather a kind of shield against media manipulation and a foundation for assessing all kinds of media. It is grounded in five core concepts:

- All media messages are constructed,
- Media messages are constructed using a creative language with its own rules,
- Different people experience the same media message differently,
- Media have embedded values and points of view, and
- Most media are organized to gain profit and/or power.[10]

Working from these foundational concepts, media-literate citizens learn to pose questions that ultimately help them critique the thousands of media messages that come at them each day.

Media critique is one level of media literacy—an essential one, given the power the media wield. But for that critique to be meaningful and significant, the critic must not be naïve. One of the reasons those in the press have historically responded so negatively to criticism is that much of it is uninformed. Media literacy—at its most foundational level—can counter the dilemma of uniformed critique; it can help ensure that citizens and journalists have shared understandings of journalism's role, its codes and conventions, its strengths, and its weaknesses. Media literacy can help news organizations around the country have more meaningful relationships with their audiences, in part by repairing the bond of trust between journalism and the public.

Trust is the foundation of any successful relationship, and it must be mutual. Citizens must, of course, be able to trust the news they receive, to consider it credible, but news professionals must also be able to trust that readers, listeners, and viewers understand the news-telling process. With mutual trust comes a better connection between the press and the public, and this connection is the very foundation of journalism in a democracy.

If the nature of media-literacy skills and the need for them are now clear, the next question becomes: How are those skills developed? In Canada, in much of Europe, and even in a handful of post-Soviet states, media literacy has become part of the national education curriculum. Beginning in primary school, students develop skills of inquiry that are applied to particular forms of media. As students get older, more advanced skills are applied to a broader array of media.

Other countries, including the United States, have yet to fully embrace the need for media literacy. Many states have incorporated elements calling for some form of media literacy into their curricular frameworks, but where efforts exist, they are likely spearheaded by individual teachers, funded through special grants, or offered as extracurricular activities or workshops by media-literacy organizations such as the National Association for Media Literacy Education or the Action Coalition for Media Education. Some schools benefit from the efforts of the movement; others don't.[11] Of course, teaching media literacy in schools does not assure a media-literate citizenry. Media are always changing, and audiences must work to continually refine their skills of inquiry and develop new strategies for new media. Like democracy, media literacy takes work and dedication.

OBLIGATION #2: CONSUME THE NEWS. The benefits of being media literate are wasted on someone who chooses not to opt in to news content. One might convincingly argue that those who don't consume media cannot be media literate; the two are mutually dependent. But people—specifically young people—are opting out of news in increasingly large numbers. Between 2001 and 2003, the media scholar David Mindich traveled the United States talking with people under forty about their news habits. What did he find? First, only about one-fifth of today's college students read a newspaper every day. Second, young people haven't abandoned newspapers in favor of new media such as the Internet (only 11 percent of eighteen- to twenty-four-year-olds list news as a major reason for logging on); rather, they have abandoned news altogether.[12]

Mindich's findings are backed up by other research, including the 2007 study *Young People and the News*, which found that while young adults may spend as much as six hours a day with media of various kinds, 24 percent of them "paid almost no attention to news, whatever the source."[13] What's more, the study found that young people aren't just tuning out the news, they have a notable aversion to it. Our modern media system with its round-the-clock operations may provide a way for audiences to access an extensive array of news content, but that same system, with its hundreds of television and radio channels, its chat rooms, and its instant messaging, provides countless ways to avoid the news.

The repercussions of this behavior are felt on multiple levels, each of which helps justify an obligation to consume the news. On a societal level, a healthy democracy depends on citizens who know what's going on. Lippmann's view of society will only be hastened when people choose to ignore matters of public concern. On an individual level, people who don't pay attention cede their power to those who do. Young people may not agree with their parents or their grandparents on many issues, but it's those generations who are paying attention and those generations who are making decisions for everyone else.

Furthermore, opting out of the news diminishes one's right to serve as a critic. Finally, and importantly, less news consumption leads to less news altogether. Already the news is becoming "a smaller star in the media universe."[14] Our media system is designed to respond to numbers—to readership, to viewership, and to listenership. If audiences are consuming entertainment and not news, the economic structure dictates more entertainment and less news.

OBLIGATION #3: DIVERSIFY NEWS SOURCES. For many people who spend hectic days running from one scheduled event to the other, consuming at least a little news can be a challenge. Shouldn't we be proud of the college student who manages to log on to the *New York Times* Web site for five minutes between classes? Or the commuter from the suburbs who listens to National Public Radio on her drive to work downtown? Or the father who sits down to the ten o'clock news after he gets the kids to sleep? After all, some news is better than no news.

Yes, it is. But citizens' obligations transcend the mere consumption of news. They also include a mandate to conscientiously diversify the sources from which that news comes. This means seeking out sources that may provide unsettling or unpleasant information that runs counter to our own beliefs.

Dewey, again, explains the need for this extra effort: Democracy relies on education that has as its essence argument. For Dewey, we come to understand what we know and what we still need to learn only when we subject our preferences to the test of debate.[15] In other words, our intelligence relies on our willingness to thoughtfully consider—and engage in debate with—those ideas that challenge our own.

Today's media landscape has made meeting the obligation to diversify both easier and more difficult. The rise of cable TV, satellite radio, Internet-based news, and digital recording devices provides access to countless sources, including those from other countries. As just one example, the Web site of the British newspaper the *Guardian* attracts fourteen million readers from all over the world; 40 percent of them come from North America.[16] This easy and immediate access is clearly valuable, but it can also prove overwhelming. The sheer vastness of available news can quickly lead to a feeling of "information overload," and every new message consulted leads to new demands—from a media-literacy perspective—for understanding and assessing the source from which the message derived.

Jerry Ceppos, who served as vice-president for news at Knight-Ridder, proposes asking a series of questions about each source we encounter. Some of these include: Are news and opinion clearly distinguished in the source? Does this source break news or merely aggregate? Are stories provided by the source based on firsthand observation or secondary sourcing? Are sources within the stories clearly identified? Are all sides asked to comment within the stories? Are errors corrected promptly and prominently?[17] For some citizens, taking the time to address these questions is unrealistic. In this case, access to an unlimited array of sources ends up hindering rather than helping the charge to diversify.

The obligation is also hindered by the natural desire to minimize dissonance in our lives. How easy it has become to simply tune in to news with a view . . . *my* view. As *Newsday* reporter Noel Holston said, purveyors of news and information that play to audiences' prejudices are everywhere.[18] And people are seeking them out. For instance, a 2006 Pew Center survey found that one-quarter of Americans want news that reflects their own viewpoint,[19] and they are very picky about choosing outlets that do so. Consumer logic has led Americans to expect getting everything just the way they want it, including their media. The *Time* magazine columnist James Poniewozik called this the ethos of "iPod America."[20] My students think of it as "Starbucks" culture. Whatever name you prefer, the idea that we can pay attention only to niche media that simply reinforce our views means we never have to enter the uncomfortable realm of disagreement with other people or with their ideas. But if we truly want to understand the multiple facets of a given topic, opting in to the news isn't enough; we need to engage with diverse sources. Otherwise, we risk entering what Poniewozik called a "happy apartheid."[21]

OBLIGATION # 4: RESPOND TO THE NEWS. Any teacher can articulate how frustrating it is to be in a classroom where students are unresponsive. The teacher wonders: Are these ideas getting through? Do students understand why this matters? Should I change my methods?

Consider, then, the analogy between the work of journalists and that of teachers. Audiences choosing not to expose themselves to news messages are analogous to empty classrooms for the teacher. If, however, audiences opt in but give no response to the news they consume, it's like the classroom scenario described above: Just as the teacher receives inadequate feedback, so also are news media left ignorant of how their information is being received. It is only when journalists get authentic feedback—beyond audience numbers—that they can genuinely respond to community needs.

On a more hopeful front, a shifting media landscape has made it far easier to reach newspeople. Contact information for reporters is frequently given at the bottom of printed news stories; Web-based news often has response features; and even in a world of shrinking staffs at mainstream news organizations, the number of ombudsmen worldwide is growing.[22] What's more, in their struggle to remain relevant in a world awash with information, news organizations are actively seeking to establish dialogue with members of the public through experiments with blogs, participatory journalism, and more.

The problem is, when audiences do respond, it's often with claims about "the media" as a collective rather than about the acts of an individual news organization or newsperson. For instance, audiences hear something on talk radio and then generalize it to all news media. Or audiences complain about news bias when what they really mean is that the news isn't biased in favor of their side of the argument. Journalists report that a good deal of feedback they receive demonstrates that many newspaper practices are indecipherable to audiences. And beyond this basic news *illiteracy* is what Jamie Gold, the readers' representative for the *Los Angeles Times*, called a distressing lack of understanding of the broader role newspapers can and should play in society.[23] This comment reveals, once again, the interrelatedness of the five citizen obligations: Useful feedback from audiences and more substantive dialogue between the press and the public depend on audiences that have developed at least foundational media-literacy skills.

OBLIGATION #5: PROTECT MEDIA AUTONOMY. The charge of a democratic media system is to provide the information and stimulate the debate necessary for productive citizen decisions. That media system must also hold those in power—whoever they may be at the time—to account. These obligations cannot be met if the freedom and independence of the press are hampered or eradicated by government interference, public apathy, or, more insidiously, economic pressures. As Ian Richards and Marty Steffens argue in this volume, increasing media concentration is hindering journalism's ability in its watchdog role and in its charge to offer diverse perspectives on issues of the day. But ownership concentration isn't the only threat to media autonomy. Two national surveys from 2007 revealed that 34 percent of Americans think the press has too much freedom, and that same number would support government censorship of the press.[24]

Journalists certainly don't get it all right all of the time. We witness problems with accuracy, accountability, and transparency. We learn about reporters who fabricate and plagiarize. And we observe a continuing slide toward infotainment. But even during the worst of these times, citizens must maintain their commitment to media autonomy and actively work to stand against incursions on that autonomy. Failure to do so will bring consequences more grave than any of the journalistic sins we have endured.

Consider the case of Armenia, a post-Soviet republic that has been working to establish itself as a democracy since its independence in 1991. In March 2008, police clashed with a group of citizens who had been protesting recent election results, and eight people were killed. Speculation began immediately about who started the violence—the protestors or the police? In response, the Armenian government declared a media blackout, requiring all Armenian media to cite only official government sources in their coverage of national news and curtailing access to media coming from outside the country, including broadcast and Internet news.[25] Even though Armenians have constitutional rights to disseminate and receive information, for twenty days they were at the mercy of their government, a government many suspected of instigating the violence. In response to the blackout, a group of Armenian editors said, "This not only fails to contribute to reducing tension in society, but even deepens an atmosphere of hatred and enmity."[26] The events in Armenia may seem far removed from anything that could happen in more established democracies with long traditions of press freedom, but even there threats abound, as evidenced by the one-third of Americans who would support government censorship of the press and by the blistering criticisms of mainstream media from bloggers and television and radio talk shows.

A SUPEREROGATORY OBLIGATION: EMPOWER PARTICIPATION BY ALL. The five obligations above speak to requirements for the citizen side of the collaborative relationship between the press and the public. The challenge is that not all citizens are equipped to meet them. Much of the literature on media consumption speaks to issues of access—to limitations faced by those who are disenfranchised and, therefore, voiceless. Article 19 of the United Nations Universal Declaration of Human Rights states that everyone has the right to seek, receive, and impart information and ideas through any media. Yet even in a democratic society, access to information is limited for some, and without access, assigning obligations is unreasonable. It becomes incumbent, therefore, on both the press and the public to use their power to bring as many people as possible into the realm of participation. This helps ensure that all who are willing have the means to exercise their moral agency and to assume their obligations toward news media.

What does empowering participation look like? It can assume a variety of forms. Organizing media-literacy workshops for underprivileged groups, supporting the ethnic press, or communicating with journalists about who is missing or underrepresented in their stories are just a few ways to help others opt in to a relationship with news media.

Justifying Citizen Obligations

As several chapters in this text have argued, if media do not use their power wisely, they fail their audiences—the citizens whose power is directly related to the information and ideas they receive. Similarly, as this chapter contends, citizens fail if they do not take advantage of what media provide. The relationship is—or ought to be—both collaborative and reciprocal.

Audience responsibilities to media are not mandated; they are *ethical* obligations rather than *legal* imperatives. In a democracy, we can easily choose to opt out entirely, and many of us do. But a number of considerations covered in Elliott and Ozar's systematic moral analysis (SMA) from the first chapter provide ethical force for the claim of citizen responsibilities.

In step one, Elliott and Ozar ask journalists to consider the courses of action available to them. Let's apply the same question to citizens. First, citizens could simply opt out of any relationship with media; they could dismiss the notion of obligations altogether. Second, they could opt in to a relationship with news media that serves their personal preferences—for instance, their desire to be entertained. Third, citizens could accept the set of obligations presented in this chapter: the obligations to develop media-literacy skills, to consume the news, to diversify news sources, to respond to the news, to protect media autonomy, and to empower participation by all.

Elliott and Ozar's second step asks us to consider role-related responsibilities. Just as journalists in a democracy have role-related responsibilities, so do citizens. Of course, citizens minimally have a responsibility to follow the laws of the land, but ethically speaking, that is not enough. A democracy without active, engaged citizens is really no democracy at all, so one of the role-related responsibilities of citizens is participation in the democratic process, and news media are an essential tool for participation. Elliott and Ozar also insist that journalists have a role-related responsibility to facilitate a collaborative relationship between the journalist and the audience. By definition, collaborative means *two-way*, *mutual*, or *shared*. This journalistic responsibility, therefore, depends on citizens assuming the same ethical responsibility to facilitate this collaboration.

Steps three and four of Elliott and Ozar's SMA ask us to consider harms and goods created by potential actions. In fact, these kinds of considerations have already informed much of this chapter, and the previous sections have touched upon the potential harms and benefits created by citizens either opting in to or out of each of the six obligations. It's worth noting, however, that in step four of the SMA, Elliott and Ozar implore moral agents to act in ways that respect all persons involved, encourage relationships, build trust, and promote the aggregate good of the community. The collaboration between journalists and their audiences cannot move forward, and the long-term common good cannot be achieved, unless the needs and responsibilities of both parties are addressed. Citizens clearly need journalists to help facilitate the conversations of our culture; without journalism, the public becomes voiceless, ignorant, and vulnerable. They also need journalists to respect them as audiences—rather than simply as consumers of a product—and to cover the news in a way deserving of their trust. Journalists need citizens to respectfully participate in the conversations they facilitate—sometimes simply as listeners (or viewers or readers), but also sometimes as informers, as questioners, as activists. Journalists must be able to trust that citizens are engaging seriously with their work. Of course, not all have the means to participate equally in this collaboration, but that remains the goal. It is incumbent on those who are empowered to be extra vigilant about the needs of those who aren't and to work toward bringing everyone into the realm of equal partnership.

In the fifth and final step of Elliott and Ozar's SMA, they present four types of actions: ethically prohibited, ethically required, ethically permitted, and ethically ideal. Based on the analysis above, the first five citizen obligations fall into the *ethically required* category and the sixth is *ethically ideal*.

We Get the Journalism We Deserve

The discipline of journalism ethics has been built largely on the missteps of those in the news profession. Each year brings new evidence of journalists, and journalism, making moral mistakes. From acts of deception, plagiarism, and fabrication to instances of the watchdog rolling over and playing dead rather than speaking truth to power, questionable behaviors are never in short supply. But news media cannot shoulder all of the blame. If journalists are doing their job in an environment where few care enough to opt in—where the latest celebrity gossip generates more attention and more response than anything else— what does this say? If we want good journalism, we must help create it by developing media-literacy skills that we can apply to consuming news messages, to diversifying our sources, to providing feedback, and to protecting media autonomy. We cannot cast stones at others. We cannot put it off until later when we have more time. We cannot make excuses. In a democratic society, we get the journalism we help create, which is nothing more or less than the journalism we deserve.

For More Information

Center for Media Literacy (www.medialit.org)
Young People and News survey (www.hks.harvard.edu/presspol/ carnegie_knight/young_news_web.pdf)
State of the First Amendment survey (www.firstamendmentcenter.org/ sofa_reports/index.aspx)
State of the News Media survey (www.stateofthenewsmedia.org)

Notes

1. James W. Carey, "The Press and Public Discourse," *Center Magazine* 20, no. 2 (1987): 5.
2. Eric Alterman, "Out of Print: The Death and Life of the American Newspaper," *New Yorker*, March 31, 2008, p. 53.
3. Walter Lippmann, cited in Alterman, "Out of Print," p. 53.
4. John Dewey, "Review of Public Opinion by Walter Lippmann," *New Republic*, May 3, 1922, p. 215.
5. John Dewey, *The Public and Its Problems* (Chicago: Gateway, 1946), 184.
6. John Durham Peters, "Public Journalism and Democratic Theory," in *The Idea of Public Journalism*, ed. Theodore L. Glasser (New York: Guilford, 1999), 114.
7. Bhikhu Parekh, "A Misconceived Discourse on Political Obligation," *Political Studies* 41 (1993): 236–51.
8. Parekh, "A Misconceived Discourse," 243.
9. These obligations are based on Wendy Barger and Ralph D. Barney, "Media-Citizen Reciprocity as a Moral Mandate," *Journal of Mass Media Ethics* 19, nos. 3–4 (2004): 191–206.

10. Center for Media Literacy, "Teacher's/Leader's Orientation Guide," *MediaLit Kit: A Framework for Learning and Teaching in a Media Age* (Santa Monica, CA: Center for Media Literacy, 2003).

11. Nellie Gregorian, "Eye on Research: Media Literacy and Core Curriculum," *Threshold* (Winter 2006): 5–7.

12. David T. Z. Mindich, *Tuned Out: Why Americans under 40 Don't Follow the News.* (New York: Oxford University Press, 2005).

13. Thomas E. Patterson, *Young People and the News,* (report by the Joan Shorenstein Center on the Press, Politics and Public Policy, John F. Kennedy School of Government, Harvard University [July 2007], 12).

14. David T. Z. Mindich, "Dude, Where's Your Newspaper?" *Chronicle of Higher Education,* October 8, 2004, p. 5.

15. Christopher Lasch, "Publicity and the Lost Art of Argument," *Gannett Center Journal* 4, no. 2 (Spring 1990): 1–11.

16. Personal communication from Margaret Holborn, Head of Education for the *Guardian,* January 15, 2008.

17. Arthur S. Hayes, Jane B. Singer, and Jerry Ceppos, "Shifting Roles, Enduring Values: The Credible Journalist in a Digital Age," *Journal of Mass Media Ethics* 22, no. 4 (2007): 262–79.

18. Noel Holston, "Some Like the News Slanted Their Way," (Minneapolis) *Star Tribune,* September 15, 2004, www.startribune.com/viewers/story.php?template=print_a&;story=4972420 (accessed September 20, 2004).

19. Pew Research Center for the People and the Press, *Online Papers Modestly Boost Newspaper Readership: Maturing Internet News Audience Broader Than Deep,* July 2006, http://people-press.org/report/282/online-papers-modestly-boost-newspaper-readership (accessed May 31, 2008).

20. James Poniewozik, "The Age of iPod Politics," *Time,* September 27, 2004, p. 84.

21. Poniewozik, "The Age of iPod Politics," 84.

22. Michael Getler, "The Ombudsman's Mailbag," PBS.org, June 4, 2008, www.pbs.org/ombudsman/2008/06/the_ombudsmans_mailbag_18.html (accessed August 4, 2008).

23. Personal communication, September 16, 2006.

24. First Amendment Center, *State of the First Amendment Survey,* 2007, www.firstamendmentcenter.org/sofa_reports/index.aspx; Project for Excellence in Journalism, *The State of the News Media: An Annual Report on American Journalism,* 2007, www.stateofthenewsmedia.org/2007 (accessed May 28, 2008).

25. Svitlana Korenovska, "Broadcasters Unplugged during State of Emergency," *Washington Times,* March 8, 2008, p. A05.

26. BBC Worldwide Monitoring, "Armenia in 'Total' Information Blockade under Emergency Rule—Editors,"BBC Monitoring Transcaucasus Unit, March 14, 2008, available via Lexis-Nexis.

PART VIII

Getting the Story

Introduction

Journalism's finest hours and worst debacles both stem, I would submit, from the same source—reporters' deep-seated drive to get the story. Good journalists are fascinated with the world and with people; they are powerfully motivated to discover interesting facts and to effectively communicate them to others.

Examples of "finest and worst" abound; here are two: First, I religiously show my students the film version of *All the President's Men* because, despite any number of ethical lapses, Bob Woodward and Carl Bernstein's dogged pursuit of the Watergate story, and of its eventual tentacles deep in a crooked Nixon administration, still represents news reporters at their best, engaged in the profession's highest calling.

Compare this, though, with CBS News's shameful coverage of President George W. Bush's National Guard service—the so-called memogate fiasco.[1] Badly sourced and shoddily researched, the story likely hastened anchorman Dan Rather's retirement from CBS News.[2] Maybe worse, the validity of the story, never seriously challenged, was lost in the noise over the purportedly forged memo.

In both examples, the drive to get the story had widespread ramifications. In the Watergate reporting, their near-obsessive resolve, combined with an insistence—by reporters and editors alike—not just to get the story, but to *get it right*, helped bring about the end of a corrupt presidency, changed the face of U.S. politics, and, for a short time at least, placed journalism among the more highly respected professions. In the "memogate" story, an insistence upon being first, even at the expense of due diligence, helped galvanize and inspire

Bush's electoral base and further exacerbated the by then growing derision of mainstream media .[3]

This topic thus motivates a deep moral ambivalence. When done well, as Patrick Plaisance concludes, "'getting the story' is an ennobling activity, one that benefits journalism and the public alike." I fully agree but would emphasize the "done well" qualifier and worry that the structure of modern journalism in fact discourages such ethically proper reporting, a worry that is only increasing as MSM struggles to retain an audience.

The phrase "getting the story" is meant here as a catchall that includes everything from the longing to root out and report on corruption, to the "scoop mentality," to camping out on the lawn of the latest scandal figure, to celebrity paparazzi. Each reflects the basic journalistic drive to acquire and disseminate truth.

That drive is, I would argue, core to reporters' mindset, manifesting in both obvious and subtle ways. It is part of the professional culture's norms and, as such, is a motivational *given*, in many ways distinct from carefully reflected upon ideals like informing the democratic polis. It is simply what reporters *do*.[4]

Its subtle impact on reporting activity is exemplified in the too-common error of broadcasting live footage without first carefully reviewing it and providing necessary context. For instance, I happened to be watching a Los Angeles morning news program on April 19, 1995, the day of the Oklahoma City bombing. One of the anchors broke away from their normal fare of entertainment stories and told the audience (and I paraphrase), "We have some footage coming into the station. It's evidently something important out of Oklahoma City, but we don't yet have details." They then proceeded to air an unnarrated live feed from the scene, including images of rescue workers carrying badly burned children out of the building's childcare center. After about a minute of this footage, they cut back to the stunned anchors, one of whom managed to stammer (I again paraphrase), "Um, we probably should not have shown that. It's clearly some kind of disaster. When we have more information, we'll be sure to pass it along. Let's now go to commercial."

It's tough to pick which of the myriad ethical lapses to start with, but in all of them, getting the story was a primary motivator. The news team knew they had something important, with dramatic footage; they also knew they would be the first Los Angeles station to air it (no other news program broadcast at that time of the morning). So they followed the journalistic default: they televised it. That is, they let the drive to get the story override their good training and ethical sensibilities.

This example highlights the negative side of the norm, but I must stress its dual nature. Without the drive to seek out and report, journalism's great historical achievements would not have been possible; indeed, arguably, journalism itself would not be possible.

This conclusion, and the "done well" dictum, thus reveal the value of Patrick Plaisance's and Lee Wilkins's chapters; both are theoretically informed and sophisticated "how to's," that is, they explain how to make sure reporting is in fact done well.

Plaisance focuses on the "mechanics of news work—the moral questions raised in the process of getting the story." He explains, "These questions deal with decision-making processes of single journalists as well as the strong cultural and professional norms and standards in the newsroom that influence journalists' behavior. [They also deal with] the realm of media effects: What are intended and unintended impacts on audiences, and how might those impacts inform our decisions and judgments about news work?"

Plaisance notes the power of the norm, calling it a journalistic "bias": "This bias . . . hints at the essence of how journalists define themselves as professionals and at a key sense of mission for the craft of reporting. It is a bias most journalists wear as a badge of honor—an embodiment of the journalistic obligation to present the news 'without fear or favor.'" But it is worthy of honor only when the stories are properly researched and reported. The trick, of course, lies in determining what "properly" entails, given the sometimes competing interests of reporters, subjects, and readers.

This in turn requires, Plaisance argues, realizing how journalists see themselves, how they define their mission. He describes four roles—the "disseminator," the "interpretive," the "adversarial," and the "populist mobilizer," each of which carries distinct ethical guidelines. Plaisance then ties these to such classical principles as the Kantian dictum to "treat persons as ends and not as mere means" and a Joel Feinberg–influenced version of "minimize harm." He concludes with a Rossian admonition to exercise one's "moral autonomy" in the often difficult task of weighing conflicting duties.

Wilkins also focuses on the harm principle, using "disaster coverage" to reveal two important aspects of being a journalist and of what it means to pursue stories. First, the objectivity-driven emotional distancing journalists often bring to disaster stories quickly breaks down when one's city is under water or being threatened by an inferno—as it should be. Journalists are persons first, persons who care deeply about what happens to their community. As such, they are governed by the same moral principles as the rest of us—in particular, she stresses, the duty to "mitigate harm."

This leads to the second point: in order to fulfill that duty, news organizations, and by implication reporters, should sometimes advocate for political or structural changes. Wilkins reaches this conclusion via a rich analysis of different types of disasters (quick/slow onset; technological/natural) and their associated stages (warning, impact, immediate post-impact, recovery, and mitigation). From these, she determines, "If journalists are serious about an ethical foundation for their work, then mitigation—how it is conceptualized and how it is implemented—needs to replace the focus on the event itself as the predominant journalistic goal.

Saving lives and reducing financial losses are worthy ethical goals," in addition to, even sometimes instead of, traditional journalistic norms like objectivity.

Therefore, Wilkins argues, the story—that which should be pursued—gets redefined: "Journalists will have to acknowledge that news is what might happen as well as what has happened." Other changes result, too, including, "a re-examination of the traditional news frames for disaster, specifically the focus on victims and decontextualized devastation"; "news routines would have to accommodate a more community and enterprise-oriented role"; "news organizations would have to be willing to grapple with, and then make policy about, how technology should impact their news coverage"; and such organizations would have to come to grips with whether they should "partner with government in the warning phase of the event."

The question, hence, is not just whether to get the story, but which ones and how? Thus, as you read, ask yourself whether you are convinced by Wilkins's arguments that the journalist's role, even the very self-conception as journalist, should be changed in these ways. Similarly, does Plaisance provide the right ethical tools to ensure that the positive aspects of "getting the story" prevail over the negative? Or would it be possible to fundamentally alter this basic motivating drive and still have a vibrant journalism? If so, what would it look like?

Notes

1. See Jarrett Murphy, "CBS Ousts 4 For Bush Guard Story," CBS News.com, January 10, 2005, http://www.cbsnews.com/stories/2005/01/10/national/main665727.shtml (accessed November 3, 2008) for an account of the story and its aftermath.

2. Following an internal investigation, CBS fired four producers. Within two months of the story's being aired, and before the investigation was complete, Rather announced his retirement. (See Howard Kurtz's November 23, 2004, story at http://www.washingtonpost.com/wp-dyn/articles/A7313–2004Nov23.html. Accessed November 3, 2008.) As of this writing, Rather is the managing editor and anchor of a television news magazine, *Dan Rather Reports*, on the cable channel HDNet.

3. Within hours of being aired, the story was being attacked by bloggers and online journalists, even as respected MSM sources such as the *New York Times* and *Washington Post* were repeating it on their pages.

4. Compare it to, for example, the academic drive to publish, lawyers' seeing the world in argumentative terms, or physicians' push to treat. Each represents a professional norm, generally if not universally true, easily justified via ethical reflection on first principles, and motivating of behavior even when not explicitly considered.

20

The Ethos of "Getting the Story"

Patrick Lee Plaisance

Editor Jones receives a call from a local resident about something interesting. Jones calls over General Assignment Reporter Smith and assigns her the story. Smith calls the resident, gathers more information, and calls several other people who can speak to the topic. She asks questions. She chats. She plays devil's advocate. She goes online to search for more details and perspectives on the topic. She drives out to the relevant scene to see it for herself. She may arrange some photos or take some video footage. She takes notes. She returns to talk with Editor Jones about the validity, importance, and focus of the story. Then she sits down at her computer to write. As the story comes together, she may make some more calls to confirm a detail or ask other questions that come to her mind. She sends her story to an editor, who reads it several times and talks to her as he edits. He sends it to a copydesk, where it is given another read and a headline and is placed on a page or posted on a Web site.

This is a generic summary of the news-production process of an archetypal story. But this straightforward account of journalism work is deceptive in its apparent simplicity. In fact, it is fraught with substantive moral, philosophical, and procedural questions at virtually every step. The product called journalism is a complex culmination of newsroom socialization, self-directed enterprise, and negotiated exchanges with superiors, subordinates, sources, and subjects. News is the result of a cascade of individual judgments, professional norms, and claims about duty, means, and consequences. It also represents the exercise of a kind of information-based power. As with almost all forms of power, its use (and occasional abuse) is continually contested. The product of journalism also exists in a particular context of media literacy: degrees of understanding of the nature and purpose of news work vary widely in our society.[1]

These have resulted in a chronic journalist–public disconnect, which is largely responsible for the persistent "credibility gap" between what audiences see and what they believe. Some news consumers expect a "just the facts" journalism in which they see detachment as a measure of credibility. They are surely disappointed in the news delivered by journalists whose measure of professionalism is not merely the ability to dispassionately convey information but to provide informed context to help audiences understand why such information is important. This is the difference between the "disseminator" and "interpretive" roles that journalism simultaneously embraces.[2] But that journalists have historically failed to adequately explain their work does not mean their work is unethical.

This chapter provides a discussion of some key ethical implications of the mechanics of news work—the moral questions raised in the process of getting the story. These questions necessarily address the individual and sociological dimensions. That is, they deal with both the decision-making processes of individual journalists and the strong cultural and professional norms and standards in the newsroom that influence journalists' behavior. Other questions address the realm of media effects: What are intended and unintended impacts on audiences, and how might those impacts inform our decisions and judgments about news work? The chapter's thesis is that, done well—ethically well—"getting the story" is an ennobling activity, one that benefits journalism and the public alike.

Who Journalists Are

The average journalist does not look like the average American. Journalists are typically more educated, less religious, more affluent, and more likely to describe themselves as socially liberal.[3] They probably have a more cosmopolitan outlook and an iconoclastic streak—that is, they're more comfortable questioning authority and more willing to entertain efforts at reform. This should not be very surprising; journalism, like most crafts and professions, tends to attract certain personality types. The type of person drawn to electrical engineering is not likely to consider an alternative career in dance. Indeed, many journalists consider their reformist stance an essential part of their professionalism. "Journalists are skeptical, confrontational and iconoclastic, which means they challenge the establishment, while conservatives want to conserve it. So the better journalists do their job, the more likely conservatives are to see them as liberal," according to the late prize-winning media critic David Shaw.[4] Philip Jones Griffith, a noted photojournalist whose work during the Vietnam War became among the defining images of that conflict, embodied this stance: "Journalists should be by their very nature anarchists, people who want to point out things that are generally not approved of. It's by criticizing that society that

humanity has made progress."[5] This attitude is one reason that so many jour-
nalism-ethics critiques often devolve into claims and counterclaims of political
bias. The on-the-ground journalistic reality tends to be quite different. The
sociologist Herbert Gans concluded his lengthy ethnographic study of journalists by saying: "In reality, the news is not so much conservative or liberal as it is
reformist; indeed, the enduring values are very much like the values of the
Progressive movement of the early twentieth century."[6] More recently, the
media critic Brent Cunningham offered yet another take on this issue: "Reporters are biased toward conflict because it is more interesting than stories without conflict; we are biased toward sticking with the pack because it is safe; we
are biased toward event-driven coverage because it is easier; we are biased
toward existing narratives because they are safe and easy. . . . Mostly, though,
we are biased in favor of getting the story, regardless of whose ox is being
gored."[7]

This bias of "getting the story" hints at the essence of how journalists
define themselves as professionals and at a key sense of mission for the craft of
reporting. It is a bias most journalists wear as a badge of honor—an embodiment of the journalistic obligation to present the news "without fear or favor."
And yet it is also the source of suspicion, distrust, and outright bewilderment
for members of the public unaccustomed to such an ethos. As Deni Elliott and
David Ozar point out in their essay at the start of this book, the journalistic
profession prides itself on its commitment to public service. "One of the central ethical values to which journalists must be committed," they wrote, "is
discerning pursuit and effective dissemination of needed information; discerning so as to recognize and distinguish the kinds of information needed by the
society being served, effective and accurate so as to be genuinely heard and
read." They go further, arguing that the profession must continue efforts to
realize a truly "collaborative" relationship with the public they serve. However,
the "disconnect" between the journalist and her public remains, in many ways,
a prominent feature of the profession. "I think we all sort of have to be ambassadors for our profession—reporters aren't particularly held in high esteem,"
said one journalist at a North Carolina newspaper. "Part of that is just the idea
that reporters are unscrupulous, and I think that goes back to the fact that
many people don't understand the rules of what we do, and haven't properly
understood the rules of how we operate."[8] Gardner, Csikszentmihalyi, and
Damon said the very nature of journalism creates a "paradoxical relationship"
between journalists and their audiences: "On the one hand, [journalism] tries
to give readers and viewers what they want; on the other, it feels responsible for
telling them what they should know even when that information is neither easy
to assimilate nor popular."[9]

Still, while the field of journalism may draw individuals of certain tempera-
ments, those individual impulses, values, and ideals are transformed by the
powerful culture created by the working environment. As Christopher Meyers

reminds us in this book's introductions, newsroom socialization processes, time constraints, power structures, and a host of other factors converge to shape and influence individual-level motivations. Research efforts to identify and quantify these various, multidimensional influences on news work continue. Shoemaker and Reese cautioned that routines and organizational constraints are likely to minimize or negate the influence of personal attitudes, values, and beliefs on media content.[10] This is not to say such influences are always determinative; McQuail, for example, warned against ruling out any legitimate degree of autonomy in the newsroom and overstating the power of workplace socialization.[11]

That this debate continues does not preclude us, however, from exploring and proposing normative claims about what journalists do and why. Journalists rightly become the object of criticism when their practices betray public service ideals, when organizational-level interests unduly influence news decisions, when they fail to properly understand the nature and dimensions of harm, or when they fail to recognize potential harm or fail to take reasonable steps to minimize it. In other words, much of the journalistic ethos revolves around the concepts of *credibility* and *harm*. These areas involve important ethical concepts that must be fully grasped by both journalists and the public if we are to have responsible newsgathering.

Journalists' Roles and Credibility

Lots of factors motivate journalists to do what they do. The gratification of seeing their name broadcast on the air, on the Web, or in print; naked ambition; the power of the press; the power of a good narrative; pride in the gift of storytelling; a desire to make a difference; a desire to get the story first. Not all these motivations are always ethically justifiable or should override other considerations in specific cases. But for any journalist worthy of the term, all of these motivations rest on a more fundamental appreciation for the central functions of the press in society.[12] Yet if the journalist is not seen as a credible source of information, then he has nothing; his work becomes propaganda or an exercise in empty egoism, or both. As a result, professional journalists go to great lengths to protect and maintain their credibility, since it is difficult, if not impossible, to rebuild once it is lost.

Before we make judgments about how well journalists do their job or whether they behave ethically in getting and reporting the story, we must understand how journalists see themselves and how they define they mission to serve the public. They simultaneously embrace four distinct roles:[13]

- the disseminator role, which reflects a view of news as "just the facts" to inform a wide audience while avoiding rumor, innuendo and unverified data;

- the interpretive role, which reflects an effort among journalists to draw on their expertise, experience and access to provide context and to help audiences make sense of facts;
- the adversarial role, which reflects the more aggressive, "watchdog" expectations of the press to scrutinize the institutions of power and to hold them up for accountability on behalf of the public;
- the populist-mobilizer role, which reflects a burgeoning belief among journalists that they ought also to help foster civic engagement and join with the public in the search for solutions.

The ways in which journalists manifest or carry out these roles raise ethical questions. For example, straightforward journalistic dissemination of information is not innocuous if it includes private information. As Cliff Christians and Candace Gauthier argue in this book, full understanding of the reasons we have to value privacy must be part of the journalistic ethos. If disclosure of private facts does not materially advance public understanding of a vital issue but instead serves only to "spice up" the story, and if that disclosure violates the reasons we all require privacy—for example, for the full development of one's self[14]—then such disclosure is unethical.

The adversarial and populist-mobilizer roles require journalists to be scrupulous about avoiding actual and apparent conflicts of interest. Autonomy is important here and is bound up closely with the notion of journalistic credibility. If news is presented with an eye toward favoring or benefiting a certain group or an individual because of a relationship or vested interest a journalist has with that entity, it invites charges of unethical failure. Autonomy refers not just to what we *can* do but to what we *ought* to do. Philosophers talk of our "moral" autonomy as our ability to control the reasons for our actions and our awareness of our obligations as moral beings. For journalists, this means that in performing their "watchdog" role as part of their public service mission, they must be careful about maintaining their independence from people who would want to use the news for their benefit, so as to subject everyone to an impartial scrutiny. If audiences, for example, learn that a news organization or a journalist is profiting directly from the subject of a news story and thus begin to wonder whose *interests* are being served by such a relationship, the journalistic credibility of the media outlet or person may be rightly called into question. Journalistic autonomy "is a lynchpin in what journalists should stand for," said Bob Steele, a prominent media ethicist. "Independence is at the heart of journalism's unique and essential role in a society."[15] The most common conflicts of interest arise on the individual and organizational level, when, for example, a journalist has a personal relationship with someone who also is being used as source for a story, or when a newsmagazine allows an advertiser to influence news content. CNBC and Maria Bartiromo, the financial news cable channel's self-described "Money Honey" anchor, drew accusations of conflicts of interest on both levels in 2006 and 2007 after she was reported to be socializing with prominent Citigroup banking executives, sharing charter jet flights with them, and joining them for black-tie events. Not only did she continue to front "objective" news segments on Citigroup, but the banking giant also happened to be a major advertiser on the channel.

Minimizing Harm

Acknowledging the potential to cause harm in the course of their work, and placing a premium on efforts to minimize that harm, are central to the journalistic ethos—indeed, "minimize harm" is the second of four primary directives offered in the Society of Professional Journalists' code of ethics. Yet, as Deni Elliott and David Ozar noted, journalists often have the duty, paradoxically, to *cause* harm.

The concept of harm has multiple dimensions and manifestations, ranging from inflicting physical pain, to damaging one's economic options, to not treating others with dignity and respect. Journalists readily acknowledge the former harms but too often forget or ignore the Kantian requirement never to treat persons as mere means. This concern often emerges in journalists' relationships with their sources. Reporters expose themselves to charges of unethical behavior, and rightly so, when they exploit individuals to get a story, showing little regard for their welfare or interests. People accustomed to dealing with the news media—public officials, community leaders, oft-quoted specialists—understand how the game is played and can usually engage the journalist in a mutually advantageous and respectful manner. But sources with less experience may be less media-savvy; excited at just being asked to comment and uninformed about the news process, they may be too trusting and thus susceptible to the unscrupulous reporter.

Kant's demand that we treat others as ends in themselves obligates journalists to assess each sources' degree of vulnerability to exploitation and to use that assessment to inform how that source is to be approached and handled. Does the potential source understand the difference between a conversation that is "on the record" and one that's "off the record"? Has the reporter adequately explained her aims and motives to allow the potential source to use his capacity for reason in deciding whether to talk? Is she aware of her possible prominence in the story and the variety of ways she may be presented? Kantian duty—and the journalistic code of professionalism—requires the journalist be able to clearly articulate honest responses to these and other questions.

As Elliott and Ozar note, however, the professional directive calls for journalists to *minimize* harm; it does not impose a requirement to *avoid* harm. Some harm may be inevitable in the course of pursuing the truth and gathering information in the spirit of public service. Indeed, when investigative work appears headed to cause explicit harm to someone's livelihood or reputation, journalists are expected to exhibit moral courage when it comes to stories that provide information considered of vital public importance. In such cases, the journalist is obligated to mitigate harm: to be careful only to cause that which is necessary to and justified by the story, particularly in cases in which those harmed are essentially innocent bystanders.

In addition to the harm attached to using sources and subjects as mere means, several other, more concrete, types of harm are possible. Story subjects can be defamed, lose reputations, have their privacy violated, or even lose their jobs.

Audience members, though, often charge they are harmed by graphic or offensive content. People can be distressed by coverage. Non-journalists are likely to see the perceived or actual harm in nearly every aspect of news work, and this is why it is important for journalists to have a clear understanding of the nature of harm. As Elliott and Ozar's "systematic moral analysis (SMA)" stresses, the concept of "harm" is fundamental to journalists' ethical pursuit of stories. It thus warrants a more nuanced analysis. Joel Feinberg's *Harm to Others* is an excellent analysis.

Harm more Narrowly Defined

Feinberg's approach requires us think about the nature of our effects on others and our obligations to them. It is of use to journalists because it moves beyond the gross generalizations often made about harm in news media and provides a way for journalists, and the news-consuming public, to better understand when their news decisions are harmful. This, combined with Elliott and Ozar's SMA, provides the tools for determining when harm-causing news decisions need to be ethically justified and how that occurs.

According to Feinberg, a harm is an act or state that "sets back" the interest of someone else, such as her reasonable interest in her career, health, reputation, or privacy. This setting back of someone's interest has to be concrete—it has to be something that explicitly makes the person's state of affairs, or his or her ability to attain reasonable goals, worse off than if the act had not been done. And it must be something that sets back *important* desires, like raising a family or accomplishing a long-term project, and not more trivial interests such as avoiding embarrassment. "Not everything that we dislike or resent, and wish to avoid, is harmful to us," Feinberg wrote. "[It is critical that we distinguish] between the harmful conditions and *all* the various unhappy and unwanted physical and mental states that are not states of harm in themselves."[16] He continued:

> [Unpleasant or objectionable] experiences can distress, offend, or
> irritate us, without harming any of our interests. They come to us,

are suffered for a time, and then go, leaving us as whole and undam-
aged as we were before. The unhappy mental states they produce are
motley and diverse. They include . . . transitory disappointments and
disillusionments, wounded pride, hurt feelings, aroused anger,
shocked sensibility, alarm, disgust, frustration, impatient restless-
ness, acute boredom, irritation, embarrassment, feeling of guilt and
shame, . . . bodily discomfort, and many more. . . . [L]ike various
pleasures of the moment, these passing unpleasantnesses are neither
in nor against one's interests. For that reason, they are not to be
classified as harms."[17]

Insisting that such relatively minor offenses be considered "harms" risks
turning us into a sinister society of paternalistic, censorious vigilantes. Likewise, ensuring a healthy, vigorous public sphere, or marketplace of ideas,
means our sensibilities will inevitably be offended, and our ideals about decency are going to be challenged and violated. As creatures of community, we
should expect to be upset or occasionally hurt in these ways, as a natural part of
living in a social system and interacting with others who have different or competing interests, perspectives, and motivations. Journalists, understandably,
become the target of people's responses to these "unhappy mental states,"
which is all the more reason journalists must be able to articulate the justification for perceived harms in their broader public service mission.

Feinberg's distinctions suggest that journalists must make critical distinctions among effects and intentions that are not often fully appreciated by
news sources, subjects, and audiences. Most of the responses and perceived
slights mentioned by Feinberg are routinely hurled at journalists in the course
of their work. Journalists must be able to articulate a response to these claims
that helps story subjects and audiences understand how journalists perceive
their professional roles in society and how forms of power are used to carry
them out.

W. D. Ross's emphasis on the reality of moral conflict, combined with his
call that we are morally obligated to minimize harm—to be committed to
"nonmaleficence"—helps clarify how we might argue that some *reasons* for
doing things ought to carry more weight than others, instead of getting tangled
in moralistic claims and counterclaims about what's harmful and what's not.
"He allows us to think of moral conflict not as conflicts of *duties* but as a conflict
of moral *reasons*," the moral philosopher Philip Stratton-Lake said.[18] Ross was
clear about the duties we have, including avoidance of harm, but his system is
wholly dependent on context. Any broad generalizations about duty that do not
sufficiently consider the facts of a specific case carry little weight in Ross's system. He cautioned that it is a mistake to presume in any ethical deliberation
that "every act that is our duty is so for one and the same reason." According
to Ross, "No act is ever, in virtue of falling under some general description,

necessarily actually right; its rightness depends on its whole nature and not on any element of it."[19] The journalist must, thus, be able to show how her public service mission is often a compelling *reason* that, in the right contexts, she is justified in, for example, compromising a news subject's privacy.

Conclusion

The journalistic ethos of getting the story, ethically understood, is a noble one, committed to the ideal of public service and grounded in the key moral principles of respecting human dignity, minimizing harm, and exercising moral autonomy. Journalists must continually be mindful of these principles in their interactions with their sources, their subjects, and their audiences. A journalist who is driven primarily by market competition to get the story first may be serving personal or organizational interests but is at risk of using others as mere means to this competitive end, and thus of violating his Kantian obligation to respecting others as ends in themselves. This Kantian duty, taken with the commitment to public service and the approach that Ross offers to see dilemmas as opportunities to articulate compelling *reasons* for decisions that may cause harm, constitute the core ethos of the story.

The journalistic ethos, however, requires continual reiteration. Just as journalistic credibility can be damaged by subordinating these principles to other motives, so can it be compromised by aloofness and disregard for calls for accountability. Journalists can always do a better job explaining of themselves— acting as "ambassadors for our profession," as one reporter put it—to an often uncomprehending public. Such explanatory efforts, in fact, reflect the essence of ethics. Credibility requires journalists to manifest these principles in their work and to be able to articulate a compelling case that disclosing private information, or providing interpretive insight, or publishing the controversial results of investigative work serves a broad public interest. Doing so will not always bring about public support or approval, but explaining one's reasons demonstrates a commitment to journalism as an ethical enterprise.

Notes

1. See chap. 19 by Wendy Wyatt in this volume.

2. David H. Weaver, Randal A. Beam, Bonnie J. Brownlee, Paul S. Voakes, and G. Cleveland Wilhoit, *The American Journalist in the 21st Century: U.S. News People at the Dawn of a New Millennium* (Mahwah, NJ: Lawrence Erlbaum, 2007).

3. See Weaver et al., *American Journalist*, for data on journalists' comparative education (p. 40), religious activity (pp. 15–16), income (p. 97), and political leanings (p. 17).

4. David Shaw, "'Bias' That Bends over Backward to Right Itself," *Los Angeles Times*, March 23, 2003, p. E33.

5. Randy Kennedy, "Philip Jones Griffiths, War Photographer, Dies at 72," *New York Times*, March 20, 2008, p. A21.

6. Herbert J. Gans, *Deciding What's News: A Study of CBS Evening News, NBC Nightly News, Newsweek and Time* (New York: Vintage, 1980), 68.

7. Brent Cunningham, "Rethinking Objectivity," *Columbia Journalism Review*, (July/August 2003): 30.

8. P. L. Plaisance and J. A. Deppa, "Perceptions and Manifestations of Autonomy, Transparency and Harm among U.S. Newspaper Journalists," *Journalism & Communication Monographs* 10, no. 6, (2009):371.

9. Howard Gardner, Mihaly Csikszentmihalyi, and William Damon, *Good Work: When Excellence and Ethics Meet* (New York: Basic Books, 2001), 48.

10. Pamela J. Shoemaker and Stephen D. Reese, *Mediating the Message: Theories of Influences on Mass Media Content* (New York: Longman, 1996), 91.

11. Denis McQuail, *Mass Communication Theory: An Introduction* (London: SAGE, 1994), 204.

12. See the chapters by Stephanie Craft (chap. 3) and Sandra Borden (chap. 4) in this volume.

13. Weaver et al., *American Journalist*; David Weaver and G. Cleveland Wilhoit, *The American Journalist in the 1990s: U.S. News People at the End of an Era* (Mahwah, NJ: Lawrence Erlbaum, 1996).

14. Jeffrey H. Reiman, "Privacy, Intimacy, and Personhood," *Philosophy and Public Affairs* 6, no. 1 (1976): 26–44; Frederick D. Schoeman, *Privacy and Social Freedom* (Cambridge: Cambridge University Press, 1992); Judith A. Swanson, *The Public and the Private in Aristotle's Political Philosophy* (Ithaca, NY: Cornell University Press, 1992).

15. Bob Steele, "The Value of Independence," http://www.poynter.org/column.asp?id=36&aid=40421 (accessed May 3, 2008).

16. Joel Feinberg, *Harm to Others: The Moral Limits of the Criminal Law* (New York: Oxford University Press, 1984), 45, 47.

17. Feinberg, *Harm to Others*, 45–46.

18. W. D. Ross, *The Right and the Good*, ed. Philip Stratton-Lake (1930; Oxford: Clarendon, 2002), xxxviii.

19. Ross, *The Right and the Good*, 24, 33.

21

Mitigation Watchdogs: The Ethical Foundation for a Journalist's Role

Lee Wilkins

Coverage of disasters reveals that journalists, though they may not always acknowledge it, typically share ethical values and goals with the people and organizations on whom they report during these events. Thus, as persons, journalists have a duty to save lives and attempt to prevent property damage during such times. Yet news routines, indeed even the definition of news itself, retard the actualization of that goal in significant ways. A focus on mitigation—coverage based on the goal of reducing loss of life and property in times of disaster for both individuals and the organizations that employ them—can change news coverage, bringing the profession into better alignment with its ethical obligations.

Disasters have a way of revealing the inner workings of organizations.[1] Katrina told Americans a lot about how the local, state, and national government functioned; about the place of poverty in urban life; and about the unique culture and traditions of New Orleans. Katrina also represents a melding of disaster categories usually regarded as distinct and separable. On the one hand, Katrina was a "quick-onset" natural hazard—the tropical storm that became a category 5 hurricane developed, hit land, and blew itself out within two weeks. Wildfires, earthquakes, and tornados are also considered quick-onset hazards. But the magnitude of damage that Katrina caused, and the way that damage occurred, also make the storm a slow-onset technological disaster. Slow-onset disasters are a long time coming. Floods, droughts, and epidemics, for example, can take weeks, months, or even years to develop. Technological hazards implicate human choice—to build certain sorts of systems, to prepare for certain sorts of events, to consider certain sorts of eventualities while failing to consider others. Katrina crossed all these boundaries.

Katrina also strained generally accepted categories and ways of gathering, producing, and publishing the news. As a quick onset disaster, Katrina placed a premium on the ability of local news media to warn of an impending event and to stay on the air (or continue to publish in hard copy or via the Internet) during the first few days after the storm made landfall.[2] Katrina played to the definition of news that emphasizes immediacy, proximity, and conveying important information in both images and in words.

Katrina as a quick-onset disaster also emphasized journalism's environmental surveillance role. That role employs traditional definitions of news and asks news organizations to do well the things that journalists have done well for most of the past hundred years. The surveillance role also places a premium on saving lives from immediate peril—the ethical duties to prevent harm through warning, to investigate systems that may fail in predictable ways and to alert the public to those possibilities, and to improve lives when possible. This traditional articulation of the surveillance function assumes a traditional understanding of objectivity: the journalistic watchdog remains apart from the organizations that produce warning messages or that implement public policy to allow human beings to create predictably fallible systems.

As a slow-onset hazard, though, Katrina also revealed some accepted ways of doing journalism that served neither journalists nor their audiences very well. There were almost no warnings about the impending event in the weeks, months, or years beforehand, even though scholars whose business it is to study disasters knew that New Orleans was in peril. The single exception to this lack of news coverage was the local newspaper, the New Orleans *Times-Picayune*, which, a year before Katrina, had warned of impending catastrophe. The *Times-Picayune* had asked an important question and answered it non-traditionally: Can the definition of news include something that *might* happen in addition to something that *has* happened?

After the storm blew itself out, journalists were faced with a story that was traditional only on the surface. The predictable narrative of governmental incompetence, what investigative reporters refer to as a system failure, dominated news reports in the weeks and months immediately after the event. But there was less reporting about the roots of the problem—the merger of FEMA into the Department of Homeland Security (DHS) after 9/11, the ability of Congress to provide oversight for the Army Corps of Engineers, and the growth of a culture of poverty in New Orleans that negated accepted means of dealing with warnings, evacuations, and reconstruction.

Katrina as a slow-onset, technological disaster asked journalists to reconsider the traditional definition of news. The storm suggested that part of that definition, in addition to surveillance, should be coverage that attempts to mitigate future harm. In other words, journalists had to anticipate, and report on, what might occur. In order to accomplish this, journalists and their new organizations would have to plan for such potential events; to reorient their definition of news from emphasis on the coverage of immediate events to revelation of the origins of events, not just their outcomes. In this context, preventing harm becomes the predominant ethical obligation[3]—one that asks journalists and their news organizations to significantly step outside their traditional roles and ways of doing things. Katrina also suggests that journalists tie themselves to community survival in ways that question some of the more superficial understandings of objectivity. Using Katrina again as an example, the journalistic watchdog lived in a house that Katrina destroyed. To rebuild the house, the journalistic watchdog had to get personally involved, first by making an ethical judgment that the house itself was worth rebuilding, and second by cooperating with others to rebuild that house within a community. Neither the initial ethical judgment that the house needed to be rebuilt nor the acknowledgement of stakeholder status within a community's larger goal fits a traditional articulation of objective journalism.

Katrina was what practiced journalists might call a systems story with a human face. First, Katrina was about the systems put in place to deal with disasters and hazards.[4] The political systems Katrina engaged had their roots in local, state, and national government. But there was culture, economics, and science as well, each having an impact on how the story was portrayed and understood. There were journalistic systems, too, including definitions of news and understandings of role, mechanisms of news delivery, and craft demands to humanize the event. Ethical decisions played a part in all of it, from the individual words and images journalists selected to what stories were covered and what staff was assigned. The thesis of this chapter is that the ethical principles that best fund such coverage can be subsumed under the notion of harm prevention, in part by being a "mitigation watchdog." Ethically informed news coverage can both report on immediate events and work to prevent harm in ways that allow citizens of a democracy to hold themselves and their social and governmental institutions to account.

Normal Accidents

The sociologist Charles Perrow[5] said it best: Things break. Mechanical systems wear out. People interact badly with machines. The weather sometimes does produce the perfect storm, and even a lesser storm can cause great devastation. The unexpected happens—predictably enough that human beings have found many effective coping mechanisms. The process of covering news of such "normal accidents" has been categorized as the "routinization of the unexpected."[6]

Scholars, too, have routinized disasters; they accept a definition of disasters that replicates common sense—an event or series of events "concentrated in time and space, in which a society or a relatively self-sufficient division of a society, undergoes severe danger, and incurs such losses to its members and physical appurtenances that the social structure is disrupted and the fulfillment of all or some of the essential functions of the society is prevented."[7]

As noted above, disasters are generally divided into the sometimes overlapping categories of "natural" and "technological." These are then categorized into five phases:

- Warning
- Impact
- Immediate post impact
- Recovery
- Mitigation

Human activity, and interaction with the natural and social environment, varies predictably depending on the phase of the disaster.[8] Scholars have linked specific government actions and news organization's proclivities to each of these phases. These empirical findings about how journalists behave can be linked to ethical understandings.[9] By exploring the ethical implications of "normal news work," defined by scholars as the field of newsroom sociology,[10] practitioners can develop new ways of thinking through disaster coverage—ways that will more effectively serve the public and community.

Warning

In natural hazards, government is often responsible for issuing warnings to other community stakeholders. In technological hazards, government has required some industries to provide information that will allow warnings about certain sorts of events to be issued. When the natural hazard is weather, news organizations have learned that investing in systems that make warnings visual and compelling produces profits.[11] The local weather forecaster is probably the best-recognized television personality in most local media markets. Quick-onset warnings conveyed through mass media about certain sorts of weather or weather-related events are generally heeded. However, warnings that require people to behave differently, particularly warnings that ask people to evacuate, meet strong individual resistance based on a host of factors, among them prior experience with similar warning messages (if you survived the last hurricane and didn't evacuate, you are less likely to respond to warning messages suggesting evacuation the next time around). These findings reinforce one of the oldest research findings in mass communication: people respond to the same message differently.

News accounts of warnings tend to make some assumptions—specifically, that audiences will be familiar with terms used in warning messages. Research indicates that members of the public often confuse such concepts as "warning" and "watch;" for example, Sattler and Marshall stress the importance of detail.[12]

Their study of coastal South Carolina found that television graphics depicting the time frames meant by "watch" and "warning" led to better awareness of the likelihood that residents would have to take action. Other events—for example, blizzards—have a technical meaning that is seldom included in news accounts.[13] And anti-terrorism warnings in London subway cars after the March 2004 Madrid train bombings were simple and specific: Don't do this. Do this.

It is unrealistic to expect that any single warning message, or even a well-thought-out message campaign, will produce the desired response in every instance. But that expectation should not encourage public officials or journalists to put less thought and effort into effectively and accurately communicating warning of specific events. Scholarship here is unequivocal: warning messages save lives.

To best communicate those messages, though, may require journalists and news organizations to enter into partnership with government, a partnership that calls into question journalistic independence.[14] Government's tendency to establish a command post, and to give journalists access to that command post, results in news stories that are told exclusively from the official point of view. This is particularly the case when the disaster limits mobility and journalists find themselves geographically restricted, thus limiting any pool of potential sources. Disasters tend to disrupt normal newsgathering and editing routines regardless of media outlet and type of disaster. Research suggests that normal fact-checking routines are truncated, though other studies have found the major media working effectively to filter out rumors.[15] These limitations, while understandable, often make it difficult for journalists at this stage of the event to report using anything other than officials sources—and those officials sources know this and sometimes take advantage of journalistic routines and limitations to frame events in their own interest. Journalists covering Hurricane Katrina, for example, thought both creatively and ethically when they decided to use "split screen" technology to show live events in New Orleans while simultaneously airing the official federal response to those events.

Most technological hazards, however, occur with little warning and pit both government and news media against private industries, such as the local chemical plant. In warning of technological hazards, journalists can find themselves confronting formidable government obstacles—for example, regulatory agencies—or difficult intellectual issues, such as reporting charges that childhood vaccines are somehow connected with the rise in childhood autism, even though current scientific evidence indicates otherwise.[16] The ethically sound approach in such cases is the best-science approach. Science is rarely definite, and scientific opinion about possible occurrences will typically includes a range of views, but it is almost always the case that some views have far stronger supporting evidence. Journalists, though, in their zeal for a perceived objectivity tend to employ a "dueling scientists" framing—they quote scientists or public officials in favor of a particular point of view and balance it with that of another

scientist or public official who is opposed.[17] Such striving for fairness is generally laudable, but when there are genuine hazards, the duty to prevent harm
outweighs such a goal and demands one discover the "weight of best scientific
opinion."

Knowing what to warn about, and at what level of intensity, demands journalism that is at once hyper-responsive to changing conditions (think tornado)
or willing to undertake expensive and long-term critical and investigative
reporting (think the decades-old proposal to bury high-level radioactive waste
under Yucca Mountain, Nevada). Institutionally, it may also require that news
organizations become part of a warning system while, simultaneously, retaining
enough independence to be critical of it—an admittedly difficult balancing act.
Warning messages also emphasize an event-centered definition of news, an
approach that, because it is profitable, is particularly difficult to dislodge.
Nonetheless, the ethical stricture of preventing harm requires that journalists
and news organizations reconsider their almost exclusive reliance on an event-
centered definition of news when the news peg is disaster. Warning about disasters that are likely to occur in the future, while an expansion of the traditional
journalistic role, is critical if the ethical values are to have a meaningful effect
on coverage.

Impact

The impact phase of any disaster often shows journalists at their very best, as
evidenced in the universally praised coverage of 9/11 and of national and local
journalistic efforts in covering Hurricane Katrina. In natural disasters, government, first at the local and then at the state and national level, is almost always
the first official responder; technological disasters follow a similar pattern. Ethically, journalists and government responders find themselves on the same
side: save lives and mitigate property damage where possible. "Prevent harm
when possible" informs many decisions at this stage of the event for all players,
including journalists.

One ethical problem to emerge in such coverage is that during this time,
journalists can and often do forge strong relationships with government officials involved in the response. While journalists understand that this partnership is born of the event, their sources often don't understand that, for the
news media, this role is a temporary one. When journalists return to their more
in-depth, critical, or investigative work, officials and other sources are often
dumbfounded, cutting off relationships that had been working well until that
point.[18]

Another problem is that visual and verbal imagery focuses on human victims, sometimes raising ethical questions about truthfulness in context and
invasion of privacy. Framing news stories primarily in terms of victims min-
imizes the role that structure, regulation, and private industry can play in

producing a context in which certain sorts of disaster are likely. The visual images of television—because they evoke the human response of empathy toward those affected—can also influence the policy making process toward a "quick" fix rather than longer term and more systemic change.[19] All of this implicates the "truth telling within context" imperative of journalism. In addition, such images, because they "catch" people at times of great stress and grief raise questions of privacy invasion.[20] The ethical issue here is whether such images merely hype a story or provide inconsequential information—after all, it wouldn't be news if people were *not* upset in such circumstances—rather than digging deeper for a story that will actually help people cope in both the short and long run.

A third problem: news coverage, particularly the visual elements of it, will emphasize "the worst" damage. In some cases, audience members and public officials, upon seeing such images, assume an entire city has been devastated rather than particular geographic areas. This lack of geographic context can sometimes be almost humorous—as when parents of international students studying in the Midwest called their children immediately after 9/11 because they assumed the entire country was in flames. But they can also have policy consequences, where aid is directed to the most devastated areas while others are ignored because they have not made the front page of the newspaper or the television screen or YouTube. Professionally, journalists can be faced with tough choices; the most compelling and focused shot may also be the least accurate in terms of the event's impact.

Fourth, some studies indicate that media accounts generally underplay rather than sensationalize the extent of a disaster, particularly in the early hours when even those charged with responding to the event may have incomplete information. Other studies have found that news accounts are inaccurate, and individual journalists, particularly when confronted with highly technical information, are sometimes confused and contradictory. Information made public without critically evaluating whether a particular source has the knowledge, expertise, and access to respond authoritatively certainly reflects the values of scoop and immediacy rather than the professional commitment to providing needed information in context. Truth telling is jeopardized.

Fifth, the world of the Web and the drive for citizen journalism and crowd-sourcing raise a different category of issues: how much should news organizations encourage citizens to put themselves in harm's way in order to fulfill these perceived responsibilities? Or, to phrase it in words that Kant would understand: should news organizations treat their readers (listeners, viewers) as a mere means to their own end—news stories and profit—or as an end in themselves? Cool cell phone video of the tornado as it weaves down the street may not be worth airing because it sends a message about a news organization's willingness to use a citizen for the organization's ends. Yet such citizen-generated content is becoming more common.[21] Institutionally, news organizations need to develop policies—and then be willing to enforce them—in order for them to work both ethically and collaboratively with their audiences during the impact phase of the event.

Finally, journalists must be aware that many in the emergency-management community view the media—and hence its representatives—with some suspicion.[22] Journalists (and their news organizations) need to understand that the need to "feed the beast" must take a backseat for first responders and many other emergency workers, whose paramount responsibility is saving lives.

Immediate Post-Impact

During the post-impact phase, emergency responses give way to the regular workings of government and private stakeholders such as insurance companies and social service agencies. Information collection continues, both by government and by private organizations involved in the response.

For journalists, this phase of disaster is the beginning of what becomes a decline in the amount of coverage. If the disaster has been significant, staff members of news organizations that have "staffed up" now find themselves physically tired. That fatigue may be psychological as well; in some cases, journalists themselves are first responders, and most news organizations do not provide counseling or other sorts of support to their employees.[23] Some may even have been affected by the disaster and now have family and other personal concerns to attend to (this was particularly true for journalists covering Katrina). The "minimize harm" principle applies just as well to news organizations who have a duty to see to the physical and psychological health of their employees.

While frames make for predictable narratives, there are certain stereotypes about how people behave during disasters that have little place in news accounts—despite their persistence in the public mind. Multiple studies suggest people seldom panic at the time of a disaster, and those who do find their escape routes blocked or they become socially isolated from others.[24] Panic is a maladaptive behavior. Thus, journalists have every reason to be skeptical, and to insist on verification, if anything other than sporadic panic is reported during a disaster. The same is true for looting, which occurs more often in times of civil unrest than during a disaster response.

In the immediate impact phase, attention shifts to concerns about rebuilding and mitigation. These are systems stories—not nearly as flashy and often requiring enterprise. In this stage of a disaster, the news organization's role begins the shift from partner with government to *watchdog*—primarily of government but also of the private sector, for example, the insurance industry. Here context becomes important and spot reporting begins to give way to more in-depth coverage. The journalistic and human tendency is to "blame" people rather than the systems people create—what psychologists call the fundamental attribution error.[25] Reporting that adopts the frame of individual responsibility and causality for the disaster's spread will not examine how the systems built or required by engineers, governments, and private industry, for example, helped exacerbate the consequences of hazards. The result is that institutions are less likely to be held to account, a failure of the watchdog role no matter how it is conceived.

All this, of course, cannot be done by individual journalists acting on their own, regardless of motive. News organizations need to be willing to support such coverage, with the understanding that it's going to cost them money in the short run while in the long run demonstrating their collaboration with the public and the community. Such an approach is also not strictly objective, in the narrowest sense of the term. For example, after Katrina, the *Times-Picayune* made an editorial decision that it was going to focus its news (as opposed to editorial) coverage on New Orleans, with the understanding that the city itself should be rebuilt. While this decision on the surface seems relatively non-contentious, if the *Kansas City Star* had made the same decision about the Missouri towns that were entirely relocated after the 1993 Midwest flood, flood-plain management and mitigation efforts could have suffered a genuine setback.[26] Taking a pro-existing-community point of view can have both empirical and moral consequences. It certainly heightens the need for serious professional debate about the role of news organizations in partnership with their communities after disasters. As will be noted later, a focus on mitigation—a long-term view of recovery—may provide an ethically based stance that simultaneously allows for critical, contextual, scientific, and policy-informed journalism, while continuing a community collaboration.

Recovery

While government often steps back to allow private industry and the citizenry to shoulder the work of rebuilding the physical environment, it continues to play a role in assessing losses, and in coordinating and planning recovery and reconstruction efforts, including policy decisions about reconstruction. Government, particularly community mental health agencies and social service agencies, also oversees and monitors the psychological response to disaster.

"By contrast, newspapers display a rapidly rising interest in disaster but lose interest very quickly as the dramatic aspects of the situation are replaced by the prosaic activities of planning and rebuilding."[27] Yet, particularly for wide-spread disasters, those prosaic activities have a greater long-term impact on readers and viewers than does the disaster itself.

Journalists lose interest for a number of nested reasons:

First, actual rebuilding is often the purview of the private sector. Documents that the government is required to disgorge can legally be withheld by banks or insurance firms. Planning meetings of private-sector responders are not subject to open-meetings laws. Provisions of the USA PATRIOT Act require that some decisions and information that were once public, such as specific spending on security-related items or personnel, are now off-limits for journalists. Even when government is doing the rebuilding, it takes time and becomes less clearly linked to the initial event.

Second, the policymaking process is complex, and journalistic coverage of the political process, particularly at the state and regional level, is less extensive than it was twenty years ago. Stories are simply dropped from the news agenda because of the lack of staff or the perceived urgency of other events.

Third, reporting on the recovery phase of the event generally emerges through in-depth and investigative work. Yet even here, previously adopted frames tend to dominate coverage. This is particularly problematic when such framing results in less airtime or a smaller news hole to examine more sys-temic causes for a particular event and the response to it. But it is during the recovery phase that alternate voices are most likely to try to catch the attention of policymakers. Stories from this "non-command-post point of view" can make for compelling reading and viewing.

Despite the temptation to move on to the next hot story, coverage of recov-ery efforts, when done properly, involves compelling business, consumer, and policy reporting. The journalistic struggle here is connecting the dots—linking policy decisions to the disaster—and being willing to "follow the money," a tough task in a journalistic culture that valorizes the immediate.

A more central struggle, in this post–9/11 environment, is the statutory requirement that the DHS be in charge of disaster response at both the state and federal levels. This authority structure has placed emergency-management and public health officials in an organizational vise, trying to work from the bottom up, while facing a top-down DHS authority structure. Because this arrangement is still relatively new, journalists may discover that one set of responders (e.g., local public health officials) actually want to talk to news media but are prohibited from doing so by supervisors from DHS, whose institutional culture is rooted in secrecy.

The journalistic response—both individual and organizational—needs to be a tenacious commitment to truth telling and the watchdog role. This is par-ticularly crucial because of the vast sums of money being allocated to homeland security functions, a newsworthy series of stories by any journalistic standard.

Mitigation

This phase represents an effort to plan for similar events so as to reduce loss of life and property damage. The mitigation phase is really about public policy evaluation and creation. For both natural and technological hazards, mitigation involves coordinating with multiple stakeholders, both private and public, and placing mitigation activities in a political context. Scholars particularly view mitigation as the most crucial phase of disasters and hazards. In fact, the United Nations declared the decade of the 1990s the decade of hazard reduction and mitigation—a worldwide effort. Yet scholarship also indicates that mitigation is the most unreported phase of the event.[28]

The Impact of Making Mitigation the Guiding Ethical Goal

If journalists are serious about an ethical foundation for their work, then mitigation—how it is conceptualized and how it is implemented—needs to replace the focus on the event itself as the predominant journalistic goal. Saving lives and reducing financial losses are worthy ethical goals. Mitigation provides a context for understanding much of what goes on both before and after a disaster. Mitigation reporting (e.g., on the development and enforcement of building codes) can save lives during and after an earthquake. Furthermore, this approach is valid internationally; it applies just as much to school construction in China as it does to apartment buildings in San Francisco. But a news focus on mitigation also has ethical implications.

For mitigation to take hold, journalists will have to acknowledge that news is what might happen, not only what has happened. Former U.S. vice president and Nobel laureate Al Gore, who began his working life as a journalist at the *Nashville Tennessean*, provides an excellent example of what this future-oriented definition of news might look like in his film, *An Inconvenient Truth*. But the future is epistemologically distinct from the present, at least as far as news is concerned, and this change would require a shift in worldview.

Part of this change needs to be a reexamination of the traditional news frames for disaster, specifically the focus on victims and decontextualized devastation. A mitigation reporting frame, for example, would require journalists to note when individuals or communities have chosen to rebuild in a floodplain or how national governments have prepared for potential epidemics. A mitigation frame thus requires understanding of science and public policy, rather than reliance on decontextualized human interest that dominates so much contemporary disaster coverage.

News routines would have to accommodate a more community and enterprise- oriented role. In some sense, this is a return to journalism's past, where news organizations were considered community citizens first and businesses second. This shift becomes more difficult when most news organizations are owned by distant conglomerates that regard them as a business just like any other. Figuring out how to monetize community connection is a significant issue for this century—one that has implications not just for disaster coverage but for many other journalistic efforts.[29]

News organizations would have to be willing to grapple with, and then make policy about, how technology should affect their news coverage. For example, should they establish a Web site template to support a community bulletin board function? What sort of mutual-aid agreements should organizations develop in anticipation of a widespread disaster such as Katrina that dismantles printing plants or broadcast facilities?

Last, how much, and under what guidelines, should news organizations partner with government in the warning phase of the event? Partnerships pit access against independence, at least in the planning phase. How should prudence be incorporated into the role of citizen journalist? In an attempt to provide better coverage, should news organizations encourage unpaid, uninsured, and perhaps ill-informed audience members to attempt to aid news organizations, even at substantial personal risk?

Mitigation reporting in the face of disaster can bring journalists, and the organizations that employ them, into alignment with their ethical obligations. It is not that the current focus on the event and its immediate aftermath is unethical so much as it is unreflective of what scholars and practitioners now know about disasters and media behavior. A better alignment with the ethical obligations of the profession can give journalists new insight into how they might better do their jobs, allowing them to serve their communities more effectively and to build on the care values journalists as professionals have developed over the past four hundred years.

Notes

1. H. Molotch and M. Lester, "News as Purposive Behavior: On the Strategic Uses of Routine Events, Accidents, and Scandals," *American Sociological Review* 39 (1975): 101–12.

2. Douglas Brinkley, *The Great Deluge: Katrina, New Orleans and the Gulf Coast* (New York: William Morrow, 2005).

3. Philosophers might link this concept of preventing harm with the duty of beneficence as articulated by W. D. Ross or with the concept of nurture that dominates the work of feminist philosophers such as Nell Noddings or Daryl Koehn.

4. D. S. Mileti, *Disasters by Design: A Reassessment of Natural Hazards in the US* (Washington D.C.: Joseph Henry, 1999).

5. Charles Perrow, *Normal Accidents: Living with High-risk Technologies* (New York: Basic Books, 1984).

6. G. Tuchman, *Making News: A Study in the Construction of Reality* (New York: Free Press, 1978).

7. C. E. Fritz, "Disasters." In *Contemporary Social Problems*, ed. R. D. Merton and Robert Nisbet (New York: Harcourt, Brace & World, 1961), 655.

8. Disasters have been studied by scholars in a variety of disciplines, most prominent among them geography, sociology, and psychology. For a review of this work, which encompasses literally thousands of separate empirical and theoretical investigations, see E. L. Quarantelli, *Inventory of Disaster Field Studies in the Social and*

Behavioral Sciences, 1919–1979 (Book & Monograph Series #20) (Newark: University of Delaware, Disaster Research Center, 1984); Dennis, S. Mileti, Thomas E. Drabek, and J. Eugene Hass, *Human Systems in Extreme Environments: A Sociological Perspective* (Boulder, CO: Institute for Behavioral Sciences, 1975); Thomas Drabek, *Human Systems in Response to Disaster: An Inventory of Sociological Findings* (New York: Springer-Verlag, 1986).

9. Findings through content analysis include using predictable narratives and frames, exaggerating or underestimating the number of victims killed or injured and the amount of property damage, focusing on officials' reports, using visual images of the worst of disasters, and perpetuating some disaster myths. All raise issues of accuracy and balance, of source dependency, and of focusing on events instead of their causes to boost ratings, circulation, and Web hits. These findings link to the ethical issues of truth telling, fairness, completeness, and role.

10. Daniel, A Berkowitz, *The Social Meanings of News: A Text Reader* (Beverly Hills: Sage, 1997). See also work by H. Gans and M. Schudson.

11. Some sorts of disasters (e.g., forest fires) lend themselves to weather-like reports as well. However, most non-weather-related disasters do not, and even some weather-related disasters, such as tornados, are notoriously difficult to predict and follow.

12. D. N. Sattler and A. Marshall, "Hurricane Preparedness: Improving Television Hurricane Watch and Warning Graphics," *International Journal of Mass Emergencies and Disasters* 20 (2002): 41–49.

13. L. Wilkins, "Television and Newspaper Coverage of a Blizzard: Is the Message Helplessness?" *Newspaper Research Journal* 6, no. 4 (1985): 51–65.

14. Such a partnership currently exists with most broadcast outlets and the National Weather Service.

15. D. Lasorsa, "Newspapers Perpetuate Few Rumors about 9/11 Crisis," *Newspaper Research Journal* 24 (2002): 10–21.

16. E. Singer and P. Endreny, "Reporting Hazards: Their Benefits and Costs," *Journal of Communication* 7 (1987):10–16.

17. For a more detailed discussion of the difficult problem of perceived objectivity, see chap. 9 by Stephen Ward and chap. 10 by Carrie Figdor, in this volume; S. Friedman, S. Dunwoodsy, and C. Rogers, *Communicating Uncertainty: Media Coverage of New and Controversial Science* (Mahwah, NJ: Lawrence Erlbaum, 1999); K. M. Wilson, "Drought, Climate Change and Uncertainty: Measuring Reporters' Knowledge of Global Climate Change," *Public Understanding of Science* 9 (2000): 1–14. J. W. Dearing, "Newspaper Coverage of Maverick Science: Creating Controversy through Balance," *Public Understanding of Science* 4 (1995): 341–61.

18. P. Driscoll and M. B. Salwen, "Riding Out the Storm: Public Evaluation of News Coverage of Hurricane Andrew," *International Journal of Mass Emergencies and Disasters* 14 (1996): 293–303.

19. L. Wilkins, "Living with the Flood: Human and Governmental Responses to Real and Symbolic Risk," in *The Great Flood of 1993: Causes, Impacts and Responses*, ed. Stanley E. Chagnon, 218–44 (Boulder, CO: Westview, 1993).

20. See chap. 14 by Clifford Christians and chap. 15 by Candace Gauthier, in this volume.

21. Further, citizens seeking to help others in times of disasters is a well-documented human response to disaster—a response news organizations can take advantage of. For scholarly analysis, see E. L. Quarantelli, "Emergent Citizen Groups In Disaster Preparedness and Recovery: An Interim Report" (Miscellaneous Rept. #33) (Newark: University of Delaware, Disaster Research Center, 1983).

22. Specific studies detailed in Thomas Drabek, *Human System Responses to Disaster: An Inventory of Sociological Findings* (New York: Springer, 1986).

23. The Dart Center for Journalism and Trauma (www.dartcenter.org) provides a wealth of resources and professional exemplars for covering disasters and hazards. The center's work also includes workshops for journalists and managers on how to deal with stress when journalists find themselves covering such events. Thanks to the Dart Center and the events of September 11, 2001, most scholars now acknowledge that journalists face the same sorts of psychological and physical stresses as other first responders. News organizations have been slower to get the message, although many journalists covering the Iraq War have taken advantage of programs or other resources like those suggested by the center.

24. See Dennis S. Mileti, *Human Systems in extreme environments* (Boulder, CO: Institute of Behavioral Science, 1975); Mileti, *Natural hazard warning systems in the United States: A research assessment* (Boulder, CO: Institute of Behavioral Science, 1975); and Mileti, *Disasters by design: A Reassessment of Natural Hazards in the United States* (Washington, D.C.: Joseph Henry Press, 1999).

25. L. Wilkins and P. Patterson, "Risk Analysis and the Construction of News," *Journal of Communication* 37 no. 3 (1987): 80–92.

26. S. A. Chagnon, ed., *The Great Flood of 1993: Causes, Impacts and Responses* (Boulder, CO: Westview, 1996).

27. Harry E. Moore, Fredrick L. Bates, Marvin V. Layman, and Vernon J. Parenton, "Before the Wind: A Study of the Response to Hurricane Carla" (Disaster study no. 19) (Washington, D.C., National Academy of Sciences—National Research Council, 1963), p. 126.

28. See, for example, L. Wilkins, *Shared Vulnerability: The Media and American Perceptions of the Bhopal Disaster* (Westport, CT: Greenwood, 1987).

29. For additional discussion, see chap. 11 by Ian Richards and chap. 13 by Marty Steffens, in this volume.

PART IX

Image Ethics

Introduction

Many people's first engagement with news ethics, I would venture, is motivated by an image: "How *could* they show something so (take your pick) obscene, violent, offensive, biased. . . ." Further, reactions frequently conflict; allowing for exceptional cases,[1] for every ten who are outraged by an image, at least five are impressed.

Photojournalists must often feel they just can't win. Take, for example, *Time* magazine's September 15, 2008, cover photo of the vice-presidential candidate Sarah Palin. The close-up image was, to my mind, a flattering photo, accompanying an equally flattering inside story, "The Education of Sarah Palin." Reaction from her supporters, however, was very different: they complained that the "obviously unbecoming" image revealed *Time*'s liberal bias. As evidence, one commentator grumbled, "You can see her chin hairs!"

In addition to sometimes ticking us off, images also draw us in, as every marketing director will attest. They attract, inform, and motivate, and often in ways the best wordsmiths can only envy. Like most instructors, when I teach this topic I rely heavily on photo slides and hard copies, letting the power of the image tell the story.

Think about historical events of the last hundred years; you recall them as images rather than words, right? Some examples: the 1937 crash of the Hindenburg; raising the flag on Iwo Jima; planes hitting the Twin Towers; Abu Ghraib.[2] Once exposed to these images, they're pretty well burned into our brains and continue to evoke powerful emotional and ethical responses.

All this makes perfect sense, say Julie Newton and Rick Williams, because our brain is wired to react to images at a more primal level than it does to words. Relying on cutting-edge evolutionary accounts of psycho-biology and ethical naturalism, Newton and Williams argue that "images . . . become 'truths' stored in memory, capable of influencing our intuitive core of knowledge before and beyond the attention of consciousness."

Their chapter first works through some challenging arguments concerning images and the production of "truth," of, in fact, different kinds of truth, all of which most powerfully affect our understanding of information via "nonconscious" or "pre-reflective" mechanisms. They then provide an interesting case study, both as a model for analysis and as a way of testing readers' intuitions.

The upshot of this for ethics is nicely captured in the chapter's epigraph (quoting George Johnson): "Plato had it wrong. It's the shadows on the wall that are real." That is, the sort of reflective analysis that makes up the traditional model of ethics must at least be supplemented, maybe even supplanted, by a more careful understanding of these unconscious processes and their impact on ethical reactions and judgments: "While conscious, rational evaluation of the ethics of a journalistic act, along the lines of Elliott and Ozar's SMA, is a goal worthy of each and every journalist, in daily practice, journalists rarely have the time or opportunity to conduct a step-by-step analysis of each act they perform." This constraint is even more telling for the photojournalist who "works in time increments as fast as 1/5000th of a second and may make hundreds or even thousands of photographs in the course of covering one event or story."

Key to an informed ethical evaluation of images, Newton and Williams contend, is how they connect to deep, evolutionarily driven intuitions. According to this view of ethical naturalism, people have evolved in ways that produce what some have called the "yuck factor," an unreflective, non-rational reaction, usually negative, to the action in question. For example, the psychology professor Marc Hauser tested people's reaction to various scenarios and concluded there is a basic gut reaction to certain options, even if there's no rationally discernible difference.[3]

From this, Newton and Williams conclude, "Because the complex decision-making that facilitates ethical behavior is supported by highly intuitive, nonconscious cognitive processes, we need a balanced, holistic approach to ethics, one that integrates rational and intuitive cognitive abilities of the human mind to enhance ethical decision making." They then provide just such an approach, the "Personal Impact Assessment," which, when combined with "logical tools, such as SMA . . . can deeply enhance understanding of the powerful effects of visual imagery on perception, memory and behavior." As noted above, they link this theory and method to a real case, one most striking because of its ordinariness. That is, they don't focus on the unusual and dramatic, but pick an everyday photo, with its revelation of everyday—and telling—reactions.

Newton and Williams's use of words like "truth" and "meaning" varies considerably from how a philosopher would employ them, and that will cause some confusion for those trained in that tradition. They acknowledge this, however, and are careful to provide stipulated definitions where appropriate. There is also heated debate in the literature about what just the "yuck factor" tells us: Should we give up on two thousand years of insistence on rational scrutiny of emotive reactions? Some reject Hauser et al.'s arguments outright;[4] others think we should take it seriously as indicative, but not conclusive of appropriate moral response.[5]

Newton and Williams's chapter, thus, is rich and sophisticated, one from which I learned a lot. It should motivate extended class conversation and, I would hope, fun debate. My take on moral intuitions is closer to Callahan's; we should very much pay attention to gut reactions, and it may be that key moral principles cannot be rationally defended but must simply be intuitively accepted.[6] I am convinced, however, that rational reflection is still indispensable to determining the right thing to do. They agree—see their holistic method—but we would probably differ on emphasis: what's more telling, the intuitive reaction or the rational analysis?

Regardless, though, of where we should come down on that problem, Newton and Williams's arguments about the pre-reflective impact of images (and, as suggested above, their long-lasting impact) seems clearly right, as does their call for a different kind of ethics education, one that gives close attention to the relationship between that impact, the intuitions it motivates, and our cognitive and ethical understandings.

Paul Martin Lester, one of the field's best-known scholars on this topic, comes at it from a very different—and complementary—orientation. While he also stresses the powerful impact of images, his is a very on-the-street approach: How should photojournalists and their editors approach sticky cases? In answering this, he also nicely articulates the photographers' ethos.

Working off, and reacting to, Elliott and Ozar's explanation of the SMA, Lester notes: "Interestingly, the only example in their chapter in which it is concluded that a journalist caused unjustified harm and should be considered ethically prohibited, is one that involves a photojournalist taking a picture during a spot news story." We shouldn't be surprised, Lester says, to see "the visual message singled out for criticism, [since] . . . photographers and their products are easy targets." He nonetheless reaches a different conclusion in the case, after a detailed application of the SMA.

This chapter was one of the more fun to edit, largely because Lester and I had good-natured disagreements about many of his conclusions. Those disagreements were informative for a number of reasons, all of which should provide insight for your own ethical reflections—which makes this a wonderful chapter with which to end the book.

First, even a tool as sophisticated as the SMA will not provide clear-cut solutions; one must still use one's informed judgment, both to interpret the facts and to determine how the steps apply. To repeat a consistent refrain in these chapter introductions, *ethics is hard work*. Second, such informed judgment is largely shaped by one's history and conceptual scheme or mindset. Ethics decision-making, of course, entails considerable interpretation, which is in turn built upon who one is, what one does, with whom one works and relates, and how one prioritizes values—that is, upon how one sees the world. Third, ethical problems look very different from the trenches, with their associated goals and pressures. If you decide to make a career of journalism (or any other profession, for that matter), you will become enmeshed in that reality. The challenge is to be able to step in and out of its culture, to be able to appreciate its norms while also critically assessing them.

Lester's chapter reflects all these insights, in part because, far better than most, he is able to keep a foot in both worlds—that of praxis and of theoretical–critical analysis, thus setting a standard for the rest of us, one I urge you to carry into your careers.

One last point: you should notice that neither chapter gives attention to the question of veracity, to whether it is ever appropriate to alter an image before printing or airing. For many photojournalists, this is the *only* question, and the answer is invariably "no." That none of these authors addresses it suggests two probable answers. Either, first, the negative answer is such a given as not to be worth discussing, or, second, we've entered such a no-man's land (given the enhanced technical capacities for making minor changes) that we need time for the problem to percolate. New technologies, in fact, give old questions new meaning: When does *enhancement* equal *alteration?* Since commercial sponsorship is now so pervasive as to make it increasingly difficult to capture "non-branded" images, has it become ethical simply to edit them out? Has the Internet generation become so accustomed to digital alterations that news credibility no longer rests (as much?) on such veracity?

My sense is that most photojournalists still treat this as an absolute—never do it. But, like all absolutes, this one is problematic: there can be ethically good reasons allowing for, even sometimes ethically requiring, alteration. Maybe it is time to change the ethos to allow for alteration, but only in those rare cases in which it is ethically justified, as determined through a process like Elliott and Ozar's SMA.

Wherever the conversation goes, trustworthiness is all the more vital. So many clearly altered images now pass through my email that the default has reversed: I simply assume it is all altered, unless I've been given reason to think otherwise. Surely this cannot be news media's standard, but what should be?

Notes

1. See the *Bakersfield Californian* drowning photo discussed in chapter 15.
2. All these photos can be easily found via a Google image search.

3. Marc Hauser, *Moral Minds* (New York: Harper Collins, 2006). Most of the scenarios explored the difference between actively participating in someone's death versus not acting to prevent it. Hauser found that most persons reacted more negatively to the active option, even when fewer lives were at stake. (Cf. the story I provide in the introduction to Part I.)

4. Cf. Peter Singer, "Should We Trust Our Moral Intuitions?" http://www. utilitarian.net/singer/by/200703--.htm.

5. This theme runs through much of Dan Callahan's later work.

6. See my "Appreciating W. D. Ross: on Duties and Consequences," *Journal of Mass Media Ethics* 18, no. 2 (2003): 1–18.

22

Visual Ethics: An Integrative Approach to Ethical Practice in Visual Journalism

Julianne H. Newton and Rick Williams

Plato had it backward. It's the shadows on the wall that are real.

—George Johnson

Twenty-first-century journalism juxtaposes words with still photographs, graphics, cartoons, video, sound, and animation in seamless presentations intended to be understood as real. As images work with words and music in short- and long-form journalistic presentations alongside advertising and entertainment media, fact and fantasy merge, dancing together in human memory as if all are real. These increasingly sophisticated messages, conveyed by media of every function and form, deserve careful attention by journalism ethicists.

Regardless of whether their purposes are deemed journalism, persuasion, entertainment, or art by media professionals and scholars, images enter the memory galleries of viewers' minds as part of the storehouse of information underlying and facilitating problem solving, decision-making, and behavior. Their forms and contexts convey meanings the brain perceives and remembers as real, or actual. Through this process, images—whatever their origin—become "truths" stored in memory, capable of influencing our intuitive core of knowledge before and beyond the attention of consciousness. These image messages can be perceived as intended, misconstrued, or even "reconstrued" as they transform in memory.

In this context, "truth" or "truths" refer to data individuals use as if they are accurate. People draw on these dynamic memory "biases" to help them make decisions and act. Though some "brain truths" may be shared to various degrees by other individuals, these thoughts more often are uniquely personal understandings of information perceived and interpreted through noncon-scious ways of knowing.[1] This process leads people to accept what looks real as "visual truth," which we define as "authentic knowledge derived from seeing."[2] "Authentic" means "not false or copied; genuine; real . . . having an origin sup-ported by unquestionable evidence . . . reliable, trustworthy, authoritative."[3] Although we could write a chapter qualifying each term in the definition (espe-cially "unquestionable"!), the important point for our discussion is that journalists not only strive to determine trustworthy information but also necessarily use visu-ally based ways of knowing—which can seem reliable even when they are not.

Media imagery carries particularly significant impact because we tend to remember what we see and because visual memories can inform and shape our perceptions and behaviors on levels more deeply and personally significant than verbal memories alone. Underscoring the import of these issues is the fact that visual journalism is rare as a mass media genre in which visual docu-ments are gathered, organized, and disseminated for the primary purpose of conveying information its practitioners intend to be perceived as real and true.

Visual journalists, therefore, carry a unique responsibility to accurately rep-resent what they see—that is, to convey a reasonable truth, which we define as the best reality a human can discern and communicate, given the subjective challenges of accurate observation, meaning making, and meaning dissemina-tion. These challenges include both intrapersonal and interpersonal characteristics of the information (or image) gatherer–maker, subject–source, disseminator (edi-tor, designer, book publisher, webmaster), and viewer–perceiver. "Intrapersonal" refers to the internal processes through which an individual brain gathers, inter-prets, and uses information. One person's brain simultaneously operates on nonconscious levels to maintain the body while perceiving and interpreting external stimuli, and on conscious levels to focus attention and reflect. In that way, one person can carry on an internal "dialogue"—or "multilogue"—on conscious and nonconscious levels within the same brain.

"Interpersonal," on the other hand, refers to the *external* process through which individuals exchange information. The two processes are interdepend-ent, which means that the internal communication (intrapersonal) influences the external communication (interpersonal), and vice versa. Challenges also include a multitude of contextual variables determining the creation, use, and viewing of any particular image. The process is so dynamic—or in flux—that brain research shows even remembering something shifts the way we will remember that same "something" the next time.

Key to our discussion of these issues is distinguishing between the concept of a "reasonable truth"—information discerned and communicated through largely conscious and often professional processes—and "personal truth," the dynamic "story of the self" on which an individual relies for navigating life and which influences how a person interprets information. In journalism practice, professionals strive to move beyond their personal truths in order to determine reasonably accurate information. The special challenge of visually derived information is that it can short-circuit conscious reason, making it appear we have determined truth objectively while we are actually heavily influenced by personal truths. Optically perceived information follows neural routes that can blend imperceptibly with nonconscious and deeply personal brain data to operate as "the given"—even for practiced journalism professionals.

This chapter addresses ethical issues of journalism practice that arise through these processes of visual knowing. We describe an *integrative approach* to ethics to help practitioners and readers develop sound professional and personal guidelines for interpreting and using journalistic images. Part of our argument is that the kind of rational, reflective systematic moral analysis (SMA) recommended by Deni Elliott and David Ozar in this book's opening chapter needs to be supplemented with a method that also focuses on humans' pre-reflective, nonconscious, intuitive cognition and memory. Our ultimate goal is to show how an individual's understanding, or "personal truth," of his or her *self story* can either hinder or contribute to a more balanced approach to journalism and to a more balanced, sustainable culture.

Truth versus Information

In their opening chapter to this volume, Elliott and Ozar note the problematic nature of using the term "truth" in discussions of ethics. They suggest using "information" instead. While we agree that a twenty-first-century understanding of the relative nature of truth renders discussions of truth problematic, we assert the significance of the visual to the formation of personal truths that influence how we interpret and thus understand the world around us. To the nonconscious brain, where each of us processes most of what we perceive and know,[4] what we see, to use the common maxim, is what we get, and—perhaps more important—what we *remember*.[5] A philosopher might say that what we *see* is the "given" at its most raw. We see, we believe, we do. In this way, visual information transforms into *personal truth* through intrapersonal processing of that information. Our lives depend on this intuitive process. We take in sensory information through the many receptors of our bodies. The brain synthesizes that information, translating electrical and chemical signals into visual patterns. All of this happens long before the conscious mind can begin to determine whether the stimulus information is accurate, much less ethical at its core. Decision-making relies primarily on information stored as memory.

Visual perception researchers believe that as much as 75 percent of the information our brains process is from visual sources. In addition, most, if not all, brain memory and processing is in image patterns. The neuroscientist Antonio Damasio writes:

Those written words now printed before your eyes are first processed
by you as verbal images before they promote the activation of yet
other images, this time nonverbal, with which the "concepts"
that correspond to my words can be displayed mentally. In this
perspective, any symbol you can think of is an image, and there may
be little leftover mental residue that is not made of images. Even the
feelings that make up the backdrop of each mental instant are
images. . . . The obsessively repeated feelings that constitute the self
in the act of knowing are no exception.[6]

Furthermore, most of the complex problem solving and decision-making
that the human mind does occurs nonconsciously as much as ten seconds
before the conscious mind even becomes aware of the decision—if it ever
becomes aware of the decision.[7] Thus, the body, via the central nervous system,
perceives, or takes in, information that the brain converts, stores, and uses in
primarily visual formats to form the basis of our "personal truths"—the beliefs
and biases that underlie our decision-making.

The neuroscientist Michael Gazzaniga takes these concerns even further.
Gazzaniga asserts the problematic nature of the conscious brain's interpretations of its own nonconscious responses:

After many years of fascinating research on the split brain, it appears
that the inventive and interpreting left hemisphere has a conscious
experience very different from that of the truthful, literal right brain. . . .
[T]he interpretive mechanism of the left hemisphere is always hard at
work, seeking the meaning of events. It is constantly looking for order
and reason, *even when there is none*. [This] leads it continually to make
mistakes. It tends to overgeneralize, frequently constructing a potential
past as opposed to a true one. . . . After many years of fascinating
research on the split brain, it appears that the inventive and interpreting
left hemisphere has a conscious experience very different from that
of the truthful, literal right brain. (emphasis added)[8]

So, what we consciously "see" is actually what we "think" we saw, the brain's
best effort to use its physiological ability, psychological motivations, and individual experiences to interpret and use the information it has gathered. However, this consciously accessible information is of secondary importance in the
nonconscious brain, where visual memory facilitates the cognitive events that
are the basis of our problem solving, decision-making, and behavior. For these
core reasons—the way humans come to "know" and act—understanding *visual
truth* matters. No matter how well the *conscious* mind understands the relative
nature of any truth, it is not possible to simultaneously bring into consciousness all the personal givens that are used to make those judgments. In the
often-millisecond-fast-brain world of problem solving and decision-making,

the nonconscious mind synthesizes relevant perceived stimuli and resulting mind-mediated, remembered reality as if they are accurate. The sheer amount of perceptual information the brain processes in any given day, or even at any given moment, means that much of our nonconscious decision-making never activates conscious awareness even though it motivates behavior. Consequently, we can expand the definition of *visual truth* to include the synthesis of meanings derived from ocularly perceived stimuli and internally formed brain images.

Journalism and Visual Truth

How does this affect journalism? Journalism, which is a form of social research when practiced well, is a profession of information gathering (perceiving), translation (interpreting, writing, photographing) and representation (framing, editing, designing, disseminating). Journalism depends on the abilities of human beings to perceive, observe, and gather data in different forms, to interpret meaning and evaluate significance, and to organize and prepare the data for dissemination to other humans. In the case of word journalism, a reporter might interview a source, using a symbol system that depends on the communication of sound and images. Good reporters have developed exceptional observational skills that help them "read" the nonverbal communication of sources as one means for judging the significance and veracity of the information conveyed. Then, the reporter arranges the information gathered into a form—news story, feature story, analysis—that includes and omits contextual data available during the original interview. The resulting story is published within a frame—a rectangular layout printed on paper or electronically transmitted and perceived via pixels on screens of varying sizes—along with other stories and advertisements that are part of the overall format of a medium. And research indicates that even one factor in that dissemination process, such as quality of the image form, can affect the extent to which we believe what we see. For example, the media psychologist Cheryl Bracken determined that viewing a newscast in high-definition television rather than on an analog TV increases the credibility of news anchors and the overall newscast.[9]

Further, as described by Damasio above, words are translated by the brain into image patterns and stored in memory in these image formats. Say the word "mother" or "hammer" and note the image(s) that come to consciousness from your memory. This is your "mind's eye," an intrapersonal communication process that is at work drawing on personal, visual truths. In their effort to get and hold readers' attention, writers vividly convey meaning through dynamic description or metaphor. Through interpersonal communication—and remember that even "mass media" necessarily depend on the individual perception of widely distributed messages—writers use their own understanding of reality to connect with the personal truths of their readers. In the case of visual journalism, a photographer or videographer might capture images and sounds with a camera and microphone. The visual journalist is also an exceptional observer, trained to watch for peak moments, called "decisive moments" by Henri Cartier-Bresson,[10] those fractions of a second in which real-world elements come together in an aesthetically appealing frame to represent the most significant or engaging moment of an event or other newsworthy activity. Just as a word reporter selects quotes and data to use in writing a story, the visual reporter selects moments while shooting and then further refines the selection down to the one frame or few seconds or minutes of moving frames that convey the story.

Our goal with this chapter is to ethically analyze such visual journalism, to develop a *visual ethics*: "the study of how images and imaging affect the ways we think, feel, behave, and create, use, and interpret meaning, for good or for bad."[11]

Defining by Function

In keeping with Elliott and Ozar's view, the primary function of visual journalism is to *inform*, to communicate knowledge. The spot news photograph that captures the key moment, much as a lead does in word journalism, epitomizes the informative function of visual journalism. A graphic condensing electoral votes to a representational map of blue and red states also operates to inform— quickly and succinctly, and sometimes misleadingly.

To *entertain* means to engage interest or amuse. Although entertaining readers may seem to run counter to the weighty ideals of high-quality journalism, much of visual journalism functions specifically to engage interest or amuse. One category of photojournalism, for example, is "wild art," standalone images with full captions highlighting general-interest topics such as weather, children in the park, or community events. Yet even hard news is not immune to the entertainment function. Photographs draw readers' eyes, engaging interest that editors hope will then transfer to news texts. The entertainment function of images dominates much of television news, spawning the category "infotainment." Although Internet news sites are still working out how design works best within the frame of a computer screen, wild art is common on the opening page.

To *persuade*, or influence opinion or behavior, is not usually considered a function of news. However, research strongly suggests that news images can skew reader perception toward a particular slant on a story, especially in long-term memory. Furthermore, news images regularly appear near advertisements, competing for viewer attention in print and Internet frames. The merger of images in the frames of print and electronic media thus carries meaning beyond conscious discourse to resonate with, confirm, and generate intrapersonal truths on nonconscious levels. Our minds—on both conscious and nonconscious levels of processing—in turn draw on those embedded truths to help us live.

Expression, or aesthetic communication, while also not typically linked with journalism, is critical to photographic and video reportage and to the design of print and electronic frames. As noted above, photojournalists strive to capture the "decisive moment" in a particularly appealing and communicative frame. The use of a particular angle of view, framing, timing, light, color, or black-and-white contrast, depth of field, blur or sharpness, wide angle or telephoto lenses, high or low grain or pixels, is a technique that integrates both technical and aesthetic dimensions. These dimensions influence understanding and meaning on nonconscious and conscious levels of cognition in ways that can be at least as influential as those derived from facts and logical analysis.

Further complicating this discussion is that these functions overlap and resonate in ways that defy clear logical analysis. Consider one well-known photograph, Alfred Eisenstaedt's 1945 image of a soldier kissing a nurse in a confetti-strewn Times Square on V-Day.[12] The image *informs*, showing viewers the spontaneous jubilation experienced at the end of World War II; *entertains*, grabbing attention and bringing pleasure to those who view it; *persuades*, encouraging viewers to join in the celebration of a U.S. victory; and *expresses*, epitomizing Eisenstaedt's abilities to capture a decisive moment with appealing composition and a bit of humor. Beyond these obvious functions, the photograph operates on individual levels based on a particular person's experiences and perceptions. Most important for our discussion is the fact that the brain does not store images in neat categories according to the function for which an image is intended.

Interaction of Function and Memory

The factor that may carry the most substantive weight in determining what we consider to be visual truth is the memory of the individual viewer or reader. The media psychologist Dolf Zillmann conducted a number of experiments that suggest the meaning remembered may very well differ from the meaning intended in published form—and even from the meaning initially perceived at the time of the first reading or viewing. In one experiment, researchers compared response to (1) a print message, (2) the same print message with a positively oriented photo, and (3) the same print message with a negatively oriented photo.[13] At the time of initial reading, meaning recall was fairly similar. Two weeks later, however, meaning recall was skewed toward the meaning conveyed by the photograph. Research is mounting to suggest that this memory effect may apply to most media messages: the lasting meaning remembered is influenced by the visuals more than by the words. Thus, for example, if a diamond ring is advertised next to a news photo about a starving child, the brain nonconsciously connects the two. Consider, as well, how juxtaposing "wild art," light-hearted moments of daily life, with significant stories affects meaning discerned from the overall frame. Gazzaniga's research further suggests the conscious mind makes up explanations for responses that the nonconscious mind has already experienced.

We therefore need a holistic ethical approach—one that considers not only conscious thinking processes common to traditional reasoned approaches to ethics, but also the nonconscious processes of thought that facilitate our perceptions, problem solving, decision-making, and behavior. Our recommended approach is integrative mind theory (IMT), which has roots in Sherrington's century-old work on the integrative nature of the nervous system.[14] We draw on past and recent IMT research to develop ways to apply complementary intuitive and rational mental processes to media and art studies. Cognitively balanced theory that blends ethical approaches based on brain science with traditional logically based analysis is needed to fully understand and respond intelligently to the complex workings of both brain and external media.

Applying SMA and IMT through Visual Ethics

We appreciate the careful and complex process detailed in Elliott and Ozar's SMA and think it can be enhanced by integrative mind and visual ethics models. To see this, let's look at an example.

On December 1, 2002, the *Sunday Oregonian* ran a feature story on Annette Steele. Opening the "Living Today" section of the paper, the story featured a six-column, above-the-fold photograph of an African American woman on her hands and knees scrubbing a kitchen floor. Below the lead photo was an image of Steele in her home, reading her Bible. Inside photographs, run with columns of text across two full pages, portrayed Steele walking home from

FIGURE 1. The *Oregonian*, December 1, 2002, used with permission. Photograph by Rob Finch. Original in color.

work and with her children and grandchildren. The focus of the story was on how Steele had worked throughout her life to support her family.

Randy Cox, the director of visuals for the *Oregonian*, reported that the decision to run the lead photograph involved considerable debate in the newsroom.[15] Some people argued *against* running the photograph, saying it portrayed an African American woman in a stereotypically negative way. Others argued *for* running the photograph, saying it was an accurate and beautiful portrayal of a hard-working woman who was proud of her life and her ability to care for and support her family. The latter group won the day.

The *Oregonian* staff in fact engaged in a kind of SMA, carefully weighing the pros and cons of leading the section with the photograph: they considered the possible courses of action, discussed whether running the photo fulfilled their journalistic role, debated the amount and kind of harm that would be produced, and asked whether that harm was justified by the corresponding benefit. From this, they determined the photo was best placed in a leading position. That is, even though staff members were concerned about negative attitudes viewers might hold about a historically underrepresented and often negatively represented group of people, they based their decision on their conscious awareness of the greater contextualized truth conveyed by the whole story: that one individual could work hard at a job some would not desire and accomplish a dignified, worthwhile life that contributed to her family's well-being.

While Elliott and Ozar's method stresses conscious, rational reflection on the informational value and context of the photograph, we focus on the pre-reflective given—the visual truth—evoked by viewing the photo. We argue the deeper "personal truth," made up of nonconscious biases stored in viewers' and readers' minds, framed their perception of the story. Whether the image was negative or positive, many readers have most likely seen, either directly (through personal experience) or indirectly (via media), African American women cleaning houses. One image in popular media viewed by millions of individuals since its release in 1939 features the house servant Mammy, played by the Oscar-winning Hattie McDaniel in "Gone with the Wind." McDaniel's portrayals have been heralded as "shrewd line readings, suggesting some measure of righteous anger directed at her white 'employers,'" and condemned as a "symbolic reminder" of a "slave past."[16] Whether seeing the image of Steele in the *Oregonian* reinforced a negative truth or enhanced a positive truth would depend on the extent to which the viewer (1) held negative or positive biases associated with similar images, (2) was aware that those biases could be nonconsciously triggered by similar images, and (3) was willing to reflect on the photograph within the context of the larger truth of one individual's life story. The viewer might skim the article, barely noticing the photograph; stop to look at the prominently displayed photograph without comprehending the context of the story; or view the photo, read the entire story and view the other photos, and actively reflect on whether the photograph reinforced or challenged stereotypes

RELATIONSHIPS/family

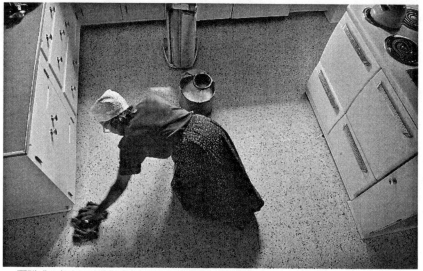

ABOVE ■ After 40 years of cleaning houses, Annette Steele still gets down on her hands and knees to scrub floors. "I chose this work," she says, "because I needed to. I had to be with my children when they needed me."

BELOW ■ With the television blaring as her grandchildren watch cartoons, Annette retreats to her dining room table and opens the Bible.

The patience of Job

She never took a handout, and her stubborn independence is the legacy she leaves her children

By Tom Hallman Jr./The Oregonian

In the early evening, while her grandchildren busied themselves in the kitchen, Annette Steele lifted the Bible from an end table and cradled it in her arms. For more than a half-century she's carved out a moment at day's end to read from the book her father handed her as she left the family's small Georgia farm.

Within this Northeast Portland house few remnants of that old life remain. A letter or two buried in a drawer, and on the shelves, hidden behind knickknacks, yellowed photographs. Her parents and her precious grandmother are gone. This Bible — a heavy, black, leather-bound edition as substantial as a big-city phone book — is the last living link to her past.

Her seven children, and certainly her grandchildren and great-grandchildren, don't share her intense faith, and to them her relationship with this Bible is a bit of a mystery.

She carried the big book to the dining room, pushed aside a pile of folded clothes and created a clearing at the end of a long table. Then she eased herself onto an old wooden chair. A self-professed "little bitty woman," she's a wiry 5-foot-2 and weighs a slim 130 pounds.

Earlier in the day she'd been on her nearly 70-year-old knees, scrubbing out yet another toilet. The years have left nicks and cuts on her fingers, and her hands are scarred from barehanded cleaning with lye.

After settling into the chair, she adjusted her glasses. When she was a girl, she jabbed herself in the right eye with a pair of scissors. In the poor, black area of rural

Photos by Rob Finch/The Oregonian

Georgia that she called home, going to a doctor was a luxury. Her grandmother calmed her down, pulled the blade and hoped for the best. The eye never healed correctly, and Annette wondered if that's why learning to read was such a struggle.

She bowed her head, reached out as if preparing to shuffle a deck of cards and ran her fingers along the Bible's frayed edges. When she felt the spirit move her, she flipped open the book to embrace the evening's message: the 34th Psalm. She tilted her head and moved close to the page in the way a scientist peers into a microscope. A power appropriate to the pulpit infused her voice: "I will extol the Lord at all times . . ."

Something crashed in the kitchen. She stopped and heard her grandson curse. "What's that?" she demanded, swiveling toward the door. "What did I hear?"

"Ship," he said sheepishly. "I said 'ship.'"

"I thought I heard something else," she said. "I better not."

She bowed her head. "I will extol the Lord at all times," she said, her voice rising and falling with a haunting rhythm. Her 14-year-old granddaughter, captivated, paused on her way up the stairs. "His praise will always be on my lips. My soul . . ."

Her grandson weekly approached with the portable phone. She patted him on the shoulder and smiled, keeping the phone pressed to her thigh until he, too, smiled. She lifted the phone to her ear. One of her clients, a Portland couple headed to the desert for the winter season, wanted Annette to clean their house. "Oh, yes," she said. "That'll be just fine. I'll see you tomorrow."

Please see **THE PATIENCE OF JOB**, Page L4

FIGURE 2. The *Oregonian*, December 1, 2002, p. L1, used with permission. Photographs by Rob Finch. Originals in color.

FIGURE 3. The *Oregonian*, December 1, 2002, pp. L4–5, used with permission. Photographs by Rob Finch. Originals in color.

of African American women. A negative response, either nonconscious or conscious, might be the conclusion that scrubbing floors is what African American women still do. A positive response, again either nonconscious or conscious, might be the conclusion that, had the viewer not seen the photograph, he or she would not know that (1) African American women still scrub floors in the twenty-first century, and (2) scrubbing floors can be an honorable occupation.

Much depends on the nonconscious biases dominating readers' and viewers' minds. Might the *Oregonian* have done better by leading with a photograph that clearly and quickly communicated a positive, family-centered image of Steele? As noted earlier, research by Zillmann and Gibson supports this idea:[17] Readers are more likely to remember the image of the African American woman on her knees scrubbing the floor than the larger context of her rich and positive life story. In an ideal world, readers would spend time thoughtfully considering the positive and more complex meaning of the story about Steele. In the real world, readers rush through most stories, catching bits and pieces—and evocative images—on the run. Had the story led with a six-column photograph of Steele at the dinner table with her family, the dominant image would have framed reader's approach (and memory) differently. The floor-washing photo—definitely important to showing the full story of Steele—could have been run smaller and inside.

While conscious, rational evaluation of the ethics of a journalistic act, along the lines of Elliott and Ozar's SMA, is a goal worthy of each and every journalist, in daily practice, journalists rarely have the time or opportunity to conduct a step-by-step analysis of each act they perform. A photojournalist, in particular, works in time increments as fast as 1/5000th of a second and may make hundreds or even thousands of photographs in the course of covering one event or story. It would be impossible to evaluate every decision to fire the shutter to capture rays of light reflected from a person or scene.

We do not support, however, the common maxim of photojournalism to "just get the picture, then worry about what to do with it." There are times—such as when taking a picture causes undue distress to a grieving mother—to put the camera down. A workable solution, we think, is to train oneself in ethical reflection, carefully thinking through tough problems when time allows, so as to be better prepared to respond ethically when under a deadline.

Similarly, readers and viewers seldom have the time to work through the steps of SMA for every image they see. A workable solution is to build the study of ethics and media into educational systems in order to enhance the judgments of users of contemporary media.[18] Third, even if readers and viewers do work through an SMA for an image of visual journalism, they are more likely to remember the content of the story the way it was framed by the photograph than how it was framed in the story. We believe the *Oregonian* staff, while acting with the highest ethical intentions, "rationalized" their intuitive responses of concern through conscious analysis, unintentionally acting unethically by leading with the photo. Integrative mind and visual ethics theories lead us to believe that the *Oregonian* staffers would have made a better decision by honoring their intuitive responses that the photo reinforced negative stereotypes rather than conveyed the story of a powerfully strong woman.

Balancing the Rational and Intuitive toward More Ethical Practices

I would like to support the idea that there could be a universal set of biological responses to moral dilemmas, a sort of ethics, built into our brains. My hope is that we soon may be able to uncover those ethics, identify them, and begin to live more fully by them. I believe we live by them largely nonconsciously now, but that a lot of suffering, war, and conflict could be eliminated if we could agree to live by them more consciously.

—Michael S. Gazzaniga, *The Ethical Brain* (2005)

Consider that we have just spent numerous pages consciously analyzing one image by translating our thinking into words. How much more complex would it be to deconstruct the thousands of images—still and moving—we see in a day? It is rare that image makers, designers, and editors, much less readers, would have the time to apply instruments such as SMA to even one image a day, much less to the hundreds of images and designs found in a daily publication and elsewhere in the media. The considerable research we have reviewed above suggests that problem solving and decision-making primarily occur on nonconscious levels of cognition and the less time allotted, for instance in making images, the more likely it is that nonconscious decision-making is the primary motivator of the behavior.

The use of SMA and similarly rational processes may, with enough time, enhance the ability of visual creators and editors to make more ethical decisions. However, doing so will facilitate only part of the desired outcome: the cultivation of a reflective, internal sense of ethics to help guide ongoing, daily decision-making. Because the complex decision-making that facilitates ethical behavior is supported by highly intuitive, nonconscious cognitive processes, we need a balanced, holistic approach to ethics, one that integrates rational and intuitive cognitive abilities of the human mind to enhance ethical decision-making.

Logical tools, such as SMA, used in tandem with methods rooted in integrative mind and visual ethics theories, can deeply enhance our understanding of the powerful effects of visual imagery on perception, memory, and behavior. One such method is the personal impact assessment (PIA), a method Williams[19] developed to draw nonconscious responses to media images into conscious awareness as a way to inform ethical media use and practice. PIA allows the viewer of an image to begin with logical, obvious nouns and adjectives, quickly shift to words associated with those terms, and, through reflection, move deeper into self-awareness. Ultimately, the goal is to move from rational analysis of the image to a deeper, more intuitive understanding of one's personal response to an image.

PIA is a simple process that may seem complex when first described. To begin, a reader or viewer spends time looking at an image—in this case, the lead photograph of Steele (see Figure 1). To conduct a PIA on the image, do the following:

- List key visual elements in the frame.
- Review the list, jotting down three or four words that each key element evokes.
- Review the associative words, selecting one for each of the key words.
- Make a new list of the selected associative words.
- Think about each associative word, and allow a word describing a part of your self to emerge. Write it down.
- Using your third list of words, write a short essay describing your

response to the image.[20] You may list the words in whatever form is easiest, and any word that comes to mind is acceptable. It is important, however, to work quickly while noting key and associative words in order to maximize the potential for intuitive, or "gut" responses rather than carefully reasoned responses.

Please see Figures 4 and 5 for our respective applications of the PIA to the Steele photo.

Newton's PIA of Annette Steele Photograph

Key words (in bold) and associative words (*italic*)

Woman: myself, *Grandmother,* mother maid
Dark: African-American, *mysterious,* sensual, bad
Skin: reveal, soft, kind, *open*
Hands: work, hurt, *wet,* care
Knees: hurt, *vulnerable,* prayer, sex
Rag: clean, *dirty,* work, small
Floor: base, ground, *lowly,* poor
Old bucket: water, container, old, *not modern*
Kitchen: domestic, center, *heart,* soul
Counter: above, *frame,* support, rest
Stove: cook, *warm,* food, nurture
Scarf: head, hair, mammy, clean, *sweat*
Light: *beauty,* joy, faith, love

Associative words (*italic*) and self words (underlined)

Grandmother: caring
Open: truthful
Vulnerable: vulnerable/trusting
Lowly: grounded
Center: heart
Warm: loving
Beauty: lovely

Mysterious: strong
Wet: fluid
Dirty: earthy
Not modern: primal
Frame: sturdy/core
Sweat: hard-working

Personal Response

Viewing the photograph takes me back to scenes in my childhood when I saw both my grandmother and her African-American maid clean our floors. It also makes me think of a time in my adult life when I was a stay-at-home mother with a toddler and having a really clean floor was important to me. Symbolically, I conclude that viewing the image taps into my own determination to care for my family and my soul in whatever manner I must. I use my strength and flexibility to endure earthly trauma, to ground me in honest, loving relationships. My own primal feminine works at the heart of my life, a lovely, pulsing, sometimes exploited, yet strong and essential core of my life.

FIGURE 4. One author's PIA, made in about a half hour, showing her response shift from the logical naming of key elements in the photograph to a deeper understanding of her intuitive response to the photograph.

Williams's PIA of Annette Steele Photograph

Key words (in bold) and associative words (*italic*)

Warmth: safe, home, *nurture*, feed
White: *sheets*, clean, pure, light
Light: *pure*, enlighten, see, wash
Kneel: *worship*, saint
Yellow: sun, flower, *grow*
Bend: old, break, *grace*
Red: hot, vibrant, *blood*, warm
Cabinets: inside, hide, *keep, protect*
Blue: *cool*, heaven, safe
Shadow: *dark*, other, inner, strength
Gingham: old, *quaint*, poor, west
Movement: *change*
Clean: pure, Mr., water, *new*

Blur: *move*, run, hide
Soap: wash, clean, *bubbles*, play
Kitchen: *sustenance*, food, feed, eat
Water: *renew*, wash, splash, fun
Nice clothes: class, special, *care*
Bucket: hole, hold, *wood*, carry
Floor: bottom, walk, *lie*
Vacuum: dirt, away, air, *work*
Scrub: *away*, dirt
Older woman: *mother*, madonna, wise
Spotless: *scrub*, clean, pure
Stove: *cook*, feed, hot
Looking down: tired, below, *serve*

Associative words (*italic*) and self words (underlined)

Nurture: giving self
Worship: humble
Blood: core
Cool: peaceful
Change: renewed
Bubbles: laughing
Care: sharing
Scrub: pure

Sheets: spirit
Grow: changing
Keep: vigilant
Dark: shadow
New: renewed
Sustenance: caring
Wood: solid/core
Away: distant
Cook: sustaining

Pure: caring
Grace: giving
Protect: father
Quaint: friend
Move: powerful
Renew: spiritual
Lie: resting
Mother: nurturing
Serve: serving

Personal Response

What this image appeals to in me is the highest order of caring and human ethical values. By rearranging the order of the parts of the inner self (as below) in order to group them by like meanings, we discover three primary related areas; caring and giving, changing and renewal, and core self or spirit. The words in these pairings suggest to me that the image conveys underlying messages about how nurturing and caring facilitate a powerful transformation of the core, spiritual self:

Nurture: Giving
Grace: Giving
Pure: Caring
Sustenance: Caring
Serve: Serving
Mother: Nurturing
Lie: Resting
Cook: Sustaining
Care: Sharing
Protect: Father
Quaint: Friend

Self Move: Powerful
Keep: Vigilant
Change: Renewed
Grow: Changing
New: Renewed
Bubbles: Laughing

Away: Distant

Sheets: Spirit
Renew: Spiritual
Blood: Core
Wood: Solid/Core
Cool: Peaceful
Worship: Humble
Dark: Shadow
Scrub: Pure
Work: Ethical

FIGURE 5. The other author's PIA, which took about one and a half hours to complete by viewing the photograph in color, demonstrates the increasing depth and complexity of understanding one can achieve by searching for intuitive responses.

Summary

So. Now what do we have? Tapping into the intuitive response of one of the authors, a white woman, reveals deep connections between her past, her sense of the archetypal feminine self, and the image of Steele. This may be exactly what the *Oregonian* staff intended. The response of the second author, a white man, also taps into archetypal qualities of a relational, strong, and spiritually centered individual but does not ascribe those qualities specifically to the feminine.

Considering the two responses in tandem, we can see an overlap of the viewers' intuitive processing of visual cues in the image. On one level, the image appears to have evoked a positive, ennobling interpretation from the viewers. Now, it is time to move back into the conscious, logical analytical process. On that level, one might argue that the authors responded to the image in a stereotypical manner, connecting the beautiful image of Steele at work with myths of hard work being good for the spirit and ennobling for an African American woman or for women in general. We could even use the PIA evidence to argue that the image evoked a stereotypical response by its use of soft light and strong colors.

What the PIA illustrates is the complexity of human response to images. As with SMA, journalists in everyday practice and viewers in everyday media use do not have time to conduct PIA on every image they want to publish or view. However, the journalist concerned about ethical practice and the viewer concerned with understanding potential media effects on her understanding of the world could cultivate a deeper awareness of ethical concerns and personal response biases by working through both SMA and PIA from time to time.

Conclusion

Through the last century our educational processes have increasingly marginalized our more primary, intuitive cognitive processes. They have mistakenly assumed conscious reason is the cognitive mode best suited for solving the most complex problems and for making the most advantageous decisions. Our educational system has mistakenly assumed that the intuitive processes are secondary, at best, and of little or no significance to thinking and being. This rationally biased pedagogical model leaves a huge *intuitive void* in both our experiences and our cognitive development. This void leaves us longing for cognitive balance, susceptible to highly sophisticated, intuitive media messages; it also marginalizes our primary mode for implementing the highest levels of holistic and ethical problem solving and decision-making.

In journalism education, the problem is exemplified in the emphasis on logically derived, so-called objective truth, which has left, again, an intuitive void.

Ancient philosophers, from Confucius to Plato and Aristotle, recognized that emotion and intuition play key roles in moral judgment. Contemporary scholars, such as Damasio and Gazzaniga, seek to undo the dominant paradigm of rational approaches to ethics by underscoring the need to consider how the brain actually makes moral judgments. We now have scientific evidence that it is actually the intuitive, nonconscious cognitive modes that are best suited for higher level, complex problem solving and decision-making. We are not the rational, logical beings we have believed ourselves to be. In fact, rational, conscious cognition is a secondary response to the more rapid, complex, and essential problem-solving functions of the nonconscious, intuitive, cognitive modes and the multiple intelligences that support them.

Journalists, whose traditions have focused on objective, logical gathering and presentation of information, would do well to acknowledge the objectively derived findings of twenty-first-century cognitive neuroscience. Visual journalists, in particular, carry a responsibility to employ recent discoveries about the power of images to influence the ways viewers respond to and interpret visual information.

We believe that the repeated practice of a method like PIA will support holistic development of ethically grounded journalism practice. Educational reform, a long-term goal, is at all levels a primary step in this process and is underway.[21] In the meantime, individuals—photographers, videographers, designers, editors, writers, animators—can advance the development of their own integrative abilities. Using SMA and other more rationally focused assessment tools will support this process by keeping the focus of the reasoned mind on ethical development and practices. Complementing those efforts with processes such as PIA, specifically designed to access the nonconscious mind and enhance creativity, problem solving, and decision-making in core cognitive modes, will help develop more balanced, ethically sound, and effective journalism practices.

By recognizing and consciously working through the arts and other visual modes, we can orchestrate the integration and enhancement of our primary rational and intuitive cognitive and mental modes as equal and complementary components of high-level, whole-mind cognition. Through this integrative-mind process, we can create an ecological well of ethically derived visual truths in nonconscious memory to guide our problem solving and decision-making from the highest levels of intellect and knowing toward more balanced and thus more ethical selves.

Our lives—and journalism's—depend on it. Our readers and viewers deserve and need it.

Notes

The epigraph is taken from George Johnson, "The Theory That Ate the World," Review of *The Black Hole War* by Leonard Susskind, *New York Times Sunday Book Review*, August 24, 2008, p. 16.

1. The term *nonconscious* is used throughout the chapter to indicate a cognitive process that is the basis for all human problem solving and decision-making. This primary process operates before and beyond conscious thought. We do not use the term *unconscious* because its use in common language tends to marginalize fundamental cognitive processes.

2. Julianne H. Newton, *The Burden of Visual Truth: The Role of Photojournalism in Mediating Reality* (Mahwah, NJ: Lawrence Erlbaum, 2001), 8.

3. *Random House Webster's College Dictionary* (New York: Random House, 1995), 92.

4. Eric Kandel, *In Search of Memory: The Emergence of a New Science of Mind* (New York: W. W. Norton, 2006).

5. Ann Marie Seward Barry, *Visual Intelligence: Perception, Image, and Manipulation in Visual Communication* (Stony Brook: State University of New York Press, 1997).

6. Antonio Damasio, *The Feeling of What Happens* (New York: Harcourt Brace, 1999), 319.

7. Chun Siong Soon, Marcel Brass, Hans-Jochen Heinze, and John-Dylan Haynes, "Unconscious Determinants of Free Decisions in the Human Brain," *Nature Neuroscience* 11 (May 2008): 543–45. See also Marcel Brass and Patrick Haggard, "To Do or Not to Do: The Neural Signature of Self-Control," *Journal of Neuroscience* 27, no. 34, (August 22, 2007): 9141–45. For classic studies on this topic, see also Antoine Bechara, Hanna Damasio, Daniel Tranel, and Antonio Damasio "Deciding Advantageously before Knowing the Advantageous Strategy," *Science* 275 (1997): 1293–95; and Benjamin Libet, Curtis A. Gleason, Elwood W. Wright, and Dennis K. Pearl, "Time of Conscious Intention to Act in Relation to Onset of Cerebral Activity (Readiness-Potential). The Unconscious Initiation of a Freely Voluntary Act," *Brain* 106 (1983): 623–42.

8. Michael S. Gazzaniga, "The Split Brain Revisited," *Scientific American Special Edition* 12 (August 2002): 27–31.

9. Cheryl Campanella Bracken, "Perceived Source Credibility of Local Television News: The Impact of Television Form and Presence, *Journal of Broadcasting & Electronic Media* 50 (December 2006): 723–41.

10. Henri Cartier-Bresson, *The Decisive Moment* (New York: Simon & Schuster, 1952).

11. Julianne H. Newton, "Visual Ethics," in *Handbook of Visual Communication*, ed. Kenneth Smith, Gretchen Barbatsis, Sandra Moriarty, and Keith Kenney, 429–43 (Mahwah, NJ: Lawrence Erlbaum, 2004).

12. Alfred Eisenstaedt, "Eisie—The icons, *The Digital Journalist*," http://www.digitaljournalist.org/issue9911/icon01.htm (accessed August 19, 2008).

13. Dolf Zillmann and Rhonda Gibson, "Effects of Photographs in Newsmagazine Reception on Issue Perception," *Media Psychology* 1 (1999): 207–28.

14. Charles S. Sherrington, *The Integrative Action of the Nervous System* (New York: Scribner, 1906).

15. Randy Cox, presentation to Introduction to Visual Communication class, Allen Hall, School of Journalism and Communication, University of Oregon, 2003.

16. Cynthia Fuchs, "Done Gone, Review of *Beyond Tara: The Extraordinary Life of Hattie McDaniel,*" *PopMatters,* http://www.popmatters.com/tv/reviews/b/beyond-tara.html (accessed August 19, 2008), para. 4.

17. Zillmann and Gibson, "Effects of Photographs."

18. Please see chap. 19 by Wendy Wyatt, in this volume.

19. Rick Williams, "Visual Illiteracy and Intuitive Visual Persuasion, Part II," *Journal of Visual Literacy* 20, no. 1 (2000): 111–24; Rick Williams, "Omniphasic Visual-Media Literacy in the Classroom, Part III," *Journal of Visual Literacy* 20, no. 2 (2000): 219–42; Rick Williams, "Transforming Intuitive Illiteracy: Understanding the Effects of the Unconscious Mind on Image Meaning, Image Consumption, and Behavior," *Explorations in Media Ecology* 2 (2003): 119–34.

20. For a more detailed description of how to conduct a PIA, see Rick Williams and Julianne H. Newton, *Visual Communication: Integrating Media, Art and Science* (New York: Lawrence Erlbaum, 2007).

21. See Elliot W. Eisner, *The Enlightened Eye: Qualitative Inquiry and the Enhancement of Educational Practice* (Upper Saddle River, NJ: Merrill, 1998); Howard Gardner, *Intelligence Reframed: Multiple Intelligences for the 21st Century* (New York: Basic Books, 1999); Howard Gardner, *The Disciplined Mind: Beyond Facts and Standardized Tests: The K–12 Education That Every Child Deserves* (New York: Simon & Schuster, 1999); and Lois Hetland, Ellen Winner, Shirley Veenema, and Kimberly M. Sheridan, with Foreword by David N. Perkins, *Studio Thinking: The Real Benefits of Visual Arts Education* (New York: Teachers College Press, 2007).

23

Ethics and Images: Five Major Concerns

Paul Martin Lester

After I told a new acquaintance that I taught at a university, she naturally asked which subject. "Visual communication," I answered quickly, "and mass media ethics." I then braced slightly for the inevitable bad joke that always followed. "Visual ethics," she replied, "sort of an oxymoron, isn't it?" Fortunately, I was ready with my usual and equally weak comeback, "Well, I always have work."

Because of the unique emotive power that pictures have over words, it seems the link between visual messages and ethical behavior is more problematic in the lay public's mind than stories and ethical dilemmas (although conflicts of interest between the political positions of media organizations and individuals and their editorial products sometimes get noticed). Consequently, still and moving images reproduced within any media are often singled out for criticism. Usually, the disapproval is justified. Most media critics name five mass communications issues associated with ethics and visual journalism: victims of violence, rights of privacy, manipulations, stereotyping, and visual-persuasion techniques used for commercial purposes.

Violent pictures sensationalize and distract readers and viewers from the story itself. The public is made to feel sorry for pampered and deteriorating celebrities when they are hounded by packs of photographers. Stage-managed sources and digitally altered pictures stretch credibility to the point where "seeing is disbelieving." Negative stereotypes of individuals from various multicultural groups are now the norm and no longer the exception. And finally, visual messages blur the distinction among advertising, public relations, and journalism until the public cannot tell the difference among the three professions.

The theory chapter by Elliott and Ozar, "An Explanation and a Method for the Ethics of Journalism," is a helpful introduction to the philosophical underpinnings that should guide professional journalism practices. Toward that end, the two philosophy professors detail a five-step systematic moral analysis procedure whose goal is to classify any journalistic action or non-action into one of four categories—an action determined to be either ethically prohibited (one that cannot be justified under any circumstances), ethically required (one that meets the profession's expectations of behavior), ethically permitted (one that meets the required category and yet cause harms that nevertheless can be justified), or ethically ideal (one that meets the required and permitted categories and prevents or avoids harms altogether).

With only one category that bans an action by a journalist outright, their system is, to their credit, obviously weighted to allow journalists to perform their role-related responsibilities and keep the public informed. Stated another way, it would be an extraordinary case in which a journalist's action is prohibited under the Elliott and Ozar's standards. Such a moral system is probably a relief for most journalism professionals, who would rather run a story than not.

Interestingly, the only example in their chapter in which it is concluded that a journalist caused unjustified harm and should be considered ethically prohibited is one that involves a photojournalist's taking a picture during a spot news story. Once again, visual messages and ethics collide.

Perhaps it should not be a surprise that a visual message is singled out for criticism in Deni Elliott and David Ozar's theory chapter. Photographers and their products are easy targets. For centuries the visual media were employed either as drawings only appropriate for the margins of great works, or as sensational, attention-getting tools to attract (mostly) illiterate patrons to public shows or the front pages of newspapers. Historically, then, images took their "place alongside oral culture as a signifier of underdevelopment."[1] Not surprisingly, photographers, especially for big city newspapers, were considered by many word reporters as lower class workers within a newsroom and dismissed as "reporters with their brains knocked out."[2] However, as philosophers, critics, and educators began to take image production as a serious art, visual literacy gradually developed into a serious study, with visual practitioners afforded a higher level of respect.

In their chapter, Elliott and Ozar use a picture taken during a tragic news situation as an example of journalistic wrongdoing. Violence and tragedy are staples of U.S. journalism because many readers are attracted to gruesome stories and photographs. "If it bleeds, it leads" is an undesirable rule of thumb. Judges of contests also have a fatal attraction. Pulitzer Prizes are most often awarded to photographers who make pictures of gruesome, dramatic moments.[3] *Milwaukee Journal* editor Sig Gissler summed up the newspaper profession's sometimes hedonistic philosophy when he admitted, "We have a commercial interest in catastrophe."[4]

Photographs have long been known to spark more emotional responses than stories. Eugene Goodman wrote, "Pictures usually have more impact on people than written words. Their capacity to shock exceeds that of language."[5] Other researchers have noted the eye-catching ability of newspaper photographs. Susan Miller explained, "Photos are among the first news items to catch the reader's eye. . . . A photo may catch the eye of a reader who doesn't read an accompanying story."[6] Roy Blackwood argued that "people who either can't read, or who don't take the time to read many of the stories in newspapers do scan the photographs."[7] Nora Ephron asserted that disturbing accident images should be printed. "That they disturb readers," Ephron wrote, "is exactly as it should be: that's why photojournalism is often more powerful than written journalism."[8]

Therefore, it is often a journalist's role-related responsibility to produce words and images that disturb sources, readers, and viewers. But, certainly, to do so in a way that causes harm without adequate and defendable justification should be ethically prohibited.

The case study in Elliott and Ozar's chapter invites us to "imagine a picture of a mother standing on the street, staring in horror as her house is engulfed in flames with her young children still in it."[9]

As a former photojournalist, my first reaction to the scenario is that the image must be a hell-of-a-picture if in one, presumably wide-angle shot, it shows the woman's anguished face, a fire out of control, and trapped children inside a house. Nevertheless, aesthetics alone should never be the determining decision-making factor in journalism, but neither, it can be argued, should an initial personal and gut reaction to a photograph's disturbing content.

The two authors conclude that the image is deemed ethically prohibited and should not be published because it causes unjustified harm:

> It is certainly legal to print such a picture, but one might argue that [the mother depicted] has a moral right to be treated with respect and not to be objectified in such a moment. The pain caused by publication of that picture is not what she deserves. In addition, it is hard to think of how publication of this picture would, in any way, assist in promoting the aggregate good. Human interest stories promote human bonding, but human bonding often occurs through the sacrifice of an individual. The harm caused this individual (assuming that the picture is published without her consent), would not benefit her or people who might find themselves in a similar situation. People do not need to see this excruciating moment in this woman's life to assist in their self-governance.

The rest of this chapter will use Elliott and Ozar's five-step systematic moral analysis to determine if the image's use can be justified despite the assumed harm to the woman in the photograph.

Step One: Identify the Courses of Action Available to the Journalist

Since the scenario begins with the photograph in hand, obviously the choice has been made by the photojournalist to take the picture and make it available for viewing. Ordinarily, however, the first choice for a photographer arriving at such a scene would be to take a picture or not. There are many reasons a journalist would *not* take a photograph of a spot news story. One of the most humanitarian reasons would be if it were possible for the photographer to help those in need of immediate assistance. Ideally, a journalist should first render aid, if it is possible to do so, then, as soon as possible, perform the requirements of the profession's role-related responsibilities. In this case, take pictures. A photojournalist is subject to criticism from the profession and condemnation from the public if she or he could have provided help but did not for the sake of a picture.

After rendering aid, it is professionally acceptable to resume the role-related duties of a photographer and record the scene. Of course, a photographer might be sensitive to the anguish of the woman and decide not to record her image out of respect for her privacy. And if she specifically asked the photographer not to take her picture, he or she might oblige. Although most news stories occur in full public view and it is legal to take such pictures in almost all cases, some photojournalists might respect the wish of the source and refrain from taking a picture. There may be other reasons for not taking pictures, too: a camera might be defective, a memory card might be full, it might be too dark, bystanders might be in the way, and so on. However, technical problems, whether a broken camera or a lack of experience, are not considered part of an ethical dilemma's decision-making process.

Given the parameters of the authors' scenario, with a decision to take the photograph already made, the only actions available to the photojournalist are whether to submit the image to the city editor or not. Although a photographer can sometimes suggest where a picture should be printed, rarely does an editor solicit the photographer's opinion.

Step Two: Does the Action Fulfill the Journalist's Role-related Responsibility?

A photojournalist is employed by a news organization for the specific purpose of providing facts in (mostly) a visual format (photojournalists are sometimes asked to provide caption information, such as names, titles, and perhaps observations and quotations). Not providing an image to an editor violates the contract the journalist has with the news entity. The only possible action that fulfills the journalist's role-related responsibility is to give the picture to the editor.

From this point on, the ethical dilemma is lifted from the photojournalist and given to the editor, who must decide whether to publish the picture and, if so, how it should be presented to the news organization's audience. In many enlightened news outlets, when a potentially controversial picture is being considered, a photographer is asked to participate in a newsroom discussion that might include other photographers, the principle reporter of the story and other journalists, and the editor-in-chief and publisher, if they are available. Regardless, the final decision to use the image is, in most cases, now up to the editor and not the photographer. Therefore, the following steps in the "decision guide" apply to the editor.

At this point an editor has two choices, with a potential corollary: *whether* to publish the picture; and, if the former, *how* to publish it.

Any decision to publish or not publish a picture should not be based only on the story of the day. Perhaps there is a larger context for this story that the reader should know. This house fire might be one of several recently started within the city limits. Fire and police officials might suspect an arsonist. Perhaps there is a problem with the electrical grid or natural gas lines within the city. Perhaps no other photograph taken during previous fires was of as high "decisive moment" quality as the imagined image briefly described in the case study. Perhaps the children and others in the house were killed or seriously injured. Maybe with high winds the house set other homes in the neighborhood ablaze and caused millions of dollars in property damage. Suppose the mother left her children alone in the house and went to drink in the neighborhood bar? Maybe there was a domestic argument and the estranged father set the fire deliberately in a murder-suicide plot. With such larger contexts for a news story, an editor might certainly be inclined to include this strong visual message along with a story on the front page because it is an important event that readers should know about as soon as possible. Whatever the specifics, it will be painful for the woman to have her situation so publicly displayed. However, the community is served by knowing of a larger social problem within the limits of their city.

If the decision by the editor, after consultation, is to not publish the picture, the authors' qualms about the scenario—the mother's plight and the (assumed) negative reaction if she and others were to see her image published in the next day's newspaper—are alleviated. If that decision is based on a professional determination of the story's low news value or a judgment of the image's low aesthetic quality, the decision can probably be justified to fellow journalists. However, if the decision is solely based on sensitivity to the woman's privacy, the editor may be accused of violating a role-related responsibility that makes journalism a unique profession.

If the choice is made to publish the image, the editor must now decide how it should be presented to readers. The editor has at least ten choices based on the importance of the story to the community. The image can be published:

On the front or inside page;
With only a caption;
With a caption and a story;
In color or in black and white;
Large or small;
With other images, in a picture spread;
With an informational graphic;
With a detailed description of the story by the reporter and photographer;
With a warning for readers that an inside page contains an image that might
  be upsetting to some readers; and
On the newspaper's website.

If this story were a "one-off" event, a tragedy, but not one within a more complicated context, an editor might be inclined to downplay the story visually by using it small and on an inside page. The justification might be that the unusual nature of the strong photograph requires publication. After all, a primary responsibility of journalism is to report the news—and an unusual, storytelling, and powerful image fits that definition. Once the photo is published, readers and viewers will learn in words and images of the woman's pain, think of their own loved ones, and be more likely to check the smoke detectors in their own homes. Hence, the aggregate good is served more by the publication of the image than without it because a reader regards the pain of another, and internalizes that sorrow so that care is transferred to immediate family members and friends, and actions are initiated to ensure that such a tragedy does not happen.

Will the Action Cause Harm?

Certainly, there are differences between running a photograph large on the front page, where it might be seen by many readers and nonreaders (in paper boxes, for example), publishing an image on an inside page (where mostly those who have purchased the paper would presumably see it), or presenting it on the newspaper's Web site (where only highly motivated viewers would see the picture). However, it is difficult to determine if the woman in the picture or if anyone who views the printed image will experience the harms described above. Additionally, how can it be determined if a "harm" is negative? For example, a reader who has a strong, emotional reaction to the image might be helped by the experience. The woman might be aided financially if the picture is used successfully in a case in which damages are sought in a lawsuit. Regardless, if the woman feels harmed in any way by the publication of the picture, her harm is offset by the potential harm that not publishing the picture might cause to readers and members of the community who might be aided indirectly by the image.

Step Four: Is Causing This Harm Justified?

For the sake of this argument, let's assume that the woman is harmed emotionally by the fact that the photograph of her anguished face amid flames and trapped children was shown on the front page of the newspaper the next day. Many times, and on a daily basis, persons, through no fault of their own, are victims of violence and consequently lose their anonymity. Some of the most important Pulitzer Prize photographs testify to the importance of documenting for the public's consumption scenes that no one would seek to witness because of their gruesome, graphic content. Nevertheless, the images and the photographers who captured these tragic moments are praised by journalists and the general public for their ability to tell in pictures what words alone can never reveal. The woman, her family, and her friends may be harmed by the publishing of such a photograph, but such publication is justified by the simple fact that the public has a right to know what happens to their fellow citizens, not out of prurient curiosity and not because of sensational consumerism, but because of the fundamental mission of journalism—to report and explain events that citizens need to know in order to navigate their lives successfully. The best stories made public combine the values of honesty, fairness, and responsibility that citizens and journalists agree upon.

Step Five: Which Type Is This Action?

To not report, even in words, the story of the woman's plight is ethically prohibited, as it cannot be justified by the role-related responsibilities of traditional journalism. If it is true that 2,500 years of Western moral philosophy can by summed up in one, compound sentence—"Do your job and don't cause unjustified harm"—then not reporting an important event in a reader's community violates that clause on both fronts.

Depending on the related news events that occurred before the case study's description and any additional information about the scenario itself, including a photograph with a story somewhere within the pages of the newspaper is ethically required, publishing a picture on the front page is ethically permitted, and putting this news story within a series of articles that speak to a larger social and economic context either in print or on the website is ethically ideal.

In the end, using Elliott and Ozar's SMA, a journalist can be thought ethical after publishing a graphically disturbing, private moment of a woman caught in a horrible situation because, as difficult as it might be, the profession is charged to provide, at times, that kind of news visually.

The mission of a photojournalist, as is the mission of all journalists, is to report news in a balanced, fair, and accurate manner. The profession can improve in quality and stature only when photographers care about those they see in their viewfinders and when editors consider the potential harm that published images might give to those pictured and those they seldom see, their readers. Journalism decisions, however, should be guided, never ruled, by sources, readers, and ethicists.

It is important to note that good, caring persons, both academics and professionals, will agree with Elliott and Ozar's conclusion to not use the photograph they described, and others will contend that the image should be used. As my father used to remark whenever there was a disagreement between two, equally valid considerations, "That's why there's horseracing." The important point is that any decision should be made through a long-term, rational, systematic process and not a quick, subjective, emotional one. The five-step analysis described in the opening chapter is an excellent method to achieve the goal of ethical professionalism.

Notes

1. Brian Goldfarb, *Media Pedagogy Media Cultures in and beyond the Classroom* (Durham, NC: Duke University Press, 2002), 19.
2. Clifton C. Edom, *Photojournalism* (Dubuque, IA: Wm. C. Brown, 1980), 26.
3. Eugene Goodwin, *Groping for Ethics in Journalism* (Ames: Iowa State University Press, 1983).
4. "Knocking on Death's Door," *Time*, February 27, 1989, p. 49.
5. Goodwin, *Groping*, 190.
6. Susan H. Miller, "The Content of News Photos: Women's and Men's Roles," *Journalism Quarterly* 52 (1975): 70–75.
7. Roy Blackwood, "The Content of News Photos: Roles Portrayed by Men and Women," *Journalism Quarterly* 60 (1983): 710–14.
8. Nora Ephron, *Scribble Scribble Notes on the Media* (New York: Alfred Knopf, 1978), 62.
9. The author of this chapter received a bachelor of journalism degree from the University of Texas at Austin with a major in photojournalism. Subsequently, he was a staff photographer for the *Times-Picayune* newspaper in New Orleans. In 1977 he was asked to cover the site of a natural-gas explosion that destroyed a home. While covering the news story, he took a close-up photograph of a woman looking in horror at her leveled house. Two images from the assignment can be found at http://commfaculty.fulterton.edu/lester/house_explosion.jpg.

Index